Understanding Cybersecurity for Smart Contracts

Sepideh HajiHosseinKhani
Arash Habibi Lashkari • Ali Mizani Oskui

Understanding Cybersecurity for Smart Contracts

Challenges, Strategies, and Trends

Springer

Sepideh HajiHosseinKhani
Behaviour-Centric Cybersecurity
Center (BCCC)
York University
Toronto, ON, Canada

Arash Habibi Lashkari
Behaviour-Centric Cybersecurity
Center (BCCC)
York University
Toronto, ON, Canada

Ali Mizani Oskui
FiCAS AG
Zug, Switzerland

ISBN 978-3-032-28862-2 ISBN 978-3-032-28863-9 (eBook)
https://doi.org/10.1007/978-3-032-28863-9

This Springer imprint is published by the registered company Springer Nature Switzerland AG
The registered company address is: Gewerbestrasse 11, 6330 Cham, Switzerland

Preface

As part of the Understanding Cybersecurity Series (UCS) knowledge mobilization program, this book, *Understanding Cybersecurity in Smart Contracts: Challenges, Strategies, and Trends*, explores the unique vulnerabilities, threats, and defense mechanisms associated with blockchain-based smart contracts. It provides a detailed analysis of critical security issues, including contract-level vulnerabilities, adversarial attack vectors, and advanced detection techniques leveraging interpretable AI and deep learning. By combining theoretical foundations, empirical datasets, and practical tools, the book offers both researchers and practitioners a comprehensive understanding of smart contract security within decentralized ecosystems.

In 2020, the first team released the online article series "Understanding Canadian Cybersecurity Laws," which received recognition and won the Gold Medal for Best Blog Column in the Business Division at the 2020 Canadian Online Publishing Awards. Building on this success, the team published the first book, *Understanding Cybersecurity Law and Digital Privacy: A Common Law Perspective*, in 2021 through Springer Nature Switzerland AG.

Continuing the research efforts, the second team launched the second article series in 2021, titled *Understanding Cybersecurity Management for FinTech (UCMF)*, accompanied by the publication of the related book *Understanding Cybersecurity Management in FinTech: Challenges, Strategies, and Trends*. This book highlights the importance of cybersecurity in financial institutions by examining recent cyber breaches and attacks, as well as the resulting financial losses.

Starting in 2022, the third UCS team launched the third online series, "Understanding Current Cybersecurity Challenges in Law," which addressed emerging trends and critical legal issues in cybersecurity globally. This six-part series explores digital jurisdictional authority and user-generated content ownership. The series is complemented by the publication of the third book, *Understanding Cybersecurity Law in Data Sovereignty and Digital Governance: An Overview from a Legal Perspective*, which offers an in-depth understanding of current cybersecurity challenges and their legal implications. Simultaneously, another team also worked on the fourth book, *Understanding Cybersecurity Management in Decentralized Finance: Challenges, Strategies, and Trends*. This book comprehensively reviews cybersecurity in blockchain technologies, analyzing platforms like Ethereum, Binance Smart Chain, Solana, Cardano, Avalanche, and Polygon. It explores cybersecurity issues in smart contracts, and related blog posts are currently being published on the ITWorldCanada website.

Beginning in 2023, the fifth UCS team embarked on developing the fifth book, *Understanding Cybersecurity on Smartphones: Challenges, Strategies, and Trends*. This book focuses on understanding cyber threats and adversaries on smartphones, examining vulnerabilities and risk management. The book offers practical solutions for securing and protecting smartphones while raising awareness of the importance of smartphone security.

In 2024, the sixth UCS team focused on understanding the criticality of cybersecurity in healthcare and advocated for robust measures to protect patient data, maintain system integrity, and mitigate evolving cyber threats in a book titled *Understanding Cybersecurity Management in Healthcare: Challenges, Strategies and Trends*. The book offers practical solutions for securing and protecting healthcare data and the environment for patients, doctors, and hospital IT teams while raising awareness of the importance of healthcare environment security.

In 2025, the UCS program proudly released two major books, each reflecting 2 years of dedicated research and writing. The seventh UCS team, which started in 2024, authored *Understandi*ng AI for Cybersecurity and Secure AI: Challenges, Strategies, and Trends, which examines how AI can serve as both a powerful defense tool and a vulnerable attack surface, addressing threats such as adversarial attacks and model poisoning while proposing strategies for secure and ethical deployment. Meanwhile, the eighth UCS team, which started in 2024, produced *Understanding Cybersecurity Management in Smart Construction: Challenges, Strategies, and Trends*, led by the Digital Construction cluster head at the Innovation Value Institute, National University of Ireland, Maynooth. This volume explores the unique security challenges of IoT, AI, and connected systems in smart construction, highlighting vulnerabilities in infrastructure, machinery, and project management platforms, and offering practical strategies to strengthen resilience across the sector.

As the latest addition to this growing body of work, Understanding Cybersecurity in Smart Contracts continues the UCS mission by addressing one of the most pressing and underexplored areas of cybersecurity. With blockchain adoption expanding rapidly across industries, the book fills a critical gap by focusing on the vulnerabilities and defenses of smart contracts. It introduces open-source analyzers, benchmark datasets, and interpretable AI models to support research, auditing, and real-world applications, making it a valuable resource for academics, developers, and security professionals alike.

Toronto, ON, Canada — Sepideh HajiHosseinKhani
Toronto, ON, Canada — Arash Habibi Lashkari
Zug, Switzerland — Ali Mizani Oskui
March 2026

Competing Interests The authors have no competing interests to declare that are relevant to the content of this manuscript.

Contents

Chapter 1
Introduction

Abstract This chapter introduces the foundational concepts of blockchain, beginning with the 2008 Bitcoin white paper by Satoshi Nakamoto and moving into Ethereum, which expands blockchain's capabilities through smart contracts. It shows how blockchains function as peer-to-peer, append-only ledgers where transactions record into linked blocks, creating a decentralized and tamper-resistant system. The lifecycle of a blockchain unfolds from genesis block creation and network launch to adoption, upgrades, maturity, and even abandonment, underscoring its dynamic nature and reliance on community support. Also, it explores the architecture of blockchain networks, nodes, blocks, and transactions, demonstrating how decentralization removes single points of failure while ensuring security and transparency through cryptography and consensus mechanisms. Additionally, it highlights the benefits of blockchain, including trust, automation, cost reduction, tokenization, interoperability, and sustainability, and shows how smart contracts enable self-executing agreements across industries. Finally, this chapter sets the stage for understanding blockchain as both a technical innovation and a transformative foundation for decentralized applications.

The concept of "blockchain" originated in the 2008 Bitcoin white paper, authored by the enigmatic figure Satoshi Nakamoto. While the term "blockchain" itself isn't explicitly mentioned in the paper, the underlying idea is clearly outlined. Essentially, transactions involving the exchange of value are processed through a peer-to-peer network and are periodically compiled into "blocks," or lists. Once a block of transactions is confirmed, it is linked, or "chained," to the previous block, creating an append-only structure. This structure, along with the protocol that governs it, forms an immutable ledger of transactions [1, 2].

The launch of Bitcoin in early 2009 marked the advent of public blockchain networks. Since then, numerous cryptocurrencies have sought to replicate Bitcoin's success as a novel form of currency. However, many early Bitcoin adopters soon recognized that the blockchain's properties could be applied beyond financial transactions. Community emerged with the aim of expanding, modifying, and building

S. HajiHosseinKhani et al., *Understanding Cybersecurity for Smart Contracts*,
https://doi.org/10.1007/978-3-032-28863-9_1

upon Bitcoin to explore new possibilities. Despite these efforts, the Bitcoin protocol is intentionally designed with limitations that make it difficult to extend. Recognizing these constraints, blockchain visionary Vitalik Buterin chose to abandon attempts to expand Bitcoin and instead developed a new, more versatile protocol from the ground up. This vision led to the creation of the Ethereum white paper in 2013 [3].

When Ethereum was launched in 2015, it quickly ascended to become one of the most valuable cryptocurrencies, second only to Bitcoin. Ethereum gained widespread acclaim for providing a platform for deploying and running smart contracts on a public blockchain. The term "smart contract" was originally coined by Nick Szabo in 1994, with the idea that many legal agreements, notarizations, and other traditional contracts could be automatically enforced using digital protocols and cryptographic signatures [4, 5]. Despite this historical backdrop, developing smart contracts on Ethereum feels more like general-purpose programming rather than a direct extension of legal contracts. The Ethereum protocol's virtual machine is Turing-complete, meaning that as long as the computations fit within the constraints of a single block, smart contract developers are limited only by their creativity [3].

So, what sets blockchain apart from other technologies you may have encountered? In the next section, we'll explore the unique characteristics that define blockchain technology.

1.1 Definition of a Blockchain

At its essence, a blockchain is a specialized data structure, specifically a linked chain of distinct "blocks." Each block in this chain references the previous one, forming a sequence, and within each block is a collection of transactions. While this structure may seem like a simple list-of-lists, the true innovation of blockchain technology lies in the protocol that governs how new blocks are added to the chain, all without a central authority. Figure 1.1 illustrates this fundamental structure.

Phase 1 The first step, called 'Genesis Creation,' involves establishing the genesis block, the very first block in a blockchain. The initial block, known as the genesis block, forms the foundation of the blockchain and is unique in that it does not reference any previous block, unlike all subsequent blocks, which are linked to their predecessors. This block contains metadata essential for initializing the blockchain's protocol and parameters, such as the blockchain's version, the initial state, and any relevant network settings.

The creation of this block involves specific coding by blockchain developers, as it cannot be mined or added by the consensus mechanisms (such as Proof of Work or Proof of Stake) that govern subsequent blocks. For example, in Bitcoin, the genesis block contains a cryptic message embedded by its creator, Satoshi Nakamoto, symbolizing both a starting point and a manifesto for decentralization. This block anchors the blockchain, setting the groundwork for transparency, immutability, and decentralized consensus that define the blockchain's lifecycle.

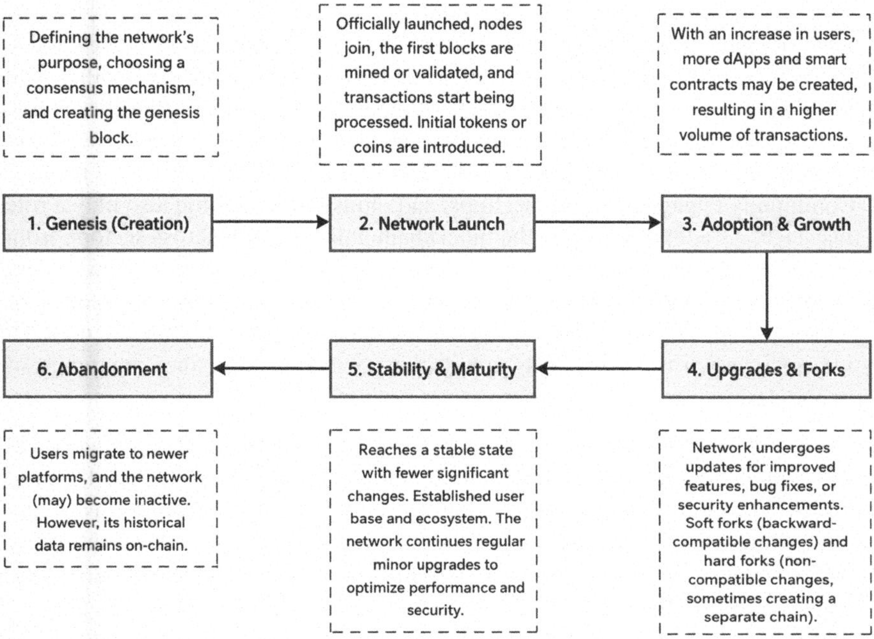

Fig. 1.1 Blockchain lifecycle

Phase 2 Following the creation of the genesis block, the next phase is the 'Network Launch.' During this step, the blockchain network goes live, enabling nodes (computers participating in the network) to connect, communicate, and begin processing transactions. Network participants configure their nodes to recognize the genesis block as the starting point, ensuring that all nodes have a shared understanding of the blockchain's history and protocol.

The network launch is a critical phase, as it marks the beginning of decentralized consensus. In this phase, the nodes collectively validate and add new blocks of transactions to the blockchain. Once the network is launched, it becomes possible to introduce the blockchain's native assets, such as tokens or coins, and open the network for users to initiate transactions, deploy smart contracts (if supported), and engage with decentralized applications. This phase establishes the blockchain as an active, publicly accessible ecosystem, laying the groundwork for its decentralized, self-sustaining operation.

Phase 3 After the network launch, the blockchain enters a phase known as 'Adoption and Growth.' This step is characterized by increasing participation, development, and utility within the blockchain ecosystem. Early adopters, including developers, miners (or validators), and users, begin interacting with the network by running nodes, mining or staking, transacting, and building decentralized applications (dApps) or smart contracts, if the blockchain supports them, thereby contributing to its expansion.

As more participants join, the blockchain's utility and value can increase, leading to network effects that drive further adoption. Developers may introduce new tools, infrastructure, and enhancements to improve the user experience, scalability, and security of the network. In blockchains that support smart contracts, this phase often sees the growth of Decentralized Finance (DeFi) projects, tokenized assets, and other applications that leverage the blockchain's decentralized, transparent nature.

Community engagement, partnerships, and industry recognition also play a role in this stage. As adoption grows, the blockchain gains traction across sectors, from finance to supply chain management, thereby promoting broader public awareness and contributing to the ecosystem's legitimacy and trustworthiness. This period of growth is crucial for a blockchain's long-term viability, as it strengthens the network by increasing security, diversifying applications, and expanding the community of users and developers.

Phase 4 As the blockchain matures, it often enters a phase of 'Upgrades and Forks,' though this depends entirely on whether the ecosystem is designed to support such adaptability. Some blockchains are built with upgradeability as a core feature, while others maintain a fixed, immutable structure that does not easily allow for changes. In this stage, the community, developers, and stakeholders collaborate to improve the network's functionality, security, and scalability. Upgrades are essential to ensure the blockchain adapts to evolving user needs, technological advancements, and security requirements. These upgrades may involve optimizations in transaction processing speed, adjustments to consensus algorithms, or enhancements in privacy features.

Some upgrades can be implemented seamlessly through backward-compatible changes, often called 'soft forks.' A soft fork allows upgraded nodes to recognize new rules, while older nodes continue to function, albeit with limited capabilities. However, significant changes may require a 'hard fork,' which creates an irreversible split in the blockchain's protocol. In a hard fork, nodes that adopt the new rules diverge from those that do not, effectively creating two separate chains with distinct histories. Hard forks can occur for various reasons, such as introducing substantial new features, addressing security vulnerabilities, or resolving ideological differences within the community.

Notable examples include the hard fork in the Ethereum blockchain after the DAO hack, which led to the creation of Ethereum and Ethereum Classic. In such cases, forks can foster innovation and improvement or even give rise to new ecosystems with unique objectives. The upgrades and forks stage are a testament to the blockchain's adaptability, ensuring that the technology remains resilient and responsive to the needs of its community and the broader industry.

Phase 5 Following upgrades and forks, the blockchain enters the 'Stability & Maturity' phase. In this stage, the blockchain has typically reached a level of reliability and robustness, with most major technical issues addressed and a stable set of protocols and features in place. The network's infrastructure, governance, and community have evolved, creating a resilient system capable of handling high transaction volumes and a variety of use cases.

During this phase, the blockchain may see fewer drastic changes, as stability and reliability become the primary focus. The network often gains wider trust, attracting more users, institutional support, and mainstream adoption. At this point, the blockchain is considered mature, having proven its longevity, security, and scalability over time and establishing itself as a trusted digital asset or service infrastructure. This phase underscores the blockchain's success in balancing innovation and stability, making it a reliable, sustainable technology for long-term applications in industries such as finance, supply chain, and public administration.

Phase 6 The final phase in a blockchain's lifecycle can be 'Abandonment,' though this depends on the specific circumstances. In this phase, the blockchain may experience a decline in active development, user engagement, and community support, eventually leading to its discontinuation. This can occur for various reasons, such as a loss of interest among developers and users, the emergence of better technologies that replace it, security issues that make the network unsustainable, or an overall lack of resources to maintain it. However, the historical data on the blockchain remains immutable and preserved indefinitely, providing a permanent archive of all past transactions and records.

As activity dwindles, nodes may go offline, transactions may no longer be processed, and the network could become vulnerable to attacks. For public blockchains, abandonment may leave users with inaccessible assets or unsupported applications, while in private or permissioned blockchains, it may mean transitioning to new solutions or platforms. Abandonment highlights the importance of continuous support and adaptation within the blockchain ecosystem, as technologies that fail to evolve with user needs or to compete with more advanced systems may lose relevance over time. In some cases, an abandoned blockchain may be revived by a new community, creating a 'relaunch' scenario. However, without a committed group of developers, users, and stakeholders, the blockchain eventually becomes inactive, effectively reaching the end of its lifecycle.

The blockchain lifecycle, from genesis to potential abandonment, reflects its dynamic nature. Starting with the genesis block, it evolves through phases of launch, growth, and adaptation, fostering innovation and utility. Maturity brings reliability and trust, while immutable historical data preserves legacy, underscoring the need for community and innovation to ensure long-term relevance.

1.1.1 The Blockchain Network

In a centralized system, a single database serves as the core of operations, holding all essential data and enabling users and applications to access, update, or retrieve information as needed. To interact with this database, a connection must be established along with the necessary permissions to modify its contents. In simple scenarios, where only one database is involved, this connection can be set up using a single IP address. However, the system's functionality is entirely dependent on the availability of this database. If it crashes, loses connectivity, or if access rights are revoked, the entire application ceases to function. This reliance highlights the centralized nature of the setup, where all data storage, permissions, and operations revolve around a single, critical point, the database, making it both the system's strength and its vulnerability.

In contrast, blockchains are designed to operate within decentralized networks. Individuals and organizations run nodes within the network, and, in many ways, these nodes function as equals. This is feasible because each node stores the complete history of every transaction that has ever occurred on the blockchain. Since every node is an independent, self-sufficient unit, there is no central point of control within the network. All nodes participate in validating and propagating transactions to their peers. Additionally, some nodes participate in creating new blocks and are rewarded with a "block reward" in the blockchain's native cryptocurrency. Unlike the centralized database example, any node in a decentralized network can join or leave at any time, without requiring special permissions or rights to read from or write to the blockchain, as long as they adhere to the established protocol. Figure 1.2 presents an overview of blockchain network architecture.

But without a single, central database to connect to, how do nodes establish connections within the network? Many smart contract developers sidestep this complexity by using services that abstract away these details behind a web API. This approach, however, involves a trade-off between tying your system to a third-party service and the intricacies of running your own Ethereum node. If you opt to run your own node, it must initiate itself by connecting to the public Ethereum network. Most major Ethereum node software comes with a predefined list of "bootnodes." These are well-known, relatively stable IP addresses that can help the node establish sufficient network peer connections. If these bootnodes are unavailable or no longer trustworthy, the node software can be configured with a custom list of bootnodes.

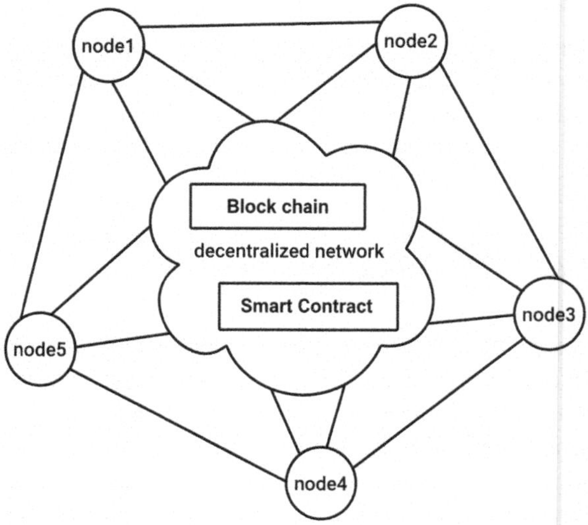

Fig. 1.2 Blockchain network architecture

1.1.2 *The Blockchain Node*

The decentralized nature of blockchain means that each node in the network is responsible for executing all operations necessary for the blockchain to function effectively. Every node is responsible for maintaining and updating a complete copy of the digital ledger, which is structured as a chain of blocks. This means that each node stores the full blockchain and may also maintain a more accessible version of the data. For instance, in Ethereum, nodes maintain a database representing the current state, which is continuously derived from and updated by the blockchain, reflecting the ledger's latest state.

In addition to storing the blockchain, a node might also participate in creating new blocks. This involves tracking transactions that have not yet been included in a block and managing the outputs of previous transactions that can be used in future transactions. These unused outputs might, for example, represent the current distribution of a blockchain's cryptocurrency.

Moreover, a blockchain node can have responsibilities beyond just maintaining the ledger. On platforms designed for smart contracts, such as Ethereum, nodes help create a decentralized computing system. To facilitate this, each node hosts a virtual machine (VM), which executes the instructions embedded in transactions whenever a new block is added to the blockchain. This allows the decentralized network to function not just as a ledger, but as a global computer that can execute code securely and transparently across all participating nodes.

1.1.3 *The Blockchain Block*

Blocks serve as the fundamental building blocks of a blockchain. Each block contains a block header, which becomes part of the blockchain and includes critical metadata. One key component of this metadata is the root hash of the block's Merkle tree. A Merkle tree is a data structure used to efficiently and securely verify the integrity of large datasets. It organizes data into a tree-like structure in which each leaf node represents a transaction hash, and each non-leaf node represents a hash of its child nodes. The root of the tree, known as the Merkle root, summarizes all the transactions in the block and provides a compact way to verify their integrity. Block headers are linked together through hash functions, with each block header incorporating the hash of the preceding block. These hash functions are designed to be collision-resistant, ensuring that it is nearly impossible to find two different inputs producing the same hash output. By embedding the hash of the previous block in each block header, the blockchain ensures that altering a single block would require changing every subsequent block as well, significantly increasing the difficulty of tampering with the blockchain and falsifying its transaction history.

The second component of a block is the block body, which contains a list of transactions that are included in that block. While these transactions may initially be

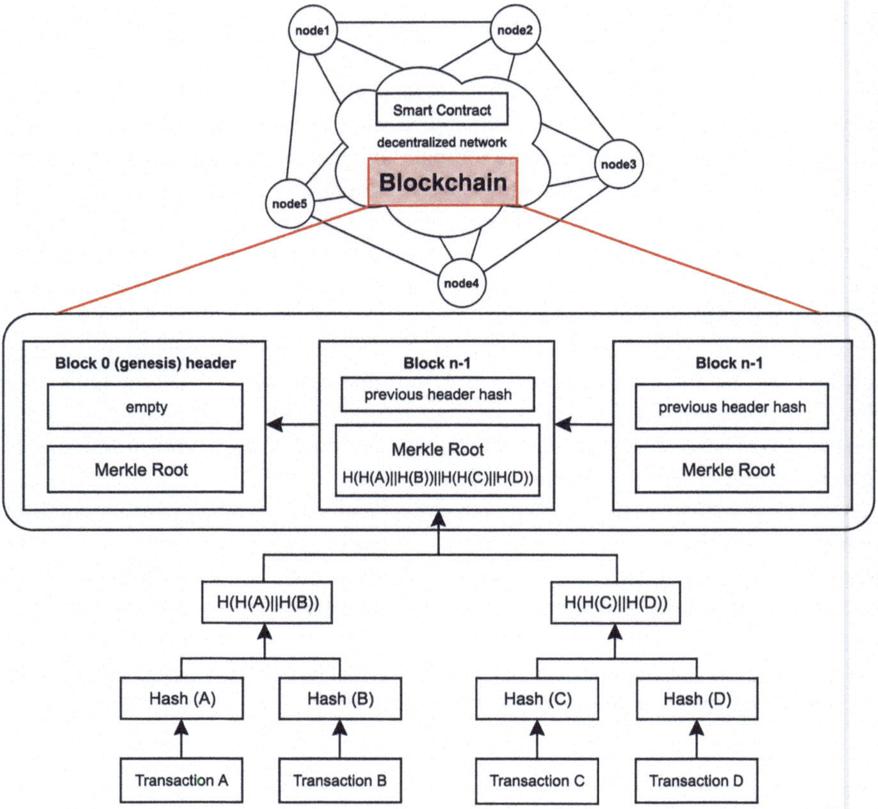

Fig. 1.3 Blockchain architecture

communicated as a list, they are organized into a Merkle tree. Figure 1.3 illustrates the components of a block and their relationship to the decentralized network.

In a Merkle tree, the leaf nodes represent the hashes of individual transactions, while the internal nodes contain the hash of their two child nodes. The properties of hash functions make it virtually impossible to find two distinct versions of a Merkle tree (of a given size) that share the same root hash value. Consequently, the single-root hash in the block header provides a secure summary of all transactions in the block and ensures they are protected by the blockchain's immutability. This structure is central to the security and integrity of the blockchain, as it prevents unauthorized modifications to the transaction history.

1.1.4 The Blockchain Transaction

The original blockchain, Bitcoin, was specifically designed as a cryptocurrency. Its distributed ledger was created to track and record Bitcoin transfers between accounts.

Because of this primary function, the data recorded on the Bitcoin blockchain are referred to as transactions. The term "transaction" can be somewhat misleading, as a single blockchain transaction can involve multiple transfers of value between various accounts. However, a transaction can also encompass multiple transfers of different tokens or other independent actions.

At a basic level, the input to a blockchain transaction must include a source address, an amount, and a digital signature. These fields define the intent of the transaction and verify that it was authorized by someone who has access to the private key associated with the source account, typically the account owner. Moreover, for a transaction input to be considered valid, it usually must be an unused output from a previous transaction.

Most blockchains do not require transactions to be authorized by the recipient. Therefore, the transaction must only specify the recipient's address and the amount to be transferred. Once a transaction is validated, its output can be used by the recipients as inputs for new transactions, continuing the flow of value across the blockchain.

1.2 The Benefits of Blockchain

Blockchain technology offers a wide range of benefits, making it a transformative tool across various industries. In addition to its widely recognized features like privacy and decentralization, it offers unparalleled transparency. All transactions recorded on the blockchain are immutable and verifiable, allowing participants to trace activities in real-time. This transparency fosters trust among users and reduces opportunities for fraud, making it ideal for sectors like finance, supply chain, and governance.

A key advantage is security. Blockchain employs advanced cryptographic techniques and consensus mechanisms to protect data from unauthorized alterations. Each block is linked to the previous one through cryptographic hashes, ensuring data integrity and making tampering nearly impossible. Furthermore, the distributed nature of the network ensures that there is no single point of failure, significantly reducing vulnerabilities to cyberattacks.

Blockchain also enhances automation through smart contracts. These self-executing contracts, embedded with code, automate processes when predefined conditions are met. This not only reduces human intervention but also minimizes errors and speeds up processes, such as payments, document verification, and supply chain management.

Interoperability is another emerging strength of blockchain systems. With advancements in cross-chain technologies, blockchains can now interact and exchange information seamlessly, fostering collaboration between previously siloed systems. This ability enhances the scalability of blockchain networks, making them suitable for complex, interconnected applications.

Blockchain also supports tokenization, which involves converting physical or digital assets into blockchain-based tokens. This feature democratizes access to investments and enables fractional ownership, providing opportunities for people to participate in previously inaccessible markets, such as real estate or fine art.

Cost-effectiveness is another notable advantage. By removing intermediaries and streamlining processes, blockchain reduces transaction costs and increases operational efficiency. For businesses, this means not only lower overheads but also faster service turnaround times.

Sustainability is an emerging focus in blockchain innovation. Newer blockchain models are adopting eco-friendly consensus mechanisms like Proof of Stake (PoS), which significantly reduce energy consumption compared to earlier models like Proof of Work (PoW). This makes blockchain a viable option for industries striving to meet sustainability goals.

Lastly, blockchain's programmability allows it to adapt to evolving needs. Custom protocols, modular architecture, and upgradable smart contracts make blockchain networks flexible and future-proof. These characteristics ensure that organizations can continuously innovate without significant disruptions to their systems.

By combining these advantages, privacy, security, transparency, automation, scalability, and sustainability, blockchain technology stands as a cornerstone for digital transformation in diverse fields ranging from healthcare to logistics, finance, and beyond.

1.3 Smart Contracts

During the **Adoption and Growth** phase of a blockchain lifecycle, as illustrated in Fig. 1.1, smart contracts can be introduced to the network. A smart contract is a self-executing program stored on a blockchain that enforces the terms of an agreement automatically when predefined conditions are met. Unlike traditional contracts, which rely on intermediaries for execution and enforcement, smart contracts leverage the blockchain's decentralized nature to provide transparency, security, and automation. Written in specialized programming languages such as Solidity, smart contracts encapsulate logic to perform actions like transferring funds, validating transactions, or managing digital assets.

Once deployed on a blockchain, a smart contract is assigned to a unique address, where its code and initial state are securely recorded on the decentralized network. This process ensures both immutability and accessibility for all network participants. Users interact with the contract by sending transactions to its address, triggering specific functions embedded in its code. These interactions update the contract's state, which is stored on the blockchain and permanently linked to its transaction history. The following section will delve into the benefits of smart contracts, highlighting their transformative potential across various applications.

1.3.1 *The Benefits of Smart Contracts*

The benefits of smart contracts span across multiple dimensions, offering transformative advantages in modern business operations. **Accuracy** is a cornerstone benefit, as smart contracts use conditional logic, such as "if-then" statements, to ensure precise execution of terms. For instance, a contract might stipulate: "If customer X pays Y units of currency, then grant access to the service package." By integrating with cryptocurrencies such as Ethereum, Bitcoin, and Litecoin, these contracts enhance overall performance and robustness. Explicit, error-free coding of terms is critical, as inaccuracies can lead to transaction failures. Automation further minimizes human errors, ensuring efficient and reliable execution.

Clear Communication and Transparency are inherent features of smart contracts, as their terms and conditions are visible to all participants on the blockchain. Once established, these terms cannot be altered, and every transaction is monitored and verified by a decentralized network of nodes. This transparency reduces the risk of fraud and eliminates the need for intermediaries, fostering trust and ensuring compliance. Unlike traditional contracts, which often require legal oversight to address breaches such as overcharging or service delays, smart contracts self-enforce agreements, ensuring accuracy and validity in every transaction.

Speed and Efficiency are achieved as smart contracts execute autonomously, triggered by predefined conditions such as a specific date, time, or payment. For example, a contract might automatically renew a subscription upon receiving payment. Unlike traditional contracts that rely on manual verification and are prone to delays, smart contracts leverage decentralized blockchain-based verification for rapid, efficient execution. This eliminates delays while ensuring secure, fast transactions without centralized control.

Security is significantly enhanced through blockchain technology. The decentralized nature of blockchain ensures that no single party controls the system, and cryptographic techniques, including encryption and the use of private and public keys, secure transactions. Each transaction must be validated by all nodes in the network, creating an additional layer of security. Research, such as that by Seijas, highlights how cryptographic methods protect against malicious activities, ensuring the integrity of smart contracts [6, 7].

Finally, **Cost Reduction** is a key advantage for businesses. By eliminating intermediaries like legal personnel, smart contracts reduce organizational expenses, streamline operations, and maximize profit margins. This is particularly beneficial for multinational corporations managing numerous contracts, as it significantly lowers traditional contract management costs.

Despite these benefits, it is important to acknowledge that the effectiveness of smart contracts relies on the quality of their code. Poorly written contracts can lead to adverse outcomes, underlining the need for meticulous design and implementation to fully leverage their potential.

1.3.2 *Smart Contracts Platforms and Languages*

Smart contract platforms provide infrastructure for creating and executing dApps, with each platform supporting specific programming languages tailored to its architecture. **Ethereum**, a leading platform, offers a versatile range of languages, including **Solidity**, known for its widespread adoption and flexibility, **Vyper**, a security-focused alternative, and **Yul**, a low-level language optimized for advanced optimizations. Platforms like **Algorand** use **PyTeal**, enabling developers to write smart contracts in Python, while **Tezos** employs **SmartPy** and **Liquidity**, emphasizing formal verification to ensure correctness and reliability. Similarly, **Cardano** supports **Aiken**, a language that prioritizes functional programming principles for secure and efficient smart contract development. Enterprise-focused platforms like **Hyperledger Fabric** rely on **ChainCode**, offering a robust framework for developing business-centric blockchain solutions.

The differences among platforms and languages can be categorized by their design goals and capabilities. For instance, **Bitcoin Script** is a non-Turing-complete language, designed to prioritize simplicity and security for Bitcoin transactions, while **Rust** and **Move**, used by high-performance platforms like **Solana** and **Aptos**, focus on scalability and efficiency. **Cairo**, employed by platforms like **StarkNet** and **StarkEx**, is tailored for zero-knowledge proof systems, enabling privacy-preserving applications. Meanwhile, **Pact** and **Kadena** emphasize readability and auditability, catering to developers who require clear, secure smart contract implementations. This diverse landscape allows developers to choose platforms and languages that align with their priorities, whether they value performance, security, scalability, or transparency, driving innovation across various blockchain ecosystems.

1.4 Chapter Summary

This chapter introduces the foundational concepts of blockchain technology, tracing its origins from the 2008 Bitcoin white paper by Satoshi Nakamoto. It explains how blockchain operates as a peer-to-peer network that processes transactions into sequential "blocks," forming an immutable ledger. While Bitcoin pioneered public blockchains, other projects like Ethereum emerged to extend blockchain's capabilities beyond financial transactions, particularly through smart contracts. Ethereum's introduction in 2015 marked a significant advancement, allowing developers to write complex decentralized applications (DApps) and execute smart contracts on a Turing-complete platform. The chapter also outlines the technical structure of blockchains, including decentralized networks and consensus mechanisms, highlighting their resilience, security, and potential for applications far beyond cryptocurrency.

References

1. Wang, S., et al.: An overview of smart contract: architecture, applications, and future trends. In: 2018 IEEE Intelligent Vehicles Symposium (IV). IEEE (2018)
2. Mohanta, B.K., Panda, S.S., Jena, D.: An overview of smart contract and use cases in blockchain technology. In: 2018 9th International Conference on Computing, Communication and Networking Technologies (ICCCNT). IEEE (2018)
3. Buterin, V.: A next-generation smart contract and decentralized application platform. White paper 3.37, 2–1 (2014)
4. Lavery, K.: Smart Contracting for Local Government Services, pp. 1–232. Praeger, Westport (1999)
5. Grigg, I.: The Ricardian contract. In: Proceedings. First IEEE International Workshop on Electronic Contracting, 2004. IEEE (2004)
6. Luu, L., et al.: Making smart contracts smarter. In: Proceedings of the 2016 ACM SIGSAC Conference on Computer and Communications Security, p. 2016
7. Bünz, B., et al.: Zether: towards privacy in a smart contract world. In: International Conference on Financial Cryptography and Data Security. Springer, Cham (2020)

Chapter 2
Fundamentals of Smart Contracts

Abstract This chapter examines the limits of traditional contracts, costly intermediaries, slow manual execution, ambiguity, and cross-border enforcement hurdles, and shows how smart contracts address them with automation, transparency, and cryptographic assurance. It maps each contract element (terms, signatures, timelines, termination, ownership, confidentiality, and governing law) into precise on-chain logic through digital signatures, timestamped milestones, automated payments or penalties, and verifiable ownership transfer, with oracles and arbitration workflows managing off-chain inputs or disputes. Then, it traces smart contracts from Szabo's 1990s concept to Ethereum's programmable era, highlighting milestones such as the DAO fork, ICOs, DeFi, NFTs, Layer-2 scaling, and enterprise adoption. Additionally, it outlines core principles, decentralization, autonomy, immutability (with cautious upgrade patterns), determinism, conditional logic, security and gas economics, oracle use, and interoperability, and details the lifecycle from creation and deployment to activation, execution and state management, upgrade or termination, and archival. In the end, this chapter frames smart contracts as a practical, scalable alternative to traditional agreements when engineered with clear specifications, secure code, and accountable governance.

Traditional contracts have long served as the foundation of business and legal transactions, but they face significant limitations in today's fast-paced, digital world. Their reliance on intermediaries, such as lawyers and notaries, adds unnecessary costs and delays, while the risk of human error, misinterpretation, and fraud can lead to disputes and costly legal battles. Enforcing these contracts, particularly across different legal jurisdictions, often proves complex and costly. Additionally, the manual processes inherent to traditional contracts hinder scalability, making them unsuitable for industries that demand speed and efficiency. To address these challenges, smart contracts have emerged as a transformative solution, providing automation, transparency, and enhanced security to revolutionize the execution and enforcement of agreements [1, 2]. This chapter begins by examining the problems and solutions associated with traditional contracts, then explores smart contracts in depth, covering their history, key characteristics, and core principles from inception through their current role in modern technology.

S. HajiHosseinKhani et al., *Understanding Cybersecurity for Smart Contracts*,
https://doi.org/10.1007/978-3-032-28863-9_2

2.1 Traditional Contracts Problems and Solutions

Traditional contracts comprise several fundamental components that define the terms and obligations between the parties. These components include **terms and conditions**, **signatures**, **verification and enforcement mechanisms**, **execution processes**, and **provisions for confidentiality and intellectual property rights**. While these elements are critical to formalizing agreements, they are often accompanied by inefficiencies, ambiguities, and vulnerabilities that can complicate their implementation and management.

The **terms and conditions** in a traditional contract outline the scope of work, obligations, and payment terms. In the provided **Contract for Services Agreement**, the "Services Provided" section specifies that ABC Web Solutions will design and maintain an e-commerce website for XYZ Retail Company, with payment divided into two milestones: 50% upon signing and 50% upon successful delivery. While clear, such language can still be ambiguous, particularly around terms like "successful delivery," which may lead to disputes. Similarly, the "Timeline" section defines project start and end dates, but adherence relies on manual oversight.

The **signatures** section in the agreement serves as proof of mutual consent and requires both parties to sign and date the document. These signatures must often be verified by intermediaries like notaries to ensure authenticity, adding time and cost to the process. The agreement also includes mechanisms for **verification and enforcement**, as seen in the "Termination" clause, which outlines the procedure for ending the contract and outlines financial obligations upon termination. However, enforcing such provisions typically requires legal intervention, which can be costly and time-consuming, especially in cross-border agreements.

The **execution process** in traditional contracts is inherently manual. For example, payments outlined in the "Payment Terms" section require human initiation and monitoring to ensure they are made when the specified milestones are met. This manual approach introduces delays and inefficiencies. Additionally, the "Confidentiality" and "Ownership and Intellectual Property Rights" sections impose obligations on both parties to safeguard proprietary information and transfer ownership of the deliverables upon full payment. However, ensuring compliance with these clauses often depends on trust and post-contract enforcement mechanisms.

Finally, the "Governing Law" section specifies the jurisdiction governing the contract, which can create challenges in cross-border agreements where different legal frameworks apply. This reliance on jurisdictional systems can complicate dispute resolution and increase costs.

The solution to these challenges lies in transitioning from traditional contracts to **smart contracts**, which leverage blockchain technology to automate terms and processes, ensure transparency, and eliminate intermediaries [1, 3]. In the following chapter, we illustrate this transition by transforming the example into a smart contract.

Contract for Services Agreement

This Services Agreement ("Agreement") is entered into as of [Date], by and between:

Company: ABC Web Solutions, Inc.

Address: 123 Business Park, City, State, ZIP

Client: XYZ Retail Company

Address: 456 Main Street, City, State, ZIP

Services Provided:

ABC Web Solutions agrees to provide the following services ("Services") to XYZ Retail Company:

Design and development of an e-commerce website.

Maintenance and technical support for the website for a period of 6 months after the launch date.

Payment Terms:

The total fee for the services is $10,000, payable as follows:

50% ($5,000) upon signing this Agreement.

50% ($5,000) upon successful completion and delivery of the website.

Timeline:

The project shall commence on [Start Date] and be completed no later than [End Date].

Ownership and Intellectual Property Rights:

XYZ Retail Company will own all rights to the website, including the source code, upon full payment of the service fees.

ABC Web Solutions will retain the right to showcase the website as part of their portfolio.

Termination:

Either party may terminate this Agreement by providing 30 days' written notice.

In the event of termination, XYZ Retail Company will be responsible for payment of all work completed up to the date of termination.

Confidentiality:

Both parties agree to keep confidential any proprietary information, trade secrets, and business information obtained during the course of this Agreement.

Governing Law:

This Agreement shall be governed by and construed in accordance with the laws of the State of [State].

Signatures:

By signing below, the parties agree to the terms of this Agreement.

ABC Web Solutions, Inc.

Name: ____________________

Title: ____________________

Signature: ________________

Date: _____________________

XYZ Retail Company

Name: ____________________

Title: ____________________

Signature: ________________

2.2 Traditional Contracts to Smart Contracts

To transition from a traditional contract to a smart contract, each component of the traditional agreement must be mapped to the programmable, automated framework of a blockchain-based smart contract [1, 4]. This process not only involves encoding the terms and conditions but also redefining how essential elements such as enforcement, execution, and confidentiality are handled. Using the **Contract for Services Agreement** as an example, we can outline the steps required for this transformation.

In a traditional contract, terms and conditions are expressed in natural language, which, although flexible, is often susceptible to ambiguity and misinterpretation. For instance, in the provided contract, the "Services Provided" and "Payment

Terms" sections outline ABC Web Solutions' responsibilities, including designing and maintaining a website, with payments split into two milestones: 50% upon signing and 50% upon delivery. In a smart contract, these terms would be converted into precise, executable logic. To implement the payment process, two conditions must be defined: **Condition 1** specifies that upon signing the agreement (validated via blockchain digital signatures), $5000 is automatically transferred from the client's account to ABC Web Solutions. **Condition 2** states that upon successful delivery of the website (verified using a hash representing the completed deliverable), the remaining $5000 is released. This approach removes ambiguity by explicitly defining "delivery" and ensures automatic enforcement of payment terms, significantly reducing the likelihood of disputes.

Moving forward, in traditional contracts, "**signatures**", whether physical or electronic, serve as proof of agreement and often require intermediaries, such as notaries, for verification. In smart contracts, this process is replaced by cryptographic digital signatures [3]. Each party signs the contract using their private key, and the blockchain automatically records and validates these signatures. This implementation ensures authenticity, prevents tampering, and eliminates the need for intermediaries, thereby reducing costs and streamlining the process.

The **"Termination"** section of a traditional contract defines the process of ending the agreement, including the financial obligations upon termination. In a smart contract, these clauses are encoded to execute automatically. For example, if either party provides 30 days' notice to terminate, the smart contract calculates the payment for work completed up to that date and automatically transfers the owed amount to ABC Web Solutions [2]. This automation eliminates the need for arbitration or litigation, ensuring that financial obligations are resolved fairly, efficiently, and without manual intervention.

Next, the **"Timeline"** section specifies the project schedule, including start and end dates. Smart contracts can automate these milestones using blockchain timestamps. To enclose the timeline conditions, Condition 1 requires the project to begin on the designated start date, while Condition 2 mandates that final delivery occur by the specified end date. Additionally, Penalty Clauses can be programmed so that if deadlines are missed, the smart contract automatically applies penalties or issues refunds. This automation enforces strict adherence to deadlines, ensuring accountability without manual oversight.

Subsequently, the "Ownership and Intellectual Property Rights" section states that XYZ Retail Company will gain full ownership of the website upon payment in full. In a smart contract, this transfer of ownership can be automated. By implementing an ownership transfer mechanism, the smart contract ensures that upon full payment, ownership rights are automatically transferred to XYZ Retail Company. This transaction is immutably recorded on the blockchain, providing verifiable proof of the transfer. This approach minimizes the risk of disputes and enhances transparency throughout the process.

The **"Confidentiality"** section in a traditional contract requires the parties to protect proprietary information; however, this cannot be enforced directly by a smart contract. Instead, secure data handling can be significantly enhanced by utilizing encryption and hashing [5]. Sensitive information can be stored on the blockchain as encrypted data or hashes, ensuring data security and providing verifiable proof of compliance with confidentiality agreements. Similarly, the **"Governing Law"** section establishes the legal framework for resolving disputes in traditional contracts. In smart contracts, decentralization enables jurisdiction-agnostic enforcement. Dispute resolution mechanisms can be embedded within the smart contract by incorporating arbitration workflows [6]. For instance, if a dispute arises, the contract can automatically trigger a process to engage third-party mediators through blockchain protocols. This approach simplifies cross-border agreements and minimizes reliance on traditional legal frameworks.

The transformation of the **Contract for Services Agreement** into a smart contract involves encoding all key components, terms, signatures, enforcement, execution, ownership, confidentiality, and jurisdiction into programmable logic on the blockchain [1, 3, 4]. This eliminates inefficiencies, ambiguities, and vulnerabilities while automating processes and enhancing security.

2.3 History of Smart Contracts

The history of smart contract invention traces back to the early 1990s when computer scientist Nick Szabo first introduced the concept in 1994 [7, 8]. Szabo envisioned smart contracts as self-executing agreements embedded with computer protocols, designed to enforce their terms automatically. His idea was grounded in reducing reliance on traditional intermediaries, such as lawyers or escrow agents, by leveraging automation and cryptographic security. At that time, the term "smart contract" referred to software that could encode business logic and execute predefined actions when certain conditions were met. Szabo proposed that these contracts could handle transactions and relationships in digital environments, much like vending machines: if specific inputs (money) were provided, the machine would automatically perform the agreed-upon action (dispensing a product). While his vision was innovative, the technological infrastructure, such as decentralized blockchains, was not yet mature enough to implement his ideas effectively.

In the mid-2000s, decentralized ledgers and cryptographic tools began to gain attention in academic and technical communities, though smart contract technology itself remained underdeveloped. In 2008, Satoshi Nakamoto released the Bitcoin whitepaper, introducing blockchain technology and programmable transactions [9, 10]. When Bitcoin launched in 2009, its scripting language enabled basic functionalities such as multi-signature wallets and time-locked transactions. These early features hinted at the potential for automated agreements, though they were limited in scope [11, 12].

By 2013, Vitalik Buterin recognized the limitations of Bitcoin's scripting language and proposed Ethereum, a blockchain designed for generalized programmability [8, 13]. The Ethereum project was crowdfunded through an Initial Coin Offering (ICO) in 2014, raising over $18 million. This marked the beginning of a platform specifically intended to support decentralized applications (dApps) and smart contracts. Ethereum's mainnet launched in 2015, introducing Solidity, a Turing-complete programming language that allowed developers to write complex smart contracts capable of executing intricate logic. This innovation transformed blockchain from a simple ledger into a platform for decentralized applications. Early use cases included token issuance, automated voting systems, and financial agreements.

In 2016, Ethereum saw its first major challenge with the Decentralized Autonomous Organization (DAO) [1]. While the DAO demonstrated the potential for large-scale smart contract-driven projects, a critical vulnerability led to a $50 million hack. This incident exposed the risks of poorly designed contracts and led to Ethereum's first hard fork, splitting the network into Ethereum (ETH) and Ethereum Classic (ETC).

The year 2017 marked the ICO boom, with startups leveraging Ethereum's smart contract capabilities to raise funds by issuing tokens. This period also saw the growth of dApps in gaming, identity management, and prediction markets. However, as Ethereum gained popularity, its scalability issues became apparent. By 2018, network congestion from applications like CryptoKitties underscored the need for improvements. Alternative platforms such as EOS, TRON, and Cardano emerged, offering faster transaction speeds and lower costs.

In 2019, smart contract adoption expanded into enterprise applications, with industries like supply chain management and finance exploring blockchain-based automation. Chainlink gained prominence by enabling secure off-chain data feeds for smart contracts, improving their utility. The following year, 2020, saw an explosion in Decentralized Finance (DeFi) [13, 14]. Platforms like Uniswap, Aave, and Compound used smart contracts to automate lending, borrowing, and trading. Yield farming emerged, introducing new incentive mechanisms for liquidity provision.

The momentum continued into 2021 with the rise of non-fungible tokens (NFTs) [8, 14]. Ethereum smart contracts underpinned NFT marketplaces like OpenSea, while Layer 2 scaling solutions such as Polygon addressed network congestion and high gas fees. In 2022, multi-chain platforms like Avalanche, Polkadot, and Cosmos facilitated cross-chain interoperability, and security practices improved with the widespread adoption of formal verification and automated auditing tools [14].

By 2023, tokenization of real-world assets such as real estate and stocks had become mainstream, with smart contracts enabling fractional ownership and automated transactions. Governments and institutions began piloting legal frameworks to integrate smart contracts into traditional contract law [14]. In 2024, modular architecture allowed developers to update and customize smart contracts more easily without redeployment, and AI integration enabled predictive analytics and autonomous decision-making in DeFi and supply chain management.

In summary, the period before 2000 was characterized by the conceptualization of smart contracts and the development of cryptographic tools, setting the stage for the creation of blockchain systems capable of realizing Szabo's vision. This evolution of smart contract technology illustrates its growing complexity and utility, transitioning from simple programmable features on Bitcoin to a cornerstone of decentralized ecosystems and real-world applications.

2.4 The First Invention of Smart Contracts

The concept of "smart contracts" was first introduced by Nick Szabo, a computer scientist and cryptographer, in 1994 [7–9]. Szabo's idea of a smart contract was to extend the functionality of traditional contracts by using computer protocols to automatically enforce, verify, or facilitate the negotiation or execution of agreements, without intermediaries.

Szabo's vision was to create self-executing contracts in which the terms and conditions of an agreement between two parties could be encoded directly in lines of code [7, 8, 14]. These smart contracts would automatically enforce the agreed-upon rules and penalties, reducing reliance on third parties such as lawyers or banks.

However, it wasn't until the development of blockchain technology, particularly with the introduction of Ethereum in 2015, that smart contracts became practical and widely implemented [1, 10, 14]. Ethereum's decentralized platform allowed for the execution of smart contracts in a secure, transparent, and tamper-resistant manner, which has since revolutionized various industries.

2.4.1 Present Day Smart Contracts

As discussed in 3.1, Smart contracts, first conceptualized by Nick Szabo in the 1990s, have evolved significantly over the past few decades. What began as a visionary idea has transformed into a powerful tool that underpins many decentralized applications today, thanks to advancements in blockchain technology.

The difference between Szabo's original concept and the modern implementation of smart contracts is substantial, driven by significant technological advancements, particularly the rise of blockchain platforms like Ethereum. Szabo's original idea of smart contracts was largely theoretical. He envisioned how digital contracts could be self-executed by incorporating the terms of the agreement directly into computer code. However, in the 1990s, there was no decentralized platform capable of implementing these contracts securely without intermediaries. In contrast, present-day smart contracts are fully implemented and widely used on decentralized blockchain platforms like Ethereum. These contracts automatically execute once predefined conditions are met [3, 4] and have practical applications in areas such as decentralized finance (DeFi) and supply chain management.

The technological landscape has also evolved significantly since Szabo's initial concept. In the 1990s, blockchain technology did not exist, and Szabo envisioned smart contracts embedded in systems such as digital payment methods. However, there was no trusted infrastructure to ensure the decentralized and secure execution of these contracts. Today, blockchain platforms like Ethereum serve as the foundation for smart contracts. Ethereum provides a decentralized virtual machine (EVM) in which smart contracts are written in languages like Solidity and executed in a secure, tamper-proof environment. Other platforms, such as Binance Smart Chain, Solana, and Polkadot, have also emerged to support smart contracts, further advancing their practical implementation.

2.4.2 Smart Contracts Core Concepts and Principles

Smart contracts are governed by several core principles and concepts that distinguish them from traditional contracts, making them a transformative force in digital transactions. One of the foundational principles is **decentralization**, in which smart contracts typically operate on decentralized blockchain platforms such as Ethereum. In decentralized systems, no single entity controls the contract, ensuring transparency and tamper-resistance. Decentralization prevents any party from altering the contract's terms once deployed, creating trust in the system by making all actions verifiable on a public ledger.

Another key concept is **autonomy**. Once a smart contract is deployed, it operates independently and executes automatically without further intervention from any party. This reduces reliance on intermediaries such as brokers, lawyers, and banks, which traditionally mediate contracts, and lowers transaction costs. Alongside autonomy, immutability is a crucial feature of smart contracts. Once deployed on the blockchain, the contract cannot be modified, ensuring its terms and conditions are preserved over time. However, this immutability comes with risks, as any bugs or flaws within the contract will persist, emphasizing the importance of thorough code audits and security measures before deployment.

Smart contracts are known for **their trustless execution, meaning** parties do not need to trust each other to follow through on the agreement. The blockchain enforces contract execution, and as long as predefined conditions are met, the contract will execute automatically, regardless of any participant's intentions or behavior. This reduces disputes and creates a fair, impartial process. In addition, **transparency** plays a critical role: the contract's code and its execution are visible and verifiable by all participants, promoting trust and accountability. This openness makes smart contracts highly reliable, as any user can inspect the contract's logic before engaging with it.

One of the strengths of smart contracts is their **deterministic behavior**. For a given set of inputs, a smart contract will always produce the same result, making it predictable and reliable. This is essential for automating business processes and agreements, as it ensures consistent outcomes every time the contract is executed. At the core of smart contracts is **conditional logic**, which allows them to operate like "if-then" programs. For example, a smart contract might specify, "if Party A sends 5 Ether, then transfer ownership of Asset B to Party A." This predefined logic enables the automation of various tasks and agreements without human intervention.

Security is another vital aspect of smart contracts, given their role in managing assets and financial transactions [4, 6]. **Security** vulnerabilities, such as reentrancy attacks, can be exploited if the code is not properly secured. Therefore, rigorous code review, formal verification, and security audits are crucial to minimizing risks. Additionally, smart contracts incur **gas costs**, fees required to execute computational resources on platforms like Ethereum. The complexity of the contract's logic directly impacts these fees, with more complex contracts requiring higher gas costs to incentivize validators to process transactions.

Smart contracts are both **self-verifying and self-enforcing**, meaning they automatically check whether conditions have been met and enforce the agreed-upon outcomes. This eliminates the need for third-party enforcement, such as courts or arbitrators, and speeds up the execution of agreements. However, for certain contracts that depend on external information, **oracles** are used [13, 15]. Oracles act as bridges between off-chain data (e.g., real-world events) and on-chain smart contracts, enabling contracts to access external information necessary for execution.

Despite immutability being a core principle, some smart contract systems support upgradability. Proxy patterns or other techniques enable upgrades and changes to the contract without compromising its original intent, addressing bugs and introducing new functionality over time. Furthermore, **interoperability** is an essential feature of smart contracts [1, 15]. They can interact with other contracts and decentralized applications (dApps) on the blockchain, enabling complex systems like decentralized finance (DeFi) protocols, decentralized autonomous organizations (DAOs), and token standards (e.g., ERC-20 and ERC-721) to function cohesively.

2.4.3 Smart Contracts Lifecyle

In the third phase of a blockchain's development, smart contracts are generated and deployed. These programs operate on the blockchain's distributed ledger, enabling automated agreement execution. The purpose of smart contract platforms is to create a "world computer" in which every node in the blockchain network hosts a synchronized virtual machine, ensuring a unified and consistent state across the entire network [1, 3].

The execution of these contracts occurs within this distributed virtual machine environment, coordinated through the blockchain's ledger and consensus algorithms.

Instructions for smart contracts are embedded within transactions, which are organized into blocks and added to the blockchain ledger. This process ensures that, when the network reaches consensus on the blockchain state, all nodes agree on the sequence in which transactions are executed.

Smart contract platforms manage this execution by running the instructions within virtual machines. These virtual machines are designed to create identical, deterministic environments on every node. In theory, when every node executes the same code in identical environments, it should produce the exact same results. This design maintains decentralization while ensuring synchronization across the "world computer" (Fig. 2.1).

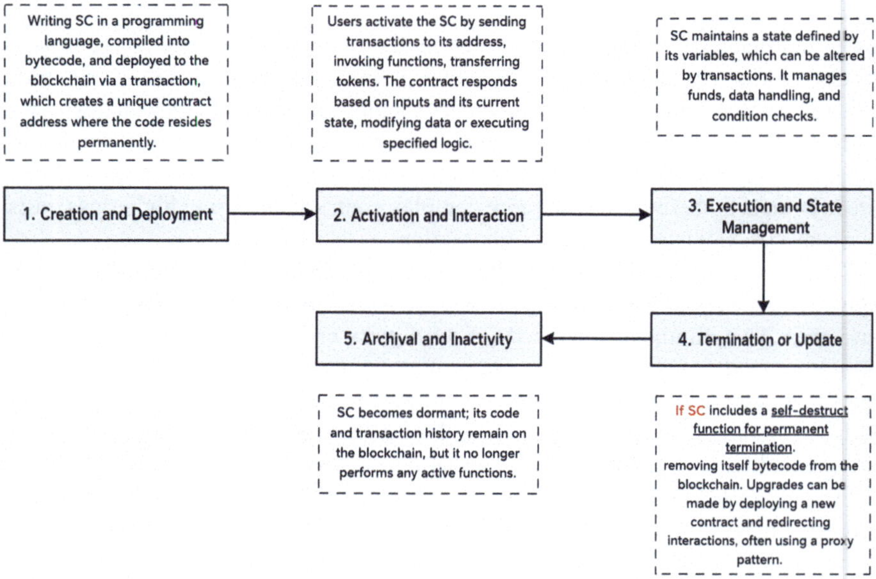

Fig. 2.1 Smart contract lifecycle

Phase 1 In the Creation and Deployment phase of a smart contract, the process begins by writing the contract code in a language compatible with the target blockchain, such as Solidity for Ethereum. This code defines the contract's functions, conditions, and logic, specifying transaction rules, roles, and state variables for storing data. Once written, the code is compiled into bytecode, a low-level language understood by the blockchain's virtual machine, like the Ethereum Virtual Machine (EVM). This compilation process translates the contract into a format optimized for secure, efficient execution on the blockchain.

After compilation, the bytecode is deployed to the blockchain via a transaction, which includes a small fee, often called "gas" on Ethereum, paid to miners or validators to cover the deployment cost. At this point, a unique contract address is created, serving as the contract's permanent identifier and location on the blockchain.

Some contracts then undergo an initial setup phase, where values such as admin privileges or token balances are assigned. This optional step ensures that the contract is properly configured for user interaction. Once deployed, the contract's bytecode and initial state are permanently stored on the blockchain. This immutability ensures transparency and security, as the code and transaction history are publicly accessible and cannot be altered.

Phase 2 Following the creation step, the Activation and Interaction phase makes the deployed smart contract fully operational and accessible to users. This phase starts when users send transactions to the contract's unique address, activating its functions. Each interaction, such as sending tokens, querying data, or invoking specific functions, initiates a response from the contract according to its programmed logic. Users can access these functions by calling the contract's methods, enabling them to interact with its predefined functionality.

During these interactions, the contract's state, represented by its variables, is updated based on the input it receives. For instance, if a user transfers tokens to the contract, the contract will update its internal records to reflect the change. Every transaction modifies the contract's state, which is permanently stored on the blockchain, ensuring transparency and traceability [2, 3]. This phase is critical because it enables the contract to execute its programmed tasks in real time, whether processing funds, verifying conditions, or handling data requests. Through this active period, the smart contract serves its intended purpose, operating independently to fulfill user requests within the blockchain environment.

Phase 3 **Moving into** the **Execution and State Management** phase, the smart contract operates dynamically, maintaining and updating its state based on each transaction it processes. The contract's state is defined by its internal variables, which store essential data such as balances, permissions, and status flags. Every time a user interacts with the contract by calling its functions, transferring assets, or querying data, the contract executes its programmed logic in response to the transaction, adjusting its state as needed. This process allows the contract to fulfill its purpose, whether it's handling funds, verifying conditions, or processing data within a decentralized application.

Each execution modifies the contract's state, which is stored permanently on the blockchain. This state management is essential for preserving the contract's integrity and continuity, as the blockchain records every change, creating a transparent and immutable history of interactions. Smart contracts in this phase often include mechanisms to facilitate secure transactions, enforce conditions, and handle data transfers, capabilities that are especially important in applications such as decentralized finance (DeFi), voting systems, and auction platforms. Interacting with these contracts involves sending requests, each of which is governed by a distinct lifecycle. The details of these requests and transaction lifecycles will be explored in Sect. 1.3.2. Through careful state management, the contract autonomously executes complex operations, reliably maintaining its functionality over time.

Phase 4 In the **Update or Termination** phase, a smart contract may require updates to address new requirements, resolve vulnerabilities, or expand its functionality. Due to their inherent immutability, smart contracts cannot be directly modified after deployment. Instead, developers deploy a new version of the contract and redirect user interactions to it, typically using a proxy pattern. In this setup, the original contract serves as a gateway, forwarding interactions to the latest version. This proxy approach allows the contract to evolve over time while maintaining its original address and continuity, ensuring a seamless user experience. Thus, this phase illustrates the adaptability of smart contracts, as they can either reach the end of their lifecycle through termination or extend their capabilities through strategic updates.

Alternatively, some contracts may simply reach the end of their lifecycle. Because they are designed to be immutable, most smart contracts cannot be changed once deployed. When a smart contract is terminated using the 'selfdestruct' function, the **bytecode** of the contract is removed from the blockchain, meaning the code itself is no longer accessible for execution. However, **transaction data** and any interactions that occurred during the contract's lifecycle remain permanently on the blockchain. These historical records, including emitted events, state changes, and transactions, are immutable and can be accessed for auditing and analysis.

Phase 5 Finally, in the **Archival and Inactivity** phase, a smart contract transitions into a dormant state, either due to intentional inactivity or a lack of ongoing interactions. Although the contract remains accessible on the blockchain, it no longer receives transactions or actively performs functions. Its bytecode, internal state, and transaction history are permanently stored on the blockchain, preserving a transparent and immutable record of all past activities.

Even though the contract is technically still in existence, it becomes functionally inactive, with no further changes to its state. This archived state allows the contract to be referenced or audited at any time, contributing to the blockchain's historical data and ensuring transparency. In this way, the Archival and Inactivity phase represents the final resting stage of a smart contract, where it ceases to operate actively but remains as a preserved artifact on the blockchain, available for future inspection or analysis.

In conclusion, the lifecycle of a smart contract reflects its journey from inception to dormancy, highlighting its transformative role within a blockchain ecosystem. Beginning with creation and deployment, the contract's code establishes its rules and functionality, ensuring a secure foundation for decentralized operations. Activation and interaction enable users to engage with the contract, dynamically updating its state via transparent, immutable transactions. Execution and state management maintain its operational integrity, enabling the contract to autonomously fulfill its intended purpose. As requirements evolve, the update or termination phase ensures adaptability or closure, preserving flexibility while upholding the contract's transactional history. Finally, in the archival and inactive phase, the contract transitions into a preserved state, contributing to the blockchain's historical transparency and auditability.

2.4.3.1 The Lifecycle of a Request

The lifecycle of a request to a blockchain platform outlines the systematic process through which a transaction progresses, from its initiation to its finalization and retrieval of results. In the following section, we present Fig. 2.2, which illustrates the proposed lifecycle and provides a detailed explanation of each step.

Step 1 The first step is the Submission of a request, where a user initiates a transaction by creating a signed message to be sent to the blockchain network. For inter-

Fig. 2.2 The lifecycle of a request

actions involving a smart contract, this request includes the contract address, the function to invoke, any required parameters, and details such as the gas limit and gas price. In non-smart contract interactions, the request typically includes the sender's and recipient's addresses, as well as the amount to be transferred. The transaction is then signed with the sender's private key, ensuring authenticity and security. This step represents the user's intent to either interact with a decentralized application or execute a simple fund transfer, and it forms the basis for all subsequent actions in the blockchain lifecycle.

Step 2 **The next step is Transaction Validation**, where the submitted transaction undergoes a series of checks to ensure it conforms to the blockchain's rules and protocols. For transactions involving smart contracts, the system verifies the existence of the contract address, the validity of the function signature, and the correctness of the provided parameters. For simple transactions without smart contracts, the system ensures that the sender's account has sufficient funds to cover the transaction amount and associated gas fees, and it validates the recipient's address format. Additionally, the transaction's cryptographic signature is verified to confirm it was signed with the sender's private key, ensuring authenticity. This validation step is critical to maintaining the integrity and reliability of the blockchain network by preventing malformed or fraudulent transactions from being processed.

Step 3 **Propagation to Network, where the validated transaction is broadcast across** the blockchain network for processing. Once the transaction is deemed valid, it is transmitted from the user's wallet or client software to a network of nodes. These nodes receive and propagate the transaction further, ensuring it reaches as many participants as possible within the decentralized network. The transaction is then added to the mempool, a temporary storage area where unconfirmed transactions await inclusion in a block. Miners or validators monitor the mempool, selecting transactions based on factors such as gas price or priority. This step ensures that the transaction becomes visible and accessible across the network, setting the stage for its eventual inclusion in the blockchain.

Step 4 Next, the Inclusion in a Block step occurs, where a miner or validator selects a transaction from the mempool to add to a new block. For transactions involving smart contracts, the miner or validator executes the contract code in the blockchain's execution environment (e.g., the Ethereum Virtual Machine) to compute the result and determine whether the transaction is valid. If the execution is successful, the transaction is included in the block, and any changes to the contract's state are prepared for updating the blockchain. For simple transactions, such as fund transfers, the miner or validator verifies the sender's balance and cryptographic signature before including it in the block. Once a set of transactions is compiled, the block undergoes a consensus process, such as Proof-of-Work (PoW) or Proof-of-Stake (PoS), to ensure agreement among network participants before it is finalized and added to the blockchain [3, 4]. This step marks the transaction as officially recorded in the blockchain ledger.

Step 5 The following step is Consensus and Block Addition, in which the block containing the transaction undergoes a consensus mechanism to ensure its validity and agreement among network participants. Depending on the blockchain's consensus protocol, such as PoW or PoS, miners or validators validate blocks. In PoW, miners solve a computational puzzle to validate the block, while in PoS, validators are selected based on their staked assets and other factors. During this process, the network ensures that the block adheres to the blockchain's rules and that it contains no double-spending or fraudulent transactions. Once consensus is achieved, the block is permanently added to the blockchain, linking it to the previous block in the chain via cryptographic hashing. This step finalizes the transaction, making it immutable and part of the blockchain's distributed ledger.

Step 6 Moving forward is Execution and State Update, where the transaction is processed and its effects are applied to the blockchain. For transactions involving smart contracts, the blockchain's execution environment (e.g., Ethereum Virtual Machine) runs the contract code to perform the requested operation, such as transferring tokens, updating balances, or executing predefined logic. If the execution is successful, the smart contract's state is updated to reflect the changes in the blockchain's ledger. Events emitted during execution, such as logs of token transfers or other significant actions, are also recorded for retrieval by external applications or users [15]. For transactions without smart contracts, this step simply updates the blockchain's state by adjusting account balances and recording the completed transaction. This stage is critical because it ensures that the blockchain reflects the most accurate, up-to-date state after every interaction.

Step 7 Confirmation, where the transaction's inclusion in the blockchain is verified and acknowledged. Once the block containing the transaction has been successfully added to the blockchain, the network begins confirming the transaction by adding subsequent blocks on top of it. Each additional block increases the transaction's confirmation level, solidifying its permanence and reducing the likelihood of reversal. For smart contract interactions, this step ensures that the executed contract state changes are now immutable and fully integrated into the blockchain. For simple transactions, it guarantees that the transfer of funds is finalized and cannot be altered. Users are typically notified of a transaction's confirmation status via their wallet or blockchain explorer, confirming that the transaction has been securely processed and recorded.

Step 8 Post-Processing and Retrieval, in which the transaction's results and associated data are accessed and analyzed. For transactions involving smart contracts, external systems or users may query the blockchain to retrieve updated contract states, such as token balances or newly stored data. Events emitted during contract execution, such as transfer logs or interaction events, are made available to applications for further processing. For non-smart contract transactions, users can retrieve transaction details, including confirmation status, transferred amount, gas fees, and other metadata, via blockchain explorers or wallet interfaces. This stage ensures transparency and provides essential insights into the transaction's outcome, enabling users and applications to act upon the finalized data.

In conclusion, the lifecycle of a blockchain request outlines the distinct stages it goes through. While some actions vary depending on whether the request involves a smart contract or a simple transaction, certain steps, such as Propagation to Network, Consensus, and Confirmation, remain consistent in both cases. This consistency reflects the fundamental nature of blockchain systems, where these steps are essential regardless of the type of request, ensuring reliability and transparency throughout the process.

2.5 Chapter Summary

This chapter explores the problems associated with traditional contracts, including their dependence on intermediaries, vulnerability to human error, and challenges in enforcement, particularly across legal frameworks. It then delves into the solutions provided by smart contracts, which eliminate intermediaries, streamline execution, and ensure transparency through blockchain technology. The chapter also highlights the core characteristics of smart contracts, such as decentralization, autonomy, and immutability, and discusses their evolution from conceptual frameworks in the 1990s to practical applications today. Through these innovations, smart contracts offer a more efficient and reliable alternative to traditional contracts, reshaping various industries by automating processes, reducing costs, and enhancing trust.

References

1. Zheng, Z., et al.: An overview on smart contracts: challenges, advances and platforms. Futur. Gener. Comput. Syst. **105**, 475–491 (2020)
2. Allam, Z.: On smart contracts and organisational performance: a review of smart contracts through the blockchain technology. Rev. Econ. Bus. Stud. **22**, 137–156 (2018)
3. Bocek, T., Stiller, B.: Smart contracts–blockchains in the wings. In: Digital Marketplaces Unleashed, pp. 169–184. Springer, Berlin, Heidelberg (2017)
4. Singh, A., et al.: Blockchain smart contracts formalization: approaches and challenges to address vulnerabilities. Comput. Secur. **88**, 101654 (2020)
5. Yuan, R., et al.: Shadoweth: private smart contract on public blockchain. J. Comput. Sci. Technol. **33**, 542–556 (2018)
6. Abdellatif, T., Brousmiche, K.-L.: Formal verification of smart contracts based on users and blockchain behaviors models. In: 2018 9th IFIP International Conference on New Technologies, Mobility and Security (NTMS), p. 2018, IEEE
7. https://www.investopedia.com/terms/s/smart-contracts.asp#:~:text=Smart%20contracts%20were%20first%20proposed,years%20before%20Bitcoin%20was%20introduced
8. https://en.wikipedia.org/wiki/Smart_contract
9. https://pontem.network/posts/the-history-of-smart-contracts
10. https://token.kitchen/history-of-smart-contracts
11. https://www.cryptoninjas.net/what-are-smart-contracts/
12. https://medium.com/@pattylawz/smart-contracts-a-brief-history-9a63c4b610e7
13. https://chain.link/education/smart-contracts
14. https://www.ibm.com/topics/smart-contracts
15. Pan, J., et al.: EdgeChain: an edge-IoT framework and prototype based on blockchain and smart contracts. IEEE Internet Things J. **6**(3), 4719–4732 (2018)

Chapter 3
Smart Contract Programming Languages and Platforms

Abstract This chapter examines the programming languages and platforms that form the foundation of smart contract development, showing how language design and platform choice influence security, scalability, and usability. It explores Solidity, the dominant Ethereum language with its contract-oriented structure, modifiers, and events; Rust, which enforces memory safety and modular design through ownership and borrowing; Aiken for Cardano, which combines functional programming with validator-based logic; and Move, which introduces resource-oriented programming for safe asset management. Furthermore, it considers Python frameworks such as PyTeal for Algorand and SmartPy for Tezos, which simplify contract writing with high-level abstractions, while Vyper and Yul on Ethereum emphasize minimalism, security, and low-level optimization. Additionally, it highlights Cairo, Pact, and Liquidity, which demonstrate advanced approaches such as zero-knowledge proof integration, declarative verification, and functional correctness, and Chaincode in Hyperledger Fabric, which illustrates enterprise-grade smart contracts with modular logic in Go, Java, or JavaScript. Beyond languages, this chapter compares platforms such as Ethereum and Binance Smart Chain for permissionless environments, Hyperledger Fabric and Corda for enterprise use, and Tezos and Cardano for their governance and formal verification features. It shows how each platform's design, from consensus models to governance, directly affects scalability, interoperability, and regulatory alignment. As a final point, it highlights that choosing a language and platform is not just a technical decision but a strategic one, shaping how contracts are developed, secured, and deployed across diverse blockchain ecosystems.

Programming languages play a fundamental role in blockchain development, serving as the foundation for writing smart contracts, developing decentralized applications (dApps), and ensuring the security and efficiency of blockchain-based systems [1, 2, 3]. Each blockchain platform is designed to support specific programming languages, chosen based on their execution models, security features, and performance considerations. For instance, Solidity, a contract-oriented language, is widely used for Ethereum smart contracts due to its Turing completeness and integration with the Ethereum Virtual Machine (EVM). Meanwhile, platforms like Hyperledger Fabric support Go, Java, and JavaScript, providing flexibility for enterprise applications. The selection of an appropriate programming language is not merely a

S. HajiHosseinKhani et al., *Understanding Cybersecurity for Smart Contracts*,
https://doi.org/10.1007/978-3-032-28863-9_3

technical decision but a strategic one, influencing factors such as security vulnerabilities, computational efficiency, and ease of development [2, 4].

Beyond programming languages, blockchain platforms differ in architecture, governance models, and consensus mechanisms, which affect their overall functionality and suitability for different applications. Some platforms, such as Ethereum and Binance Smart Chain, emphasize decentralized, permissionless environments, while others, like Hyperledger Fabric and Corda, cater to private, permissioned use cases. The choice of a platform determines aspects such as scalability, transaction throughput, interoperability, and regulatory compliance. Given these variations, conducting a comparative analysis of blockchain platforms and their associated languages is essential to understanding how they align with different development needs. This chapter provides a structured evaluation of blockchain platforms alongside the programming languages they support, helping developers and organizations make informed decisions when selecting the most suitable combination for their projects [1, 5].

3.1 Overview of Different Programming Languages

In traditional legal agreements, contracts specify terms and conditions, with enforcement governed by established legal frameworks, such as courts or arbitration. In contrast, smart contracts transform these terms into computer-executable code that resides on the blockchain. The critical enabler of this transformation is the use of specialized programming languages designed for smart contract development [1, 4]. These languages, such as Solidity, Vyper, Pact, and Liquidity, provide syntax and structures that allow contractual obligations, rights, and conditions to be encoded in a way that is both precise and automatically enforceable. Unlike human-readable text, which requires interpretation, code ensures deterministic execution, making the contract self-enforcing once deployed [2, 3].

In this section, we implement the smart version of the Services Agreement (see Sect. 2.1) using the previously introduced programming languages. Each language offers distinct design philosophies and execution models, yet all serve the same purpose: enabling the seamless transition of a traditional legal contract into a trustless, automated smart contract. The flowchart below illustrates the roadmap for this transition, mapping the progression from textual terms to programmable instructions and finally to deployable smart contracts on blockchain platforms (Fig. 3.1).

3.1.1 Solidity

Solidity is a contract-oriented programming language designed for developing smart contracts on Ethereum and similar blockchain platforms [1, 6]. Influenced by C++, Python, and JavaScript, Solidity combines the strengths of these languages to

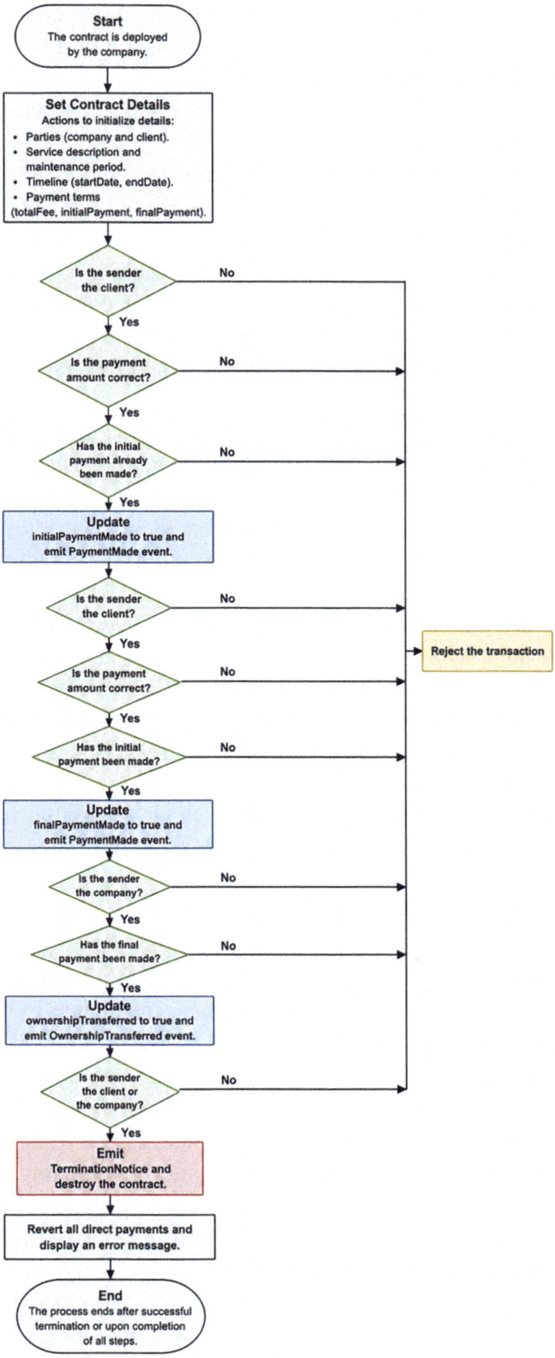

Fig. 3.1 Flowchart illustrating the process of creating a smart contract

optimize its performance. C++ provides low-level memory control and efficient execution, which are essential for managing gas consumption in blockchain environments. Python offers readability and simplicity, with intuitive, clean syntax, while JavaScript provides dynamic features and event-driven programming, making Solidity well-suited for decentralized applications.

As a statically typed language, Solidity requires developers to explicitly define variable data types, reducing errors and improving reliability during compilation [2]. A typical Solidity smart contract comprises several key components, each crucial to its functionality. At the beginning of every contract is the pragma version, which specifies the required compiler version to maintain compatibility and prevent unexpected behavior during deployment. Import statements follow, allowing the inclusion of external libraries and reusable code, which fosters modular, maintainable design.

The foundation of a Solidity smart contract lies in its state variables, which store persistent data on the blockchain. These variables can represent various data types, such as numerical values, strings, addresses, or logical conditions. For example, a state variable might store an integer or an address identifying the contract owner. Functions are the primary means of interaction within a contract and contain the logic that governs its behavior. They allow users to read or modify state variables and are categorized by their visibility: public, private, internal, or external. Getter functions retrieve data, while setter functions update the contract's state.

Modifiers are another crucial feature in Solidity [5]. They are reusable code snippets that enforce conditions or restrictions on functions. For instance, an "onlyOwner" modifier can ensure that only the contract's owner can execute specific functions. Events are equally important for maintaining transparency, as they log key interactions on the blockchain, making them accessible for tracking and debugging. For example, an event might be triggered whenever a value in the contract is updated.

Additionally, Solidity contracts often implement fallbacks and receive functions to handle special cases. The receive function processes plain Ether transfers, while the fallback function manages invalid function calls or Ether transfers with accompanying data. Together, they enhance the contract's resilience by ensuring it can handle unexpected input without failure.

To illustrate these concepts, consider the "ServicesAgreement" (in Sect. 2.1), which includes state variables to store key information such as the company and client addresses, the total fee, project timeline, and delivery status. It features a constructor that initializes the agreement by setting the company as the deployer and defining the client, start date, and end date. The contract employs modifiers to restrict access to specific actions, ensuring that only authorized parties (the company or the client) can perform functions such as terminating the agreement or transferring ownership. Additionally, events are used to log critical actions such as payments, website delivery, and ownership transfer, providing transparency and traceability on the blockchain.

```
-Identifier: MIT
pragma solidity ^0.8.0.

contract ServicesAgreement {
    // State variables
    address public company; // ABC Web Solutions
    address public client;  // XYZ Retail Company
    uint public totalFee = 10000 ether; // Fee in Wei
(simulated as Ether for demo)
    uint public halfFee = totalFee / 2;
    uint public startDate;
    uint public endDate;
    uint public launchDate;
    bool public isWebsiteDelivered = false;
    bool public isTerminated = false;

    // Ownership transfer status
    bool public ownershipTransferred = false;

    // Events
    event PaymentReceived(address indexed farom, uint
amount);
    event WebsiteDelivered();
    event AgreementTerminated(address terminatedBy, uint
timestamp);
    event OwnershipTransferred();

    // Modifiers
    modifier onlyCompany() {
        require(msg.sender == company, "Only the company can
perform this action");
        _;
    }

    modifier onlyClient() {
        require(msg.sender == client, "Only the client can
perform this action");
        _;
    }

    modifier notTerminated() {
        require(!isTerminated, "The agreement has been
terminated");
        _;
    }
```

```
    // Constructor
    constructor(address _client, uint _startDate, uint _
endDate) {
        company = msg.sender; // Company is the deployer of
the contract
        client = _client;     // Client's address
        startDate = _startDate;
        endDate = _endDate;
    }

    // Function to make a payment
    function makePayment() external payable onlyClient
notTerminated {
        require(msg.value == halfFee, "Payment must be 50%
of the total fee");
        emit PaymentReceived(msg.sender, msg.value);
    }

    // Function to confirm website delivery
    function confirmDelivery() external onlyCompany
notTerminated {
        require(block.timestamp <= endDate, "Cannot deliver
after the agreed timeline");
        isWebsiteDelivered = true;
        emit WebsiteDelivered();
    }

    // Function to transfer ownership
    function transferOwnership() external onlyCompany
notTerminated {
        require(isWebsiteDelivered, "Ownership can only be
transferred after website delivery");
        require(ownershipTransferred == false, "Ownership
has already been transferred");
        ownershipTransferred = true;
        emit OwnershipTransferred();
    }

    // Function to terminate the agreement
    function terminateAgreement() external notTerminated {
        require(msg.sender == company || msg.sender ==
client, "Only parties in the agreement can terminate");
        isTerminated = true;
```

```
        emit AgreementTerminated(msg.sender, block.
timestamp);
    }

    // Fallback function for receiving Ether
    receive() external payable {
        emit PaymentReceived(msg.sender, msg.value);
    }

    // Fallback function to handle invalid calls
    fallback() external {
        // Optional custom logic for fallback
    }

    // Function to withdraw funds by the company
    function withdrawFunds() external onlyCompany
notTerminated {
        require(address(this).balance >= totalFee, "Cannot
withdraw before receiving full payment");
        payable(company).transfer(address(this).balance);
    }

    // Function to check remaining time for completion
    function timeRemaining() external view returns (uint) {
        if (block.timestamp >= endDate) {
            return 0;
        }
        return endDate - block.timestamp;
    }
}
```

3.1.2 Rust

Rust is a statically typed programming language renowned for its focus on performance and memory safety, achieved through its distinctive ownership model. Drawing inspiration from foundational languages such as C, C++, and the Meta Language, Rust integrates key features that underpin its robust design [4]. C and C++ are well-suited for low-level memory control and performance optimization, making Rust well-suited for systems programming. Meanwhile, Meta Language introduces advanced type system concepts and pattern matching, enhancing code expressiveness and safety without compromising efficiency.

A Rust program is structured around several key components, with the main function, "fn main()", serving as the program's entry point. Functions are defined using the "fn" keyword and can accept parameters and return values, with return types specified using the -> operator. These functions play a central role in organizing and executing the program's logic. By default, variables in Rust are immutable, a design choice inspired by functional programming to encourage safer, more predictable code. To make a variable mutable, the mut keyword must be explicitly declared. Constants, defined with the const keyword, hold values that remain fixed throughout the program's execution, ensuring stability and clarity in the code.

Rust offers a broad range of data types, including scalar types like integers, floating-point numbers, characters, and booleans, as well as compound types such as tuples and arrays. This diversity allows developers to handle both simple and complex data structures while maintaining strict type safety. Control flow is managed using constructs such as if statements for conditional logic and loops (while, for, and do) for iteration, enabling efficient and expressive logic implementation. One of Rust's defining features is its ownership and borrowing system, which ensures memory safety without a garbage collector. Ownership rules dictate that each value has a single owner, and upon transfer of ownership, the original owner loses access. Borrowing allows functions to temporarily access values without taking ownership, providing flexibility in function calls while maintaining memory integrity.

Modules in Rust help organize code into reusable, logical components, promoting modularity and maintainability. They group related functions, structs, and other items, and public items can be exposed using the pub keyword. This modular approach makes it easier to manage large codebases and encourages code reuse across different parts of a project. Rust also includes powerful macros, such as "println!", which simplify repetitive tasks through meta-programming, enhancing productivity while keeping the code concise and maintainable.

To translate the given "ServicesAgreement" (in Sect. 2.1) into Rust, we can structure the program using the main components of the language, including variables, functions, control flow, ownership, and modules. Each section of the contract will be represented as a "struct", and its associated operations will be encapsulated in functions. This approach illustrates Rust's design philosophy, in which data is encapsulated in structs, logic is implemented in functions, and memory safety is ensured through ownership and borrowing. Additionally, the modular design allows us to organize the code effectively for clarity and scalability.

The Rust implementation captures the essence of the contract by defining the parties, services, payment terms, and confidentiality as structured data. Functions are used to display, update, and manage the agreement. Ownership rules ensure that modifications are tracked safely. Control flow is used to validate timelines and payment conditions, while constants and "enums" provide clear representations of governing laws and agreement statuses. This design reflects the detailed precision and reliability that Rust offers for managing structured data and operations.

```rust
// Modules for better organization
mod contract {
    use chrono::{NaiveDate, ParseError};

    // Struct to define a party involved in the contract
    pub struct Party {
        pub name: String,
        pub address: String,
    }

    // Struct for service details
    pub struct Service {
        pub description: String,
        pub duration_months: u8,
    }

    // Struct for payment terms
    pub struct Payment {
        pub total_fee: f64,
        pub upfront_fee: f64,
        pub completion_fee: f64,
    }

    // Enum for contract status
    pub enum Status {
        Active,
        Terminated,
        Completed,
    }

    // Main contract struct
    pub struct Contract {
        pub company: Party,
        pub client: Party,
        pub services: Vec<Service>,
        pub payment: Payment,
        pub start_date: NaiveDate,
        pub end_date: NaiveDate,
        pub status: Status,
    }

    impl Contract {
        // Function to create a new contract
```

```
        pub fn new(
            company: Party,
            client: Party,
            services: Vec<Service>,
            payment: Payment,
            start_date: &str,
            end_date: &str,
        ) -> Result<Self, ParseError> {
            Ok(Self {
                company,
                client,
                services,
                payment,
                start_date: NaiveDate::parse_from_str(start_
date, "%Y-%m-%d")?,
                end_date: NaiveDate::parse_from_str(end_
date, "%Y-%m-%d")?,
                status: Status::Active,
            })
    // Define payment terms
    let payment = Payment {
        total_fee: 10_000.0,
        upfront_fee: 5_000.0,
        completion_fee: 5_000.0,
    };

    // Create contract
    let contract = Contract::new(
        company,
        client,
        services,
        payment,
        "2024-01-01",
        "2024-06-30",
    );

    match contract {
        Ok(c) => c.display(),
        Err(e) => println!("Error creating contract:
{}", e),
    }
}
```

```
}

// Function to display contract details
pub fn display(&self) {
    println!("Contract for Services Agreement");
    println!("Company: {}", self.company.name);
    println!("Client: {}", self.client.name);
    println!("Services Provided:");
    for service in &self.services {
        println!(
            "- {} (Duration: {} months)",
            service.description, service.duration_months
        );
    }
    println!("Payment Terms:");
    println!(
        "Total Fee: ${}, Upfront: ${}, Completion: ${}",
        self.payment.total_fee, self.payment.upfront_fee,
self.payment.completion_fee
    );
    println!(
        "Timeline: From {} to {}",
        self.start_date, self.end_date
    );
    println!("Status: {:?}", self.status);
}
}
}

use contract::{Contract, Party, Payment, Service};
use chrono::NaiveDate;

fn main() {
// Define parties
let company = Party {
name: String::from("ABC Web Solutions, Inc."),
address: String::from("123 Business Park, City,
State, ZIP"),
};

let client = Party {
name: String::from("XYZ Retail Company"),
address: String::from("456 Main Street, City, State, ZIP"),
```

```
};

// Define services
let services = vec![
Service {
    description: String::from("Design and development of an
e-commerce website"),
    duration_months: 6,
},
Service {
    description: String::from("Maintenance and technical
support for 6 months"),
    duration_months: 6,
},
];
```

3.1.3 Aiken

The Aiken programming language, specifically designed for writing smart contracts on the Cardano blockchain, draws its inspiration from foundational languages such as Haskell, OCaml, and Elm, each contributing essential features to Aiken's design. Haskell influences Aiken's functional programming nature, including strong static typing and lazy evaluation, which enhances safety and precision in contract execution. OCaml brings efficient compilation and module-based organization, promoting modular and scalable code design. Elm, known for its simplicity and focus on developer experience, contributes intuitive syntax and predictable functional constructs, making Aiken more accessible by abstracting much of the complexity often associated with functional programming languages.

An Aiken program is organized into modules, which act as namespaces to structure the code effectively. These modules begin with the module keyword, followed by their name, and can define constants, types, functions, validators, and core components of smart contract logic. Aiken's import system allows developers to bring in external functionality from other modules, enabling modularity and code reuse, a design choice inspired by both OCaml and Haskell to enhance maintainability and scalability in decentralized applications. By combining these influences, Aiken provides developers with a powerful yet simplified environment for building secure and efficient smart contracts on Cardano.

Constants are fixed values that remain unchanged throughout the program and are declared using the const keyword. For example, a minimum transaction threshold can be set as a constant for validation purposes. Aiken supports the definition of custom types using the type of keyword, enabling developers to create data structures that align with the domain logic. Type aliases can also be used to simplify complex types and improve code clarity. Functions are the core building blocks of an Aiken program, defined by their name, parameters, and body. These functions allow developers to express logic in a clean, functional manner. Validators, on the other hand, are a special type of function critical to smart contracts as they verify whether a transaction adheres to predefined conditions. Validators typically return a boolean value (True or False) to determine the success or failure of a transaction.

The Aiken version of "ServicesAgreement" (in Sect. 2.1) defines constants for the payment terms: the total service fee is $10,000, payable in two installments of $5000 each. These constants make the logic clear and reusable. A custom type of Agreement is then defined to encapsulate all relevant contract details, including the parties' names, the list of services, payment statuses, start and end dates, and whether the agreement has been terminated.

The "validate_payment" function checks if both payments have been received by validating the "first_payment_received" and "second_payment_received" fields of the agreement. Similarly, the "validate_timeline" function ensures that the current date falls within the project timeline and that the contract has not been terminated. The main function, which serves as the contract's entry point, combines both validations. It ensures that payments are complete and that the agreement remains valid within the timeline.

This implementation abstracts the agreement terms into logical components and uses functional programming principles to verify the conditions. For example, if the first payment of $5000 is not received or if the project timeline has expired, the contract validation will fail. This ensures that the contract is automatically enforced based on predefined conditions, making it ideal for deployment on the Cardano blockchain.

```
module ServicesAgreement


// Define constants for the payment terms
const total_fee = 10_000
const first_payment = total_fee / 2
const second_payment = total_fee / 2

// Define a custom type for the agreement details
type Agreement {
    company: String
    client: String
    services: List(String)
    total_fee: Int
    first_payment_received: Bool
    second_payment_received: Bool
    start_date: String
    end_date: String
    terminated: Bool
```

```
}

// A function to validate the payment conditions
fn validate_payment(agreement: Agreement) -> Bool {

agreement.
first_payment_received && agreement.second_payment_received
}

// A function to validate the project's timeline and
termination status
fn validate_timeline(agreement: Agreement, current_date:
String) -> Bool {
    agreement.start_date <= current_date && current_date <=
agreement.end_date && !agreement.terminated
}

// Main validation function for the agreement
fn main(agreement: Agreement, current_date: String)
-> Bool {
    validate_payment(agreement) && validate_
timeline(agreement, current_date)
}
```

3.1.4 Move

The Move programming language, specifically designed for blockchain and smart contract development, draws on languages including Rust, C, and OCaml, each of which plays a crucial role in shaping its security, performance, and flexibility [2, 5]. Rust influences Move's memory safety and resource management through its ownership model, ensuring that assets and resources on the blockchain are managed safely without garbage collection. C provides low-level control and efficiency, enabling optimal performance crucial for blockchain transactions. OCaml contributes to Move's modular design, static typing, and functional programming capabilities, enhancing the language's predictability and robustness.

Originally developed by Meta (formerly Facebook), Move is now widely adopted in blockchain ecosystems such as Aptos and Sui, where security and flexibility are critical. A Move program is structured using modules and scripts. Modules serve as containers for custom data types, resources, and functions, encapsulating the logic and state that can be reused and extended. Scripts are executable programs that interact with modules to perform specific actions on the blockchain, such as transferring assets or executing decentralized logic. The influence of Rust ensures resource safety within modules, while OCaml's modularity helps maintain clean, maintainable code, making Move a powerful and reliable language for blockchain development.

The key components of Move include variables, resources, and functions. Variables in Move are immutable by default and must be explicitly defined with types, ensuring strict type safety. If a variable needs to be modified, it must be declared mutable using &mut. Resources are a unique and fundamental feature of Move. They are custom-defined structures that cannot be copied or implicitly discarded, making them ideal for representing blockchain assets like tokens. A resource is declared as a struct with the key property, which allows it to be stored persistently on the blockchain. Functions in Move are used to manipulate data and resources, with explicit parameter and return type definitions. They can be public to enable external access or marked as entry functions to make them executable within a transaction. Move provides mechanisms to interact with blockchain storage, such as "move_to" for storing resources in accounts and "borrow_global" or "borrow_global_mut" for reading or modifying resources.

To demonstrate these components, let's convert "ServicesAgreement" (in Sect. 2.1) to Move contract. We represent it as a **module** that captures the essential elements of the contract, such as services, payment terms, ownership rights, and termination. Move's resource-oriented model is particularly well-suited to this type of agreement, as it allows us to securely manage state changes and enforce contract terms through logic [4]. The key components of the contract, **variables**, **resources**, and **functions**, are used to model the different aspects of the agreement.

In this version, we define a **resource** named "ServiceContract" that holds the necessary information, such as the service description, payment status, and timeline. Functions are used to initialize the contract, update payment status, and manage ownership transfer once the terms are fulfilled. The use of &signer ensures that only authorized parties (ABC Web Solutions and XYZ Retail Company) can perform actions such as signing the contract, making payments, or terminating the agreement. Additionally, Move's strict immutability and type safety guarantee that the contract's terms cannot be tampered with and that resources, such as ownership rights, are securely transferred.

```
module ServicesAgreement {


    // Define a resource representing the Service Contract
    struct ServiceContract has key {
        company: address,        // Address of ABC Web
Solutions
        client: address,         // Address of XYZ
Retail Company
        service_details: vector<u8>, // Description of
services
```

```
        payment_made: u64,      // Total payment made
        total_fee: u64,         // Total fee agreed upon
        ownership_transferred: bool, // Tracks
ownership status
        start_date: vector<u8>,
        end_date: vector<u8>
    }

    // Initialize the service agreement
    public entry fun create_contract(
        company: &signer,
        client_address: address,
        service_details: vector<u8>,
        total_fee: u64,
        start_date: vector<u8>,
        end_date: vector<u8>
    ) {
        let contract = ServiceContract {
            company: signer::address_of(company),
            client: client_address,
            service_details: service_details,
            payment_made: 0,
            total_fee: total_fee,
            ownership_transferred: false,
            start_date: start_date,
            end_date: end_date
        };
        move_to(company, contract); // Store the contract in
the company's account
    }

    // Function to make a payment
    public entry fun make_payment(client: &signer,
amount: u64) {
        let contract_ref = borrow_global_mut<ServiceContract
>(signer::address_of(client));
        assert!(amount > 0, 0); // Ensure a valid
payment amount
        contract_ref.payment_made = contract_ref.payment_
made + amount;

        // Check if payment is complete
        if (contract_ref.payment_made >= contract_ref.
total_fee) {
```

```
                contract_ref.ownership_transferred = true;
            }
        }

        // Function to terminate the contract
        public entry fun terminate_contract(company: &signer) {
            let contract_ref = borrow_global_mut<ServiceContract
>(signer::address_of(company));
            contract_ref.ownership_transferred = false;
            contract_ref.payment_made = 0; // Reset payment
        }

        // Function to get contract status
        public fun get_contract_status(client: &signer): bool {
            let contract_ref = borrow_global<ServiceContract>(si
gner::address_of(client));
            contract_ref.ownership_transferred
        }
}
```

3.1.5 Python (PyTeal, SmartPy)

Python programming is a popular language that has significantly influenced the development of other languages, including those used for smart contract creation [1, 7]. As a result, two distinct libraries have been introduced for this purpose: PyTeal and SmartPy.

PyTeal is a Python library that allows developers to write **Algorand Smart Contracts** in a high-level, Pythonic way. The PyTeal code is compiled into **TEAL** (Transaction Execution Approval Language), the low-level assembly-like language executed on the Algorand blockchain. Smart contracts in PyTeal are typically divided into two categories: **stateless** and **stateful** contracts. Stateless contracts are used for lightweight tasks such as transaction verification, while stateful contracts maintain persistent data at the global or local level.

Instead of traditional variables, PyTeal operates with expressions and values. The two main types are Bytes, used for strings or hashes, and Int, which represents integers. Smart contracts rely on accessing state data through **global state** and **local state**. Global state stores key-value pairs accessible across the contract, while local state stores user-specific data. State management operations like "App.globalPut()" and "App.globalGet()" allow contracts to store and retrieve data, while "App. localPut()" and "App.localGet()" perform similar actions at the user level.

In PyTeal, logic is expressed using conditional evaluations and logical operators. PyTeal provides operators such as And, Or, Not for combining conditions, and comparison operators like Eq, Gt, and Lt. Contracts also rely on transaction attributes accessed via the "Txn" object, such as "Txn.amount()" for transaction amounts or "Txn.sender()" for the sender's address. Control flow is structured using PyTeal constructs such as Cond, which evaluates conditions sequentially, and Seq, which executes multiple operations in sequence.

In this PyTeal implementation of the "ServicesAgreement" (in Sect. 2.1), we illustrate the essential components of a smart contract, **stateful logic, conditions, and state management**, to enforce key terms like service milestones, payment conditions, ownership transfer, and termination clauses. The smart contract tracks payments, project milestones, and agreement state using both **global state variables** and **transaction attributes**. For example, global state can be used to store the "project_status", "payment_completed", and "ownership_status", ensuring both parties' obligations are verifiable on the blockchain.

The smart contract first verifies that an initial payment of $5000 (in microAlgos) is made upon signing the agreement, using "Txn.amount()" and logical conditions such as Eq. The next milestone checks whether the project is complete and whether the remaining $5000 has been paid. Once both payments are confirmed, the contract updates the "ownership_status" to transfer ownership to the client (e.g., App.globalPut(Bytes("ownership_status"), Int(1))). A termination clause can also be implemented by allowing either party to trigger termination with a special transaction, ensuring payments are prorated for completed work up to that point. **Confidentiality** and portfolio rights are not directly enforceable in blockchain logic, but milestone-based payments and ownership transfers provide accountability and fairness.

```
from pyteal import *


# Define Global State Keys
payment_stage = Bytes("payment_stage")  # Payment milestone:
1 = Initial, 2 = Final
project_status = Bytes("project_status")  # 1 = In Progress,
2 = Completed
ownership_status = Bytes("ownership_status")  # 1 =
Transferred to Client

# Approval Program
def approval_program():
    initial_payment = Int(5000000)  # $5,000 in microAlgos
    final_payment = Int(5000000)    # Remaining $5,000 in
microAlgos

    # Conditions for Initial Payment
    initial_payment_condition = And(
```

```
        Txn.amount() == initial_payment,
        Txn.application_id() == Int(0),  # Contract creation
        App.globalGet(payment_stage) == Int(0)
    )

    # Conditions for Final Payment
    final_payment_condition = And(
        Txn.amount() == final_payment,
        App.globalGet(project_status) == Int(2),  # Project
marked as completed
        App.globalGet(payment_stage) == Int(1)
    )

    # Update Global State after Initial Payment
    initial_payment_update = Seq([
        App.globalPut(payment_stage, Int(1)),  # Payment
stage to Final Payment
        App.globalPut(project_status, Int(1)),  # Project in
Progress
        Approve()
    ])

    # Update Global State after Final Payment
    final_payment_update = Seq([
        App.globalPut(payment_stage, Int(2)),  # Payment
Completed
        App.globalPut(ownership_status, Int(1)),  #
Ownership Transferred
        Approve()
    ])

    # Termination Clause: Either party can terminate
    termination_condition = Txn.type_enum() == TxnType.
ApplicationCall

    # Logic Conditions
    program = Cond(
        [initial_payment_condition, initial_payment_update],
        [final_payment_condition, final_payment_update],
        [termination_condition, Approve()],
    )

    return program
```

```
# Clear State Program
def clear_state_program():
    return Approve()

# Compile
if __name__ == "__main__":
    approval = approval_program()
    clear_state = clear_state_program()

    print(compileTeal(approval, mode=Mode.Application,
version=3))
    print(compileTeal(clear_state, mode=Mode.Application,
version=3))
```

SmartPy is a high-level smart contract programming language designed specifically for the Tezos blockchain. It is Python-based, making it intuitive for Python-familiar developers to write and test smart contracts efficiently. The structure of a SmartPy program revolves around defining a contract class, specifying its storage, and implementing entry points that allow interactions with the contract. Testing and simulation are integral parts of SmartPy, with built-in tools to validate the contract's behavior before deployment.

Storage is a fundamental component in SmartPy, as it persists data across transactions. Storage variables are initialized within the contract's constructor using "self.init()". For example, a storage variable such as count can be initialized to 0, and the contract owner's address can be stored using "sp.address". Functions in SmartPy, known as entry points, are defined using the "@sp.entry_point" decorator. These functions are the endpoints through which external actors interact with the contract, modifying its state or triggering certain behaviors. Entry points accept parameters, which are passed as structured inputs via "sp.record", and can validate inputs or enforce access control via conditions. For example, to ensure only the contract's owner can call a function, sp.verify is used to compare the sender's address (sp.sender) with the stored owner's address. The "sp.verify" command raises an error and halts execution if the specified condition is not met.

In SmartPy, the "ServicesAgreement" (in Sect. 2.1) can be represented as a smart contract that captures the key components, such as parties involved, services provided, payment terms, ownership rights, and termination clauses. The contract will store persistent information such as the **service provider** (ABC Web Solutions) and the **client** (XYZ Retail Company), along with the **project fee**, **payment milestones**, and the agreement's **timeline**. Entry points will serve as interaction points to ensure the terms are executed securely, such as confirming payments, marking milestones as complete, and allowing either party to terminate the agreement with proper notice. SmartPy's sp.verify ensures that only authorized parties, such as the provider or client, can perform specific actions, such as payment approvals or project terminations.

To illustrate this, the contract will include storage initialization for critical variables: the **total fee**, milestones, and project ownership status. It will define entry points for tracking **payments**, updating **project status** (e.g., marking the completion of website delivery), and handling ownership transfers once payment is complete. The sp.sender keyword ensures that only the authorized client can confirm the payment, while security checks prevent unauthorized access. Conditions such as a termination clause can be implemented through an entry point that allows either party to terminate the agreement, with an additional record of the **amount due for completed work** up to the termination date. Through SmartPy's testing framework, the agreement can be simulated to ensure payments are processed, project milestones are enforced, and ownership rights are transferred securely. This smart contract provides transparency and automates execution, reducing the need for manual enforcement of contract terms.

```
import smartpy as sp


# Contract for Services Agreement
class ServicesAgreement(sp.Contract):
    def __init__(self, company, client, total_fee, start_
date, end_date):
        # Initializing the storage
        self.init(
            company=company,                              # ABC Web
Solutions
            client=client,                                # XYZ
Retail Company
            total_fee=total_fee,                          # Total
service fee
            payment_made=sp.mutez(0),                     # Total
payment received
            payment_due=sp.mutez(total_fee),              #
Remaining payment
            service_completed=False,                     #
Project status
            start_date=start_date,                        # Project
start date
            end_date=end_date,                            # Project
end date
            ownership_transferred=False,                  #
Ownership transfer flag
```

```
            terminated=False,                      #
Termination flag
            terminated_by=None                     # Who
terminated the contract
        )

    # Entry point to make a payment
    @sp.entry_point
    def make_payment(self):
        sp.verify(~self.data.terminated, "Contract
terminated")  # Check termination
        sp.verify(sp.sender == self.data.client, "Only
client can pay")  # Authorization
        sp.verify(self.data.payment_due > sp.mutez(0), "No
payment due")
        sp.verify(sp.amount > sp.mutez(0), "Payment must be
greater than 0")

        # Update payments
        self.data.payment_made += sp.amount
        self.data.payment_due -= sp.amount

    # Entry point to mark project as completed
    @sp.entry_point
    def complete_project(self):
        sp.verify(~self.data.terminated, "Contract
terminated")
        sp.verify(sp.sender == self.data.company, "Only
company can mark completion")
        sp.verify(self.data.payment_made >= sp.split_
tokens(self.data.total_fee, 50, 100),
                  "At least 50% payment required to mark
completion")

        self.data.service_completed = True


    # Entry point to transfer ownership
    @sp.entry_point
    def transfer_ownership(self):
        sp.verify(~self.data.terminated, "Contract
terminated")
        sp.verify(sp.sender == self.data.company, "Only
```

```
company can transfer ownership")
        sp.verify(self.data.service_completed, "Service must
be completed")
        sp.verify(self.data.payment_due == sp.mutez(0),
"Full payment required")

        self.data.ownership_transferred = True


    # Entry point to terminate the contract
    @sp.entry_point
    def terminate_contract(self):
        sp.verify(sp.sender == self.data.client or sp.sender
== self.data.company,
                  "Only parties can terminate the contract")
        sp.verify(~self.data.terminated, "Contract already
terminated")

        self.data.terminated = True
        self.data.terminated_by = sp.sender

# Test Scenario
@sp.add_test(name="Services Agreement Test")
def test():
    scenario = sp.test_scenario()

    # Test accounts
    company = sp.test_account("ABC Web Solutions")
    client = sp.test_account("XYZ Retail Company")

    # Initialize contract
    total_fee = 10_000_000  # 10,000 XTZ in mutez
    start_date = sp.timestamp_from_utc_now()
    end_date = start_date.add_days(30)
    contract = ServicesAgreement(
        company=company.address,
        client=client.address,
        total_fee=sp.mutez(total_fee),
        start_date=start_date,
        end_date=end_date
    )

    scenario += contract
```

```
    # Client makes first payment (50%)
    scenario.h1("Client makes the first payment")
    scenario += contract.make_payment().run(sender=client,
amount=sp.mutez(5_000_000))

    # Company marks project as completed
    scenario.h1("Company marks the project as completed")
    scenario += contract.complete_project().
run(sender=company)

    # Client makes the remaining payment
    scenario.h1("Client makes the remaining payment")
    scenario += contract.make_payment().run(sender=client,
amount=sp.mutez(5_000_000))

    # Company transfers ownership to the client
    scenario.h1("Company transfers ownership")
    scenario += contract.transfer_ownership().
run(sender=company)

    # Terminate the contract
    scenario.h1("Client terminates the contract")
    scenario += contract.terminate_contract().
run(sender=client)
```

3.1.6 Vyper

Vyper is a contract-oriented programming language designed for writing Ethereum smart contracts, drawing inspiration from languages such as Python, Solidity, and Ada, each of which contributes to its emphasis on simplicity, readability, and security [4, 5]. Python influences Vyper's clean and readable syntax, making it accessible to developers and easy to audit for vulnerabilities. Solidity provides foundational concepts for Ethereum smart contracts, but Vyper refines and simplifies these features to minimize risk. Ada, known for its use in safety-critical systems, aligns with Vyper's strict typing and design philosophy, ensuring secure, predictable contract behavior by reducing error-prone functionality.

Vyper contracts are structured with essential components such as state variables, functions, events, mappings, and modifiers. State variables represent persistent data storage on the blockchain and are declared at the contract level. These variables use strict types such as int128 for signed integers, uint256 for unsigned integers, bool for Boolean values, address for Ethereum addresses, and mapping for key-value associations. Mappings are a key feature, widely used to associate keys with values, such as tracking user balances within a contract. By combining Python's simplicity, Solidity's blockchain expertise, and Ada's focus on safety, Vyper provides a secure, minimalist approach to smart contract development, reducing the attack surface and making contracts easier to understand and maintain.

Functions form the backbone of a Vyper contract, encapsulating its logic and behavior. Functions are explicitly defined and can include modifiers such as @public, which allows external access, "@view" for read-only functions that do not alter the contract state, and @pure for computation-based functions without state access. Events in Vyper enable logging of specific actions, such as transfers or updates, and these logs can later be accessed by external tools for monitoring purposes. Vyper also supports constructors, which initialize the contract state upon deployment, as well as fallback functions like "default", which execute when a call does not match any existing function.

Here is the Vyper version of the given "ServicesAgreement" (in Sect. 2.1), demonstrating all the elements of a Vyper smart contract such as state variables, functions, events, and mappings. This implementation ensures transparency, immutability, and the security of the terms outlined in the agreement.

In this smart contract, state variables store key information about the company, client, project timelines, and payment details. A mapping is used to track client payments, and events are included to log milestones such as payments, project completion, or termination notices. Functions are defined to initiate the agreement, process payments, check project progress, and allow termination of the contract under proper conditions. Access control is maintained through checks, such as verifying that the contract deployer is the service provider.

```
# Vyper Contract: Services Agreement


# State Variables
company: public(address)
client: public(address)
project_start_date: public(uint256)
project_end_date: public(uint256)
total_fee: public(uint256)
balance_paid: public(uint256)
project_completed: public(bool)
termination_notice: public(bool)
termination_date: public(uint256)

# Events
event PaymentMade:
    sender: indexed(address)
```

```
    amount: uint256

event ProjectCompleted:
    date: uint256

event TerminationInitiated:
    sender: indexed(address)
    date: uint256

# Constructor: Initialize contract with key details
@external
def __init__(_client: address, _start_date: uint256, _end_
date: uint256):
    self.company = msg.sender
    self.client = _client
    self.project_start_date = _start_date
    self.project_end_date = _end_date
    self.total_fee = 10_000 * 10**18  # $10,000 in wei
    self.balance_paid = 0
    self.project_completed = False
    self.termination_notice = False

# Make Payment
@external
@payable
def make_payment():
    assert msg.sender == self.client, "Only the client can
make payments."
    assert self.balance_paid < self.total_fee, "Total fee
already paid."
    assert msg.value > 0, "Payment amount must be greater
than zero."
    self.balance_paid += msg.value
    log PaymentMade(msg.sender, msg.value)

# Mark Project as Completed
@external
def complete_project():
    assert msg.sender == self.company, "Only the company can
complete the project."
    assert self.balance_paid >= self.total_fee, "Full
payment not received yet."
    self.project_completed = True
```

```
    log ProjectCompleted(block.timestamp)

# Terminate Agreement
@external
def terminate_agreement():
    assert msg.sender == self.company or msg.sender == self.
client, "Only company or client can terminate."
    self.termination_notice = True
    self.termination_date = block.timestamp
    log TerminationInitiated(msg.sender, block.timestamp)

# Check Payment Balance
@external
@view
def check_balance() -> uint256:
    return self.balance_paid

# Refund Remaining Balance (if terminated early)
@external
def refund_balance():
    assert self.termination_notice == True, "Agreement not
terminated yet."
    assert msg.sender == self.client, "Only the client can
request refund."
    remaining_balance: uint256 = self.total_fee - self.
balance_paid
    send(self.client, remaining_balance)
```

3.1.7 Yul

Yul is an intermediate-level, low-level programming language designed to act as an intermediate representation (IR) for compiling efficient bytecode for the Ethereum Virtual Machine (EVM). It draws its core design from foundational languages such as C, Assembly, and Solidity, each contributing key aspects to its performance and functionality. C provides Yul with low-level control over memory and efficient execution, making it ideal for fine-tuning smart contract performance. Assembly influences Yul's direct access to machine-level instructions, giving developers precise control over storage and computation. Solidity serves as a higher-level counterpart, where Yul integrates seamlessly within Solidity's optimization pipeline, focusing on compiling smart contracts into highly efficient EVM bytecode.

A Yul program consists of statements enclosed within braces {} and supports low-level control over operations, enabling developers to optimize gas consumption and improve execution efficiency. Yul provides core components such as variables, functions, control structures, and direct memory and storage manipulation. Its low-level nature enables precise data allocation and retrieval, which are essential for optimizing performance-critical sections of smart contracts. By combining C's efficiency, Assembly's control, and Solidity's smart contract logic, Yul bridges the gap between human-readable code and highly optimized bytecode, ensuring both flexibility and performance in Ethereum smart contract execution.

Variables in Yul are dynamically typed and initialized with the let keyword, and each value aligns with the EVM's 256-bit word size. Functions in Yul are defined using function keyword, enabling the creation of reusable code blocks. Functions accept parameters and can return values using arrow notation. The control flow in Yul includes if statements, loops such as for, and the switch construct, which allow developers to manage conditional execution and repetitive tasks. Yul also provides built-in operations like add, sub, mul, and div, enabling direct interaction with the EVM's arithmetic and logical capabilities.

Memory and storage manipulation are central to Yul programming. Memory is managed via mstore and mload: mstore(offset, value) stores a value at a specified memory offset, and mload(offset) retrieves it. Persistent storage, on the other hand, uses sstore and sload, which interact with the blockchain's storage layer. These mechanisms allow Yul to handle temporary and permanent data effectively. The simplicity of Yul's syntax, combined with its ability to access low-level EVM instructions, makes it a powerful tool for developers seeking optimization.

Let's demonstrate the "ServicesAgreement" (in Sect. 2.1) in Yul language. The program starts by defining critical variables for the payment structure: "totalFee" stores the total service cost, and "milestone1" and "milestone2" represent payment stages. The "validatePayment" function validates incoming payments, ensures they meet the agreed-upon milestones, and updates the total "paidAmount". To simulate project completion, the "isProjectComplete" variable is set to 1. A second function, "finalizeOwnership", checks whether "paidAmount" equals "totalFee" and whether the project is complete; if so, it transfers ownership by writing 1 to memory.

The program uses mstore to simulate memory operations for tracking payments and ownership. For instance, mstore(0x60, paidAmount) stores the current payment progress, while mstore(0x80, ownershipTransferred) records ownership status. The terminateAgreement condition, represented with the variable terminated, ensures that if the agreement is canceled, the payment progress is stored using sstore to reflect a final status.

```
{
    // Variables for the service agreement terms
    let totalFee := 10000        // Total project fee in USD
    let milestone1 := 5000       // Payment for the first
```

```
milestone
    let milestone2 := 5000        // Payment for the second
milestone
    let paidAmount := 0           // Tracks total payments
    let isProjectComplete := 0    // 0 = Incomplete, 1 =
Complete
    let ownershipTransferred := 0 // 0 = Not transferred, 1
= Transferred

    // Function to validate payments based on milestones
    function validatePayment(amount) -> success {
        success := 0
        if or(eq(amount, milestone1), eq(amount,
milestone2)) {
            paidAmount := add(paidAmount, amount)
            success := 1
        }
    }

    // Function to finalize ownership transfer
    function finalizeOwnership() {
        if and(eq(paidAmount, totalFee),
eq(isProjectComplete, 1)) {
            mstore(0x40, 1) // Store 1 at memory location
0x40 to indicate transfer
            ownershipTransferred := 1
        }
    }

    // Simulate first milestone payment
    if validatePayment(5000) {
        mstore(0x60, paidAmount) // Store payment progress
in memory
    }

    // Simulate project completion
    isProjectComplete := 1

    // Simulate second milestone payment and finalize
ownership
    if validatePayment(5000) {
        finalizeOwnership()
    }
```

```
    // Termination condition check
    let terminated := 0
    if eq(terminated, 1) {
        sstore(0, add(paidAmount, 0)) // Store termination
status and payment progress
    }

    // Store final status in memory
    mstore(0x80, ownershipTransferred) // Ownership status
stored at memory location 0x80
}
```

3.1.8 Cairo

Cairo is a programming language developed specifically for generating STARK-based proofs, widely used in blockchain environments like StarkNet for validity rollups and scalable computation. It is influenced by languages such as Assembly, Python, and Haskell, each contributing to Cairo's focus on performance, simplicity, and formal verification. Assembly provides Cairo with low-level, hardware-efficient control over computations, enabling optimal performance in proof generation. Python influences Cairo's clean, readable syntax, making it accessible to developers and easy to audit for correctness. Haskell, known for its strong emphasis on formal reasoning and mathematical rigor, contributes concepts such as verifiable computation and proof-based logic, which are essential to zero-knowledge proof systems.

A Cairo program is structured with key components such as functions, variables, assertions, and directives. Functions play a central role in encapsulating logic and defining sequences of computational steps. They accept input parameters and return output values, enabling modular and reusable code. The syntax for defining functions in Cairo follows a clear format, where the function body contains a series of computations and typically ends with a return statement. Assertions ensure that program conditions hold true, promoting correctness and verifiability, while directives allow developers to control compilation and proof generation efficiently. By integrating Assembly's performance, Python's accessibility, and Haskell's mathematical rigor, Cairo enables developers to write scalable, verifiable programs crucial for blockchain scalability and privacy.

Variables in Cairo have explicit types, with felt (Field Element) being the primary type, representing integers within a finite field. Variables can store single values or collections, such as arrays, and are declared using the let keyword, followed by the variable name, type, and value. Assertions are an essential part of Cairo programs, used to enforce correctness by ensuring specific conditions hold true during execution. For example, an assert statement ensures that two values are equal; if they are not, the program fails. Additionally, Cairo includes built-in tools like hashing, output handling, and signature verification. To enable these tools, the %builtins directive is used to declare necessary built-ins, such as output for printing or returning results.

Directives are another important structural component in Cairo. They configure the program and can include settings like %builtins for built-in tools or %lang to specify the language version. All these components come together to form a deterministic, verifiable Cairo program.

Let's demonstrate the "ServicesAgreement" (in Sect. 2.1) in the Cairo language. Variables store critical terms of the contract, such as the company name, client name, service description, and payment details. For clarity, "service_fee" is split into two payments ("initial_payment" and "final_payment") to ensure they add up correctly, with an assertion verifying that the total equals $10,000. Key dates, such as the project's start and end dates, are also defined as variables. Additionally, the maintenance period is specified as 6 months. Ownership is indicated programmatically by a binary value (1 for ownership transfer), ensuring the logic aligns with the contract terms.

Finally, the %builtins output directive enables us to display all relevant details of the agreement, such as payment breakdowns, ownership confirmations, and project timelines, during program execution. This structured representation mirrors the logic and ensures correctness while providing a verifiable computational model of the services agreement.

```
%builtins output


# This Cairo program represents a simplified Services
Agreement Contract
func main() -> ():
    # Company and Client Details as constants
    let company_name : felt = 'ABC Web Solutions, Inc.';
    let client_name : felt = 'XYZ Retail Company';
    let service_fee : felt = 10_000;
    let initial_payment : felt = service_fee / 2;   # 50%
Payment at Signing
    let final_payment : felt = service_fee / 2;     # 50%
Payment on Delivery

    # Service Information
    let services_provided : felt = 'E-commerce website
design and maintenance';
    let maintenance_period : felt = 6;  # Maintenance period
in months

    # Payment Assertions
    # Ensures the sum of payments matches the total
service fee
```

```
let total_payment : felt = initial_payment + final_payment;
    assert total_payment = service_fee;

    # Project Timeline
    let start_date : felt = '2024-01-01';
    let end_date : felt = '2024-06-30';

    # Ownership Confirmation
    let ownership_transfer : felt = 1;  # 1 indicates
transfer of ownership upon payment completion

    # Output contract details for verification
    %{
        output.write("Company: ABC Web Solutions, Inc.");
        output.write("Client: XYZ Retail Company");
        output.write("Service: E-commerce website design and
maintenance");
        output.write("Fee: 10,000");
        output.write("Initial Payment: 5,000");
        output.write("Final Payment: 5,000");
        output.write("Ownership transferred: Yes");
        output.write("Start Date: 2024-01-01");
        output.write("End Date: 2024-06-30");
        output.write("Maintenance Period: 6 months");
    %}
    return ();
end
```

3.1.9 Pact

Pact is a declarative, open-source, Turing-incomplete programming language specifically designed for secure, high-performance, and auditable smart contracts. It draws inspiration from SQL, Haskell, and JavaScript, each contributing essential features to its design. SQL influences Pact's schema-based approach to data handling, allowing structured storage and efficient querying of data similar to database tables. Haskell contributes to Pact's declarative nature and its focus on correctness and safety, making it easier to reason about smart contract behavior. JavaScript inspires Pact's accessible syntax and modular structure, ensuring that developers with varying skill levels can easily adopt and implement it.

A Pact program is organized into modules, which encapsulate a set of smart contract functions and define the contract's public API. Within a module, variables, constants, and schemas are declared, along with functions that define the contract's core logic and operations. Schemas, heavily influenced by SQL, specify table structures, ensuring safe and consistent data handling within the contract. Pact places a strong emphasis on security through keysets, which provide robust access control by ensuring that only authorized entities can perform specific actions. By integrating SQL's structured data handling, Haskell's safety-focused logic, and JavaScript's modularity and ease of use, Pact offers a powerful yet user-friendly environment for developing secure, scalable, and auditable smart contracts.

Variables in Pact can be constants, declared with "defconst", or bindings, which are defined and manipulated within functions using "let". Functions are created using "deffun" to encapsulate specific pieces of logic and accept parameters for customization. The language supports error handling through constructs such as "enforce", which validates conditions, and "enforce-one", for more complex logical checks. Persistent data storage in Pact is managed via tables, which must conform to predefined schemas to ensure type safety. Authorization mechanisms are integrated into the language, with keysets ensuring that only specific keys can access or modify resources. Transactions in Pact are atomic operations that guarantee consistency and safety.

To illustrate these concepts, consider the "ServicesAgreement" (in Sect. 2.1) translated into a Pact smart contract. The contract is structured into a module named the services agreement. An agreement schema defines the data structure for the agreement, including fields such as company information, services, payment terms, timeline, ownership, and other clauses. A table stores these structured agreements. The contract includes functions for creating, updating, querying, and terminating agreements, as well as enforcing authorization and validating specific conditions.

The creation agreement function initializes the agreement between two parties and specifies all essential details. Payments are handled through the record-payment function, ensuring that each payment matches the specified terms. Ownership rights are managed by the finalize-ownership function, which verifies receipt of full payment before transferring ownership of the intellectual property. Termination of the agreement is managed through the terminate-agreement function, which calculates payment for completed work and updates the agreement's status. Authorization is enforced through a keyset, ensuring that only authorized parties can modify the agreement or invoke its functions.

```
(module services-agreement 'admin-keyset
    ;; Define a schema for the services agreement
    (defschema agreement-schema
      company: string
      companyAddress: string
      client: string
      clientAddress: string
      services: [string]
      totalFee: decimal
```

```
      paymentTerms: [object]
      timeline: object
      ownershipRights: object
      confidentiality: bool
      governingLaw: string
      status: string)

    ;; Define the agreements table
    (deftable agreements:agreement-schema)

    ;; Create a new services agreement
    (deffun create-agreement (agreementId:string
company:string companyAddress:string client:string
clientAddress:string services:[string] totalFee:decimal
paymentTerms:[object] timeline:object ownershipRights:object
confidentiality:bool governingLaw:string)
      (enforce (not (exists agreements agreementId))
"Agreement already exists")
      (insert agreements agreementId {
        'company: company,
        'companyAddress: companyAddress,
        'client: client,
        'clientAddress: clientAddress,
        'services: services,
        'totalFee: totalFee,
        'paymentTerms: paymentTerms,
        'timeline: timeline,
        'ownershipRights: ownershipRights,
        'confidentiality: confidentiality,
        'governingLaw: governingLaw,
        'status: "active"
      }))

    ;; Record a payment for the services
    (deffun record-payment (agreementId:string
amount:decimal)
      (let ((agreement (read agreements agreementId))
            (remaining-fee (- (at 'totalFee agreement)
(reduce + 0.0 (map at 'amount (at 'paymentTerms
agreement))))))
        (enforce (> amount 0.0) "Payment amount must be
greater than zero")
        (enforce (>= remaining-fee amount) "Payment exceeds
```

```
remaining balance")
        (update agreements agreementId
          { 'paymentTerms: (append (at 'paymentTerms
agreement) [{ 'amount: amount, 'timestamp: (time) }]) })))

    ;; Finalize ownership transfer
    (deffun finalize-ownership (agreementId:string)
      (let ((agreement (read agreements agreementId))
            (total-paid (reduce + 0.0 (map at 'amount (at
'paymentTerms agreement)))))
        (enforce (= total-paid (at 'totalFee agreement))
"Full payment not completed")
        (update agreements agreementId
          { 'ownershipRights: { 'transferred: true, 'owner:
(at 'client agreement) } })))

    ;; Terminate an agreement
    (deffun terminate-agreement (agreementId:string)
      (let ((agreement (read agreements agreementId)))
        (enforce (= (at 'status agreement) "active")
"Agreement is not active")
        (update agreements agreementId
          { 'status: "terminated" })))

    ;; Query agreement details
    (deffun get-agreement (agreementId:string)
      (read agreements agreementId)))
```

3.1.10 Liquidity

Liquidity is a high-level programming language for creating smart contracts on the Tezos blockchain, drawing its core inspiration from OCaml, Haskell, and Michelson [8]. OCaml provides Liquidity with a strong foundation in static typing, pattern matching, and functional programming, enabling developers to write concise, reliable code. Haskell influences Liquidity's focus on formal verification and functional purity, enhancing its ability to ensure correctness and security in critical applications. Michelson, the native language of Tezos, plays a crucial role by defining the low-level instructions that Liquidity compiles to, ensuring seamless compatibility with the Tezos ecosystem.

A Liquidity smart contract is structured with several key components, including declarations, an entry point, types, reusable functions, and storage definitions. The entry point, or main function, encapsulates the contract's logic, processes inputs, updates storage, and determines transaction outcomes. Types and storage definitions help ensure that the contract handles data securely and consistently, minimizing errors. Reusable functions improve modularity and maintainability; a design concept derived from OCaml's and Haskell's functional paradigms. Liquidity's integration of OCaml's static typing, Haskell's formal verification, and Michelson's low-level execution makes it a powerful language for developing secure, efficient, and verifiable smart contracts within the Tezos ecosystem.

The variables in Liquidity are declared using the let keyword for immutability or let rec for recursive functions. Functions encapsulate specific operations and can manipulate storage or process inputs. The main function, required for every contract, takes two arguments: parameter and storage, and returns a tuple consisting of operations and the updated storage state. Storage defines the contract's state, such as an integer counter or a more complex structure like a record or a map. Types are a fundamental part of Liquidity, allowing developers to define data structures that ensure consistency throughout the contract. Supported types include basic types such as integers, strings, and booleans, as well as more advanced structures like lists, maps, and records.

To illustrate these concepts, let's convert "ServicesAgreement" (in Sect. 2.1) into the Liquidity format. It defines types to represent each part of the agreement, including service details, client and company information, payment terms, termination conditions, confidentiality clauses, governing law, and signatures. These elements are organized within the storage structure, which serves as the contract's state and ensures that all essential details of the agreement are preserved on the chain.

The contract's main function is to serve as the entry point for interactions, allowing two primary operations: signing the agreement and terminating the contract. When representatives from both parties sign the contract, their names are recorded in the signed field, thereby activating the agreement. For termination, the function checks whether the notice period provided meets the agreed-upon condition before invalidating the signatures and effectively ending the agreement. By formalizing the agreement in this manner, the contract ensures transparency, reduces the potential for disputes, and provides an immutable record of terms and interactions, all while leveraging the security and reliability of the Tezos blockchain.

```
(* Define types for the contract *)
type service_details = {
  description: string;
  timeline: string;
  payment_terms: string;
}

type client_details = {
  name: string;
  address: string;
}
```

```
type company_details = {
  name: string;
  address: string;
  portfolio_rights: bool;
}

type termination_details = {
  notice_period_days: int;
  partial_payment_due: bool;
}

type confidentiality = {
  mutual_agreement: bool;
}

type governing_law = string


type signatures = {
  company_rep: string;
  client_rep: string;
}

type storage = {
  services: service_details;
  client: client_details;
  company: company_details;
  termination: termination_details;
  confidentiality: confidentiality;
  law: governing_law;
  signed: signatures option;
}

(* Initialize the storage with the given details *)
let%init storage = {
  services = {
    description = "Design and development of an e-commerce
website. Maintenance and support for 6 months.";
    timeline = "Start: 2024-12-01, End: 2025-03-01";
    payment_terms = "50% upfront ($5,000), 50% upon delivery
($5,000)";
  };
  client = {
```

```
      name = "XYZ Retail Company";
      address = "456 Main Street, City, State, ZIP";
    };
    company = {
      name = "ABC Web Solutions, Inc.";
      address = "123 Business Park, City, State, ZIP";
      portfolio_rights = true;
    };
    termination = {
      notice_period_days = 30;
      partial_payment_due = true;
    };
    confidentiality = {
      mutual_agreement = true;
    };
    law = "State of California";
    signed = None;
  }

(* Main entry point for contract interaction *)
let main (parameter, storage) =
  match parameter with
  | ("sign", company_rep, client_rep) ->
      (* Signing the agreement *)
      let new_signed = Some { company_rep; client_rep } in
      let new_storage = { storage with signed = new_
signed } in
      ([], new_storage)
  | ("terminate", notice_given_days) ->
      (* Handling contract termination *)
      if notice_given_days >= storage.termination.notice_
period_days then
        let new_storage = { storage with signed = None } in
        ([], new_storage)
      else
        failwith "Insufficient notice period for termination."
  | _ ->
      failwith "Invalid parameter."
```

3.1.11 Chaincode

Chaincode in Hyperledger Fabric is the equivalent of a smart contract and defines the business logic for processing transactions on the blockchain. It draws its primary influence from languages such as Go, Java, and Node.js, with Go being the most widely adopted. Go contributes to Chaincode's efficient memory management, concurrency model, and simplicity, making it ideal for high-performance, scalable distributed systems. Java offers robustness, cross-platform compatibility, and mature development tools that support enterprise-grade applications. Node.js offers event-driven, non-blocking I/O functionality, making it a suitable choice for asynchronous transaction processing and fast, real-time applications.

A Chaincode program follows a specific structure, including two key functions: Init and Invoke. The Init function is called when the chaincode is instantiated or upgraded and initializes the ledger state, such as setting default data or configuration values. The Invoke function processes transaction requests and routes them to the appropriate business logic, performing operations such as reading and writing data to the ledger. This modular structure is influenced by Go's function-based programming and Java's method-driven logic, enabling developers to build reusable, maintainable code. The flexibility in supporting multiple programming languages ensures that organizations can select the best development environment for their needs, combining Go's performance, Java's stability, and Node.js's real-time responsiveness to create secure and efficient smart contracts in enterprise blockchain applications.

The main components of chaincode include variables, functions, and ledger access methods. Variables are used to manage state and configurations within the chaincode, such as defining keys and values stored in the ledger. Functions, on the other hand, are divided into core functions like Init and Invoke, and custom functions that implement specific business logic, such as adding, querying, or modifying assets. The ledger access methods are provided by the Hyperledger Fabric SDK and include functions such as "PutState" to write data to the ledger, "GetState" to read data, "DelState" to delete data, and "GetQueryResult" to perform rich queries when CouchDB is used as the state database.

To represent the given "ServicesAgreement" (in Sect. 2.1) as a chaincode in Hyperledger Fabric, the elements of the contract would be structured into variables, functions, and ledger access methods. The contract terms would be stored as key-value pairs on the blockchain ledger, ensuring immutability and transparency. Variables would represent critical elements such as the names and addresses of the parties (Company and Client), service descriptions, payment terms, timelines, ownership rights, termination clauses, and confidentiality agreements. For instance, variables such as "companyName", "clientName", "servicesProvided", "paymentTerms", and "timeline" would encapsulate these details in a serialized format.

Functions within the chaincode would handle operations on this data. For example, an "InitContract" function would initialize the contract by storing all agreement terms on the ledger at deployment time. A "QueryContract" function would allow users to retrieve the agreement details using unique identifiers such as a contract ID. The "UpdatePaymentStatus" function could handle updates to payment milestones, and a "TerminateContract" function would enforce the termination clause, ensuring appropriate state changes on the ledger. By leveraging ledger access methods such as "PutState" and "GetState", these functions would securely store and retrieve contract details, providing a decentralized, tamper-proof implementation of the agreement. This chaincode model exemplifies how legal agreements can be translated into programmable, enforceable blockchain code.

```
package main

import (
    "encoding/json"
    "fmt"

    "github.com/hyperledger/fabric-contract-api-go/
contractapi"
)

// ServiceContract represents the agreement between
two parties
type ServiceContract struct {
    ContractID          string `json:"contractID"`
    CompanyName         string `json:"companyName"`
    CompanyAddress      string `json:"companyAddress"`
    ClientName          string `json:"clientName"`
    ClientAddress       string `json:"clientAddress"`
    ServicesProvided    string `json:"servicesProvided"`
    PaymentTerms        string `json:"paymentTerms"`
    PaymentStatus       string `json:"paymentStatus"` //
Paid, Partial, or Pending
    Timeline            string `json:"timeline"`
    OwnershipDetails    string `json:"ownershipDetails"`
    TerminationStatus   string `json:"terminationStatus"` //
Active or Terminated
    Confidentiality    string `json:"confidentiality"`
    GoverningLaw        string `json:"governingLaw"`
}

// SmartContract provides functions for managing the service
agreement
type SmartContract struct {
    contractapi.Contract
}

// InitContract initializes a new contract on the ledger
func (s *SmartContract) InitContract(ctx contractapi.
TransactionContextInterface, contractID string, companyName
string, companyAddress string,
    clientName string, clientAddress string,
servicesProvided string, paymentTerms string,
```

```
timeline string,
    ownershipDetails string, confidentiality string,
governingLaw string) error {

    // Initialize with status "Pending" and "Active"
    contract := ServiceContract{
        ContractID:          contractID,
        CompanyName:         companyName,
        CompanyAddress:      companyAddress,
        ClientName:          clientName,
        ClientAddress:       clientAddress,
        ServicesProvided:    servicesProvided,
        PaymentTerms:        paymentTerms,
        PaymentStatus:       "Pending",
        Timeline:            timeline,
        OwnershipDetails:    ownershipDetails,
        TerminationStatus:   "Active",
        Confidentiality:    confidentiality,
        GoverningLaw:        governingLaw,
    }

    contractJSON, err := json.Marshal(contract)
    if err != nil {
        return fmt.Errorf("failed to marshal contract:
%v", err)
    }

    // Save to ledger
    return ctx.GetStub().PutState(contractID, contractJSON)
}

// QueryContract retrieves the contract details from
the ledger
func (s *SmartContract) QueryContract(ctx contractapi.
TransactionContextInterface, contractID string)
(*ServiceContract, error) {
    contractJSON, err := ctx.GetStub().GetState(contractID)
    if err != nil {
        return nil, fmt.Errorf("failed to read from ledger:
%v", err)
    }
    if contractJSON == nil {
        return nil, fmt.Errorf("contract %s does not exist",
```

```
contractID)
    }

    var contract ServiceContract
    err = json.Unmarshal(contractJSON, &contract)
    if err != nil {
        return nil, fmt.Errorf("failed to unmarshal
contract: %v", err)
    }
    return &contract, nil
}

// UpdatePaymentStatus updates the payment status of the
contract
func (s *SmartContract) UpdatePaymentStatus(ctx contractapi.
TransactionContextInterface, contractID string,
paymentStatus string) error {
    contract, err := s.QueryContract(ctx, contractID)
    if err != nil {
        return err
    }

    contract.PaymentStatus = paymentStatus


    updatedContractJSON, err := json.Marshal(contract)
    if err != nil {
        return fmt.Errorf("failed to marshal updated
contract: %v", err)
    }

    return ctx.GetStub().PutState(contractID,
updatedContractJSON)
}

// TerminateContract updates the contract termination status
func (s *SmartContract) TerminateContract(ctx contractapi.
TransactionContextInterface, contractID string) error {
    contract, err := s.QueryContract(ctx, contractID)
    if err != nil {
        return err
    }
```

```
    contract.TerminationStatus = "Terminated"

    updatedContractJSON, err := json.Marshal(contract)
    if err != nil {
        return fmt.Errorf("failed to marshal terminated
contract: %v", err)
    }

    return ctx.GetStub().PutState(contractID,
updatedContractJSON)
}

func main() {
    chaincode, err := contractapi.
NewChaincode(&SmartContract{})
    if err != nil {
        fmt.Printf("Error creating chaincode: %s", err.
Error())
        return
    }

    if err := chaincode.Start(); err != nil {
        fmt.Printf("Error starting chaincode: %s", err.
Error())
    }
}
```

In summary, the availability of diverse programming languages and paradigms explored for implementing smart contracts highlights a common goal: creating secure, transparent, and efficient contractual automation across different blockchain ecosystems. Each language contributes unique strengths to this objective. Solidity, with its Ethereum-native design, focuses on extensive interaction with the blockchain through constructs such as state variables, functions, and events. Rust, known for its memory safety and modularity, excels at encapsulating secure logic via structs and borrowing, translating contract logic into reusable components.

Aiken and Move bring domain-specific optimizations to Cardano and emerging ecosystems, respectively, emphasizing modular design, type safety, and transaction validation through validators or resource-based logic. Meanwhile, high-level Python frameworks such as PyTeal and SmartPy simplify complex blockchain logic by abstracting low-level details, offering expressive syntax to enforce conditions and manage persistent state effectively.

Vyper and Yul adopt more specialized roles: Vyper prioritizes simplicity and security for Ethereum-based contracts, while Yul targets optimization through low-level EVM interactions. These languages demonstrate how abstraction and optimization coexist to balance clarity with performance. Similarly, Cairo, Pact, and Liquidity offer advanced features such as formal verification, functional programming, and data-centric constructs to enhance security and correctness in the Tezos and StarkNet environments.

Finally, Chaincode in Hyperledger Fabric stands out for its focus on permissioned blockchains, relying on business logic encapsulated in modular functions and ledger access methods. Its design reflects the needs of enterprise solutions requiring tamper-proof data and transparency through a distributed ledger.

Together, these languages and frameworks illustrate a comprehensive view of smart contract development, tailored to diverse blockchain ecosystems. They combine static and dynamic typing, functional and imperative paradigms, and high- and low-level abstractions to ensure that smart contracts remain robust, auditable, and adaptable across varying use cases.

3.2 Overview of Different Platforms

The previous section highlighted the existence of multiple programming languages for developing smart contracts. In this section, we will focus on various blockchain platforms that support smart contract development. However, platforms such as Bitcoin, which do not primarily facilitate smart contract creation, will not be the subject of our study.

3.2.1 Ethereum

Ethereum, one of the most prominent blockchain platforms, was created by Vitalik Buterin in 2013 and officially launched in July 2015 following a successful 2014 crowdfunding campaign [3, 6]. Buterin, a Canadian-Russian programmer, conceived the idea of Ethereum to go beyond Bitcoin's original design by creating a platform capable of executing smart contracts, self-executing programs that automatically enforce agreements without intermediaries. The project was co-founded by several key figures, including Gavin Wood, Joseph Lubin, Anthony Di Iorio, and Mihai Alisie, who were instrumental in its development and early success.

Ethereum's development is supported by multiple programming languages that serve different parts of its ecosystem. The most significant implementation, Geth (Go Ethereum), is written in Go and provides a full node for the Ethereum network. The original cpp-ethereum client (also known as Aleth) was written in C++, offering low-level memory control and efficient performance in Ethereum's early implementations. Rust, another high-performance language, powers the OpenEthereum (formerly Parity) client, known for its modular design and efficiency. At the core of Ethereum's smart contract development is Solidity, a purpose-built, contract-oriented programming language that allows developers to write and deploy self-executing smart contracts. Solidity's syntax draws inspiration from JavaScript, making it relatively easy for developers to adopt, while offering features for writing contracts that handle financial transactions, token issuance, or complex application logic. Vyper, another programming language, focuses on simplicity and security, targeting applications that require enhanced safety guarantees.

Ethereum's architecture is designed around a decentralized, Turing-complete virtual machine called the Ethereum Virtual Machine (EVM). EVM executes smart contracts on top of the blockchain and ensures that they behave deterministically, with all nodes in the network agreeing on the outcomes. Ethereum uses a proof-of-stake (PoS) consensus mechanism (after transitioning from proof-of-work during the Ethereum 2.0 upgrade), which reduces energy consumption while maintaining security and decentralization. The platform's architecture supports decentralized applications (dApps) by enabling developers to deploy smart contracts that can interact with one another, creating an ecosystem in which applications can operate without relying on centralized servers.

The key features developed through the programming languages Go, C++, and Rust are fundamental to Ethereum's overall performance, modularity, and scalability, shaping the platform's robust and efficient infrastructure. Go is chosen for its simplicity, concurrency model, and support for network-based applications, making it ideal for Geth's role as a full node that syncs quickly and processes transactions efficiently. C++ contributes to Ethereum's core by providing low-level memory control and high-performance execution, both critical to Ethereum's early implementation and continuing to influence efficient protocol design. Rust is known for its memory safety, speed, and concurrency, making it ideal for the OpenEthereum client, which benefits from Rust's support for modular design and its ability to reduce runtime errors. Together, these languages enhance Ethereum's overall stability, allowing it to process thousands of transactions reliably, scale its infrastructure, and maintain security while supporting the execution of dApps and smart contracts. This combination of robust backend technologies ensures that Ethereum remains a leading platform for blockchain innovation, from DeFi applications to decentralized governance models and NFTs.

3.2.2 Solana

Solana, a high-performance blockchain platform known for its speed and scalability, was created by Anatoly Yakovenko in 2017. Yakovenko, a former engineer at Qualcomm, envisioned Solana as a solution to the limitations of existing blockchains, particularly regarding transaction speed, scalability, and high fees. Along with co-founders Greg Fitzgerald and Raj Gokal, Yakovenko developed a blockchain platform capable of handling thousands of transactions per second without compromising security or decentralization. The Solana network officially launched in March 2020 and quickly gained traction as a go-to platform for decentralized applications (dApps), decentralized finance (DeFi), and non-fungible tokens (NFTs).

The Solana blockchain is primarily developed using Rust, a programming language chosen for its memory safety, performance, and speed, which are essential for handling high-throughput applications. Rust allows developers to build highly efficient programs without compromising security, making it well-suited to Solana's design. Additionally, the development environment supports C and C++ for specific use cases, giving developers flexibility to optimize smart contracts and applications. The Solana programming model also includes Solana Program Library (SPL), a collection of on-chain programs and utilities, similar to Ethereum's ERC standards, that streamline development and functionality.

Solana's architecture is fundamentally different from many traditional blockchains, relying on a unique Proof of History (PoH) mechanism combined with Proof of Stake (PoS) consensus to achieve high scalability. Proof of History is a cryptographic clock that timestamps transactions before they enter the blockchain, creating a verifiable order of events and reducing the time required for consensus. This innovation allows Solana to process thousands of transactions per second and achieve block times as low as 400 ms. Its PoS component ensures network security by selecting validators based on their stake to validate and confirm transactions. Solana also uses parallel transaction execution through a feature called Sealevel, which enables multiple smart contracts to run simultaneously, further increasing throughput.

By leveraging Rust and its architectural innovations, Solana integrates several key features that optimize its performance and developer experience. Smart contracts, known as programs in the Solana ecosystem, are designed using Rust to achieve efficiency and low latency. Developers can create programs for various use cases, such as token issuance, decentralized exchanges, and lending protocols, with minimal overhead. Solana's SPL token standard simplifies the creation of custom tokens and stablecoins, while Sealevel allows these programs to interact concurrently without creating bottlenecks. Additionally, Solana integrates Gulf Stream, a transaction-forwarding mechanism that reduces memory pool congestion and enables near-instant confirmations. The combination of Rust's performance, Proof of History's timestamping, and Sealevel's parallelism enables Solana to support high-demand applications such as DeFi protocols, NFT platforms, and gaming ecosystems, while maintaining low fees and high transaction speeds. This efficiency has positioned Solana as a leading blockchain for developers seeking scalable, real-time decentralized applications.

3.2.3 Cardano

Cardano, a third-generation blockchain platform, was created by **Charles Hoskinson** in **2015**. Hoskinson, one of Ethereum's co-founders, founded Cardano to address the scalability, sustainability, and interoperability issues in earlier blockchain networks. The platform was developed through a research-first approach by **IOHK (Input Output Hong Kong)**, a blockchain engineering company co-founded by Hoskinson. Cardano was officially launched in September 2017 and quickly became known for its rigorous academic approach, with a strong emphasis on peer-reviewed research and formal methods to ensure the security and robustness of its network.

The Cardano platform is primarily developed using Haskell, a functional programming language known for its precision and mathematical rigor. Haskell allows for the implementation of Cardano's core components with a high degree of formal verification, making it well-suited for building reliable and secure blockchain systems. Smart contracts on Cardano are developed using Plutus, a custom smart contract language based on Haskell. Plutus brings functional programming principles directly to smart contract development, enabling developers to write contracts that are more secure and verifiable than those in traditional languages like Solidity. Additionally, Marlowe, a domain-specific language designed for financial contracts, simplifies the development of decentralized finance (DeFi) applications on Cardano.

Cardano's architecture is designed around a multi-layered approach that separates the settlement layer (for token transactions) from the computation layer (for smart contract execution). The Cardano Settlement Layer (CSL) handles ADA transactions and ensures fast, secure, and low-cost transfers, while the Cardano Computation Layer (CCL) executes smart contracts and dApps. This separation enhances scalability, as improvements or changes to one layer do not affect the other. The network initially operated on a proof-of-stake (PoS) consensus mechanism known as Ouroboros, a protocol designed to be energy-efficient and secure, backed by peer-reviewed cryptographic research. With ongoing updates, Cardano has evolved into Ouroboros Praos, enhancing decentralization and scalability while maintaining security.

Cardano integrates several unique features through its programming language choices and layered architecture. The use of Haskell and Plutus allows developers to leverage formal verification, ensuring that smart contracts behave predictably and reducing the likelihood of vulnerabilities. Plutus contracts run within a highly secure environment called Plutus Core, providing sandboxed execution that minimizes the risk of contract failures. Additionally, Cardano supports native tokens that can be created and managed without smart contracts, unlike Ethereum's token standards. This feature reduces complexity and costs while enabling a wide range of applications, from NFTs to stablecoins. With Marlowe, non-technical users can design and deploy financial contracts using a visual interface, broadening accessibility for DeFi developers. Through its layered architecture, secure smart contract framework, and emphasis on formal methods, Cardano positions itself as a scalable, sustainable, and secure platform for decentralized applications and enterprise use cases.

3.2.4 Aptos

Aptos is a next-generation Layer-1 blockchain platform designed to deliver high scalability, reliability, and security for decentralized applications. It was founded in 2021 by Mo Shaikh and Avery Ching, former Meta engineers who played key roles in developing the Diem blockchain (formerly known as Libra) before its cancellation. The Aptos project emerged from the desire to build on the innovations developed during the Diem project and to introduce a blockchain optimized for high throughput and low latency. The platform officially launched its mainnet in October 2022, gaining attention as a promising blockchain with cutting-edge performance optimizations and a developer-friendly environment.

Aptos is primarily developed using Move, a programming language specifically created for writing smart contracts and secure on-chain applications. Originally designed during the Diem project, Move focuses on resource-oriented programming, ensuring that assets such as tokens are treated as first-class resources that cannot be accidentally duplicated or deleted. This design feature helps prevent common vulnerabilities, such as double-spending and reentrancy attacks, which have plagued many other blockchain platforms. Additionally, Aptos integrates infrastructure components built with traditional languages such as Rust, known for its safety and performance, providing a strong foundation for the blockchain's node software and underlying architecture.

The architecture of Aptos is centered on a modular, scalable design that combines several advanced features to achieve high throughput and low finality times. One of its core innovations is the Block-STM (Software Transactional Memory) parallel execution engine, which allows multiple transactions to be processed simultaneously while ensuring consistency and correctness through conflict detection. This parallel processing mechanism differentiates Aptos from traditional blockchains like Ethereum, where transactions are executed sequentially. By leveraging Block-STM, Aptos can achieve sub-second transaction finality and handle thousands of transactions per second, making it highly scalable for large-scale decentralized applications. The platform also uses a Byzantine Fault Tolerant (BFT) consensus protocol that ensures fault tolerance and high security, allowing the network to maintain consensus even in the presence of malicious actors or failures.

The integration of Move into Aptos brings several important features that enhance the security, flexibility, and efficiency of smart contracts. Move's resource-oriented programming model prevents asset duplication and improper token handling, reducing the risk of exploits. It also offers fine-grained control over data ownership and permissions, making it suitable for applications involving complex financial transactions, gaming assets, and more. Aptos supports on-chain upgrades without disrupting the network, allowing for continuous innovation and improvement of smart contracts. Developers can create and update applications seamlessly, making it easier to deploy decentralized finance (DeFi) protocols, non-fungible token (NFT) marketplaces, and other applications. With its combination of Move's secure contract model, parallel execution via Block-STM, and a modular architecture, Aptos provides a robust and scalable environment for next-generation dApps while addressing the limitations of existing blockchains in speed, security, and user experience.

3.2.5 Algorand

Algorand, a highly scalable and secure blockchain platform, was created in 2017 by Silvio Micali, an MIT professor and recipient of the Turing Award. Micali, known for his pioneering work in cryptography, founded Algorand to solve the "blockchain trilemma" by achieving scalability, security, and decentralization simultaneously. The platform was officially launched in June 2019, and its innovative approach quickly gained attention for providing fast, efficient, and low-cost transactions, making it suitable for a wide range of decentralized applications, including financial services, tokenized assets, and DeFi projects.

Algorand's core software is primarily developed in Go, a statically typed language known for its simplicity and performance, ensuring efficient execution and low-latency processing. Certain components of the network's tooling and infrastructure are also written in Python and C/C++, making the platform versatile and easy to extend. Developers can write Algorand smart contracts using TEAL (Transaction Execution Approval Language) and PyTeal, a Python-based framework that simplifies smart contract development by translating Python code into TEAL. TEAL is an assembly-like, deterministic language designed to provide high security and efficient execution of Algorand's Layer-1 smart contracts.

Algorand's architecture is designed to achieve high throughput and security through its unique Pure Proof of Stake (PPoS) consensus mechanism. Unlike traditional Proof of Stake systems that rely on a small group of validators, PPoS selects validators at random and in proportion to their stake, ensuring decentralized consensus while mitigating centralization risks. The network achieves block finality within seconds and can handle thousands of transactions per second, making it highly scalable. The architecture is designed with a dual-layer approach, where Layer-1 handles core functionalities such as asset creation, atomic swaps, and simple smart contracts, while Layer-2 supports more complex, off-chain computations that can interact with Layer-1 for final settlement.

Through TEAL and PyTeal, Algorand integrates several key features that enhance its performance and security. TEAL's design ensures smart contracts run efficiently and securely by enforcing strict logic and deterministic execution, thereby minimizing vulnerabilities commonly associated with smart contract development. Developers can create Algorand Standard Assets (ASA) directly on Layer-1, without relying on external protocols, enabling the issuance of tokens, stablecoins, and

NFTs at low fees. The platform also supports atomic transfers, allowing multiple transactions to be grouped and executed as a single unit, making it ideal for financial applications that require complex, multi-party operations. Algorand's architecture and programming model also include rekeying capabilities, allowing accounts to update their cryptographic keys without changing their public addresses, enhancing security and usability. By combining TEAL's secure contract logic, Go's efficient performance, and a scalable consensus mechanism, Algorand has established itself as a robust blockchain for decentralized finance, enterprise applications, and cross-border payments.

3.2.6 Tezos

Tezos is a decentralized, self-amending blockchain platform designed to address governance, scalability, and security issues in existing blockchain networks. It was founded by Arthur Breitman and Kathleen Breitman in 2014, with the whitepaper released the same year under Arthur's pseudonym "L.M. Goodman." Tezos gained widespread attention in 2017 when it conducted one of the largest initial coin offerings (ICOs) at the time, raising over $230 million. The platform officially launched its mainnet in September 2018. Tezos was designed from the start to prioritize on-chain governance, allowing the network to upgrade itself without requiring hard forks, which can create fragmentation in blockchain ecosystems.

Tezos is primarily developed in OCaml, a functional programming language known for its strong type system and mathematical precision, which helps minimize errors and enhance network security. The use of OCaml ensures that critical components of the platform, such as its consensus mechanism and governance model, are rigorously verified. Smart contracts on Tezos are written using Michelson, a low-level, stack-based language designed for formal verification of contract logic. For developers who prefer higher-level languages, SmartPy (based on Python) and LIGO offer more user-friendly alternatives that compile to Michelson.

The architecture of Tezos is built around three core layers: the network layer, the consensus layer, and the transaction layer. The network layer handles communication between nodes, ensuring that information is distributed efficiently across the system. The consensus layer, initially based on a Liquid Proof of Stake (LPoS) mechanism, ensures secure block validation and participation from token holders who delegate their staking rights to validators, known as "bakers." The transaction layer handles the execution of smart contracts and transactions, with a focus on security and determinism. Tezos's self-amending design allows its architecture to evolve seamlessly, as proposed protocol upgrades are voted on by the community and implemented without disrupting the network.

Tezos integrates several important features through its programming languages and architecture. The use of OCaml enables precise development of key protocol components, ensuring that upgrades and changes can be implemented with minimal risk of bugs or vulnerabilities. Michelson, although low-level, is specifically designed for formal verification, a mathematical method used to prove the correctness of smart contracts and to prevent issues such as reentrancy attacks and logic errors. This makes Tezos particularly attractive for applications involving high-value assets or complex financial agreements. The platform also supports token standards like FA1.2 (similar to Ethereum's ERC-20) and FA2, which allows for the creation of various token types, including fungible, non-fungible (NFTs), and multi-asset tokens. Additionally, Tezos's on-chain governance mechanism allows developers and users to propose, discuss, and implement protocol changes without forking. This adaptability, combined with its robust formal verification capabilities, makes Tezos an ideal blockchain for long-term projects in decentralized finance, gaming, and enterprise applications.

3.2.7 Liquid

Liquid Network, a sidechain-based blockchain platform, was created by Blockstream, a blockchain technology company founded in 2014 by Adam Back and other prominent figures in the Bitcoin community. The Liquid Network officially launched in October 2018 as a solution to address Bitcoin's limitations in transaction speed and privacy, aiming to enable faster settlement for large-value transfers between exchanges and traders. The platform primarily serves as a settlement layer for Bitcoin and focuses on enhancing liquidity and transaction confidentiality for users across exchanges, brokers, and institutions.

Liquid Network's development is based on the Elements blockchain platform, a fork of Bitcoin Core. The platform itself is developed in C++, the same programming language that powers Bitcoin, ensuring high compatibility with the Bitcoin ecosystem. In addition to C++, certain infrastructure components, such as cryptographic and wallet utilities, rely on Python and Rust for building specific tools and applications. By using C++ and Bitcoin Core as its foundation, Liquid maintains Bitcoin's proven security model while introducing new features, including federated consensus, asset issuance, and confidential transactions.

The architecture of the Liquid Network centers on its federated sidechain design, which means it is separate from the Bitcoin mainnet yet operates in tandem via a two-way peg mechanism. Liquid uses a federation of trusted members (such as exchanges and financial institutions) to validate transactions, rather than relying on Bitcoin's proof-of-work consensus. The network's assets, including pegged Bitcoin (L-BTC), are backed 1:1 with Bitcoin locked on the mainnet. When users send Bitcoin to the Liquid Network, it is locked in a multisignature wallet, and an equivalent amount of L-BTC is minted on the Liquid sidechain. This design allows for fast confirmation times, usually within 1 min, compared to Bitcoin's average 10-min block intervals.

One of the key features Liquid integrates using its programming framework is the ability to issue confidential assets, which go beyond standard Bitcoin transactions by hiding the transaction amount and asset type using Confidential Transactions

(CT). This cryptographic feature, implemented via range proofs and Pedersen commitments, ensures privacy without compromising network security. Developers and users can create custom assets, such as stablecoins, tokenized securities, and other digital assets, directly on the Liquid sidechain thanks to its flexible asset issuance capabilities. Additionally, Liquid's architecture supports atomic swaps, enabling trustless asset exchanges between parties [9]. Overall, the use of C++ and its integration into the Elements platform enable Liquid to maintain a Bitcoin-like structure while providing enhanced features, including high-speed transactions, asset privacy, and interoperability, making it ideal for institutional financial applications.

3.2.8 StarkNet

StarkNet is a blockchain platform developed by StarkWare Industries, a company founded in 2018 by Eli Ben-Sasson, Uri Kolodny, Michael Riabzev, and Alessandro Chiesa [10]. StarkWare focuses on scalability and privacy solutions for blockchains using zero-knowledge proofs (ZKPs), particularly STARK proofs (Scalable Transparent ARguments of Knowledge). StarkNet was introduced as part of StarkWare's scaling solutions to enhance Ethereum's capacity by offloading computations to a Layer-2 network while maintaining security and decentralization.

StarkNet's core development relies heavily on the Cairo programming language, which StarkWare created to optimize zk-STARK proof generation. While Cairo forms the foundation for StarkNet's smart contract infrastructure, other supporting parts of its ecosystem are built using traditional programming languages such as Rust, C++, and Python. Cairo is designed to efficiently represent and execute computations in a proof-friendly way, making it essential for StarkNet's scalability mechanisms. By using Cairo, StarkNet ensures that computational processes are verifiable off-chain but are validated through on-chain proof verification, maintaining a high level of integrity and trust.

StarkNet's architecture operates as a Layer-2 solution on Ethereum using zk-rollups to achieve scalability and reduce gas fees. The architecture comprises core components such as sequencers, which order and bundle transactions; provers, which generate zk-STARK proofs off-chain; and verifiers, which are Ethereum smart contracts that validate submitted proofs. StarkNet's rollup mechanism aggregates numerous transactions off-chain and submits them as a single proof to the Ethereum blockchain. This minimizes the on-chain computational load while preserving Ethereum's security properties. The platform also includes an L1-L2 bridge that enables seamless interaction between Ethereum and StarkNet, ensuring interoperability and data consistency across both layers.

The integration of Cairo into StarkNet is central to its features, particularly in achieving scalability and efficiency. Cairo enables developers to write smart contracts optimized for zk-STARK proof generation, reducing computational costs and gas consumption compared to native Ethereum contracts. The language's composability ensures that various contracts can interact, enabling the creation of complex decentralized applications without performance bottlenecks. Cairo also facilitates mass processing of transactions off-chain while providing cryptographic guarantees of correctness when verified on-chain. This results in significantly reduced transaction fees and enhanced throughput, making StarkNet a highly scalable and secure environment for decentralized applications. By leveraging Cairo's proof-friendly nature and zk-rollup architecture, StarkNet achieves Ethereum-compatible security, composability, and cost efficiency at scale.

3.2.9 Kadena

Kadena is a high-performance, scalable Layer-1 blockchain platform designed to provide enterprise-grade solutions while maintaining decentralization and security [5]. It was co-founded in 2016 by Stuart Popejoy and Will Martino, both former blockchain experts at JPMorgan, where they worked on the bank's internal blockchain project, Juno. Drawing on their experience in financial systems and distributed ledgers, they designed Kadena to address the scalability and performance issues inherent in existing blockchains such as Bitcoin and Ethereum. Kadena officially launched its mainnet in 2020, offering a unique hybrid approach by combining a public chain with a permissioned chain for enterprise use cases.

Kadena's core development is centered on its custom-built smart contract language, Pact. Pact is a human-readable, high-level, and secure programming language designed specifically to reduce the risk of errors and vulnerabilities in smart contracts. One of its key strengths is its built-in support for formal verification, allowing developers to mathematically prove the correctness of their contract logic, which is critical for applications involving complex financial transactions and sensitive data. Unlike many low-level languages such as Solidity, Pact is designed to be easily understood by both developers and non-developers, offering greater transparency and auditability. Kadena's underlying infrastructure, including its consensus engine, is developed in Haskell for its strong type-checking and reliability, which contribute to the protocol's security.

Kadena's architecture is unique for its use of Chainweb, a parallel-chain design that connects multiple chains to enhance throughput and scalability. Unlike traditional blockchains that operate on a single chain, Kadena's Chainweb allows multiple chains to process transactions simultaneously, significantly increasing the network's transaction capacity while maintaining strong security through braided chains. Each chain in Chainweb runs its own blockchain instance, but they are interconnected and work in tandem to ensure the entire network remains secure and synchronized. Kadena also integrates a proof-of-work (PoW) consensus mechanism, but unlike Bitcoin, its architecture optimizes energy consumption and scalability by distributing the workload across multiple chains.

The integration of Pact as the core programming language enables Kadena to offer a range of powerful features for developers and businesses. Pact's human-readable syntax enables rapid development and simplifies contract auditing, reducing the time and cost of deploying decentralized applications. Its support for formal verification ensures that critical contracts, such as those for DeFi protocols or supply chain management, are less prone to bugs and exploits. Another key feature is Kadena's gas station service, which allows businesses to cover transaction fees for their users, making the user experience frictionless and enterprise-friendly. Additionally, Kadena's architecture supports cross-chain transactions within its multi-chain environment, enabling assets and data to move seamlessly across different chains without requiring complex bridging mechanisms. Through its combination of scalable architecture, secure smart contracts, and developer-friendly programming tools, Kadena positions itself as a blockchain capable of handling large-scale industrial and financial applications while addressing the limitations of traditional blockchain networks.

3.2.10 Hyperledger Fabric

Hyperledger Fabric, a permissioned blockchain platform designed for enterprise use, was created under the Hyperledger Project, an open-source collaborative effort launched by the Linux Foundation in 2016. It was initially contributed by IBM and Digital Asset, with IBM playing a significant role in its development. Fabric is designed to address the privacy, scalability, and performance requirements of enterprise blockchains, making it a leading solution for businesses seeking to implement distributed ledger technology without the constraints of a public blockchain.

Hyperledger Fabric is primarily developed in Go (Golang), a statically typed language known for its simplicity, efficiency, and support for concurrency, which is essential for building scalable, high-performance blockchain systems. Key components of its modular architecture, such as peer nodes, chaincode execution, and ordering services, are implemented in Go. In addition to Go, some components and tools are built using Java and Node.js, providing developers with flexibility in building and deploying chaincode (smart contracts) and applications that interact with the blockchain network. By supporting multiple languages, Fabric ensures that developers from diverse backgrounds can easily integrate and develop business logic across industries.

The architecture of Hyperledger Fabric is modular and highly customizable, enabling enterprises to tailor the platform to their specific requirements. One of its core architectural features is the separation of transaction ordering, validation, and execution into distinct roles within the network. The ordering service is responsible for establishing the order of transactions, ensuring consistency across the network. Peers in the network are responsible for executing smart contracts (chaincode) and validating transactions. Unlike public blockchains like Bitcoin or Ethereum, Fabric uses a pluggable consensus model that allows organizations to choose the consensus mechanism best suited to their use case, such as crash fault tolerance (CFT) or Byzantine fault tolerance (BFT). Fabric operates in a permissioned environment, where all participants are authenticated, ensuring that only authorized entities can access or contribute to the network.

Hyperledger Fabric integrates several key features through its programming language and modular design. With chaincode written in Go, Java, or Node.js, developers can easily create smart contracts to automate business processes while ensuring privacy and security. The modular architecture allows organizations to define private data collections that restrict access to sensitive information, enabling secure, confidential transactions between select participants without exposing data to the entire network. Another major feature is its channel-based architecture, which allows participants to create separate sub-networks within the main Fabric network, ensuring data isolation and fine-grained access control. This is particularly important for industries like finance and supply chain, where privacy is critical. Additionally, Fabric supports asset modeling and tokenization, enabling businesses to create, transfer, and manage digital assets efficiently. By combining Go's performance, Java and Node.js's flexibility, and Fabric's modular architecture, the platform provides a robust environment for building scalable, secure enterprise applications tailored to industries such as finance, healthcare, and logistics.

In a nutshell, the variety of blockchain platforms reflects their diverse designs, architectures, and development ecosystems, each tailored to specific performance, security, and scalability goals. At the core of these platforms lie a combination of programming languages, consensus mechanisms, and innovative architectural features that define their utility across decentralized finance (DeFi), non-fungible tokens (NFTs), enterprise applications, and scalable decentralized applications (dApps).

Ethereum and Cardano focus on robust dApp ecosystems and smart contract development, with Ethereum relying on the versatility of Solidity and Vyper and Cardano leveraging Haskell and Plutus for formal verification. While Ethereum has evolved into a general-purpose decentralized platform, Cardano adopts a research-driven approach to address scalability and security using a layered architecture. Similarly, Solana and Aptos emphasize high transaction throughput. Solana achieves this through Rust, its Proof of History mechanism, and parallel execution (Sealevel), while Aptos relies on its Move programming language, resource-oriented programming, and modular execution with Block-STM.

Algorand and Tezos focus on security, efficient execution, and formal verification of smart contracts. Algorand, using TEAL and PyTeal, combines high-speed processing with its Pure Proof of Stake consensus mechanism, making it suitable for scalable applications. Tezos emphasizes governance and self-amendment, integrating Michelson for secure smart contract execution and on-chain upgrades. Meanwhile, StarkNet introduces scalability and zero-knowledge proof-based verification through its Cairo programming language and zk-rollup architecture, designed to offload computations while preserving Ethereum compatibility.

On the enterprise side, Hyperledger Fabric and Kadena cater to permissioned blockchains and business applications. Fabric's modular architecture, Go-written chaincode, and support for private channels make it ideal for secure, enterprise-specific solutions. Kadena's Chainweb architecture and Pact programming language focus on scalability and formal verification, ensuring secure contract execution while maintaining cross-chain interoperability.

Liquid Network and StarkNet enhance existing ecosystems by addressing specific limitations. Liquid Network, built on Bitcoin's foundation using C++, optimizes liquidity and transaction speed with confidential transactions, making it ideal for financial transfers. In contrast, StarkNet focuses on scalability and security using zero-knowledge proofs, enhancing Ethereum's capacity through its Layer-2 solution.

These platforms showcase how different design choices, programming languages such as Rust, Haskell, and Move, consensus mechanisms such as Proof of Stake, Proof of History, and zk-rollups, and architectural innovations such as parallel execution, Layer-2 solutions, and modular design shape their unique contributions. While Ethereum remains a central player for dApp development, platforms like Solana, Aptos, and Cardano offer solutions for scaling, security, and efficiency. Meanwhile, enterprise platforms such as Hyperledger Fabric and Kadena address business-oriented use cases with privacy and formal verification, demonstrating blockchain's versatility and potential across industries.

3.3 Comparative Analysis of Programming Languages and Platforms

This section compares smart contracts programming languages based on three key criteria: language syntax and ease of use, security features and vulnerabilities, and performance and scalability. The differences arise from their underlying paradigms, the learning curve they impose, and their alignment with developer priorities, such as familiarity, security, and efficiency. Each language's performance and scalability are shaped by the blockchain platform it operates on, highlighting unique strengths and limitations tailored to specific applications. Similarly, their security features reflect distinct design principles and optimization for varying contexts, underscoring the trade-offs between usability, robustness, and adaptability.

First, let's compare smart contract languages based on their level of abstraction. Some languages offer high-level, user-friendly syntax that simplifies development, while others provide lower-level control, enabling greater optimization and execution efficiency. Solidity, Vyper, Move, Pact, Liquidity, ChainCode, and Python-based frameworks (PyTeal, SmartPy) are high-level languages that prioritize readability and ease of development. Solidity and Vyper, for instance, are designed for Ethereum, with Vyper focusing on security and simplicity. Move, used in Aptos and Sui, offers resource-oriented programming, while Pact emphasizes formal verification for Kadena. ChainCode, primarily written in Go or JavaScript, is used in Hyperledger Fabric, making it more accessible to developers familiar with enterprise applications. These languages abstract away low-level execution details, making smart contract development more approachable while sacrificing some control over performance optimizations.

In contrast, Yul and Cairo are lower-level languages that provide finer control over execution and optimization. Yul serves as an intermediate representation for Solidity, enabling developers to write highly efficient EVM bytecode, while Cairo is designed for STARK-based zero-knowledge proofs, making it crucial for scalable, efficient cryptographic computations. Rust stands between these categories; although it is a general-purpose systems language, it is increasingly used for smart contracts on platforms like Solana due to its memory safety and performance benefits. These lower-level languages demand a deeper understanding of system behavior but enable greater efficiency, making them ideal for performance-critical applications.

The second key comparison lies in their programming paradigms, where some languages follow imperative principles, focusing on step-by-step state manipulation, while others adopt a more declarative, functional approach that emphasizes immutability and high-level logic. Solidity, Rust, Move, ChainCode, Yul, and Cairo primarily follow the imperative paradigm, where developers define explicit steps to manipulate state. Solidity and Move are contract-oriented languages designed specifically for blockchain environments, while Rust is a general-purpose systems language increasingly used in blockchain applications like Solana. ChainCode, often written in Go or JavaScript, follows enterprise logic structures, and Yul serves as an intermediate representation for optimized EVM execution. Cairo, optimized for zero-knowledge proof computations, also follows an imperative approach but is specialized for cryptographic applications.

On the other hand, Pact, Liquidity, Aiken, and SmartPy lean toward a declarative and functional paradigm, focusing on immutability, stateless computations, and high-level logic expressions. Pact simplifies smart contract logic with built-in formal verification, reducing errors and vulnerabilities. Liquidity, inspired by OCaml, ensures strong type safety, making it ideal for Tezos smart contracts. Aiken, designed for Cardano, also follows a functional style, enhancing security and predictability. Meanwhile, SmartPy, a Python-based framework for Tezos, integrates functional programming principles while maintaining Python's readability.

Moving forward, memory management varies significantly across languages in how they handle resource allocation, ownership, and deallocation. Some languages, like Rust and Move, implement a manual memory management model through ownership and borrowing rules, ensuring memory safety at compile time. This prevents issues such as memory leaks and data races, making it highly efficient but requiring developers to carefully manage resource lifetimes. Similarly, Yul, a low-level intermediate representation for the Ethereum Virtual Machine (EVM), gives developers direct control over memory and storage, optimizing execution but requiring precise memory management. In contrast, Python-based frameworks (PyTeal, SmartPy), Pact, Liquidity, and ChainCode (Go- or JavaScript-based) rely on automatic memory management via garbage collection (GC). While GC simplifies development by handling memory deallocation, it can introduce execution pauses that may be unsuitable for performance-critical blockchain applications.

Another key distinction lies in stack-based vs. heap-based execution. Solidity, Vyper, and Cairo primarily use stack-based memory models, in which data is stored on a local stack, reducing computational overhead but imposing constraints on storage size. Solidity and Vyper, designed for EVM execution, use a structured segmentation of storage, memory, and the stack, with persistent storage incurring high gas fees. Cairo, optimized for zero-knowledge proofs, follows a similar approach to ensure efficient cryptographic computation. On the other hand, Rust, Move, ChainCode, and Python-based languages allow for heap allocation, providing greater flexibility in memory use but potentially introducing additional performance overhead.

Blockchain-specific storage models also play a crucial role in memory management strategies. Solidity, Vyper, and Yul require careful gas optimization since EVM storage operations are expensive, incentivizing developers to minimize unnecessary writes. Move and Aiken introduce resource-oriented programming, enforcing strict rules to prevent accidental duplication or deletion of digital assets and ensure secure memory handling. Pact and Liquidity, as functional languages, emphasize immutability, reducing unintended memory modifications but increasing storage requirements because new instances are created rather than modifying existing ones. Overall, Rust and Move prioritize strict memory safety; Solidity and Vyper optimize for gas-efficient stack execution; and Python-based frameworks simplify memory management through garbage collection, each reflecting a balance among performance, security, and ease of development in blockchain programming.

Another important factor when comparing languages is their cross-platform compatibility/. Many smart contract languages are blockchain-specific, meaning they are designed to work exclusively within a particular blockchain environment. Solidity, Vyper, and Yul are tightly integrated with the Ethereum Virtual Machine (EVM), making them unsuitable for non-EVM blockchains but highly compatible with Ethereum-based networks such as Binance Smart Chain and Polygon. Similarly, Cairo is specific to StarkNet, while Aiken is designed exclusively for Cardano, limiting their use outside their intended ecosystems. Move, originally developed for Libra/Diem, is now used in Aptos and Sui, but its adoption remains confined to Move-compatible blockchains.

On the other hand, some languages exhibit cross-platform capabilities or are adaptable beyond a single blockchain. Rust, while not a smart contract language by design, is widely used across multiple blockchain platforms, including Solana, Polkadot, Near, and Substrate-based chains, making it one of the most flexible options. Python-based frameworks like PyTeal and SmartPy bring smart contract functionality to Algorand and Tezos, respectively, while their general-purpose nature makes them easier to adapt across different ecosystems. ChainCode, primarily written in Go or JavaScript, supports Hyperledger Fabric, a platform designed for enterprise blockchain solutions that can be deployed across different infrastructures.

The next key distinction is the level of security prioritization in each language. When evaluating the security of smart contract languages, the level of built-in security enforcement and vulnerability mitigation strategies is a crucial factor. Some languages are designed with security as a core principle, incorporating formal verification and strict execution rules to prevent common vulnerabilities, while others offer greater flexibility but require developers to manually implement security best practices.

Languages like Vyper, Pact, Liquidity, and Move prioritize built-in security enforcement by minimizing complexity and reducing the attack surface [4]. Vyper, a more secure alternative to Solidity, removes low-level operations and features like function overloading, making contracts more predictable and less prone to vulnerabilities such as reentrancy. Pact further enhances security by integrating formal verification, enabling developers to mathematically prove the correctness of their smart contracts before deployment. This approach drastically reduces unexpected behaviors and security flaws. Liquidity, designed for Tezos, follows functional programming principles, ensuring immutability and strong type safety, making contracts resistant to unintended modifications. Move, originally developed for the Libra/Diem project and now used in Aptos and Sui, introduces resource-oriented programming, helping prevent issues such as asset duplication and ensuring safe state transitions.

Other languages, including Solidity, Yul, and ChainCode, provide flexibility but require developers to implement their own security measures to mitigate vulnerabilities. Solidity, the most widely used smart contract language, has been targeted by numerous attacks, including reentrancy, integer overflows, and improper access control. While newer versions introduce security features like SafeMath libraries, reentrancy guards, and custom error handling, these protections depend on developers actively implementing them. Yul, as a low-level Ethereum IR language, enables extensive optimizations but lacks built-in security checks, leaving developers responsible for preventing vulnerabilities. ChainCode, primarily written in Go or JavaScript for Hyperledger Fabric, relies on the security mechanisms of its host language. This dependence means it inherits the strengths and weaknesses of the underlying execution environment, making it susceptible to buffer overflows and injection attacks if not carefully managed.

Languages like Cairo and Aiken prioritize deterministic execution and formal security guarantees to mitigate risks. Cairo, used in StarkNet, benefits from its zero-knowledge proof-based execution, making contract manipulation computationally infeasible. Aiken, designed for Cardano, enforces strong type safety and eliminates many common vulnerabilities at the language level, reducing the likelihood of execution errors or security breaches.

Finally, the level of community support and the number of applications developed using each language vary significantly, reflecting their adoption and maturity in the blockchain ecosystem [2]. Solidity stands out as the most widely supported language, being the primary choice for Ethereum smart contracts. Its vast developer base, extensive documentation, and numerous decentralized applications (dApps) make it the dominant force in smart contract programming. The strong ecosystem surrounding Solidity includes a wealth of libraries, frameworks, and development tools, making it easier for developers to build and deploy applications efficiently.

Rust, though not a smart contract language by design, has gained significant traction in blockchain development, particularly with platforms like Solana and Polkadot. Its emphasis on performance and safety has attracted a growing community, and while its adoption is still developing compared to Solidity, it has a strong foundation of developers contributing to its expansion. Move, originally created for Facebook's Diem project, has found new life in projects like Aptos and Sui, leading to a gradual increase in both its community and application base. However, compared to Solidity and Rust, it remains in its early stages of widespread adoption.

Languages like Vyper and Cairo have a more niche appeal. Vyper, designed as a security-focused alternative to Solidity, has a smaller community and fewer applications, largely due to its stricter syntax and reduced feature set. While it appeals to developers who prioritize security, its limited adoption means fewer resources and libraries are available. Cairo, developed by StarkWare, specializes in zero-knowledge proof systems, making it a key language for projects like StarkNet. Though its use case is highly specialized, it has an active, engaged community focused on cryptographic applications rather than on general-purpose smart contract development.

Other languages, such as Aiken, Pact, Liquidity, and ChainCode, cater to specific blockchain ecosystems rather than general-purpose smart contract development. Aiken is designed for Cardano, Pact is tailored for Kadena, Liquidity is built for Tezos, and ChainCode is used in Hyperledger Fabric. While these languages have dedicated communities, their application bases remain relatively small due to their niche focus. They thrive within their ecosystems but do not enjoy the same level of widespread adoption as Solidity or Rust.

Yul, unlike other languages on this list, is primarily used as an intermediate language for Ethereum, focusing on low-level optimizations rather than direct application development. As a result, its community is primarily composed of developers working on compiler optimizations and EVM efficiency improvements, rather than those building dApps. This has limited its community engagement and the number of projects that rely on it directly.

In comparing smart contract languages, it becomes evident that each language is tailored to specific needs, balancing usability, security, performance, and ecosystem support. High-level languages like Solidity, Vyper, and Move prioritize accessibility, making smart contract development more approachable while introducing trade-offs in security and execution efficiency. In contrast, lower-level languages such as Yul and Cairo offer greater control over execution and optimizations but demand a deeper technical understanding. Similarly, the divergence in programming paradigms, with some languages embracing functional approaches for greater security and predictability while others focus on imperative logic for flexibility, highlights the fundamental trade-offs developers must consider.

The overall maturity and adoption of a language are also crucial factors, as a strong community provides extensive resources, tools, and real-world applications that enhance development efficiency. Solidity leads in community support and application deployment due to its dominance in Ethereum and EVM-compatible chains, while Rust is gaining traction in performance-driven blockchain ecosystems. Other languages, such as Move, Pact, and Aiken, are growing within their respective platforms, offering innovative security models but facing adoption challenges. Ultimately, selecting a smart contract language depends on the developer's priorities, whether they value ease of use, security, performance, or ecosystem support, each language offering distinct advantages and limitations within the evolving blockchain landscape.

NO	Language	Compatible Blockchain	Accounting Model	Contract Storage	Fees Depend On	Programming Style	Pros	Cons
1	Solidity	Ethereum	Account-based	Stateful	Tx computation	Procedural	Decentralized, flexible for complex apps, strong developer community, widely supported tools	High gas costs, potential for insecure code
2	Rust	Solana	Account-based	Stateless	Num. Signers, data size	Procedural	High-performance, memory safety, parallel transaction processing	Complex design, steep learning curve
3	Aiken	Cardano	UTXO	Stateful	Tx size, Tx computation	Approval	Type safety, supports both on-chain and off-chain components, strong functional paradigm	Complexity for purely on-chain programming
4	Move	Aptos	Account-based	Stateless	Tx computation, data size	Procedural	Enhanced safety with linear types, modular structure, platform adaptability	Platform-specific adaptations required, complexity in multi-participant contracts

NO	Language		Compatible Blockchain	Accounting Model	Contract Storage	Fees Depend On	Programming Style	Pros	Cons
5	Python	PyTeal	Algorand	Account-based	Stateful	Constant	Procedural	Predictable, low-cost transactions, efficient consensus mechanism	Limited smart contract complexity
		SmartPy	Tezos	Account-based	Initial storage set via constructor, embedded in Michelson	Tx computation, data size	Declarative, functional	Uses python syntax, meta-programming, strongly typed with type inference	Limited external data use, Michelson-dependent
6	Vyper		Ethereum	Account-based	Stores state on-chain	Gas usage	Procedural	Emphasizes security, minimalism, readability, simplify code auditing	Limited features compared to solidity, smaller ecosystem
7	Yul		Ethereum	Account-based	Stores state on-chain	Gas optimization	Low-level, procedural	Optimized for low gas costs, high-performance code	Limited ecosystem requires advanced expertise
8	Cairo		StarkNet StarkEx	Account-based	Uses STARK proofs for data verification	Gas usage, StarkNet-specific	Procedural	Scalable, verifiable computations, ideal for layer-2 solutions	Limited to StarkNet/StarkEx environments

9	Pact	Kadena	Account-based	Immutable data	Transaction complexity	Declarative	Focuses on security, reduced errors, ideal for business-critical apps	Turing-incompleteness limits complex logic
10	Liquidity	Tezos	Account-based	Explicit value storage	Gas usage	Functional	Formal verification, strong typing, suited for high-security applications	Limited adoption, steep learning curve
11	ChainCode	Hyper ledger fabric	Permissioned ledger model	Couch DB data base, docker containerized storage	Transaction complexity	Procedural	Enterprise-focused, secure private transactions, scalable deployment	Limited to Hyper ledger fabric ecosystem

3.4 A Sample of SC

Ethereum and Solidity are selected as the primary focus of this book due to their central role in advancing smart contract development and dApps. As the leading blockchain platform for general-purpose smart contract execution, Ethereum has achieved widespread adoption across sectors such as decentralized finance (DeFi), non-fungible tokens (NFTs), and decentralized governance. Its robust and flexible architecture, powered by the EVM, supports Turing-complete contracts and fosters a thriving ecosystem for building and deploying complex applications without intermediaries. With continuous development, including its transition to proof-of-stake (Ethereum 2.0), Ethereum is designed for scalability, energy efficiency, and long-term sustainability, making it an ideal platform for innovative blockchain research and development.

Solidity, Ethereum's native contract-oriented programming language, complements this focus by offering a developer-friendly syntax specifically tailored for creating smart contracts. Its seamless integration with the EVM facilitates the deployment of self-executing contracts that can manage financial transactions, asset tokenization, and application logic. Solidity's extensive adoption and active developer community provide abundant support, libraries, and tools, making it ideal for rapid prototyping and scalable development. Given Solidity's dominance in the blockchain ecosystem, research on Solidity-based vulnerability detection, optimization, and formal verification is highly relevant and has broad real-world applications. This focus on Ethereum and Solidity supports the exploration of critical challenges in security, scalability, and interpretability within the most widely adopted and continuously evolving smart contract platform.

3.5 Chapter Summary

This chapter provides a comprehensive exploration of smart contract programming languages and platforms, highlighting their unique features and applications. It begins with an overview of programming languages for smart contracts, such as Solidity, Pact, Liquidity, and Chaincode, and examines their suitability for various blockchain platforms and use cases. The chapter then presents sample implementations of smart contracts in these languages, showcasing their syntax, core functionalities, and approaches to automating agreements. Finally, a detailed comparative analysis of these languages highlights their strengths and limitations across key dimensions, including syntax, ease of use, security, and scalability.

References

1. Parizi, R.M., Amritraj, Dehghantanha, A.: Smart contract programming languages on blockchains: an empirical evaluation of usability and security. In: Blockchain–ICBC 2018: First International Conference, Held as Part of the Services Conference Federation, SCF 2018, Seattle, WA, USA, June 25–30, 2018, Proceedings, vol. 1. Springer International Publishing (2018)

2. Zou, W., et al.: Smart contract development: challenges and opportunities. IEEE Trans. Softw. Eng. **47**(10), 2084–2106 (2019)
3. Wang, S., et al.: An overview of smart contract: architecture, applications, and future trends. In: 2018 IEEE Intelligent Vehicles Symposium (IV). IEEE (2018)
4. Valerievitch, T.A., et al.: Overview of the languages for safe smart contract programming. Proc. Inst. Syst. Program. RAS. **31**(3), 157–176 (2019)
5. Kim, I.-S.: Survey on smart contract programming languages. Electron. Telecommun. Trends. **35**(5), 134–138 (2020)
6. Solorio, K., Kanna, R., Hoover, D.H.: Hands-On Smart Contract Development with Solidity and Ethereum: From Fundamentals to Deployment. O'Reilly Media (2019)
7. Coblenz, M., et al.: Smarter smart contract development tools. In: 2019 IEEE/ACM 2nd International Workshop on Emerging Trends in Software Engineering for Blockchain (WETSEB). IEEE (2019)
8. Doan, T.T.H., Thiemann, P.: A formal verification framework for Tezos smart contracts based on symbolic execution. In: Asian Symposium on Programming Languages and Systems. Springer, Singapore (2024)
9. Weingaertner, T., et al.: Smart contracts using blockly: representing a purchase agreement using a graphical programming language. In: 2018 Crypto Valley Conference on Blockchain Technology (CVCBT). IEEE (2018)
10. Yaseen, H., Hassan, S.I.: A systematic review on privacy preservation techniques for smart contracts in blockchain using machine learning. In: 2024 International Conference on Cognitive Robotics and Intelligent Systems (ICC-ROBINS). IEEE (2024)

Chapter 4
Smart Contracts Applications

Abstract This chapter explores the wide-ranging applications of smart contracts across industries such as finance, supply chain, healthcare, real estate, governance, and beyond. By automating agreements, smart contracts eliminate intermediaries, reduce costs, and enhance transparency and trust while enabling innovation in areas like DeFi, DAOs, provenance tracking, medical records, and digital ownership. It also examines their core advantages over traditional contracts, including automation, decentralization, accuracy, fraud prevention, and global accessibility. At the same time, it highlights significant challenges, from technical issues such as scalability, interoperability, and oracle dependence to legal and regulatory uncertainties surrounding enforceability, jurisdiction, and privacy compliance. Finally, this chapter illustrates both the transformative potential and the pressing limitations of smart contracts, underscoring the need for technical improvements and regulatory clarity to achieve their full adoption in modern digital ecosystems.

Smart contract applications span diverse industries, including finance, supply chain management, healthcare, real estate, and governance, each leveraging blockchain technology to enhance efficiency, transparency, and security. By automating contractual agreements, smart contracts eliminate intermediaries, reducing costs and minimizing the risk of human error or fraud. Their deterministic execution ensures that predefined conditions are met before transactions are processed, making them highly reliable for various use cases.

This chapter categorizes these applications and provides a structured analysis of their adoption across sectors, highlighting the factors driving their growing relevance. Additionally, it explores the advantages of smart contracts over traditional agreements, emphasizing their ability to execute transactions autonomously, prevent disputes, and enhance trust through transparency and immutability. Despite their advantages, smart contracts face significant technical and legal challenges that impact their widespread adoption. Scalability issues, security vulnerabilities, and interoperability constraints hinder seamless integration across different blockchain platforms. Moreover, the legal and regulatory landscape remains ambiguous, as many jurisdictions struggle to define the enforceability of smart contracts and their compliance with existing laws. This chapter examines these limitations, discussing the need for advancements in blockchain technology, improved security

S. HajiHosseinKhani et al., *Understanding Cybersecurity for Smart Contracts*,
https://doi.org/10.1007/978-3-032-28863-9_4

frameworks, and evolving legal frameworks to support the continued growth and adoption of smart contracts in modern digital transactions.

4.1 Categorization and Analysis of Smart Contract Applications

Smart contracts have emerged as a pivotal technology, transforming a wide range of industries by enabling automation, security, transparency, and efficiency. Their self-executing nature, governed by predefined rules encoded on the blockchain, eliminates intermediaries and streamlines complex processes. This section explores the diverse applications of smart contracts and categorizes their impact across domains such as decentralized finance (DeFi), governance, supply chain management, healthcare, intellectual property, real estate, legal compliance, energy, gaming, and telecommunications. By analyzing their role in each sector, we highlight how smart contracts drive innovation, optimize operations, and redefine traditional business models.

4.1.1 Finance & DeFi (Decentralized Finance)

DeFi is reshaping the financial system by leveraging smart contracts to automate transactions and remove the need for intermediaries such as banks. These contracts enable transparent, trustless, and programmable financial services across multiple domains. In payments, the power peer-to-peer transfers, stablecoins, CBDCs, and micropayments. In lending and borrowing, they facilitate collateralized loans, flash loans, and automated liquidations. Smart contracts also underpin decentralized exchanges (DEXs), liquidity pools, and hybrid trading systems, while supporting yield farming, staking, and governance through predefined rules that incentivize participation.

Beyond core financial services, smart contracts expand into insurance, risk management, and asset tokenization. Decentralized insurance platforms automate claim verification and payouts, often with oracles for parametric triggers. Tokenization enables fractional ownership of assets such as real estate, bonds, and equities, improving accessibility and efficiency. Overall, DeFi transforms finance into a transparent, decentralized ecosystem that enhances accessibility and innovation, though it also raises challenges of security, scalability, and regulation.

4.1.2 Governance & DAOs (Decentralized Autonomous Organizations)

DAOs transform governance by using smart contracts to automate decision-making and financial management, replacing centralized hierarchies with on-chain governance. Token holders vote through governance tokens, and smart contracts enforce these outcomes, managing treasury allocations without intermediaries. This structure ensures transparent, rule-based operations while giving stakeholders direct participation in shaping policies and the distribution of resources.

Smart contracts also extend governance into political and identity systems. They enable transparent, tamper-proof e-voting, including mechanisms such as quadratic voting that balance influence among stakeholders. Decentralized identity and reputation frameworks further enhance trust by enabling self-sovereign identity management and on-chain recording of user contributions that influence governance authority. Altogether, DAOs and decentralized voting systems redefine governance by reducing fraud, ensuring transparency, and fostering inclusive participation, creating a resilient alternative to traditional centralized structures.

4.1.3 Supply Chain & Logistics

Smart contracts are revolutionizing supply chain and logistics by automating operations, enhancing transparency, and ensuring compliance without intermediaries. They enable provenance and traceability by recording every stage of a product's lifecycle on the blockchain, allowing manufacturers, retailers, and consumers to verify authenticity, certify quality, and prevent fraud, particularly in areas such as luxury goods and pharmaceuticals, where anti-counterfeiting is critical. By securely automating product authentication and compliance, smart contracts create trust across the supply chain.

When integrated with IoT, smart contracts extend automation to logistics and shipment management. Sensors provide real-time data on conditions such as temperature and location, enabling smart contracts to autonomously confirm deliveries, execute payments, or trigger alerts if deviations occur. This is especially vital in food and cold-chain supply systems, where farm-to-table transparency and temperature monitoring ensure safety and quality. Overall, by combining blockchain, IoT, and smart contracts, supply chains become more secure, efficient, and tamper-proof, supporting a resilient and accountable global trade ecosystem.

4.1.4 Healthcare & Medical Industry

Smart contracts are transforming healthcare by decentralizing data management, securing clinical research, and automating insurance processes. In medical records, they enable patient-controlled access to tamper-proof health data, improving privacy and interoperability across institutions while eliminating reliance on centralized databases. Clinical trials also benefit from blockchain-registered data and automated consent management, ensuring transparency, ethical compliance, and real-time verification of trial integrity.

In insurance and billing, smart contracts automate claims processing, validate medical data, and reduce fraud by preventing the use of forged documentation. They also support dynamic, usage-based insurance models that adjust premiums based on medical history and real-time health metrics, offering greater transparency and personalization. Overall, the integration of smart contracts into healthcare fosters a secure, efficient, and patient-centric system that enhances trust, reduces costs, and ensures compliance across medical and insurance services.

4.1.5 Intellectual Property & Digital Content

Smart contracts are reshaping intellectual property and digital content by ensuring transparent ownership, automated licensing, and secure monetization. NFTs are among the most prominent applications, using smart contracts to verify authenticity and establish immutable ownership of digital assets such as art, collectibles, and in-game items. This automation not only prevents fraud and unauthorized reproduction but also guarantees resale royalties and seamless ownership transfers, empowering creators and players to trade assets with real-world value without relying on centralized platforms.

Beyond NFTs, smart contracts transform copyright, licensing, and intellectual property protection. In music and entertainment, they automate royalty distribution, executing revenue splits in real time and ensuring creators are fairly compensated without intermediaries. Blockchain timestamping further secures patents and trademarks by providing indisputable proof of ownership and streamlining licensing agreements. Overall, integrating smart contracts into IP management reduces fraud, enhances efficiency, and creates a more decentralized and equitable digital economy for artists, innovators, and businesses.

4.1.6 Real Estate & Land Management

Smart contracts are revolutionizing real estate and land management by automating property transactions, leases, and land registries, replacing traditional paperwork and intermediaries with secure, transparent, and efficient processes. Property deeds and titles recorded on blockchain create tamper-proof ownership records that eliminate forgery, disputes, and unauthorized changes. Tokenization further enables fractional ownership, allowing investors to purchase property shares, receive automated rental income, and enjoy greater liquidity in real estate markets without relying on traditional institutions.

Beyond sales and investments, smart contracts streamline rental agreements by automating rent payments and enabling escrow-based dispute resolution, ensuring timely transactions and secure property handovers. Governments are also adopting blockchain-based land registries, as seen in Sweden and Georgia, to guarantee immutable ownership verification and reduce corruption. Overall, by embedding smart contracts into property transactions and registries, blockchain enhances trust, reduces fraud, and makes real estate more accessible, transparent, and efficient.

4.1.7 Legal & Compliance

Smart contracts are transforming legal and compliance processes by automating enforcement, enhancing transparency, and reducing reliance on intermediaries. Traditional agreements and regulatory procedures often involve delays, manual oversight, and errors, but smart legal contracts execute predefined terms automatically, handling payments, penalties, or terminations without human intervention. This not only speeds up enforcement and lowers costs but also embeds regulatory compliance directly into contract logic, ensuring businesses adapt seamlessly to evolving tax, environmental, or industry standards.

They also play a vital role in identity and financial compliance. Decentralized KYC systems allow users to securely store verified credentials on blockchain, granting access via smart contracts when needed, improving both efficiency and privacy. Similarly, AML monitoring becomes proactive as smart contracts autonomously flag suspicious transactions and trigger real-time reports. By integrating into legal, regulatory, and financial frameworks, smart contracts create a more secure, efficient, and self-executing compliance ecosystem that strengthens trust and reduces administrative burdens.

4.1.8 Energy & Sustainability

Smart contracts are transforming energy and sustainability by enabling decentralized energy trading, automating carbon tracking, and ensuring transparent eco-certification. Traditional energy markets depend on centralized intermediaries, but blockchain-based smart contracts allow direct peer-to-peer (P2P) energy exchanges, as seen in projects like the Brooklyn Microgrid. Producers with surplus renewable energy can sell directly to consumers, with contracts automating pricing, validation, and payments in real time. They also support tokenized Renewable Energy

Certificates (RECs), providing verifiable proof of sustainable energy generation and consumption.

Beyond trading, smart contracts strengthen carbon offset and sustainability initiatives by ensuring transparent, tamper-proof tracking of carbon credits, preventing fraud and double-counting. In supply chains, they automate eco-certification, ensuring that only verified, environmentally responsible suppliers can register their products, reducing the risk of greenwashing. Overall, by embedding automation and transparency into energy and sustainability systems, smart contracts promote efficiency, accountability, and trust, advancing a decentralized and greener future.

4.1.9 Gaming & Metaverse

Smart contracts are reshaping gaming and the metaverse by automating ownership, enabling decentralized economies, and ensuring trustless interactions. Unlike traditional games controlled by centralized developers, blockchain-based systems grant players verifiable, immutable ownership of digital assets and automate in-game transactions. Play-to-Earn (P2E) models showcase this shift by rewarding players with tokenized, tradeable cryptocurrency for their achievements, as seen in games like Axie Infinity.

NFT integration further strengthens this ecosystem by turning in-game items such as skins, weapons, or characters into unique, permanent assets that can be traded across platforms. In the metaverse, smart contracts govern digital landownership and commerce, powering platforms like Decentraland and The Sandbox, where users buy, sell, or rent virtual property as NFTs. From avatar customizations to digital events, all transactions are transparently executed through smart contracts. Altogether, this technology creates a decentralized, player-driven economy where gaming and virtual worlds empower users with true ownership and real-world value.

4.1.10 Telecommunications & IoT

Smart contracts are transforming telecommunications and IoT by automating transactions, enhancing security, and decentralizing communication networks. Traditional systems rely on centralized infrastructure, which introduces inefficiencies and vulnerabilities, whereas blockchain-based smart contracts enable trustless, self-executing processes. A key application is Machine-to-Machine (M2M) payments, where devices autonomously transact without human oversight, such as vehicles paying tolls or smart meters billing for real-time energy use. This also supports flexible micropayment models in which devices dynamically charge based on actual consumption rather than on fixed fees.

Beyond financial automation, smart contracts secure communications and data integrity in telecom and IoT networks. Decentralized messaging apps use them to enforce end-to-end encryption, preventing breaches and censorship by removing reliance on central servers. Similarly, tamper-proof data transmission ensures sensitive information in healthcare, supply chains, or autonomous vehicles remains immutable and verifiable, creating audit trails and reliable decision-making inputs. Altogether, integrating smart contracts into IoT and telecom ecosystems fosters decentralized, efficient, and secure digital infrastructures for the future.

The widespread adoption of smart contracts is revolutionizing industries by introducing decentralized, automated, and trustless solutions. From DeFi's financial transformations to DAO governance, secure supply chain tracking, healthcare data management, and beyond, smart contracts are reshaping the digital and physical worlds. Their ability to enforce agreements programmatically, enhance transparency, and mitigate fraud makes them indispensable in modern applications. However, challenges such as security vulnerabilities, scalability limitations, and regulatory concerns must be addressed to fully unlock their potential. As technology matures, smart contracts will continue to evolve, fostering a more decentralized, efficient, and secure digital ecosystem across various sectors.

4.2 Factors (The Advantages of Smart Contracts Over Traditional Contracts)

The shift from traditional contracts to smart contracts is driven by fundamental improvements in efficiency, security, automation, and cost reduction. Traditional contracts rely on intermediaries, extensive paperwork, and manual enforcement, making them susceptible to inefficiencies, disputes, and delays. Smart contracts, on the other hand, leverage blockchain technology to enable self-executing, transparent, and tamper-proof agreements. This section explores the key features that make smart contracts a superior alternative to traditional contracts.

4.2.1 Automation and Self-Execution

Smart contracts bring automation and self-execution to diverse industries, eliminating inefficiencies caused by manual oversight and intermediaries. In DeFi, platforms like Aave and Compound use them to autonomously manage lending, collateral, and repayments, while flash loans enable instant, uncollateralized borrowing within a single transaction block. Supply chains replace manual invoicing with self-executing contracts that trigger payments upon delivery verification, reducing errors and disputes. In healthcare, decentralized platforms such as Nexus Mutual automate insurance claims, ensuring instant, unbiased payouts once conditions are met. Telecommunications and IoT also benefit, with smart contracts enabling autonomous machine-to-machine payments, such as smart meters paying for energy or self-driving cars handling tolls, demonstrating how automation enhances efficiency, transparency, and accessibility across sectors.

4.2.2 Transparency and Trust

Smart contracts enhance transparency by operating on the blockchain, making agreements immutable and publicly verifiable, unlike traditional, opaque contracts that are prone to manipulation. In governance, DAOs rely on this transparency to ensure tamper-proof voting and fair fund distribution, while in healthcare, smart contracts secure patient data access through immutable consent records, reducing fraud and breaches. Supply chains also gain reliability as product provenance is permanently recorded, preventing counterfeiting and unauthorized alterations. In gaming and the metaverse, transparency ensures that digital assets like NFTs maintain verifiable ownership histories, eliminating duplication and fraud. Across sectors, smart contracts create trust by embedding transparency directly into processes that traditionally relied on intermediaries.

4.2.3 Security and Tamper Resistance

Smart contracts strengthen security by leveraging blockchain's immutability and cryptography to prevent forgery, alteration, and loss of records, thereby addressing key weaknesses in traditional systems. In real estate, they secure land titles against fraud, as seen in blockchain-based registries in Sweden and Georgia, while in intellectual property, NFTs and timestamps protect creators from copyright infringement and automate royalty distribution. Legal and compliance processes such as KYC and AML also benefit, with smart contracts ensuring transparent, tamper-proof identity and transaction records, reducing fraud and errors. Even in gaming and the metaverse, they safeguard digital assets and identities against counterfeiting, giving users verifiable, secure ownership. Across industries, smart contracts provide a level of security that traditional paper-based or centralized systems cannot match.

4.2.4 Cost and Time Efficiency

Smart contracts reduce costs and delays by eliminating intermediaries such as banks, lawyers, and notaries, enabling instant, automated contract execution across industries. In DeFi, the power of peer-to-peer loans, payments, and swaps on platforms like Uniswap cuts fees compared to traditional banking. In healthcare, they streamline insurance by automating claims and ensuring immediate payouts, while in real estate, they simplify ownership transfers and enable tokenized investments without costly legal services. Energy markets also benefit, as smart contracts support peer-to-peer trading of surplus energy, bypassing centralized utilities. Across these sectors, smart contracts lower barriers, eliminate inefficiencies, and make transactions faster, cheaper, and more accessible.

4.2.5 Decentralization and Intermediary-Free Execution

Smart contracts eliminate inefficiencies and biases of centralized institutions by enabling peer-to-peer transactions on decentralized networks governed by immutable code. In supply chains, they automate shipment verification and payments, reducing delays and disputes, while in DeFi, stablecoins like USDC and DAI allow instant transfers without banks or payment processors. Telecommunications and IoT also benefit as devices autonomously execute service payments through smart contracts, bypassing centralized providers. Similarly, in gaming and the metaverse, platforms like Decentraland ensure true digital ownership by recording asset transactions on the blockchain, freeing users from centralized operators' control. Across industries, decentralization through smart contracts enhances efficiency, transparency, and user autonomy.

4.2.6 Accuracy and Reduced Human Error

Traditional contracts are vulnerable to human errors in drafting, interpretation, and execution, leading to financial losses, disputes, or unenforceable agreements. Smart contracts eliminate these risks by encoding deterministic rules on immutable blockchain networks, ensuring agreements are executed with mathematical precision and no room for miscommunication or deviation. In healthcare, this accuracy is particularly valuable for medical record management and insurance claims. Smart contracts integrated with Self-Sovereign Identity (SSI) frameworks ensure secure, cryptographically authorized access to patient records, preventing unauthorized modifications or prescription errors. Insurance processes also benefit, as claims are automatically executed when predefined conditions are met, for example, instant payouts for flight delays triggered by real-time tracking data, removing inefficiencies, disputes, and fraud.

Legal and compliance processes also benefit from smart contract precision, especially in areas such as tax reporting and regulatory compliance. Traditional tax filing relies on manual calculations and data entry, which often lead to errors, delays, or even penalties. Smart contracts automate these processes by accurately tracking transactions in real time and instantly calculating obligations such as VAT, corporate taxes, or import duties. This not only prevents miscalculations and tax evasion but also ensures full compliance without constant manual oversight. By eliminating human error across industries, smart contracts create more accurate, efficient, and trustworthy systems for executing agreements and meeting regulatory standards.

4.2.7 Global Accessibility and Cross-Border Transactions

Traditional contracts are often limited by geographical and jurisdictional barriers, requiring harmonization across legal systems and the involvement of intermediaries for currency exchange, compliance, and verification. These processes make international trade, finance, and agreements slow, costly, and complex. Smart contracts eliminate such barriers by operating on decentralized blockchain networks, executing transactions seamlessly across borders without requiring local legal reconciliation. In finance, this transformation is evident in DeFi and payments, where blockchain-based stablecoins like USDC and DAI enable instant, low-cost global transfers. Solutions such as the Bitcoin Lightning Network and Ethereum Layer 2 platforms like Optimism and Arbitrum further enhance scalability and efficiency, making global remittances and settlements faster, cheaper, and more inclusive, especially for unbanked populations that have traditionally been excluded from international finance.

The impact extends to industries such as supply chain and real estate, where traditional cross-border operations are heavily burdened by paperwork, regulations, and jurisdictional restrictions. In logistics, smart contracts automate customs duties, verify shipments with IoT integration, and trigger payments upon delivery confirmation, reducing delays and compliance disputes while ensuring transparency. In real estate, tokenization enables fractional ownership of properties worldwide, allowing investors to bypass restrictive legal processes and participate in global markets with ease. For example, investors can securely purchase real estate tokens representing ownership interests in properties abroad and automatically receive rental income through smart contracts. By streamlining these traditionally localized and regulation-heavy processes, smart contracts make international trade and investment more efficient, accessible, and transparent.

4.2.8 Programmability and Flexibility

Unlike traditional contracts that require manual oversight to manage complex conditions or multi-step agreements, smart contracts introduce programmability, enabling dynamic, automated execution. By integrating oracles, supporting multi-signature approvals, and enabling nested contract interactions, they adapt to real-world conditions without human intervention. This flexibility is particularly valuable in finance, where platforms like Aave use smart contracts to implement flash loans, instant, uncollateralized loans that must be repaid within a single transaction block, or to enforce automated liquidations, ensuring lending agreements are executed securely and without counterparty risk. Such programmability streamlines financial operations by replacing intermediaries with code that executes precisely and reliably.

Gaming, the metaverse, and healthcare also benefit significantly from smart contract programmability. In gaming, dynamic NFTs (dNFTs) evolve according to logic encoded in smart contracts, allowing characters and assets to progress in real time while granting players true ownership and tradeability across decentralized marketplaces such as The Sandbox and Decentraland. In healthcare, programmability enhances insurance and prescription systems by automating claims processing with real-time data verification and ensuring medications are issued only under authorized conditions, reducing fraud and errors. Together, these applications demonstrate how programmability elevates smart contracts beyond static agreements into adaptive, secure systems that power complex, real-world interactions across industries.

4.2.9 Fraud Prevention and Immutable Recordkeeping

Traditional contract management is vulnerable to fraud, forgery, and disputes because records can be altered, lost, or misinterpreted. Smart contracts address these issues by recording every transaction on an immutable blockchain ledger, ensuring permanent auditability and preventing unauthorized modifications. This transparency is especially valuable in governance and DAOs, where secure voting and transparent fund allocation reduce risks of election fraud and financial mismanagement. Similarly, in sustainability initiatives such as carbon credit trading, smart contracts eliminate double-counting and unverifiable claims by tokenizing credits and integrating IoT-based environmental data, ensuring accurate, tamper-proof emissions tracking.

In gaming and the metaverse, smart contracts safeguard digital economies by preventing fraudulent duplication of virtual assets. Traditional centralized platforms often face risks of hacking and asset duplication, which erode scarcity and value. By recording each NFT-backed asset immutably on the blockchain, smart contracts guarantee uniqueness, enforce true ownership, and preserve asset value. This allows players to securely trade items like skins, weapons, and collectibles in decentralized marketplaces, independent of centralized control, thereby ensuring trust and resilience in digital economies.

In a nutshell, Smart Contracts represent a paradigm shift in contract execution, offering advantages that traditional contracts cannot match. By eliminating intermediaries, automating enforcement, enhancing security, and reducing costs, they streamline processes across diverse industries. Their transparency ensures trust, their decentralization removes unnecessary bureaucracy, and their programmability enables dynamic and adaptive contract execution. While challenges such as legal recognition and security vulnerabilities remain, the widespread adoption of smart contracts continues to reshape financial systems, supply chains, and digital economies. As blockchain technology evolves, smart contracts are poised to become the foundation of a more efficient, secure, and globally accessible contract management system.

4.3 Issues and Challenges

While smart contracts offer numerous advantages over traditional contracts, their adoption is not without challenges. Several technical and legal obstacles must be addressed to ensure their reliability, security, and compliance with existing regulatory frameworks. This section explores two primary challenges faced by smart contracts: technical limitations and legal and regulatory hurdles.

1. **Technical Limitations Issues**

   Despite their automation and security benefits, smart contracts face several technical challenges that affect their scalability, security, and integration with external systems. One major concern is security vulnerabilities. Since smart contracts are immutable once deployed, any coding error or vulnerability can be exploited permanently. High-profile attacks, such as the DAO hack in 2016, have demonstrated that bugs in smart contract logic can lead to significant financial losses. Unlike traditional software, smart contracts cannot be easily patched once deployed to the blockchain, requiring extensive auditing and rigorous security testing before deployment.

   Another significant issue is scalability. Blockchain networks, particularly Ethereum, which hosts most smart contracts, face congestion and high transaction fees during peak usage periods. Smart contract execution relies on network validators, making transactions slow and costly when demand spikes. Layer 2 scaling solutions, such as rollups and sidechains, aim to mitigate this issue, but their widespread adoption is still underway.

   Interoperability is also a key challenge. Most smart contracts operate within their respective blockchain ecosystems, limiting their ability to interact seamlessly with other blockchains or traditional systems. Cross-chain communication protocols, such as Polkadot and Cosmos, aim to address this challenge, but seamless interoperability between smart contracts and traditional databases, payment systems, and enterprise solutions remains a work in progress.

   Additionally, external data dependency is a technical hurdle. Many smart contracts rely on off-chain data, such as stock prices, weather conditions, or election results, which must be retrieved from external sources known as oracles. However, the accuracy and reliability of these oracles can be compromised, leading to incorrect contract execution. Oracle attacks, such as price manipulation in DeFi platforms, highlight the risks of relying on unverified or centralized data sources.

   Lastly, the legal enforceability of smart contracts remains uncertain. Traditional legal systems recognize written, signed agreements, but smart contracts, which are executed programmatically, may lack clarity on dispute resolution. If a smart contract produces unintended outcomes due to programming errors or unexpected inputs, determining liability and enforcement mechanisms becomes challenging.

2. **Legal and Regulatory Challenges**

Smart contracts also face significant legal and regulatory hurdles that hinder their widespread adoption. One of the primary concerns is regulatory uncertainty. Many jurisdictions lack clear guidelines regarding the legal status of smart contracts. While some countries, such as the United States and the United Kingdom, have taken steps toward recognizing smart contracts as legally binding, many others have yet to establish concrete legal frameworks. Without standardized regulations, businesses and individuals may hesitate to rely on smart contracts for critical agreements.

Another major issue is jurisdiction and cross-border legal compliance. Since blockchain networks operate globally, enforcing smart contracts across different legal systems can be complex. A contract executed on a blockchain might be valid under one country's laws but unenforceable in another. Traditional legal systems rely on jurisdictional authority, whereas blockchain operates in a decentralized manner, making it difficult to determine which laws apply in disputes.

Data privacy and regulatory compliance, such as the General Data Protection Regulation (GDPR), also pose challenges. Blockchains are inherently transparent and immutable, meaning that once personal data is recorded on-chain, it cannot be modified or deleted. This conflicts with privacy laws that grant individuals the right to have their data erased or modified. Ensuring that smart contracts comply with these regulations requires innovative solutions, such as zero-knowledge proof and off-chain data management, but these approaches are still evolving.

Additionally, dispute resolution and legal recourse are problematic in smart contract implementations. Traditional contracts include clauses specifying how disputes will be resolved, often through arbitration or court proceedings. However, smart contracts execute automatically based on pre-coded rules, leaving little room for intervention if an error occurs or an agreement needs to be amended. Decentralized dispute resolution mechanisms, such as blockchain-based arbitration platforms, are being developed, but they are not yet widely accepted within mainstream legal systems.

Furthermore, compliance with anti-money laundering (AML) and know-your-customer (KYC) regulations presents a challenge. Many smart contract applications, particularly in decentralized finance (DeFi), operate without requiring users to disclose their identities. While this promotes financial inclusivity and privacy, it also raises concerns among regulators regarding illicit activities, such as money laundering and terrorism financing. Governments and financial institutions are exploring ways to integrate KYC-compliant smart contracts while maintaining the benefits of decentralization.

Lastly, the interpretation and intent of contracts remain ambiguous in smart contract law. Traditional legal contracts allow for interpretation based on intent, context, and judicial discretion. Smart contracts, however, are strictly code-based and execute predefined conditions without considering subjective factors. If a contract is poorly written or ambiguous, there may be no legal recourse to amend or reinterpret it, leading to unintended financial losses or unfair enforcement.

Inc. conclusion, while smart contracts offer revolutionary improvements in automation, efficiency, and security, their adoption is hindered by significant technical and legal challenges. Security vulnerabilities, scalability limitations, and reliance on external data present risks that must be addressed through robust coding practices, auditing, and technological advancements. Likewise, regulatory uncertainty, jurisdictional conflicts, and privacy concerns pose obstacles to widespread legal acceptance. Overcoming these issues requires collaboration between blockchain developers, policymakers, and legal experts to create frameworks that support innovation while ensuring compliance and security. As smart contracts continue to evolve, addressing these challenges will be crucial to unlocking their full potential in mainstream applications.

4.4 Chapter Summary

This chapter provides a comprehensive exploration of smart contract applications, beginning with their categorization across industries such as finance, supply chain management, healthcare, and governance, and highlighting their distinct functionalities and use cases. It then examines the advantages of smart contracts over traditional contracts, emphasizing their ability to automate processes, eliminate intermediaries, enhance transparency, and improve security through decentralized execution. However, despite these benefits, smart contracts face significant challenges, including technical limitations such as scalability issues, security vulnerabilities, and integration complexities with off-chain data. Additionally, legal and regulatory concerns, including enforceability, jurisdictional conflicts, and the lack of standardized frameworks, pose obstacles to widespread adoption. By analyzing these aspects, this chapter provides valuable insights into both the potential and limitations of smart contracts, offering guidance for developers, policymakers, and businesses seeking to implement blockchain-based solutions effectively.

Chapter 5
Designing and Developing Smart Contracts

Abstract This chapter introduces the foundations of smart contract design and development, focusing on Solidity as the primary programming language for Ethereum and other EVM-based platforms. It explains Solidity's syntax, core data types, and programming constructs, including state variables, functions, modifiers, constructors, events, and inheritance, showing how these components interact to define secure, efficient, and reusable contracts. In addition, it explores how traditional legal agreements convert into self-executing smart contracts, presenting a detailed case study of a freelance contract that translates roles, conditions, payments, and deadlines into Solidity code. Alongside practical implementations, it highlights the challenges of contract conversion, from legal ambiguity and reliance on oracles to high gas costs, immutability concerns, and security vulnerabilities such as reentrancy. Lastly, it provides both a practical and conceptual foundation for smart contract development, balancing Solidity's strengths with the limitations and risks developers must address to create robust and enforceable digital agreements.

Before building powerful decentralized applications, it is essential to grasp the language and architectural patterns that underpin smart contract development. Solidity, Ethereum's contract-oriented programming language, provides the structure and tools needed to create programmable logic that governs transactions, asset transfers, access controls, and other core components of blockchain-based systems [1, 2]. This section lays the groundwork for writing Solidity contracts by first introducing the language's syntax and semantics, then diving into the essential building blocks: state variables, functions, events, constructors, and modifiers. By understanding how these elements are defined, interact, and execute within the Ethereum Virtual Machine (EVM), developers gain confidence and competence to design secure and efficient smart contracts from the ground up [1, 3].

S. HajiHosseinKhani et al., *Understanding Cybersecurity for Smart Contracts*,
https://doi.org/10.1007/978-3-032-28863-9_5

5.1 Fundamentals of Smart Contract Development in Solidity

Smart contract development begins with mastering the language that drives the logic behind decentralized applications. Solidity, the most widely used programming language for Ethereum-based smart contracts, enables developers to encode contractual agreements directly into blockchain-executable code [1, 2]. Before diving into writing secure and functional contracts, it is crucial to understand the foundational elements of Solidity, its syntax, structure, data types, and the principles that govern its execution. This section introduces the essential components of Solidity, starting with a breakdown of its syntax and language rules, followed by a closer examination of how smart contracts are structured using state variables, functions, events, and special-purpose constructors and modifiers. Through this foundation, readers will build the knowledge required to confidently write and reason about smart contracts that interact securely and efficiently on the blockchain [1, 3].

5.1.1 Understanding Solidity: Basics and Syntax

Solidity is the primary language for writing smart contracts on the Ethereum blockchain and other EVM-compatible platforms [2, 4]. It is statically typed, meaning that variable types are declared at compile time, and contract logic is compiled into bytecode for deployment [1, 2]. Solidity has been designed with security and determinism in mind, as the blockchain environment requires code execution to be transparent, predictable, and tamper-resistant [1, 3].

A Solidity program begins with a pragma directive, which specifies the intended compiler version. This is essential to ensure compatibility and prevent unexpected behavior due to language changes:

```
pragma solidity ^0.8.0;
```

In this example, the ^ symbol ensures that the compiler version used is 0.8.0 or later, but not 0.9.0 or later. This helps avoid breaking changes in future versions.

A smart contract in Solidity is similar to a class in object-oriented programming. It encapsulates variables and functions, defining a set of rules for on-chain interactions:

```
contract MyFirstContract {
    uint public number;
    function setNumber(uint _number) public {
        number = _number;
    }
    function getNumber() public view returns (uint) {
        return number;
    }
}
```

In the above example, “number” is a state variable, and the two functions are publicly accessible. The “view” keyword indicates that the “getNumber” function does not modify the blockchain state.

5.1.1.1 Data Types, Function Behavior, and Core Constructs in Solidity

Solidity, the primary language for writing smart contracts on the Ethereum blockchain, offers a rich, expressive set of features for managing logic, storage, and interactions. Understanding its data types, function properties, and foundational constructions is essential for designing robust, efficient contracts.

Understanding Data Representation in Solidity

Solidity provides a variety of data types tailored for different use cases, each carefully optimized for Ethereum’s storage model [2]. At the simplest level, developers can define Boolean values using the “bool” type to represent logical conditions, such as whether a user is active:

```
bool public isActive = true;
```

For numeric operations, Solidity supports both signed (int) and unsigned (uint) integers, with bit widths ranging from 8 to 256 in 8-bit increments. The commonly used “uint256” aligns with the Ethereum Virtual Machine (EVM) word size, making it efficient for most operations:

```
uint256 public balance;
int8 public temperature;
```

The “address” type is used to store and interact with Ethereum addresses. This becomes critical when sending Ether or calling other contracts:

```
address public userAddress;
```

Textual data can be stored using “string” for dynamic UTF-8 encoded text, or “bytes” for raw byte storage. While “bytes32” represents a fixed-size 32-byte array, “bytes” is dynamic and more flexible:

```
string public name = "Sepideh";
bytes32 public hashValue;
```

Solidity also supports “arrays”, which may be fixed or dynamically sized, and **structs**, which allow grouping multiple related values into custom data structures:

```
string[] public messages;
struct User {
   string name;
   uint age;
}
```

For mapping relationships, “mappings” serve as hash tables connecting key-value pairs. These are essential for storing data like balances or ownership records:

```
mapping(address => uint256) public balances;
```

These types are foundational and are chosen with gas efficiency and purpose in mind [4]. For example, developers often prefer “uint256” over smaller types for simplicity and EVM compatibility, even when only a subset of 256 bits is needed.

5.1.1.2 Function Visibility and Behavioral Modifiers

Functions in Solidity are not just blocks of logic; they control the ways in which a contract can be interacted with [1]. One crucial aspect of this control lies in visibility modifiers, which determine where a function can be accessed:

- public: Accessible both within the contract and externally via transactions or calls.
- external: Intended for external use only; cannot be called internally without using this.
- internal: Available only within the contract and contracts that inherit from it.
- private: Accessible only within the current contract.

Each visibility level serves a specific role in encapsulation and security. For instance, helper functions that shouldn't be exposed to users are typically marked "internal" or "private".

Beyond visibility, Solidity allows defining **behavioral modifiers** that communicate how a function interacts with the blockchain's state [1, 2]:

- view: Ensures the function reads the state but does not modify it.
- pure: Indicates the function neither reads nor writes state; useful for pure computations.
- payable: Enables the function to accept Ether, making it critical for financial operations.

Here's an example combining visibility and behavior:

```
function calculate(uint x, uint y) public pure returns
(uint) {
   return x + y;
}
```

5.1.1.3 Constructor and Initialization

Every smart contract needs a well-defined state from the moment it is deployed. Solidity achieves this using a special "constructor" function that runs only once, during deployment. It is commonly used to set ownership or initialize key variables:

```
contract SimpleWallet {
   address public owner;

   constructor() {
       owner = msg.sender;
   }
}
```

This pattern ensures that the contract deployer becomes the initial owner, and that access to sensitive operations can be restricted accordingly.

5.1.1.4 Handling Ether Transfers: Payable, Receive, and Fallback

For contracts that involve value transfer, functions must be explicitly marked "payable" to receive Ether [2]:

```
function deposit() public payable {
    // Funds are added to the contract's balance
}
```

Solidity also defines special functions for receiving Ether directly:

- receive(): Automatically called when Ether is sent with no data.
- fallback(): Invoked when data is sent that doesn't match any function signature, or if receive() is missing.

These functions enhance the contract's robustness in handling unexpected interactions.

5.1.1.5 Events and Off-Chain Logging

To support transparency and traceability, Solidity allows contracts to emit "events", which are stored in transaction logs. Frontend applications and analytics tools can track these events in user interfaces, for monitoring, or for audits.

```
event NumberChanged(uint oldNumber, uint newNumber);
function update(uint _new) public {
    emit NumberChanged(number, _new);
    number = _new;
}
```

Logs created via "emit" are not accessible within the contract, but they are vital for external observers using platforms like Etherscan or DApps.

5.1.1.6 Inheritance and Reusability

One of Solidity's powerful features is "inheritance", which enables a contract to derive from one or more base contracts. This allows the reuse of established logic, such as access control, across multiple contracts. For example:

```
contract Ownable {
   address public owner;
   constructor() {
       owner = msg.sender;
   }
   modifier onlyOwner() {
       require(msg.sender == owner, "Not the owner");
       _;
   }
}
contract SecureContract is Ownable {
   function sensitiveAction() public onlyOwner {
       // Action only allowed for the owner
   }
}
```

By inheriting from "Ownable", the "SecureContract" immediately benefits from ownership verification logic, avoiding repetitive code. This modularity is key to building secure and scalable smart contract systems.

These building blocks, data types, function behavior, constructor logic, Ether transfer mechanisms, events, and inheritance, collectively form the foundation of every Solidity smart contract. A firm grasp of these concepts allows developers to move confidently from basic contract design to more advanced decentralized application development.

5.1.2 Key Components of a Smart Contract in Solidity

A Solidity smart contract comprises several fundamental components that work together to enable interaction, enforce logic, and manage state on the blockchain. These include state variables, functions, modifiers, events, constructors, special functions for Ether handling, and user-defined types such as structs and mappings. Understanding each component and its contribution to a smart contract's operation is crucial for effective development.

State Variables: State variables are declared at the contract level and store values permanently on the blockchain. For example:

```
uint public balance;
address public owner;
```

These values persist between function calls and represent the contract's state. Since storage operations are costly in terms of gas, it's essential to optimize the use and updates of state variables [4].

Functions: Functions define the behavior of the contract. They can be called internally or externally, depending on their visibility. They are the main mechanism through which the contract state is read or modified. For example:

```
function deposit() public payable {
   balance += msg.value;
}
```

Functions can also return values and accept parameters, just like functions in other programming languages.

Modifiers: Modifiers are a special kind of function that changes the behavior of other functions. They are most commonly used to implement access control:

```
modifier onlyOwner() {
   require(msg.sender == owner, "Not authorized");
   _;
}
function withdraw() public onlyOwner {
   payable(owner).transfer(balance);
}
```

The underscore _ represents where the modified function's code will be inserted.

Events: Events allow the contract to log data on the blockchain, which external users can access via transaction logs [1, 5]. Events are critical for building responsive dApps:

```
event DepositReceived(address indexed sender, uint amount);
function deposit() public payable {
   emit DepositReceived(msg.sender, msg.value);
}
```

Constructors: A constructor is executed only once when the contract is deployed and is typically used to initialize contract state:

```
constructor(uint _initialBalance) {
   balance = _initialBalance;
   owner = msg.sender;
}
```

Fallback and Receive Functions: Solidity provides special functions to manage Ether sent to the contract without calling a specific function:

```
receive() external payable {
   // Handles plain Ether transfers
}
fallback() external payable {
   // Handles calls to undefined functions
}
```

These are crucial for building contracts that can accept Ether payments directly.

Structs and Mappings: Structs and mappings help organize and access data efficiently:

```
struct Voter {
   bool voted;
   uint vote;
}
mapping(address => Voter) public voters;
```

Structs group related data, while mappings provide a hash table mechanism for fast lookups.

Understanding how each component operates and interacts is key to writing robust and maintainable smart contracts. In the next sections, we will explore how to apply these components in practice by translating real-world agreements into smart contract form.

5.2 Converting Traditional Contracts into Smart Contracts

The shift from traditional legal contracts to smart contracts represents more than a simple change in medium; it is a transformation in how agreements are defined, enforced, and experienced. In conventional systems, contracts are enforced through trust in human behavior, third-party intermediaries, and legal systems. Smart contracts, by contrast, are self-executing programs where contractual clauses are represented as logical conditions written in code. This paradigm enables automatic enforcement of agreements, removes reliance on intermediaries, and enhances transparency and security.

The process of converting a traditional contract into a smart contract begins with a thorough analysis of the legal document itself. Every element, party, condition, obligation, deadline, and consequence must be identified and translated into a format that can be expressed programmatically. This process is not always linear or direct, especially when legal language is ambiguous or external factors influence contract terms. The goal of the smart contract is not to replace the law but to capture enforceable logic that executes deterministically on-chain. In the sections that follow, we explore the methodology behind this translation process, provide an in-depth case study, and examine the challenges involved in such conversions.

5.2.1 Steps for Translating Legal Terms into Code

Translating legal language into Solidity code requires a structured approach that bridges the gap between legal semantics and technical constructs. The first step is to identify the parties involved and represent them using Ethereum addresses. These addresses serve as digital identities that interact with the contract. Roles such as "client," "service provider," or "escrow agent" are defined by state variables, and access to specific functions is controlled by modifiers that enforce permissions.

Next, the contract's obligations and conditions must be clearly understood and broken down into programmable logic. This includes deadlines, payments, penalties, triggers for state changes, and the flow of funds. Conditions such as "payment upon completion" or "refund if late" become required statements that enforce those terms within Solidity functions. Deadlines are typically handled using a block. Timestamp, allowing time-sensitive clauses to be integrated naturally into the blockchain environment.

The contract should then be modeled as a state machine, where each phase, such as initiation, in progress, completion, or cancellation, corresponds to a specific state in the contract's life cycle [3]. Transitions between these states are triggered by function calls, and state variables keep track of the contract's progress. Each function must include appropriate validations to ensure that only valid transitions occur.

Payment mechanisms are central to most contracts, and Solidity supports them through payable functions and safe value transfers via transfer() or call(). All funds involved in the contract should be handled securely and only moved when clearly defined conditions are met. For transparency and traceability, Solidity events should be emitted to record key actions, such as task completion, payment transfers, or cancellations, so that front-end applications or monitoring systems can respond accordingly.

Finally, rigorous testing is critical [6, 7]. Before deployment, the contract should be thoroughly tested across different scenarios using development frameworks such as Remix, Truffle, or Hardhat. These tools help simulate contract behavior, identify logical errors, and measure gas usage to ensure the contract is efficient and secure.

5.2.2 *Case Study: Successful Conversion of a Freelance Agreement*

Let us now examine a practical example that demonstrates how a simple, real-world contract can be translated into a functioning smart contract. This case study builds on the freelance agreement introduced earlier: the client (John) hires a web designer (Sarah) to deliver a responsive website by a fixed deadline. John agrees to pay 3 Ether, 1 Ether as an upfront deposit, and the remaining 2 Ether upon delivery. If the work is not delivered within a grace period of 7 days beyond the deadline, John has the right to cancel the contract and claim a full refund. The contract uses an escrow mechanism to securely manage funds.

To turn this agreement into a smart contract, we construct it step-by-step using Solidity. At each step, we focus on one portion of the code and its purpose within the broader contractual logic. This incremental approach not only clarifies the technical translation of legal clauses but also strengthens the reader's understanding of Solidity fundamentals in context.

5.2.2.1 Declaring State Variables

The first step is to define the main actors and contractual parameters. We introduce two address variables to store the client's and the freelancer's Ethereum addresses. We also declare unsigned integers for the two payment amounts and the project deadline. Additionally, boolean flags are used to track whether the project is completed or the contract has been canceled.

```
address public client;
address public freelancer;
uint public upfrontAmount = 1 ether;
uint public remainingAmount = 2 ether;
uint public deadline;
bool public isCompleted;
bool public isCancelled;
```

These variables represent the contract's persistent state. The public visibility keyword allows anyone to view the values stored in these variables through automatically generated getter functions. This transparency aligns well with the nature of blockchain contracts.

5.2.2.2 Using Modifiers for Access Control

To ensure that only the authorized parties can interact with sensitive functions, we define two **modifiers**. These modifiers encapsulate permission logic and are attached to functions that require identity checks.

```
modifier onlyClient() {
   require(msg.sender == client, "Only client allowed");
   _;
}
modifier onlyFreelancer() {
   require(msg.sender == freelancer, "Only freelancer
allowed");
   _;
}
```

The required statement verifies the identity of the function caller (msg.sender). If the condition is not met, execution halts, and an error message is returned. The underscore _ represents the placeholder for the function's original logic, which is inserted there during execution.

5.2.2.3 Constructor: Setting Up the Contract

When the contract is first deployed, the constructor is executed once. This is where we set the initial values of client, freelancer, and deadline. We also check that the correct amount of Ether (1 Ether upfront) is sent with the transaction.

```
constructor(address _freelancer) payable {
   require(msg.value == upfrontAmount, "1 ETH upfront
required");
   client = msg.sender;
   freelancer = _freelancer;
   deadline = block.timestamp + 30 days;
}
```

The msg.value keyword holds the amount of Ether sent to the contract upon deployment. By checking it, we ensure the client deposits the correct upfront amount. The block.timestamp gives the current block's timestamp in seconds, allowing us to set a time-based deadline.

5.2.2.4 Marking Work as Completed

Once Sarah (the freelancer) has completed the project, she should mark it as such in the contract. This is done through a function that can only be called by her, which changes the contract's state and emits an event for tracking:

```
event WorkCompleted(address freelancer);
function markCompleted() public onlyFreelancer {
   require(!isCompleted, "Already completed");
   isCompleted = true;
   emit WorkCompleted(msg.sender);
}
```

Events like WorkCompleted are useful for emitting logs that can be captured off-chain by user interfaces or block explorers. They help with auditability and user feedback in decentralized applications.

5.2.2.5 Releasing Final Payment

Once the freelancer has marked the work as completed, the client must release the remaining payment. This function first checks that the work is complete and that the contract contains the appropriate funds. It then transfers 2 Ether to the freelancer and emits a payment confirmation event:

```
event PaymentReleased(address to, uint amount);
function releasePayment() public onlyClient {
   require(isCompleted, "Work not completed");
   require(address(this).balance >= remainingAmount,
"Insufficient balance");
   payable(freelancer).transfer(remainingAmount);
   emit PaymentReleased(freelancer, remainingAmount);
}
```

The use of address(this) retrieves the Ether balance held by the contract, and transfer() safely sends the funds to the specified address.

5.2.2.6 Cancelling the Contract

If the deadline passes and the work is not marked as completed, the client can cancel the agreement and retrieve all funds. This function can only be called by the client, and only after the deadline plus a grace period:

```
event ContractCancelled(address by);
function cancelContract() public onlyClient {
   require(block.timestamp > deadline + 7 days, "Cannot
cancel yet");
   require(!isCompleted, "Already completed");
   isCancelled = true;
   payable(client).transfer(address(this).balance);
   emit ContractCancelled(msg.sender);
}
```

This mechanism ensures that the freelancer has a fair opportunity to complete the work on time and protects the client in the event of non-delivery.

5.2.2.7 Fallback Ether Reception

To ensure the contract receives additional funds, we include a special function called receive(). This is invoked when Ether is sent directly to the contract without specifying a function call:

```
receive() external payable {}
```

Including this function ensures that the contract remains compatible with wallet-based Ether transfers, adding flexibility to fund management.

5.2.2.8 Final Smart Contract

After assembling all of these elements, the complete smart contract looks as follows:

```
pragma solidity ^0.8.0;
contract FreelanceEscrow {
    address public client;
    address public freelancer;
    uint public upfrontAmount = 1 ether;
    uint public remainingAmount = 2 ether;
    uint public deadline;
    bool public isCompleted;
    bool public isCancelled;
    event WorkCompleted(address freelancer);
    event PaymentReleased(address to, uint amount);
    event ContractCancelled(address by);

    modifier onlyClient() {
        require(msg.sender == client, "Only client allowed");
        _;
    }
    modifier onlyFreelancer() {
        require(msg.sender == freelancer, "Only freelancer
allowed");
        _;
    }
    constructor(address _freelancer) payable {
        require(msg.value == upfrontAmount, "1 ETH upfront
required");
        client = msg.sender;
        freelancer = _freelancer;
        deadline = block.timestamp + 30 days;
    }
    function markCompleted() public onlyFreelancer {
        require(!isCompleted, "Already completed");
        isCompleted = true;
        emit WorkCompleted(msg.sender);
    }
```

This case study highlights not only how a specific traditional agreement can be modeled as a smart contract, but also how each Solidity concept, from variables and functions to events, access control, and Ether management, contributes to the delivery of a secure, autonomous, and enforceable digital agreement.

```
    function releasePayment() public onlyClient {
        require(isCompleted, "Work not completed");
        require(address(this).balance >= remainingAmount,
"Insufficient balance");
        payable(freelancer).transfer(remainingAmount);
        emit PaymentReleased(freelancer, remainingAmount);
    }
    function cancelContract() public onlyClient {
        require(block.timestamp > deadline + 7 days, "Cannot
cancel yet");
        require(!isCompleted, "Already completed");
        isCancelled = true;
        payable(client).transfer(address(this).balance);
        emit ContractCancelled(msg.sender);
    }

    receive() external payable {}
}
```

5.2.3 Challenges in Contract Conversion

Despite the elegance and automation that smart contracts offer, converting traditional contracts into Solidity is not without its challenges. One of the most significant issues lies in the ambiguity of natural language. Legal agreements often use flexible or context-dependent language, such as "reasonable effort" or "prompt delivery," which are difficult to interpret and encode in deterministic logic. Unlike humans, smart contracts cannot interpret intent; they require strict and precise conditions. As a result, developers must often work closely with legal professionals to clarify contract terms before implementing them in code.

Another difficulty arises from the need for external data, which is common in traditional agreements but inaccessible on-chain. For instance, conditions based on currency exchange rates, weather data, or real-world delivery confirmations require the use of oracles, external services that feed off-chain data into the blockchain. Integrating oracles adds complexity and introduces potential points of failure or manipulation.

Cost is also a practical concern. Every operation on the blockchain consumes gas, and complex contracts can become prohibitively expensive to deploy or interact with [4]. Developers must carefully optimize storage and logic to minimize unnecessary computation and avoid redundant operations. Additionally, smart contracts are immutable by design, which means that once deployed, the contract code cannot be changed. This lack of flexibility can be problematic if bugs are discovered after deployment or if the contract needs to evolve. While upgradable patterns using proxy contracts can mitigate this, they introduce additional complexity.

Finally, security remains a constant concern. Poorly written smart contracts are vulnerable to a range of attacks, including reentrancy, integer overflows, denial-of-service, and front-running. As the infamous DAO attack of 2016 demonstrated, a single overlooked vulnerability can have catastrophic consequences. Thus, rigorous testing, formal verification, and professional audits are not optional; they are essential components of any responsible contract development process.

5.3 Chapter Summary

This section offers a comprehensive foundation in smart contract development by introducing the Solidity programming language and its essential constructs. It begins with a detailed overview of Solidity's syntax, type system, and execution model, highlighting its alignment with object-oriented principles and its suitability for decentralized environments. The discussion then transitions to the key architectural components of a smart contract, including state variables, functions, modifiers, constructors, and event logging mechanisms, demonstrating how each element contributes to the contract's secure, deterministic behavior on the Ethereum blockchain. Emphasis is placed on Solidity's support for inheritance, modularity, and structured data handling through constructs like structs and mappings, empowering developers to write reusable, readable, and efficient code. Despite these capabilities, Solidity development also presents challenges, including complex gas optimization, limitations in error handling, and risks associated with contract immutability and attack vectors such as reentrancy. By thoroughly examining both the language's technical strengths and inherent constraints, this section equips readers with a nuanced understanding of how to responsibly design and implement smart contracts, setting the stage for real-world applications in the chapters that follow [3, 8].

References

1. Vacca, A., et al.: A systematic literature review of blockchain and smart contract development: techniques, tools, and open challenges. J. Syst. Softw. **174**, 110891 (2021)
2. Lj, Đ.I.: The utilization of Solidity programming language in blockchain. Vojnoteh. Glas. **72**(1), 363–387 (2024)
3. Tolmach, P., et al.: A survey of smart contract formal specification and verification. ACM Comput. Surv. **54**(7), 1–38 (2021)

4. Hegedűs, P.: Towards analyzing the complexity landscape of Solidity based Ethereum smart contracts. In: Proceedings of the 1st International Workshop on Emerging Trends in Software Engineering for Blockchain (2018)
5. Guirguis, M, Papasavvas, M.: Ethereum smart contracts programming and financial modeling using Solidity. Available at SSRN 4726143 (2024)
6. Guo, H., et al.: Smart contract code repair recommendation based on reinforcement learning and multi-metric optimization. ACM Trans. Softw. Eng. Methodol. **33**(4), 1–31 (2024)
7. Eshghie, M., et al.: SoliDiffy: AST Differencing for Solidity smart contracts. arXiv preprint https://arxiv.org/abs/2411.07718 (2024)
8. Singh, A., et al.: Blockchain smart contracts formalization: approaches and challenges to address vulnerabilities. Comput. Secur. **88**, 101654 (2020)

Chapter 6
Smart Contract Vulnerabilities

Abstract This chapter examines the landscape of smart contract vulnerabilities, emphasizing how even small coding flaws can trigger catastrophic losses due to the immutability and transparency of blockchain systems. It explores high-profile incidents such as The DAO hack and the Poly Network exploit to demonstrate the real-world consequences of insecure code. The discussion classifies vulnerabilities into three categories: language-level issues in Solidity (including reentrancy, integer overflow and underflow, unchecked external calls, unprotected selfdestruct, locked Ether, misuse of tx.origin, floating pragmas, variable shadowing, and default visibility), EVM-level vulnerabilities (such as short address attacks and storage overlap in delegatecall patterns), and blockchain protocol-level flaws (including timestamp dependence, transaction-order dependence or front-running, replay risks from missing chain identifiers, and deceptive honeypot contracts). Throughout, annotated code snippets and detailed explanations show how these weaknesses manifest in practice, equipping readers with both conceptual and technical insight. Finally, this chapter underscores that securing smart contracts requires vigilance at every layer, language, virtual machine, and protocol to prevent exploits and build resilient decentralized systems.

Ethereum smart contracts are self-executing programs that run on the blockchain and manage digital assets without intermediaries. However, a small bug in a smart contract can lead to catastrophic consequences. Smart contracts are immutable once deployed, meaning vulnerabilities cannot be patched easily. Over the past years, attackers have exploited these bugs to steal or lock up millions of dollars' worth of cryptocurrency. The most famous example is *The DAO* hack in 2016, where a flaw allowed an attacker to siphon ~3.6 million Ether (about $50–60 million at the time), forcing an unprecedented Ethereum hard fork to recover the funds. Since then, the scale of exploits has only grown—e.g. the Poly Network hack in 2021 allowed a hacker to withdraw over $600 million by abusing a smart contract vulnerability. These incidents highlight why understanding smart contract vulnerabilities is crucial for developers, auditors, and the community.

In this chapter, we provide an in-depth look at Ethereum smart contract vulnerabilities, focusing on those in Solidity, the dominant language for Ethereum. We will analyze how and why these vulnerabilities occur, categorize the different types,

S. HajiHosseinKhani et al., *Understanding Cybersecurity for Smart Contracts*,
https://doi.org/10.1007/978-3-032-28863-9_6

compare their prevalence and severity, and discuss real-world exploits (such as the DAO and Poly Network hacks) to ground each concept. We will also examine actual vulnerable code snippets with annotations to illustrate how the weaknesses manifest in code. The goal is to equip beginners, developers, and auditors with a comprehensive understanding of common and dangerous Solidity vulnerabilities as of 2025, enabling them to recognize and avoid these pitfalls.

6.1 In-depth Analysis of Vulnerabilities

Smart contract vulnerabilities often arise from the unique aspects of blockchain programming combined with developer mistakes. Unlike traditional software, smart contracts operate in a decentralized, immutable environment; once deployed, contract code cannot be changed or patched. This high-stakes context means a single error can lead to irreversible loss of funds. Additionally, all contract code and transactions are public, allowing attackers to study contracts to identify weaknesses and exploit them in real time. In decentralized finance (DeFi), where contracts may manage tens of millions of dollars, the incentive for attackers is enormous, and attacks often occur within seconds of a vulnerability being discovered. Ethereum smart contract vulnerabilities can be classified into several distinct categories. Below, we outline the most common types, with a particular focus on Solidity-written contracts. Figure 6.1 illustrates the taxonomy of these vulnerabilities. For each type of vulnerability, we describe the issue and explain why it occurs, often providing a real example for context.

6.1.1 Solidity: Language-Level Vulnerabilities

The Language-Level category encompasses vulnerabilities arising from the inherent characteristics, design limitations, or common misuse of the Solidity programming language. These issues typically stem from how developers interact with language features such as variable declarations, function visibility, versioning, or external calls. Vulnerabilities such as reentrancy, integer overflows/underflows, and unchecked external calls often stem from insufficient safeguards in Solidity's default behavior or from neglecting secure programming patterns. Others, such as uninitialized state variables, variable shadowing, or floating pragma versions, emerge from subtle syntactic or semantic missteps that can have serious security implications. This category also includes misuse of constructs such as tx.origin for access control, a lack of restricted write permissions, or reliance on gas-dependent loops, all of which may lead to exploitability due to poor handling at the language level. As such, these vulnerabilities are grouped together because they are directly tied to how Solidity code is written, interpreted, and executed on the Ethereum Virtual Machine (EVM).

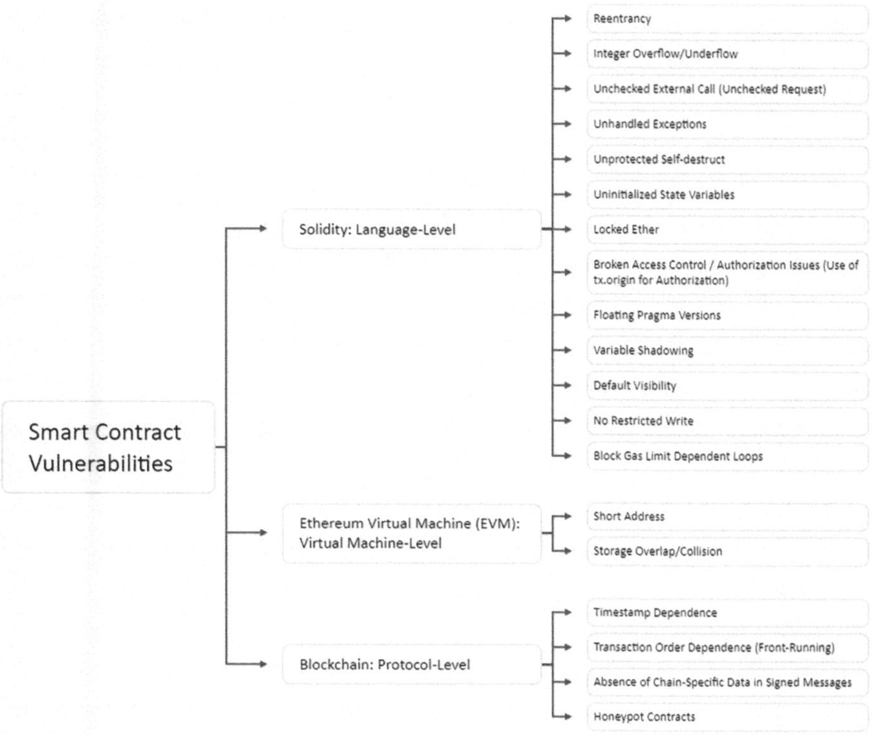

Fig. 6.1 Smart contract vulnerabilities taxonomy

1. **Reentrancy:** This is a vulnerability where a contract calls an external contract, and that external call invokes back into the calling contract (re-entering it) before the first call finishes. If the calling contract isn't carefully designed, the attacker's malicious contract can repeatedly invoke the victim contract's function, wreaking havoc on the victim contract's state. The classic example is failing to update balances *before* sending funds. An attacker can withdraw funds multiple times by recursively re-entering the withdrawal function, draining the contract's funds. *The DAO hack* was caused by a reentrancy bug—the contract allowed repeated "splitDAO" withdrawals before updating the balance, leading to ~$60 M loss. Reentrancy is often mitigated by the check-effects-interactions pattern (update state first, then call out) or using reentrancy guards.

    - Consider the following simplified Solidity contract that manages user deposits and withdrawals. A user can deposit Ether into the contract and later withdraw it.

```
// SPDX-License-Identifier: MIT
pragma solidity ^0.8.0;

contract Vulnerable {
    mapping(address => uint256) public balances;

    function deposit() public payable {
        balances[msg.sender] += msg.value;
    }

    function withdraw(uint256 amount) public {
        require(balances[msg.sender] >= amount,
"Insufficient balance");

        (bool sent, ) = msg.sender.call{value:
amount}("");
        require(sent, "Failed to send Ether");

        balances[msg.sender] -= amount;
    }
}
```

In this contract, the withdraw function is meant to check whether the user has sufficient balance, send them Ether, and finally deduct that amount from their balance. However, the vulnerability lies in the ordering of operations. The contract performs an external call to msg.sender using call{value: amount}("") *before* it updates its internal balances mapping.
To understand why this matters, consider what actually happens when that line is executed. The Ethereum Virtual Machine (EVM) pauses the current contract's execution and transfers control to the external address, in this case, the msg. sender. If msg.sender is a regular wallet, the transfer simply succeeds or fails. But if msg.sender is a contract, it can run arbitrary code via it receive() or fallback() function. At this point in execution, the vulnerable contract has not yet reduced the sender's balance. That means the contract still reflects a full balance, even though it's in the middle of a funds transfer.

To visualize the sequence:

1. The user initiates a withdraw(1 ether) call.
2. The contract checks balances[msg.sender] > = amount, which is true.
3. The contract executes msg.sender.call{value: amount}("").
4. The EVM hands control to msg.sender's contract code (if it exists).
5. The vulnerable contract is paused, its state still shows the full balance.
6. Only after this external call returns do the vulnerable contract execute balances[msg.sender] – = amount.

This timeline reveals the core issue: between steps 3 and 6, the contract is exposed. During this time, its state says the user still has the full balance, even though funds are in the process of being withdrawn. This window is the reentrancy vulnerability. The contract assumes that no changes will be made from the outside during mid-execution, which is incorrect.
The problem is not that an attacker has acted maliciously, but that the contract allows itself to be interrupted and externally influenced before finalizing its internal logic. It breaks the principle of maintaining an internally consistent state throughout execution. This vulnerability lies entirely within the logic of the withdrawal function itself, specifically in how it calls out to another address before completing its own updates.

2. **Integer Overflow/Underflow:** If arithmetic operations in Solidity exceed the range of the data type, they would *wrap around* silently in older versions of Solidity. For example, with an unsigned 256-bit integer, adding 1 to 2^256–1 (the maximum value) wraps around to 0. Unless the code checks for overflow, an attacker can exploit this to produce unintended values. One notorious case was the *"batchOverflow"* exploit in 2018, in which a token contract's batch transfer function failed to guard against overflow. Attackers passed extremely large values, causing an overflow that bypassed balance checks and allowed them to "create" astronomical token amounts. *Modern Solidity (> = 0.8)* now automatically reverts to overflow/underflow, largely eliminating this risk. However, older contracts (or any arithmetic done inside an unchecked{ } block) remain vulnerable if not using a library like SafeMath.

   - Consider a simple token contract written in a version of Solidity prior to 0.8.0, where arithmetic operations do not automatically include overflow or underflow checks.

```
  // SPDX-License-Identifier: MIT
  pragma solidity ^0.6.0;

  contract SimpleToken {
     mapping(address => uint256) public balances;

     function transfer(address recipient, uint256 amount)
public {
         require(balances[msg.sender] >= amount, "Not enough
balance");

         balances[msg.sender] -= amount;
         balances[recipient] += amount;
     }
  }
```

In this contract, the transfer function seems straightforward. It checks whether the sender has enough tokens, then subtracts amount from the sender's balance and adds it to the recipient's balance. However, the vulnerability lies in the fact that arithmetic operations are unchecked. Specifically, the subtraction balances[msg.sender] − = amount and the addition balances[recipient] + = amount are performed without verifying whether they cause the values to wrap around.

Let's step through the flow when this function is called in a vulnerable environment.

A user with a balance of 100 tokens calls transfer() to send 150 tokens. The contract evaluates require(balances[msg.sender] > = amount), which fails correctly and prevents the transfer. However, imagine the logic was slightly more complex, or this check was missing in some path. If balances[msg.sender] is 100 and amount is 150, then the subtraction operation 100–150 would not throw an error. Instead, in pre-0.8.0 Solidity, it would wrap because unsigned integers have a fixed size. The result would be a very large number close to 2^256.

This behavior is invisible at runtime. The contract doesn't signal an error, and the resulting state becomes completely incorrect. Instead of failing, the sender's balance would be set to an enormous value due to underflow. Similarly, if a user has the maximum possible uint256 balance and transfers more tokens to themselves, the addition might overflow, resetting their balance to a small or zero value if not handled correctly.

The vulnerability occurs at the precise moment these arithmetic operations are executed, when the contract assumes that addition and subtraction will behave safely. Since earlier versions of Solidity lacked built-in guardrails, any such operation must be explicitly protected using helper libraries like SafeMath. Without these protections, contracts are vulnerable not because of what is visibly wrong, but because what seems fine can silently fail at the arithmetic level.

Visualization of this vulnerability is implicit in understanding the numerical limits of the uint256 type. When a value exceeds the maximum (for overflow) or goes below zero (for underflow), it wraps around to the opposite end of the allowed range, breaking assumptions about logic and control flow. This breakdown doesn't trigger a visible fault in the EVM, it just causes the state to change in a mathematically invalid way.

3. **Unchecked External Call (Unchecked Request):** Contracts often call external functions (e.g., sending Ether or invoking another contract). In Solidity, low-level calls like address.call() or send() return a boolean success value rather than throwing on failure. A common mistake is failing to check this return value. An *unchecked call* can silently fail, and the code will continue as if it succeeded. This can lead to an inconsistent state or missed behavior (for instance, a payment failing, but the contract still marks an invoice as paid). In some cases, it can be exploited to cause a denial-of-service attack (an attacker can deliberately make a call fail by breaking some logic) [1, 2]. Another aspect is calling *untrusted addresses without validation*—for example, a contract might let a user specify another contract address to call (perhaps intended for

plugin logic), but if not restricted, an attacker could point it to a malicious contract. This *unchecked request* could allow the attacker to execute arbitrary code in the caller contract's context. In essence, failing to handle external calls—both their targets and their success/failure—carefully is a major source of vulnerabilities.

- **Unchecked External Call (Unchecked Request):** Consider a simple example where a contract attempts to send Ether to a recipient using a low-level call, as shown in the following Solidity code:

```
// SPDX-License-Identifier: MIT
pragma solidity ^0.8.0;
contract UncheckedCall {
    function sendEther(address payable recipient) public
payable {
        recipient.call{value: msg.value}(""); // no check
for success
    }
}
```

This function sends Ether to the recipient using the call{value: msg.value}("") syntax. It's a low-level call, meaning it returns a boolean value indicating success or failure. However, the function neither stores nor inspects the returned value. It simply initiates the call and moves on.

The vulnerability lies in what happens next, or rather, what *doesn't* happen. The contract assumes the transfer succeeded, even though the recipient contract might have rejected the Ether (by reverting in its fallback), run out of gas, or encountered internal logic that prevented acceptance. None of this is visible to the sender unless the result is explicitly checked. From the perspective of the contract's state, nothing has gone wrong, even though the Ether was never received.

This vulnerability becomes significant when the call's result is expected to trigger a state change, send funds, or fulfill a critical step in a larger logic sequence. Because the call is not checked, the contract continues execution based on a false assumption that the external action succeeded. This silent failure can undermine the rest of the contract's logic.

The vulnerability exists immediately after the call is executed. If the return value is not captured and tested, the contract cannot distinguish between success and failure. In visual terms, the execution path forks silently: one path leads to success, the other to failure, but the contract blindly proceeds without noticing the fork. That ignorance creates uncertainty in the contract's state and logic.

To better understand when and where this vulnerability is present, imagine the execution timeline as follows. The contract begins execution and reaches the external call point. It sends a message and funds to the external address. The

EVM waits for a response: either success (true) or failure (false). If the contract captures that return value, it can react accordingly. If it doesn't, as in this case, the outcome of that external execution is thrown away, leaving the contract oblivious to what happened outside its walls. This silent omission is vulnerable.

4. **Unhandled Exceptions:** This is related to the above. Prior to Solidity 0.6, send() and call() did not throw on failure, allowing errors to be easily ignored. Even with newer Solidity, using low-level calls can bypass Solidity's automatic reversion on failure. If a developer doesn't handle the possibility of an exception being thrown or a return value of false, the contract might assume an action (like a money transfer) succeeded when it actually didn't. An example is a withdrawal function that uses send() to pay a recipient. If the recipient's fallback function runs out of gas and causes the send to fail, the withdrawal function might not notice the failure and still deduct the balance, resulting in a loss of Ether. The proper pattern is to use functions like transfer() (which throws on failure) or check the returned bool of call(), and revert or handle the error accordingly.

   - This vulnerability exists not because the call is inherently dangerous, but because the contract fails to check the result of the call, and proceeds as if it succeeded. This can lead to incorrect assumptions, unrecorded failures, and broken logic, all stemming from a single missing check. Consider the following Solidity code, which defines a basic contract that interacts with another contract by calling one of its functions:

```
// SPDX-License-Identifier: MIT
pragma solidity ^0.8.0;
interface IReceiver {
  function notify() external;
}
contract Unhandled {
  function trigger(address receiver) public {
    IReceiver(receiver).notify(); // exception not handled
  }
}
```

In this contract, the trigger function calls the notify function of another contract. The assumption here is that the call to notify() will succeed. However, if notify() reverts for any reason, perhaps due to internal logic failure or invalid conditions, the exception is not caught or handled in the trigger function. Solidity's default behavior is to propagate reverts, meaning the whole transaction fails. But this propagation is not always sufficient, especially when the call is wrapped in control logic or embedded in loops or fallback behaviors where partial failure is acceptable or expected.

Now imagine that instead of allowing the call to fail the entire transaction, the contract had multiple operations around this call. If the exception isn't handled, it could silently cause part of the execution to fail while allowing the rest to pro-

ceed based on incorrect assumptions. Vulnerability arises because the contract has no logic to respond to or recover from the failed call, it assumes success and takes no action otherwise.
Another common scenario is when exceptions arise from low-level calls like call(), delegatecall(), or send(), which do not automatically revert the entire transaction on failure. Unlike high-level function calls, which revert by default, these low-level operations return a boolean value indicating success or failure. If the return value is not checked, any failure is silently swallowed. This is where unhandled exceptions are most dangerous: when the contract believes everything succeeded, but in reality, part of its logic was skipped or failed silently.
The moment the vulnerability exists is when the contract performs an action that could throw or fail but lacks logic to verify success, to intentionally revert, or to gracefully degrade behavior. Visually, if we imagine the function as a sequence of steps, the vulnerability appears as a gap where a critical condition might have failed, but the contract continues as though nothing went wrong. It's a missing decision point, where a check should exist but doesn't.
To illustrate this clearly, consider an example using a low-level call:

```
(bool success, ) = address(otherContract).call(abi.encodeWithSignature("
doSomething()"));
// no check for success , unhandled exception if
'doSomething()' fails
```

Here, the success variable holds the result of the call, but it is never evaluated. If doSomething() fails, success will be false, but the contract proceeds as if it succeeded. This failure is unhandled, and any logic that depends on doSomething() being executed correctly is now operating on false assumptions.

5. **Unprotected Self-destruct:** In Solidity, a contract can be destroyed with selfdestruct(address), sending its remaining Ether to a specified address. This is intended for contract upgrades or recovering funds from a broken contract. However, if the self-destruct function (often named something like destroy() or historically suicide()) is not properly restricted, *anyone* could call it. An attacker could then kill the contract and steal the Ether by specifying their own payout address. Even if the Ether goes to a fixed address (e.g., the contract creator), an attacker calling self-destruct will still permanently disable the contract's functionality, which can be devastating. A real incident was the *Parity multisig wallet bug (2017)*—a library contract had a publicly callable self-destruct (due to an initialization function oversight), which a user invoked, locking up ~$150 million worth of Ether in all wallets that depended on that library (since the library code was wiped out). Always ensure only an authorized owner can trigger self-destruct, if it's used at all.

- To understand the Unprotected Self-destruct vulnerability, it helps to examine the precise execution flow within a contract that includes the selfdestruct function but does not adequately control access to it. This vulnerability does not stem from the presence of selfdestruct itself, since this opcode can be used for legitimate purposes such as contract upgrades or decommissioning, but from the absence of proper authorization mechanisms guarding its use.

Consider the following simplified Solidity contract:

```
// SPDX-License-Identifier: MIT
pragma solidity ^0.8.0;
contract Terminable {
  address public owner;
  constructor() {
    owner = msg.sender;
  }
  function terminate() public {
    selfdestruct(payable(msg.sender)); // no
access control
  }
}
```

In this contract, the function terminate() executes selfdestruct, which deletes the contract from the blockchain and sends its remaining Ether balance to the address provided, in this case, msg.sender. The intention may have been to allow only the contract owner to terminate the contract, but that restriction is missing. There is no check such as require(msg.sender == owner) to ensure that only a trusted party can perform this irreversible action.

The vulnerability emerges the moment the terminate() function is made publicly callable without restriction. As soon as any user calls it, the EVM executes the selfdestruct opcode, which removes the contract's bytecode and state from the blockchain. The function does not throw an error or pause; it executes instantly and permanently. The contract cannot interact with you again, and all of its stored data is lost.

Visually, the contract's execution path begins when a transaction invokes the terminate() function. The function makes no decision or validation before executing selfdestruct, meaning there is no protective logic, no authorization layer, no gate. Execution continues straight into the selfdestruct call, and at that precise moment, the contract ceases to exist. The vulnerability lies in the absence of a conditional branch before this final operation, a simple if or require statement that could have prevented unauthorized access.

From a structural perspective, the vulnerability is not in the opcode itself but in its exposure. When selfdestruct is not protected by access control, it becomes a latent threat, waiting to be triggered by any caller. Even if the contract holds critical logic or manages user funds, it can be instantly wiped from the chain by any account that reaches this function. The lack of barriers is what transforms a powerful tool into a dangerous vulnerability.

6. **Uninitialized State Variables:** In Solidity, state variables that are not explicitly initialized will be set to the default value (e.g., 0 for uint, false for bool, address(0) for address). If a developer mistakenly assumes an uninitialized variable has a different value or uses it before setting it, it can lead to unexpected behavior. For instance, imagine a public address owner; that was never set—it would default to the zero address. If the contract then uses owner for access control (e.g., require(msg.sender == owner)), nobody would be able to call that function (since no one can have the zero address as sender), or worse, if there's an initialization function open to anyone, an attacker could call it to become the owner. Another scenario: uninitialized local storage variables can accidentally point to other storage slots, causing *storage corruption.* While not always directly exploitable by attackers, these bugs can introduce severe inconsistencies. The key is always explicitly initializing critical variables (like owner) and being careful with storage variables (Solidity's compiler often warns about uninitialized storage refs now).

   - To understand the Uninitialized State Variables vulnerability, it's important to examine how Solidity handles storage allocation and what happens when a state variable is declared but not explicitly initialized. This vulnerability does not involve any overtly unsafe behavior on the surface, but rather arises from how the EVM assigns default storage slots and values when initialization is omitted.

Consider the following Solidity contract:

```
// SPDX-License-Identifier: MIT
pragma solidity ^0.8.0;
contract UninitializedExample {
  address public owner;
  address public target;
  function setTarget() public {
    Dummy d;
    d = new Dummy(); // no assignment to state variable
  }
}
contract Dummy {
  address public creator;
  constructor() {
    creator = msg.sender;
  }
}
```

In this contract, the setTarget function declares a local variable d of type Dummy, and deploys a new instance of the Dummy contract. However, this deployment is not assigned to any persistent state variable. Suppose, instead, that Dummy d; was declared as a state variable but never initialized. If a contract defines a state variable of a reference type like address, uint, or even another contract, and fails to initialize it in the constructor or during deployment, Solidity will assign a default value and a default storage slot. This behavior is subtle and dangerous.

The vulnerability occurs when a contract either relies on uninitialized variables in control logic or exposes them to external use without accounting for their default state. For instance, an uninitialized address variable defaults to the zero address (0x0). If the contract later uses that variable in access control, fund transfer, or delegatecall contexts, it will inadvertently allow operations targeting unintended or invalid addresses. More critically, in complex contracts or upgradeable proxy patterns, if a storage variable that should have been explicitly set remains uninitialized, it may silently overlap with another variable due to storage-slot misalignment. In such cases, what appears to be a benign omission results in one part of the contract inadvertently overwriting or reading from the wrong location in storage.

In terms of execution flow, the vulnerability manifests the moment the contract is deployed and a state variable is declared without being assigned. Solidity allocates a storage slot for that variable but does not mark it as unused or incomplete. It treats the slot as valid, and assigns the default value, zero for integers, false for booleans, 0x0 for addresses. The problem is not that the value is invalid, but that the developer may not have expected it to be implicitly set at all. The logic that follows will then operate on assumptions about values that were never explicitly established.

Visualizing this behavior, imagine a contract with a series of storage slots. When a state variable is declared but not initialized, Solidity places it into a slot as if it were ready to use. There is no runtime error or compilation warning unless specifically caught by a linter. From that point forward, any function that reads from this variable pulls a value that has never been meaningfully set. If this variable is later used in conditions, transactions, or interactions, the outcome may diverge completely from what the developer intended because the logic operates on a placeholder rather than an explicit value.

7. **Locked Ether:** This refers to contracts that *inadvertently lock funds*, meaning Ether gets stuck with no way to get it out. This often isn't an "attack" but a vulnerability in the sense of a *bug* that causes loss of funds. It can happen if a contract is payable (can receive Ether) but lacks any withdrawal function or self-destruct—thus any Ether it receives is trapped forever. Another cause is if the only withdrawal function is somehow broken (e.g., requires an impossible condition). One high-profile example was the Parity library incident: when the library self-destructed, all Ether held in the wallets was locked because the code to move it was gone. Locked Ether bugs are usually developer errors rather than something attackers exploit (since an attacker generally can't directly profit from locking someone else's Ether, aside from griefing). Nonetheless, they rep-

resent a dangerous pitfall in smart contract design. Proper testing and the inclusion of withdrawal mechanisms (or the use of established templates) can avoid this.

- To understand the Locked Ether vulnerability, we need to examine how Ether can become permanently inaccessible in a smart contract, not due to any active malicious behavior, but because of incomplete or incorrect contract design. This vulnerability arises when a contract can receive Ether but lacks a mechanism to send it back out, effectively trapping it on-chain forever.

Consider the following Solidity contract:

```
// SPDX-License-Identifier: MIT
pragma solidity ^0.8.0;
contract LockedEther {
  // Contract accepts Ether via receive function
  receive() external payable {}
  // No function to withdraw or transfer Ether
}
```

This contract contains a receive() function, which allows it to accept plain Ether transfers. Any account that sends Ether directly to the contract address will see the transfer succeed, and the Ether will be stored in the contract's balance. However, the key point is that the contract has no function to send Ether. There is no withdraw(), transfer(), or selfdestruct() call available to return the funds. Solidity enforces strict encapsulation, meaning Ether stored in a contract cannot leave unless a function explicitly instructs the EVM to send it elsewhere.
The vulnerability is not in the fact that Ether can be sent in, this is normal, but in the absence of any code path to send it back out. From the moment the first receive() call is triggered, and Ether is transferred into the contract, that value is added to the contract's balance. This is recorded by the Ethereum state. But since there is no withdrawal function or logic to handle outbound Ether movement, the funds remain in place indefinitely. No user, not even the contract creator, can access them.
If we visualize the lifecycle of Ether in this contract, it starts externally when someone sends a transaction with Ether to the contract. The receive() function is triggered, executes successfully, and deposits Ether into the contract. At this point, the contract's balance increases. However, the execution path to recover the Ether simply does not exist. The control flow enters the contract but has no corresponding exit. The internal state can see and account for the funds, but no operation can release them.
This creates a form of logical deadlock. The vulnerability appears the moment Ether is accepted into a contract that has no exit mechanism. It is not an execution-

time failure, nor a runtime exception. It is a design-level oversight, a missing piece of logic that leaves the contract permanently holding value it cannot release.

8. **Broken Access Control/Authorization Issues (Use of tx.origin for Authorization):** Some developers mistakenly use tx.origin to authenticate users, believing it represents the caller of a function. However, tx.origin refers to the original external account that initiated the transaction chain, not necessarily the current caller of the function. This creates a serious security risk when a contract interacts with other contracts. For example, an attacker can deploy a malicious contract and trick a privileged user (e.g., the owner) into calling it. The attacker's contract then calls the vulnerable contract on their behalf, and since tx.origin is still the owner's address, the authorization check passes. This results in unauthorized access, even though the immediate caller was a malicious contract. The best practice is to use msg.sender instead, which accurately reflects the current direct caller of the function. Using tx.origin for sensitive checks such as ownership or access control is strongly discouraged.

    - To understand the Use of tx.origin for Authorization vulnerability, we need to follow how Solidity provides access to two different sender-related variables, msg.sender and tx.origin, and how substituting one for the other, particularly in access control, introduces unintended and unsafe behaviors. This vulnerability doesn't result from a failing function or a broken opcode, but from using the wrong contextual value at a critical point in contract logic.

Start by examining the following Solidity contract:

```
// SPDX-License-Identifier: MIT
pragma solidity ^0.8.0;
contract TxOriginAuth {
  address public owner;
  constructor() {
    owner = msg.sender;
  }
  function sensitiveAction() public {
    require(tx.origin == owner, "Not authorized");
    // privileged logic here
  }
}
```

In this contract, access to the sensitiveAction function is protected by a require statement that checks whether tx.origin equals the owner address. At first glance, this seems secure: if the original account that started the transaction is the owner, the function proceeds; otherwise, it fails. However, this logic misuses tx.origin in place of msg.sender, which is the correct value to reference for authorizing function calls.

To understand where the vulnerability lies, it is important to observe the sequential evaluation of a transaction's call stack. When a user initiates a transaction, tx.origin is set to their external account address and remains constant through all nested calls across contracts. msg.sender, on the other hand, reflects the immediate caller, the last address in the call chain. The crucial difference is that while msg.sender changes with each call, tx.origin stays fixed at the original external account that initiated the entire transaction.

The vulnerability arises when tx.origin is used in place of msg.sender for authorization. This logic assumes that only the original transaction sender matters, ignoring the possibility that the call may have passed through one or more intermediary contracts. In terms of flow, when sensitiveAction() is called, the require(tx.origin == owner) condition is evaluated. If the transaction was initiated by the owner, the check passes, even if the immediate caller is a completely different contract. The state of the contract assumes the caller is trusted solely because of the transaction's origin, not because of who is interacting with the contract at that moment.

Visualizing this execution helps clarify vulnerability. Imagine a straight path from an external wallet to this contract's function. The tx.origin reflects the external wallet at the top of the stack. But now consider a new path, where the wallet first interacts with an intermediary contract, which then calls this one. The tx.origin is still the external wallet, even though the msg.sender within this contract is now the intermediary. The contract, unaware of this middle layer, still passes the check. The authorization condition is bypassed, not through any exploit in the logic, but because the logic is referencing the wrong identity context.

9. **Floating Pragma Versions:** Solidity contracts typically begin with a version of pragma declaration like pragma solidity ^0.8.0. While this ensures compatibility with a range of compiler versions, using a floating pragma (with ^) instead of locking to a specific version can inadvertently introduce security issues. For example, a contract written and tested under version 0.8.4 might later be compiled under 0.8.10, where subtle behavior changes or newly introduced bugs could affect the contract's logic. This becomes especially dangerous when using external libraries or upgradable contracts, where a small version shift can lead to incompatibility or unexpected results. To avoid these issues, developers should pin their pragma to an exact compiler version during development and deployment (e.g., pragma solidity 0.8.4) to ensure deterministic behavior and reduce the risk of future compiler-induced vulnerabilities.

   - To understand the Floating Pragma Versions vulnerability in Solidity, we need to follow what happens during compilation and how version declarations affect contract behavior. This vulnerability does not arise from a specific function or piece of executable logic in the contract, but from the version directive at the top of the file, which silently controls the entire compiler behavior. The vulnerability exists when a developer uses a pragma directive that allows multiple compiler versions rather than locking to a specific one, which introduces inconsistencies and unpredictability in how the contract compiles over time.

Consider the following example of a Solidity contract with a floating pragma:

```
// SPDX-License-Identifier: MIT
pragma solidity ^0.6.0;
contract PragmaExample {
  function get() public pure returns (uint256) {
    return 42;
  }
}
```

Here, the pragma line pragma solidity ^0.6.0; tells the compiler to use any version greater than or equal to 0.6.0 but less than 0.7.0. At first, this seems reasonable, it allows the contract to stay compatible with updates and fixes within the same major version range. However, this flexibility is also the source of the vulnerability. It introduces environmental dependencies into the contract. If the compiler version available in the deployment environment differs from the one originally tested, subtle differences in behavior, security defaults, or syntax interpretations may arise. The vulnerability exists from the moment this contract is compiled. When the developer runs the compiler, Solidity uses the latest available version within the permitted range. If a new patch version introduces a change, such as stricter checks, different handling of arithmetic operations, or new warnings, the compiled bytecode might differ, even though the source code is unchanged. This affects testing, auditing, and reproducibility, and can result in deployed contracts behaving differently than intended or previously observed.

From a sequence perspective, vulnerability becomes active during the compilation step. The pragma directive is interpreted, the compiler resolves the version range, and compilation proceeds with whichever version falls within the range and is installed. The actual logic of the contract may remain unchanged, but the way the compiler treats that logic could vary. For instance, a floating pragma might compile under version 0.6.8 during development, but later compile under version 0.6.12 in production, where certain safety checks or optimizations have changed. This introduces a disconnect between what the developer expects and what is actually deployed.

This vulnerability is subtle and hard to detect because it doesn't show up during contract execution or even necessarily during testing. Its impact is found in the underlying assumptions about what the code does and how it gets compiled into bytecode. Without locking the compiler version, those assumptions are not guaranteed to hold in the future or across different environments.

10. **Variable Shadowing:** Shadowing occurs when a local variable inside a function or block has the same name as a state variable or inherited variable. This results in the local variable "shadowing" the outer one, meaning the local variable will be used while the outer one is ignored. Although Solidity doesn't throw an error

in such cases, this behavior can introduce subtle bugs that are hard to detect. For example, a developer might believe they are updating a state variable but are actually only modifying a temporary local copy, leading to logic flaws or state inconsistencies. This can break access control, accounting, or other critical contract logic. Shadowing can also occur in inheritance hierarchies, where a derived contract defines a variable with the same name as one in its parent. Best practice is to avoid using duplicate names and rely on clear, distinct variable naming conventions. Tools like linters or the Solidity compiler with appropriate warnings enabled can help catch these mistakes during development.

- To understand the Variable Shadowing vulnerability in Solidity, we must follow how variable scope and declaration order influence which value is actually being used during contract execution. This vulnerability exists when a local variable inside a function or inner scope is declared with the same name as a state variable. When this happens, the local variable "shadows" or hides the state variable within that scope, meaning the state variable becomes inaccessible and any reference to that name will point to the local one instead. This can lead to unintended behavior, where the contract appears to be working with persistent data but is in fact working only with a temporary local copy.

Consider the following Solidity contract:

```
// SPDX-License-Identifier: MIT
pragma solidity ^0.8.0;
contract ShadowingExample {
  uint256 public value;

  function setValue(uint256 _value) public {
    uint256 value = _value; // shadows the state variable
  }
}
```

Here, the contract declares a public state variable value that is intended to store persistent data on the blockchain. The setValue function is supposed to update this variable. However, within the function, the line uint256 value = _value; declares a new local variable with the exact same name. This local variable exists only within the scope of the function and does not modify the state variable at all. The assignment operation affects only the local copy, which disappears as soon as the function ends. As a result, the state variable remains unchanged, even though the function appears to be setting it.

The vulnerability begins the moment the function defines a local variable that shares its name with a state variable. During compilation, Solidity resolves references to the innermost scope first. Because of this, any usage of value within the function refers to the local version, not the state variable. This substitution is silent, no error is thrown, and the compiler does not prevent it unless specific warnings are enabled. Therefore, the function executes without issue, but its behavior diverges from the developer's likely intention.

Visually, we can imagine the contract's top-level storage layout containing the state variable value. When the function setValue is called, the EVM creates a new local variable in memory named value. All subsequent operations within that function target this memory space instead of the storage slot where the actual state variable resides. This is where the logic branches away from expectations: the state variable remains untouched because all interactions occur in a separate, temporary memory region.

In more complex contracts, especially those with inheritance or nested scopes, this vulnerability can become harder to spot. For example, a child contract might declare a variable with the same name as one in a parent contract, unintentionally overriding it in some contexts but not others. This can lead to inconsistencies, broken modifiers, and unexpected access-control behavior, again, not because the code is invalid, but because it references the wrong version of a variable due to naming collisions.

11. **Default Visibility:** Solidity functions and state variables have visibility specifiers, public, private, internal, and external, that control their accessibility. If no visibility is explicitly specified, functions default to public, potentially exposing internal logic to external users. This oversight may allow unintended users to invoke critical functions, changing contract behavior or transferring funds. A known example is early contracts that forgot to mark helper or initialization functions as private, enabling attackers to exploit them and gain unauthorized control. Developers must always define visibility explicitly to avoid accidental exposure.

    - To understand the Default Visibility vulnerability in Solidity, it is essential to look at how the language treats functions and variables that are declared without an explicit visibility specifier. Solidity offers several visibility modifiers, public, external, internal, and private, each controlling who can access a function or state variable and from where. When visibility is not specified, Solidity assigns a default, which may not align with the developer's intention. This implicit behavior introduces a subtle vulnerability, especially in earlier versions of Solidity, where the defaults were either overly permissive or not immediately obvious.

Consider the following contract written in a version of Solidity prior to 0.5.0:

```
// SPDX-License-Identifier: MIT
pragma solidity ^0.4.24;
contract VisibilityExample {
  uint256 balance;
  function setBalance(uint256 _value) {
    balance = _value;
  }
}
```

In this code, the function setBalance is defined without a visibility modifier. In this version of Solidity, such a function defaults to public. This means it is callable by any external account, even though the developer may have assumed it was internal or private. The function appears simple and isolated, but because visibility is not explicitly declared, it becomes part of the contract's public interface. As a result, any external caller has access to it. The state variable balance is also declared without a visibility modifier. In this case, it defaults to internal, which is safer but not transparent to someone reading the contract without knowledge of default behavior.

The vulnerability manifests during compilation and deployment. At the time of compilation, Solidity assigns a default visibility to functions that lack one. The compiled bytecode reflects this, and the function is included in the externally accessible interface. Once deployed, any external account or contract can interact with the function, even if that wasn't the developer's intent. The critical moment is not when the function is executed, but when it is interpreted by the compiler without an explicit directive. That silent default alters the contract's external accessibility and potentially exposes internal logic.

When the contract is called later, a transaction sent to the setBalance function is processed as a valid external call because the compiler has implicitly made the function public. There is no runtime failure, no warning, and no indication that the function was exposed unintentionally. The developer may have expected the function to be used only within internal logic, but instead it becomes a doorway into the contract's internal state manipulation. This mismatch between assumed behavior and the actual access scope is the vulnerability.

The absence of a visibility specifier is the sole trigger of this vulnerability. The language does not consider it an error; it silently applies a default. This design, while syntactically valid, can mislead developers, especially those coming from other languages where functions are private by default. In contracts with financial logic, governance roles, or sensitive operations, a single unintended public function can change the threat surface entirely.

12. **No Restricted Write:** This vulnerability occurs when a contract allows public access to critical variables or fails to restrict functions that modify storage. A prominent example was the Parity multi-signature wallet attack, in which an improper restriction allowed an attacker to reinitialize the library contract and gain ownership, enabling them to call selfdestruct. This vulnerability highlights the necessity for rigorous access control, especially in library contracts used by multiple clients.

    - To understand the No Restricted Write vulnerability in Solidity, we must follow how contracts manage access to state-modifying functions and what happens when those functions lack proper restrictions. This vulnerability emerges not from incorrect syntax or broken logic, but from the absence of control, specifically, the failure to ensure that only authorized users can modify critical contract state. It lives in the gap between the intention to protect data and the lack of enforcement in the code.

Take the following Solidity contract as an example:

```
// SPDX-License-Identifier: MIT
pragma solidity ^0.8.0;
contract Configurable {
  uint256 public interestRate;
  function setInterestRate(uint256 _rate) public {
    interestRate = _rate;
  }
}
```

At first glance, this contract defines a state variable interestRate that can be changed using the setInterestRate function. However, there is no access control mechanism in place. The function is marked public by default, which means any external caller can invoke it. There is no check to ensure that the caller is the contract owner or any designated administrator. The vulnerability begins the moment the function is declared without a restriction on who can call it. Because no condition governs access to this state-changing logic, the variable becomes openly writable from any external source.
When this contract is compiled, the setInterestRate function is included in the public interface. Upon deployment, the function can be called by anyone on the network. During execution, as soon as a transaction invokes setInterestRate, the caller-provided new value is written directly to storage. The EVM does not question the sender's authority unless the contract explicitly does. That responsibility lies with the developer, and in this example, it has been omitted. State changes execute immediately, with no validation of who is making the change or whether they are authorized to.
The vulnerability is not in the behavior of the function itself, setting a value is straightforward and syntactically correct. The problem lies in the assumption that only trusted parties will interact with the contract. Solidity does not enforce access control automatically; developers must implement their own modifiers, such as onlyOwner, to control who can write to the contract's storage. Without such checks, the function is exposed, and the contract's internal state becomes mutable by any participant on the network.
Visualizing the control flow, the contract receives a transaction, identifies the function signature, matches it to setInterestRate, and executes it without challenge. The internal state is updated, and the transaction is completed. No condition is checked along the way. The execution path is flat, no branches, no requirements, just direct writing to persistent storage. This simplicity is what makes vulnerability easy to miss and, in effect, dangerous.

13. **Block Gas Limit Dependent Loops:** Smart contracts must be carried out within the block gas limit, a protocol-level constraint on computational cost. Functions that include unbounded loops (e.g., iterating over an array of unknown

or dynamic length) are vulnerable to Denial-of-Service (DoS) if the data grows large. For instance, a function that pays rewards to all users in a list may work initially but become uncallable over time as the list grows and gas usage exceeds the block limit. Attackers can exploit this by inflating the data (e.g., registering fake users) to permanently block the function. Even without malicious intent, such patterns result in contracts that “break” as they scale. This issue highlights the need for gas-aware design patterns. Recommended mitigation strategies include breaking operations into smaller chunks (pagination), allowing users to process their own rewards (pull-over-push pattern), or implementing time-based logic to spread computation across transactions.

- To understand the Block Gas Limit Dependent Loops vulnerability in Solidity, it is necessary to examine how the Ethereum Virtual Machine (EVM) processes loops and how the fixed block gas limit affects execution. This vulnerability arises when a loop within a contract function depends on a dynamic or unbounded data structure, such as an array or mapping with an unknown or growing size. The vulnerability is not about a direct failure in logic, but rather about designing a contract that includes potentially unbounded iteration without considering the finite amount of gas available in a single transaction.

Consider the following Solidity contract that allows users to add entries and later clear them:

```
// SPDX-License-Identifier: MIT
pragma solidity ^0.8.0;
contract LoopExample {
  address[] public users;
  function register() public {
    users.push(msg.sender);
  }
  function clearAll() public {
    for (uint256 i = 0; i < users.length; i++) {
       delete users[i];
    }
  }
}
```

This contract maintains a dynamic array of user addresses and provides a clearAll() function to iterate through and delete them. The vulnerability arises from the loop in clearAll(), which iterates through the entire user’s array. First, this may work without issue when the array is small. However, because each operation within the loop consumes gas, and because the total amount of gas allowed per block is capped, this function will eventually fail to complete if users.length becomes too large. The vulnerability begins to manifest the moment the loop's execution cost approaches or exceeds the block gas limit.

When a user calls clearAll(), the EVM begins executing the loop, processing one iteration at a time. With each deletion, gas is consumed. If the number of users is too large, the function consumes more gas than the maximum allowed per block, causing the transaction to revert before the loop completes. This behavior is not an immediate bug, but a gradual degradation in usability. Over time, as more users register, the clearAll() function becomes unusable, leaving the contract in a state where that logic cannot be executed.

The vulnerability is embedded directly in the loop's structure and in the assumption that it will always finish. Solidity and the EVM do not automatically optimize or break up expensive loops; they rely entirely on the contract's logic to manage resource usage. In this case, the contract assumes that the loop will complete regardless of the number of users, but that assumption becomes invalid under Ethereum's gas constraints. Execution breaks not because the loop is syntactically invalid, but because the EVM runs out of gas while trying to carry it out.

Visualizing the control flow, the contract begins the function call, enters the for loop, and iterates over the array, performing deletion on each step. With a small array, this completes successfully. With a large array, the gas meter ticks toward the block gas limit, and at some point, execution halts. The function fails, the transaction reverts, and no changes are applied. The vulnerability, therefore, is temporal and structural; it may not be evident during testing or early deployment but becomes critical as the contract's data grows over time.

6.1.2 Ethereum Virtual Machine (EVM): Virtual Machine-Level Vulnerabilities

Virtual Machine-Level category includes vulnerabilities that originate from the underlying behavior and architecture of the Ethereum Virtual Machine itself, rather than from the high-level Solidity language. These issues arise from the way the EVM processes low-level data structures, manages memory, and encodes addresses. Vulnerabilities such as short address attacks exploit the way the EVM handles input data padding and parsing during transaction execution, potentially leading to misaligned parameters and unintended behavior. Similarly, storage overlap or collision occurs when different variables or contracts inadvertently share the same storage slot, typically due to improper use of delegate calls or manual manipulation of storage layout. These vulnerabilities are grouped in this category because they stem from the EVM's low-level operational semantics, independent of higher-level code logic, and often require a deep understanding of bytecode execution and storage mechanisms to detect and mitigate them.

14. **Short Address:** This is a less common but interesting low-level bug that exploits how Ethereum's transaction encoding works. Ethereum ABI encodes

function arguments to 32-byte slots. In early days, some contracts (or dApp front-ends) didn't properly validate the length of address inputs. An attacker could provide a *malformed shorter data payload* for a function that expects an address and some value. The EVM's *autopadding* of arguments would then mis-align the parameters—effectively concatenating part of the value with the address. This could result in the function seeing a much larger value than intended. For example, if a transfer function takes (address _to, uint _amount), and the attacker provides a _to that is missing the last byte, the EVM will shift the bytes such that what the contract reads as _amount is astronomically high (because it includes the leftover bits of the address). If the contract didn't check for this, it might transfer an excessive amount. This short-address vulnerability is primarily due to *frontend/contract mismatches* and was mitigated in most Ethereum clients by enforcing parameter size checks. It's a cautionary tale that even the underlying encoding mechanism can introduce bugs if inputs aren't validated.

- To understand Short Address vulnerability, it is necessary to examine how the Ethereum Virtual Machine handles function argument encoding, particularly when dealing with address types and the structure of the calldata. This vulnerability does not reside in the Solidity code itself, but in how the EVM decodes inputs when they are passed in improperly formatted transactions. The issue arises when an address parameter, which should be 20 bytes, is passed a shorter value in a low-level call, and the receiving contract does not verify the calldata length before using it. This causes the EVM to incorrectly shift the remaining arguments, potentially leading to the misinterpretation of inputs or the silent corruption of function behavior.

Consider a function written in Solidity that receives an address and a uint256 value:

```
// SPDX-License-Identifier: MIT
pragma solidity ^0.8.0;
contract TokenTransfer {
  function transfer(address to, uint256 amount) public {
    // Logic using 'to' and 'amount'
  }
}
```

When this function is compiled, it expects the calldata to contain the function selector followed by 32 bytes for the address (even though addresses are only 20 bytes) and another 32 bytes for the uint256 amount. However, if this function is called using a low-level interface such as call() and the calldata is crafted manually, an input with fewer than the expected 32 bytes for the address field can still be passed. EVM does not reject the transaction outright. Instead, it performs a left-aligned padding of the provided data, which shifts the remaining arguments into the wrong positions in memory.

The vulnerability begins the moment a transaction with a short address, say, 18 or 19 bytes instead of the expected 20, is submitted and accepted by a client that does not enforce strict argument length validation. When this calldata reaches the contract, the function selector is used to route the transaction to the transfer function, and the contract attempts to read the address and amount parameters based on their assumed positions in memory. But due to the short address, the uint256 amount is misaligned, resulting in either a corrupted read or the use of the wrong value entirely.

The core of the vulnerability is the reliance on implicit padding behavior without verifying that the calldata is the correct length. Since Solidity does not insert automatic runtime checks for argument size at this level, a contract function will interpret whatever is in the expected memory slots, even if the data was not properly aligned. This makes vulnerability exist precisely at the point where a contract reads functional arguments from calldata, assuming their alignment is correct, without validating their actual position.

In the execution flow, the contract starts by identifying the function selector and routing the call. It then loads the address and uint256 parameters from memory based on static offsets. If the calldata was shortened, those offsets are incorrect. The contract proceeds with the logic using parameters that may now contain unexpected or incomplete data. This silent misalignment does not throw an error, because the contract is technically working within EVM's rules, it just operates on faulty assumptions about the structure of its inputs.

15. **Storage Overlap/Collision:** Ethereum contracts have flat 2^256 slot storage. High-level languages map variables to storage slots in a deterministic way. But edge cases in how storage is allocated can lead to overlaps. For instance, certain compiler bugs or using delegatecall to a library that assumes a different storage layout can cause one contract's variables to overwrite another's. The vulnerability here is that different EVM implementations or compilers *might handle storage packing slightly differently*, leading to scenarios where a contract's data overlap and be corrupted without anyone noticing. In practice, a known issue was with multiple inheritance and storage layout changes between Solidity versions—if not handled, upgrading a contract could inadvertently overlap storage for different variables. While not a direct "attack vector" that an external user can easily trigger, it's a serious pitfall for developers (especially when writing proxy contracts or low-level assembly). Another example at EVM level was the old "EVM opcode gas cost" issues—e.g., *DoS with EXT codesize* and *call depth attack* (now historical footnotes: attackers could exploit the fixed call stack depth or perform operations that were extremely cheap gas-wise to clog up execution in early Ethereum days). These have been largely resolved by protocol updates (Ethereum removed the fixed call depth and adjusted opcode costs), but they illustrate that some vulnerabilities derive from the EVM execution model itself.

    - To understand the Storage Overlap/Collision vulnerability in Solidity, it's necessary to look at how variables are laid out in storage and how delegatecall-based architectures, particularly proxy patterns, rely on that layout remaining consistent. This vulnerability occurs when two contracts, usually a proxy and its logic (or implementation) contract, have mismatched storage layouts, causing them to unintentionally read from or write to the same storage slots. The result is that state variables in one contract overwrite or corrupt those in the other, even though they are declared independently. The vulnerability is not the result of faulty execution but of incorrect assumptions about how contract storage behaves across delegation boundaries.

To illustrate where and when this vulnerability exists, consider a simplified proxy pattern in which a base contract (proxy) uses delegatecall to forward execution to another contract (logic/implementation) that defines the application logic. In Solidity, delegatecall executes code from the implementation contract in the proxy's storage context. This means the logic contract's variables must align perfectly with the proxy's storage layout.

```
// SPDX-License-Identifier: MIT
pragma solidity ^0.8.0;
contract Proxy {
  address public implementation; // stored at slot 0
  function upgrade(address _impl) public {
    implementation = _impl;
  }
  fallback() external payable {
     address _impl = implementation;
     assembly {
       calldatacopy(0, 0, calldatasize())
       let success := delegatecall(gas(), _impl, 0,
calldatasize(), 0, 0)
       returndatacopy(0, 0, returndatasize())
       switch success
       case 0 { revert(0, returndatasize()) }
       default { return(0, returndatasize()) }
     }
  }
}
```

This proxy holds a single variable, implementation, at storage slot 0. It forwards all unknown function calls to the address held in that slot using delegatecall. Now consider the logical contract:

```
contract Logic {
   uint256 public counter; // also at slot 0
   address public owner;   // at slot 1

   function increment() public {
     counter += 1;
   }
}
```

In this logic contract, counter is the first declared variable and thus occupies slot 0, while owner occupies slot 1. But when increment() is called through the proxy, the logic contract's code is executed in the proxy's storage, so counter + = 1 writes to slot 0, which is where the proxy's implementation address is stored. This causes the storage overlap. The proxy expects slot 0 to contain an address that determines where to route logic calls. However, the logic contract thinks slot 0 is reserved for a number that tracks state. This mismatch causes one to corrupt the other's data.

The vulnerability is active the moment the two contracts declare variables that share overlapping slot indices and then execute logic using delegatecall. There is no runtime error or revert; the EVM simply writes to whatever slot the logic contract tells it to, without knowing it's being used differently by the proxy. Solidity does not have built-in awareness of storage layout consistency across contracts, it relies entirely on the developer to ensure alignment through convention or tooling.

To visualize this, imagine a linear storage array in which each slot represents a 32-byte chunk of persistent data. The proxy thinks slot 0 contains the implementation address. The logic contract thinks slot 0 contains a counter. When the logic is executed in the proxy's context, the counter increment operation modifies the implementation address instead. The proxy then loses track of which contract to delegate to. Conversely, a write to slot 1 in the logic contract might accidentally overwrite an entirely different piece of the proxy's state if it had any more variables, resulting in additional corruption.

6.1.3 Blockchain: Protocol-Level Vulnerabilities

Protocol-Level category comprises vulnerabilities that arise from the fundamental design and operational characteristics of the Ethereum blockchain protocol itself, rather than from the smart contract code or the EVM. These issues stem from how transactions are processed, ordered, and verified within the decentralized network. For example, timestamp dependence exploits the fact that miners have partial control over block timestamps, allowing them to manipulate time-sensitive logic in contracts. Transaction order dependence (commonly known as front-running) exploits the public mempool and the non-deterministic order of transactions, allowing malicious actors to reorder or insert transactions for financial gain. The absence of chain-specific data in signed messages can enable replay attacks across different chains, allowing a valid signature on one chain to be reused maliciously on another. Honeypot contracts, while deceptive by design, rely on subtle protocol behaviors or external transaction conditions to trick users into initiating interactions that appear profitable but are ultimately inescapable. These vulnerabilities are grouped in this category because they exploit the mechanics and assumptions of the blockchain protocol itself, often requiring mitigation strategies beyond smart contract code, such as network-level defenses or protocol improvements.

16. **Timestamp Dependence:** Ethereum miners have the ability to set the timestamp of a block (within a reasonable bound, typically within ~15 s of the "real" time). If a smart contract uses block.timestamp (or now) to make decisions, for example, a lottery that gives a prize if a bet is placed in an "odd" second, or a contract that releases funds only after a certain time, a miner might bias this value. For instance, a miner seeing a pending transaction that will yield them a reward if the timestamp meets a condition could choose a timestamp that satisfies that condition (as long as it's within the allowed delta). In most cases, timestamp manipulation is minor (a few seconds), so it can't drastically change game outcomes unless the game's logic is naive (e.g., using timestamp % 10 for randomness is unsafe). But there have been proofs-of-concept where a betting contract that relied on timestamp for randomness was exploitable. Rule of thumb: timestamps can be used for broad timing (e.g., daily limits) but not for precise random outcomes or critical conditions.

    - To understand the Timestamp Dependence vulnerability in Solidity, we must examine how contracts access and rely on block timestamps, and where in execution this reliance introduces fragility. This vulnerability occurs when a contract uses the block.timestamp global variable for critical control flow, particularly for security checks, randomness, or conditional logic that affects user permissions or financial transfers. The vulnerability itself is not caused by a syntax error or a broken function, but by trusting a data source that block producers can subtly manipulate within a small but exploitable range.

    Consider the following Solidity contract, which uses block.timestamp to decide whether a user can withdraw funds:

```
// SPDX-License-Identifier: MIT
pragma solidity ^0.8.0;
contract TimedWithdrawal {
  uint256 public unlockTime;
  address public owner;
  constructor(uint256 _delayInSeconds) {
    owner = msg.sender;
    unlockTime = block.timestamp + _delayInSeconds;
  }
  function withdraw() public {
    require(msg.sender == owner, "Not the owner");
    require(block.timestamp >= unlockTime, "Too early to
withdraw");
    payable(msg.sender).transfer(address(this).balance);
  }
  receive() external payable {}
}
```

In this example, the unlockTime is calculated during deployment based on the current block.timestamp. The withdraw function then checks if the current timestamp has reached or passed this threshold. The contract assumes that block.timestamp provides a secure, reliable measure of real-world time. However, the Ethereum protocol allows block producers, miners or validators, to influence the timestamp of the blocks they create, within certain protocol-defined constraints. The vulnerability arises during the execution of any function, like withdraw, that evaluates a condition based on block.timestamp. At that exact moment, the contract relies on the timestamp to reflect real time. But since miners can adjust it slightly (typically by a few seconds), the condition might evaluate differently than expected. A miner who creates the current block can adjust the timestamp within a valid range, potentially making time-based conditions pass or fail earlier or later than the actual wall-clock time would suggest.

From a control flow perspective, the contract reads block.timestamp and compares it to unlockTime. If the block's timestamp is just barely enough to satisfy the condition, the logic proceeds. The contract assumes this timestamp is precise, but in reality it is subject to influence by the entity producing the current block. This assumption introduces a risk, especially if the timestamp is used for decisions that affect security or value transfer, such as lotteries, unlock conditions, bidding deadlines, or randomized winner selection.

Visualizing this in execution, the timeline begins at contract deployment, where unlockTime is defined relative to the current block's timestamp. Later, during function calls such as withdraw, the current block's timestamp is compared against the stored value. The vulnerability arises when the decision logic depends on this value, assuming it is unalterable or outside adversarial control. The EVM does not enforce strict accuracy or trustworthiness for timestamps, it simply reports what the block producer declares, within reason.

17. **Transaction Order Dependence (Front-Running):** In Ethereum, the order of transactions in a block is not strictly first-come-first-serve; miners (or more generally, the network) determine ordering, often prioritizing higher gas price transactions. This leads to *front-running*, where an attacker can observe a pending transaction in the mempool and quickly submit their own transaction with a higher gas price to get executed before, or manipulate the order. Many contracts are vulnerable to order manipulation if they, for example, allow a user to set some value and another to act on it within the same block, or if there's a public function that executes an action based on current state that an attacker can preempt. A concrete case is decentralized exchanges (DEXes) and automated market makers: an attacker can observe a large trade coming (one that will move the price) and execute a quick trade right before and after it ("sandwiching") to profit at the user's expense. Another example was in ICO bidding or Ethereum Name Service auctions—someone could outbid or modify their bid after seeing yours, if the protocol didn't guard against it. Transaction-order dependence isn't a bug in the code *per se*; it's more of a design vulnerability. Contracts that require fairness must employ strategies such as commit-reveal schemes (where actions are hidden in the first phase) or impose a time delay to prevent instantaneous sniping. **Front-running** is one of the most pervasive issues in DeFi—not an exploit that "breaks" the contract, but a vulnerability that can be abused to consistently gain an advantage.

    - To understand the Transaction Order Dependence vulnerability, also referred to as Front-Running, it's essential to observe how smart contracts process transactions in the context of Ethereum's public, asynchronous network. This vulnerability does not arise from incorrect code but from a specific assumption in contract logic: that the order of transaction execution will match the order of submission or the user's intention. In reality, Ethereum miners or validators choose the order of transactions within a block, which introduces a layer of unpredictability when two or more transactions interact with the same contract state within a short time window.

```
// SPDX-License-Identifier: MIT
pragma solidity ^0.8.0;
contract SimpleAuction {
  address public highestBidder;
  uint256 public highestBid;
  function bid() public payable {
    require(msg.value > highestBid, "Bid not high
enough");
    highestBid = msg.value;
    highestBidder = msg.sender;
  }
}
```

In this example, the contract maintains a highestBid and a highestBidder. A user can call the bid function, sending Ether to try to become the new highest bidder. The contract checks whether the sent value exceeds the current highest bid and, if so, updates the state accordingly. The vulnerability begins not in the function's logic itself, which is correct in isolation, but in the assumption that once a transaction is sent to the bid function, its outcome is determined only by the state at the time of submission.

In practice, once a user submits a bid transaction, it enters the public mempool, an open list of pending transactions visible to everyone, including miners and other network participants. Until it is mined, it does not affect the contract's state. During this window, another transaction can be submitted with knowledge of the first one. If two bids are submitted close together, the final order of execution depends not on submission time, but on how the miner arranges the block.

The vulnerability materializes during block assembly. The miner or validator may include transactions in any order they choose, usually based on gas price incentives. Even if a user sends a higher bid first, another participant observing the mempool may submit a slightly higher bid with a higher gas price, leading the miner to include and execute it first. In this scenario, the first bidder's transaction is processed afterward, at which point their bid no longer meets the required condition and fails.

From the contract's point of view, everything works as expected. The required statement enforces the correct rule, and the state is updated consistently. However, the vulnerability lies in the timing assumption that the state a user saw when submitting their transaction would still be valid when the transaction executes. This breaks down because Ethereum is a shared, global state machine in which visibility of intent certainly precedes execution.

Visually, the sequence starts when the first transaction is broadcast to the network. At that point, the msg.value is greater than the current highestBid, and the bidder assumes the transaction will succeed. Before it is mined, a second transaction with a higher bid is sent and mined first, updating the contract state. When the original transaction is eventually mined, the condition it relies on has changed, causing it to fail. The vulnerability, therefore, lies in the temporal window between transaction broadcasting and block inclusion, during which assumptions about the current state are invalidated by the execution of other transactions.

18. **Absence of Chain-Specific Data in Signed Messages:** In multi-chain environments, contracts or protocols that rely on off-chain signed messages (e.g., approvals, withdrawals, or authorizations) must incorporate chain-specific identifiers, such as chainId or a domain separator, to distinguish the intended context. If this separation is missing, the same message can be valid across multiple environments, enabling replay attacks. For instance, a transaction signed for the Ethereum mainnet might also be valid on a testnet or forked chain if chainId is not enforced during signature verification. This vulnerability allows an attacker to reuse a legitimate message or transaction in an unintended context, potentially executing sensitive actions like transfers or approvals without additional user consent. The Ethereum ecosystem addressed this after the 2016 DAO hard fork by incorporating chain ID into the transaction signature structure (EIP-155), but smart contracts that perform off-chain message verification

must still manually enforce domain separation. Failing to do so is a critical protocol-level design flaw in today's cross-chain DeFi and messaging systems.

- **Absence of Chain-Specific Data in Signed Messages:** To understand the Absence of Chain-Specific Data in Signed Messages vulnerability, we need to focus on how off-chain messages are signed and later verified on-chain. In Ethereum and other EVM-based networks, it is common for users to sign structured messages off-chain with their private keys and then submit those signatures to smart contracts for validation. The purpose is to enable actions such as delegated approvals, meta-transactions, or cross-contract authorizations without requiring the user to send an actual transaction. The vulnerability arises when the message format being signed and later validated lacks a unique identifier that ties it to a specific blockchain network, such as a chainId. Without such contextual binding, the same message can be considered valid across multiple chains that share compatible infrastructure.

Consider a contract that verifies a message signature to authorize a certain action:

```
    // SPDX-License-Identifier: MIT
    pragma solidity ^0.8.0;
    contract MessageVerifier {
      address public trustedSigner;
      constructor(address _signer) {
        trustedSigner = _signer;
      }
      function execute(bytes32 messageHash, bytes memory
signature) public view returns (bool) {
        bytes32 ethSignedMessage = prefixed(messageHash);
        return recoverSigner(ethSignedMessage, signature) ==
trustedSigner;
      }
      function prefixed(bytes32 hash) internal pure returns
(bytes32) {
        return keccak256(abi.encodePacked("\x19Ethereum Signed
Message:\n32", hash));
      }
      function recoverSigner(bytes32 message, bytes memory
sig) internal pure returns (address) {
        (bytes32 r, bytes32 s, uint8 v) = splitSignature(sig);
        return ecrecover(message, v, r, s);
      }
      function splitSignature(bytes memory sig) internal pure
returns (bytes32 r, bytes32 s, uint8 v) {
        require(sig.length == 65, "Invalid signature length");
```

```
        assembly {
          r := mload(add(sig, 32))
          s := mload(add(sig, 64))
          v := byte(0, mload(add(sig, 96)))
        }
    }
}
```

This contract assumes that the messageHash was signed by a trusted off-chain signer, and it verifies the signature against that hash. However, there is no guarantee that this hash contains any data that uniquely identifies the blockchain network the message is intended for. If the original signed data was something like a simple approval, say, "Approve user X to spend Y tokens", and no chainId or contract address was embedded into that message before signing, then the same message and signature pair can be accepted by contracts on other chains as well.

The vulnerability becomes active when the smart contract accepts and verifies an off-chain-generated signature. If the original message does not include contextual identifiers such as the chainId, the smart contract address, or domain-specific values, the smart contract cannot determine whether the signature was intended for this chain or another. Because EVM chains often share identical logic and tooling, a valid signature on one network can be replayed on another network if the underlying message is too generic.

From an execution-flow perspective, when a user signs a message, their wallet uses only the structured data presented to them. The wallet hashes the message and applies their private key to produce a signature. This signature is valid for the data, but not for the chain, unless the data explicitly includes chain-specific identifiers. Once the message and signature are sent to the contract, the contract recovers the signer address and checks its trust level. But nowhere in this verification does the contract confirm the intended execution context of the signature because the original message lacked the necessary data.

Visualizing this, we can imagine a message floating in the ecosystem: it contains no information about what chain it was signed for, just that it authorizes an action. This message is cryptographically valid, but the lack of specificity makes it portable. Any compatible contract on any chain with the same verification logic will accept it as legitimate. The vulnerability resides in the absence of boundary conditions; there is no limit encoded into the data that says, "this signature is only meant for Ethereum Mainnet" or "only valid in contract X."

19. **Honeypot Contracts:** Honeypots are deceptive smart contracts designed to appear vulnerable while actually being traps for attackers. These contracts might expose seemingly exploitable functions, such as public withdrawal functions or large unlocked balances, but contain hidden logic that ensures only the creator can interact with them successfully. Others who attempt to "exploit" the

contract end up transferring funds to the attacker instead. Honeypots represent a unique kind of protocol-level threat: they don't directly harm the blockchain, but they manipulate attackers' assumptions about publicly visible smart contract logic. While not a vulnerability in the contract itself, they exploit the transparency and trust assumptions of the blockchain environment and serve as cautionary examples of how visibility can be used against even malicious users.

- **Honeypot Contracts:** To understand the Honeypot Contracts vulnerability, it's important to follow the way a smart contract can be deliberately constructed to appear vulnerable, but in fact is designed to prevent any successful interaction from unauthorized users while luring them into attempting one. The vulnerability does not stem from a flaw in logic or unintended behavior, but from a mismatch between what the contract's public-facing code suggests and what it actually does at runtime. Honeypots exploit the transparency of smart contract source code and the predictability of Ethereum's virtual machine to mislead observers, creating a deceptive environment in which the contract appears to allow value extraction but actually contains hidden constraints.

Consider a simplified version of a contract that pretends to expose an exploitable withdrawal function:

```
// SPDX-License-Identifier: MIT
pragma solidity ^0.8.0;
contract Honeypot {
  mapping(address => uint256) public balances;
  constructor() payable {
    balances[msg.sender] = msg.value;
  }
  function deposit() public payable {
    balances[msg.sender] += msg.value;
  }
  function withdraw(uint256 _amount) public {
    require(balances[msg.sender] >= _amount, "Insufficient
balance");
    (bool success, ) = msg.sender.call{value: _
amount}("");
    require(success, "Transfer failed");
    balances[msg.sender] -= _amount;
  }
  function getBalance() public view returns (uint256) {
    return address(this).balance;
  }
}
```

From a surface-level reading of the code, this contract appears simple: it allows users to deposit and withdraw Ether. A user might infer that if some logic flaw were introduced, like failing to update balances or allowing reentrant behavior, they could exploit it to drain funds. However, in a honeypot, such a contract includes carefully placed checks or hidden mechanisms that prevent anyone except the creator or specific addresses from succeeding in those operations. For instance, there could be a subtle condition inside withdraw() that always fails for external users, or a fallback function that behaves differently when triggered by unauthorized addresses.

The vulnerability arises when a user or tool examines the contract and determines it is exploitable based on the visible code. During execution, when a transaction attempts to invoke what appears to be an accessible or flawed function, the contract's internal logic diverges from expectations. A conditional check might silently block the action, or internal state might be wired in such a way that even correctly formed calls are reverted. The contract gives the illusion of access or a reward path, but it is, in fact, unachievable unless a specific, hardcoded condition is met.

In terms of execution, the honeypot contract behaves normally through most of its functions, such as deposit() or getBalance(), reinforcing the illusion of legitimacy and usability. However, the key function, the one that appears to release funds, includes embedded logic that discriminates against all addresses except the deployer or another whitelisted address. This logic might be deeply nested, involve seemingly benign state variables, or use unconventional patterns, such as contract self-calls or modified revert messages, to confuse observers.

Visually, the interaction can be described as a closed loop. A user initiates an action expecting it to reach a certain point, such as a withdraw() sending Ether, but the flow is intercepted just before completion by a condition that causes a revert. This flow is not revealed by a casual reading of the code and may even be obscured by misleading variable names or opaque state changes. The critical divergence between what is expected and what actually happens is where the vulnerability lives.

In conclusion, what binds these vulnerabilities together is their ability to remain hidden, often appearing harmless or entirely invisible during development and testing. Many, such as uninitialized variables or floating pragma versions, do not trigger compiler errors or halt execution but quietly introduce long-term instability. Others, such as unchecked external calls or the misuse of tx.origin, reflect a deeper misunderstanding of the execution context and the intricacies of Ethereum's security model. Structural vulnerabilities, including block gas limit-dependent loops or the lack of chain-specific data in signed messages, illustrate the importance of designing systems that anticipate scalability challenges, cross-chain interoperability, and adversarial exploitation.

Through visualization and annotated source code, it becomes evident that these vulnerabilities are not abstract concepts. Instead, they are embedded in the logic, the placement of conditions, and the sequencing of operations. A single unchecked assumption, a publicly exposed function without access control, a low-level call lacking a return value check, an unbounded loop over a dynamic array, or a signature valid across multiple chains can open the door to severe exploitation. In the immutable, permissionless environment of Ethereum, such oversights can have significant consequences.

Taken together, these categories represent the major known classes of vulnerabilities affecting Ethereum smart contracts. However, real-world exploits often involve a combination of these issues. For example, a DeFi attack may use a flash loan to exploit atomic execution, manipulate a price oracle via an economic vulnerability, and ultimately trigger a reentrancy flaw in a lending protocol. Having outlined the types and sources of these vulnerabilities, the next step is to conduct comparative analysis to determine which are most frequent and which cause the greatest damage in practice.

6.2 Vulnerabilities Analysis

Not all vulnerabilities are equally likely or equally severe. Here we compare vulnerability types across a few dimensions: how commonly they occur in real-world contracts, how easy they are to exploit, and the potential impact (severity) of an exploit. This comparative view helps prioritize what developers and auditors should focus on.

6.2.1 Frequency vs. Severity

Solidity, EVM, and blockchain-level vulnerabilities can be meaningfully compared by analyzing them along two key axes: frequency and severity. Frequency refers to how commonly these vulnerabilities appear in real-world smart contracts, while severity denotes the potential damage an exploit can cause. This kind of comparative analysis is essential for prioritizing audit efforts, secure development practices, and risk mitigation strategies.

Among the most dangerous vulnerabilities are those that rank high in both frequency and severity. Reentrancy, for example, remains one of the most devastating issues in Ethereum smart contracts, best exemplified by the infamous DAO hack. Despite its well-known status, it continues to occur due to subtle interaction patterns and developers' misunderstanding of external call behavior. Integer overflow and underflow were historically widespread before Solidity 0.8.0 introduced built-in checks. When exploited, they can cause severe economic losses, especially in financial protocols. Transaction Order Dependence (commonly associated with front-running attacks) is another high-frequency, high-impact issue, particularly problematic in DeFi applications, where attackers can reorder or sandwich transactions to unfairly extract value.

Some vulnerabilities, though not necessarily widespread, pose significant risks when they do appear. Unprotected selfdestruct operations can irrevocably terminate a contract, making it one of the most catastrophic yet rare vulnerabilities. Similarly, using tx.origin for authentication opens a contract to phishing-style privilege escalations and is considered a critical mistake. Storage collisions, often introduced by incorrect use of delegatecall and proxy patterns, are infrequent but can have a high impact, leading to corrupted or overwritten contract state.

There is another category of vulnerabilities that occur frequently but tend to be of medium or low severity. These include unhandled exceptions, default visibility settings, floating pragma versions, and unchecked external calls. While not always immediately exploitable, such oversights can lead to unintentional exposure of functionality, unexpected behavior, or the accumulation of security debt. For example, failing to declare function visibility explicitly may inadvertently expose internal logic to external users. Similarly, relying on floating pragma versions introduces the risk of breaking changes or compiler inconsistencies in production contracts.

At the protocol level, issues such as timestamp dependence and the lack of chain-specific data in signed messages reflect broader design concerns. Timestamp manipulation can affect contract logic dependent on time-based conditions, such as lotteries or staking periods. More subtle but equally important is the failure to incorporate chain-specific information into signatures, which makes cross-chain replay attacks feasible, a vulnerability that has gained more attention with the proliferation of L2s and cross-chain protocols.

Finally, honeypot contracts, while not vulnerabilities in the traditional sense, exploit user expectations by appearing easy to exploit while containing hidden traps. These malicious contracts are increasingly common and highlight the blurred line between technical vulnerability and social engineering. They serve as a reminder that smart contract security encompasses not only code correctness but also adversarial thinking and awareness of deceptive patterns.

In conclusion, a robust security posture requires focusing on both the most frequent and most damaging vulnerabilities. While automated tools are effective at identifying common, lower-risk issues, high-severity vulnerabilities, particularly those involving access control, contract lifecycle functions, and transaction ordering, demand thorough manual review and design-level mitigation. Addressing protocol-specific risks and emerging threats, such as honeypots and cross-chain attacks, further underscores the need for a holistic and proactive approach to smart contract security.

6.2.2 Ease of Detection

Analyzing the ease of detection for various smart contract vulnerabilities reveals how different types of flaws pose distinct challenges during security assessments. Some vulnerabilities are straightforward to identify using static analysis tools or linters, while others require a deeper understanding of execution context, runtime behavior, or even adversarial modeling. This comparative analysis evaluates each vulnerability across three detection difficulty tiers, Easy, Moderate, and Hard, based on how readily they can be discovered using modern auditing techniques and tooling.

To begin with, language-level vulnerabilities like unchecked external calls, default visibility settings, floating pragma versions, and variable shadowing are generally easy to detect. These issues are syntactic or structural in nature and can be flagged reliably by tools like Slither, MythX, or even Solidity compiler warnings. Their detection does not depend on runtime context, making automated scans highly effective. Similarly, unhandled exceptions and block gas-limit-dependent loops are easily identifiable by static tools that analyze control flow and loop structures, though determining their exploitability may require additional insight.

Other vulnerabilities fall into the moderate range of detection difficulty. Reentrancy, while well-known, often eludes naive detection because it depends on dynamic interactions between contracts and requires modeling external call sequences. Integer overflows and underflows were harder to catch prior to Solidity 0.8.0, but are now much easier unless developers intentionally disable overflow checks. Vulnerabilities like uninitialized state variables and locked ether require more contextual awareness; tools may flag them, but manual analysis is often necessary to determine their relevance and potential for exploitation. The use of tx.origin for authorization also falls into this moderate zone: while tools can detect its use, determining whether it's misused in a dangerous way typically requires a closer inspection of the business logic.

At the highest end of the spectrum, hard-to-detect vulnerabilities are those deeply tied to execution semantics or protocol-level behavior. For instance, storage overlap or collision issues often occur in upgradable contracts that use delegatecall and are difficult to identify without mapping out storage layouts and inheritance hierarchies. Short address attacks are another example; they are mitigated on modern networks, but still pose subtle threats on non-standard clients or custom interfaces. Timestamp dependence and transaction ordering dependence (front-running) involve temporal or mempool-based behavior that is invisible to static analysis. Detecting these issues typically requires adversarial modeling or formal verification. Similarly, the absence of chain-specific data in signed messages, a vulnerability exploitable via replay attacks, demands an understanding of cryptographic context and cross-chain architecture, making it one of the more advanced cases to diagnose.

Honeypot contracts represent a special case. They are deliberately crafted to deceive both human readers and tools by hiding malicious intent under the guise of exploitable bugs. Detecting honeypots requires not only symbolic execution but also the simulation of attacker behavior and economic incentives, which lie far beyond the capabilities of traditional static tools. As a result, honeypots are arguably among the most challenging to identify reliably without dynamic analysis or threat emulation.

In summary, while many Solidity-level bugs are easily surfaced using automated tooling, a significant portion, particularly those involving contract upgradeability, inter-contract communication, or blockchain-level dynamics, demand nuanced, manual review. Effective security audits, therefore, must go beyond tool outputs and incorporate design-level reasoning, threat modeling, and runtime simulation to uncover subtle or sophisticated vulnerabilities. As the smart contract ecosystem matures, so too must our approaches to identifying and mitigating these risks.

6.2.3 Relative Prevalence

When comparing the relative prevalence of vulnerabilities across Solidity, EVM, and blockchain protocol layers, it becomes evident that not all threats occur with equal frequency in deployed smart contracts. Some issues are endemic to beginner-level coding practices or outdated compiler usage, while others are more niche and tied to complex design patterns or advanced attack surfaces. The distribution of vulnerabilities also reflects broader trends in development maturity, tooling adoption, and ecosystem evolution.

Among Solidity language-level vulnerabilities, issues such as default visibility, unhandled exceptions, unchecked external calls, and floating pragma versions are among the most commonly encountered in real-world contracts. Their high prevalence is largely due to their subtlety and to the fact that many are introduced inadvertently by developers unfamiliar with Solidity's strict behavior. These bugs are especially common in contracts that haven't been audited or were built with older versions of the language, where such protections weren't enforced by default. Similarly, block gas-limit-dependent loops, while not inherently dangerous in every case, are relatively common, especially in contracts involving unbounded iterations over dynamic storage arrays.

Slightly less prevalent but still frequently observed are vulnerabilities like integer overflows (especially in pre-Solidity 0.8.0 codebases), reentrancy, and insufficient access control (no restricted write). These issues are well-known and widely documented, yet continue to appear in deployed contracts, particularly in forks of existing DeFi projects, amateur deployments, or unaudited NFT contracts. Reentrancy attacks, while not occurring in every vulnerable contract, remain among the most repeated exploit types in the wild due to their high potential payout and relatively low barrier to execution once the vulnerability is identified.

On the other hand, certain Solidity-level bugs like uninitialized state variables, use of tx.origin for authorization, and unprotected selfdestruct commands are much less prevalent in mature codebases. These issues are relatively rare, partly because they are easily caught by security-focused compilers or linters, and partly because awareness around their dangers has improved. Locked Ether scenarios, while not uncommon, tend to arise from poor contract design rather than malicious behavior, and are increasingly avoidable due to modern development practices and improved language features.

At the EVM level, short-address vulnerabilities have largely become obsolete on modern Ethereum mainnet clients and are rarely observed today. However, they may still appear in low-quality or custom client configurations, or in testnet contracts where signature verification or argument decoding is improperly handled. Storage overlap or collision, though uncommon in traditional contracts, is becoming increasingly relevant with the rise of upgradable proxy patterns, especially in complex DeFi protocols where modularity and delegation via delegatecall are standard. These vulnerabilities, while less frequent in general codebases, are much more common in the subset of contracts that employ upgradability and proxy designs.

At the protocol level, transaction ordering dependence (front-running) is one of the most prevalent and persistent risks in production environments. It is especially rampant in DeFi applications, NFT mints, and any contract that involves competitive participation or open mempool interactions. Although less prominent, timestamp dependence still appears regularly in contracts that use block timestamps for randomness or time-based logic, despite long-standing warnings against this practice. Replay vulnerabilities arising from the absence of chain-specific data in signed messages are less widespread but have become more of a concern with the proliferation of L2s and cross-chain bridges, where signing schemes are often reused without adaptation to different chains.

Honeypot contracts occupy a unique place in this analysis. While not traditionally categorized as vulnerabilities, their prevalence has grown substantially, particularly on public testnets and less-regulated networks like Binance Smart Chain. Honeypots are deliberately constructed to exploit user greed and superficial code reviews. They often mimic common bug patterns, like accessible withdraw() functions, while containing hidden logic that prevents actual exploitation. Their growing presence underscores the need for deeper and more adversarial code evaluation, even when apparent bugs seem easy to exploit.

Taken together, this prevalence analysis reveals that the most commonly encountered vulnerabilities are not necessarily the most complex ones, but often the simplest, most human-prone coding mistakes. As the Solidity ecosystem matures, and best practices become more widely adopted, some vulnerabilities have become less prevalent, while new risks tied to protocol complexity and inter-chain communication are beginning to rise in prominence. This underscores the need for continuous education, tooling evolution, and a shift toward proactive rather than reactive security practices.

6.2.4 Impact and Damage

The impact and damage potential of smart contract vulnerabilities vary widely across technical layers, some can lead to complete loss of contract funds or irreversible permission takeovers, while others may cause operational disruption or increase the risk of future exploitation. Understanding the comparative severity of these issues is essential for assessing risk exposure and prioritizing mitigation strategies. Below is a consolidated analysis examining the severity of each vulnerability when exploited, based on historical incidents, theoretical potential, and systemic consequences.

Among Solidity-level vulnerabilities, reentrancy is by far one of the most damaging. When successfully exploited, it can drain entire contract balances, as seen in the infamous DAO hack and repeated copycat attacks across DeFi platforms. Similarly, integer overflow and underflow, especially in versions of Solidity prior to 0.8.0, can result in manipulated balances, bypassed limits, or stolen funds, depending on where arithmetic errors are used in sensitive logic. Both of these issues can cause catastrophic financial loss with little to no warning.

Unprotected self-destruct functions also rank high in impact, despite being relatively rare. If an attacker triggers the self-destruction of a critical contract, the contract's code and data are permanently erased from the blockchain, resulting in an unrecoverable service failure and, in many cases, complete asset loss. Another serious issue is unrestricted write access. If key functions controlling roles, token issuance, withdrawals, or protocol parameters are left unguarded, a malicious user can seize control of the contract. This opens the door to governance manipulation, fund theft, or disabling of core functionality. Use of tx.origin for authorization also poses high risk, as it enables phishing-style attacks where a contract misinterprets the original sender, giving attackers unintended access to protected logic.

Some vulnerabilities cause moderate but still significant damage. For instance, uninitialized state variables can lead to unintended exposure of ownership or misconfigured settings that allow unauthorized interactions. Locked Ether, while not resulting from malicious behavior, causes permanent loss of funds due to faulty fallback functions or missing withdrawal paths. These issues affect usability and financial utility but typically don't compromise protocol security or control. Block gas limit-dependent loops also fall into this category; they can create denial-of-service conditions, freezing contract functionality, or blocking key interactions without causing direct loss of assets.

At the lower end of Solidity-related impact are default visibility, floating pragma versions, and variable shadowing. These tend to result in indirect risk: for instance, a public function that should have been internal may expose sensitive logic, or a mismatched compiler version may introduce subtle differences in behavior. While these issues are unlikely to cause direct damage on their own, they can compound into larger vulnerabilities when combined with other flaws.

Moving into the EVM layer, storage overlap and collision, especially in upgradable proxy architectures, can be extremely destructive. When storage layouts across proxy and logic contracts are misaligned, critical variables such as balances, owner addresses, or function pointers can be overwritten or corrupted. This often results in permanent loss of contract integrity and access. Short address attacks, while mostly outdated, could, under specific conditions, allow argument misalignment, resulting in transfers of funds to unintended recipients or logic branching into unsafe states. However, the practical damage of these today is minimal due to improvements in ABI parsing and transaction validation.

On the blockchain protocol level, front-running vulnerabilities, such as transaction order dependence, remain highly impactful. Attackers can exploit mempool transparency to insert or reorder transactions for profit, often draining liquidity pools, manipulating auction prices, or capturing MEV. Timestamp dependence can enable subtle but effective manipulation of time-based logic, such as reward schedules or lottery outcomes, although its direct damage is usually smaller unless part of a larger exploit. The absence of chain-specific data in signed messages is especially dangerous in multi-chain ecosystems, as it opens up replay attacks that can duplicate valid signatures across networks, resulting in unintended contract interactions and fund movement.

Finally, honeypot contracts represent a deceptive but potent threat. While technically not flawed from the creator's perspective, they are intentionally crafted to appear exploitable while locking users into losing positions. The damage here is more psychological and financial, targeting overconfident users and automated bots. In aggregate, honeypots represent significant economic traps rather than architectural weaknesses, yet their impact on victims can be financially severe.

In summary, the vulnerabilities with the highest impact are those that enable fund theft, contract destruction, or hijacking of control. These include reentrancy, unrestricted writing, storage collisions, and improper use of the selfdestruct function. Moderate-impact vulnerabilities may not compromise entire systems but often disrupt usability, lock funds, or create indirect pathways for exploitation, as seen in issues like timestamp manipulation and locked Ether. Lower-impact flaws, while not immediately dangerous, often enable more serious bugs or gradually weaken the overall integrity of a contract if left unaddressed. This layered understanding forms the foundation for designing secure smart contracts and conducting meaningful security audits.

High-impact vulnerabilities such as reentrancy, storage collisions, and broken access control are especially critical because they often lead to catastrophic financial loss or irreversible contract damage. These types of issues should be treated as top priorities during both development and security review. However, the most frequently encountered vulnerabilities in practice are not always the most severe. Many contracts contain low-severity but widespread issues, such as unchecked external calls, floating pragma versions, and missing visibility modifiers on functions. Although less dramatic in their immediate consequences, these flaws significantly expand the attack surface and contribute to the accumulation of technical debt over time.

The difficulty of detection adds another important layer to the risk assessment. While many language-level vulnerabilities can be effectively identified through static analysis tools, more subtle and context-dependent threats, including front-running, storage layout mismatches in proxy contracts, and deceptive mechanisms such as honeypots, require deeper contextual reasoning, behavioral analysis, and an adversarial mindset. As a result, a sound security strategy cannot depend solely on automation. It must incorporate a comprehensive approach that combines static and dynamic analysis, manual code inspection, and tailored threat modeling based on the contract's logic and use case.

Emerging risks such as cross-chain replay attacks and intentionally misleading contract structures further reflect the growing complexity of the decentralized ecosystem. As smart contracts continue to expand into new domains and use cases, the supporting security infrastructure must evolve in parallel. This evolution depends on stronger educational programs, more rigorous development practices, and a proactive, design-centered approach to security that emphasizes prevention from the outset.

Taken together, this comparative analysis reveals that the most serious threats to smart contract security are not necessarily the most technically complex. Often, they are the ones most easily overlooked during development and auditing. These vulnerabilities typically stem from incorrect assumptions, outdated coding practices, or a limited understanding of Ethereum's execution model. Despite their apparent simplicity, they have been responsible for some of the most damaging and costly exploits in blockchain history. Likewise, the most dangerous vulnerabilities, such as those that grant full control over a contract or cause irreversible logic failure, can often be triggered by a single transaction, leaving no opportunity for recovery. These are not gradual or recoverable issues; they result in immediate and complete breakdowns of trust and functionality.

Therefore, achieving meaningful smart contract security requires more than identifying and fixing surface-level bugs. It calls for a deep and contextual understanding of how contract code interacts with its execution environment and how it may be manipulated by adversarial actors. Developers and auditors must focus not only on frequently occurring vulnerabilities but also on those with the most severe potential impact and structural implications. Only by adopting a comprehensive perspective that accounts for frequency, severity, detectability, and systemic consequences can the Web3 community create secure, reliable decentralized systems capable of withstanding real-world threats.

Vulnerability	Most common	Most dangerous	Real-world example/details
Reentrancy	✓	✓	DAO Hack (2016), Fei Protocol/Rari Capital Hack (2022), Lendf.me Hack (2020) via ERC-777 token reentrancy
Broken access control/ authorization issues	✓	✓	Poly Network Hack (2021), Parity Wallet Hack (2017); access control flaws gave attackers ownership rights
Integer overflow/ underflow	✓	✓	batchOverflow exploit (2018), ProxyOverflow; arithmetic bugs allowed minting of billions of tokens
Unchecked low-level calls (unhandled exceptions)	✓	✓	Failure to check return values in low-level calls can result in stuck funds and partial logic failures
Denial of service (DoS) patterns	✓	✓	King of the ether game DoS, gas limit attacks, self-destruct misuse led to unusable contracts
Front-running and race conditions	✓	×	DEX order sniping, sandwich attacks in liquidity pools; frequent in DeFi without commit-reveal schemes
Unchecked external calls and code injection	×	✓	Malicious delegatecall or plugin usage lets attackers execute arbitrary code in contract context

Vulnerability	Most common	Most dangerous	Real-world example/details
Unprotected self-destruct	×	✓	Parity Multisig Freeze (2017); a user self-destructed the shared library, freezing ~$150 M
Oracle manipulation	×	✓	bZx protocol exploits; manipulated price oracles led to undercollateralized borrowing
Flash loan exploit chains	×	✓	Flash loans used in conjunction with other bugs to drain funds without initial capital (e.g., bZx, harvest)

6.3 Chapter Summary

This chapter provides a comprehensive exploration of vulnerabilities in Ethereum smart contracts, emphasizing the technical, architectural, and environmental factors that contribute to insecure contract behaviors. It begins with an in-depth analysis of how smart contract vulnerabilities arise from the inherent characteristics of Solidity programming, Ethereum's execution model, and blockchain-specific dynamics such as transaction ordering and miner influence. The discussion then categorizes vulnerabilities into language-level issues, virtual machine-level pitfalls, and protocol-level risks, systematically examining phenomena such as reentrancy attacks, unchecked arithmetic operations, broken access control mechanisms, and blockchain-specific exploits like timestamp manipulation and front-running. Real-world incidents, including the DAO attack, the Parity multisig wallet failure, and the Poly Network exploit, are integrated throughout to contextualize the theoretical risks with tangible consequences. Particular emphasis is placed on identifying the most common and most dangerous vulnerabilities, with comparative analysis revealing patterns of frequent developer oversight and highlighting the catastrophic outcomes of authorization flaws and reentrancy weaknesses. Through annotated source code examples, this section bridges conceptual understanding with practical vulnerability recognition, training readers to critically evaluate smart contract logic for subtle but consequential security flaws. By rigorously dissecting both the technical vulnerabilities and the broader security landscape of Ethereum smart contracts, this section equips readers with the analytical skills and cautionary insights necessary to design, implement, and audit smart contracts with heightened security awareness in the complex and adversarial blockchain environment.

References

1. Luu, L., et al.: Making smart contracts smarter. In: Proceedings of the 2016 ACM SIGSAC Conference on Computer and Communications Security (2016)
2. Zhou, S., et al.: SoK: decentralized finance (DeFi) attacks. In: Proceedings of the 44th IEEE Symposium on Security and Privacy (S&P) (2023)

Chapter 7
Real and Potential Smart Contract Threats

Abstract This chapter analyzes the real and potential threats that emerge from smart contract vulnerabilities, showing how flaws at the language, EVM, and architectural levels translate into practical exploit scenarios. It organizes threats into thematic categories, including control flow manipulation, unauthorized access and privilege escalation, state corruption, financial exploits, EVM-level attacks, timing and miner influence, cross-chain and off-chain replay, and deceptive contract behaviors. Each category is illustrated with technical details, for instance, how reentrant withdrawals, unchecked external calls, and cross-function reentrancy repeatedly surface as common threats, while unprotected selfdestructs, storage collisions, and delegated reentrancy pose the most catastrophic risks. Through this dual lens of frequency and severity, it demonstrates that common threats often arise from habitual coding practices, while less frequent but more severe issues can irreversibly destroy functionality, lock funds, or corrupt entire protocols. At the end, this chapter underscores the importance of structured threat modeling, combining defensive coding, rigorous auditing, and architectural foresight to protect decentralized systems against both frequent exploits and rare but devastating failures.

Understanding the security posture of smart contracts requires more than just identifying vulnerabilities; it demands a close examination of the concrete threats those vulnerabilities enable [1, 2]. While vulnerability may appear benign in isolation, it often leads to serious exploits that undermine the reliability, correctness, and safety of contract execution [1, 3]. This chapter explores the diverse range of threats arising from the smart contract vulnerabilities discussed in the previous chapter, illustrating how these flaws can lead to exploitable behaviors, including unauthorized fund transfers, control-flow manipulation, contract destruction, and logic corruption [4, 5]. By unpacking these threats in detail, we provide critical insights into the practical implications of insecure smart contract design [1, 2].

S. HajiHosseinKhani et al., *Understanding Cybersecurity for Smart Contracts*,
https://doi.org/10.1007/978-3-032-28863-9_7

7.1 Exploring the Origins of Threats

As decentralized applications grow in complexity and adoption, smart contracts have become increasingly attractive targets for exploitation [1, 4]. Exploits in smart contracts often stem not only from conventional programming bugs but also from deeper design flaws, execution-environment assumptions, and adversarial interactions that arise in open, permissionless systems [3]. The purpose of this chapter is to systematically examine the major categories of threats that smart contracts face. Rather than focusing solely on individual vulnerabilities, we organize these threats thematically, according to how they disrupt contract behavior, state integrity, financial flows, or execution semantics [6]. For each category, we define the general threat class, explain its technical underpinnings, and illustrate how specific vulnerabilities manifest within it. This structured approach provides a foundational understanding for both developers and security analysts, enabling them to reason more precisely about attack surfaces, anticipate the evolution of threats, and design more resilient decentralized protocols [1, 7].

7.1.1 Control Flow Manipulation

Control Flow Manipulation refers to threats that disrupt the intended execution sequence of a smart contract. These threats exploit flaws in how contract functions handle state updates, external interactions, or looping logic. Unlike traditional programming environments, smart contracts execute deterministically on the blockchain with strict ordering rules. However, their reliance on inter-contract communication and immutable deployment creates opportunities for adversaries to interfere with the control flow, often in ways that are difficult to detect until after exploitation. These manipulations can cause unauthorized function calls, incorrect state transitions, or execution deadlocks, resulting in financial loss, security breaches, or contract paralysis. Understanding these threats is critical because they exploit the very execution model of smart contracts and often require architectural safeguards rather than superficial code fixes [2, 6].

- **Reentrant Execution:** Reentrant execution is a threat in which an external contract reenters a function before the original execution context completes, enabling it to repeatedly invoke vulnerable logic and exploit outdated internal state.
  Reentrancy exploits arise when a smart contract performs an external call to another contract before updating its own critical state variables. If the recipient is a contract with executable code, typically through a fallback() or receive() function, it can call back into the original contract, re-triggering the function that made the call. If the original contract assumes state changes have already been made, this recursive access allows the attacker to perform actions multiple times within the same transaction, often draining funds or bypassing access controls.

A classic example of this threat is a withdrawal function that transfers Ether to a user and then sets their balance to zero [6]. If the Ether recipient is a contract, it can reenter the withdrawal function before the balance is updated, triggering another withdrawal [1]. This loop continues until the contract's funds are exhausted. Another variant is cross-function reentrancy, in which the attacker reenters a different but related function that shares a vulnerable state [5]. In more advanced cases, reentrancy occurs through delegatecall or library inheritance, making the reentrant path less obvious and more difficult to detect through standard auditing.

The risk of reentrant execution persists even in seemingly read-only functions [1]. So-called "read-only reentrancy" occurs when a view function invokes external logic that alters the caller's behavior or other system components. While Solidity now offers some protection, such as checks, effects, and interaction patterns, and the use of reentrancyGuard modifiers, any design that relies on external interaction must be rigorously reviewed for reentrant access points [6]. This threat is commonly associated with vulnerabilities such as: Reentrancy, Unchecked External Call, Unhandled Exceptions, Delegatecall Misuse, and Uninitialized State Variables.

- **Cross-Function Logic Corruption:** Cross-function logic corruption is a threat in which an attacker invokes multiple contract functions in an unintended sequence, exploiting shared state or assumptions across those functions to subvert intended behavior [2, 5].

  This threat arises in contracts that expose several public or external functions that interact with a shared internal state [3]. While each function may appear safe in isolation, their combined use, particularly when invoked from an attacker-controlled context, can result in a logic flow that violates contract assumptions. The vulnerability lies in the assumption that function calls occur in a predictable sequence or that critical values are only modified through a specific pathway.

  For instance, consider a token contract where one function updates a user's balance while another issues a reward based on the same balance. If the reward function is called during a transaction that has not yet completed its balance updates, the attacker can inflate the rewards received by calling the functions out of order. In contracts with withdrawal, refund, or approval logic, the ability to exploit race conditions or incomplete state transitions across function boundaries can lead to loss of funds or permanent corruption of internal records.

  This form of logic corruption becomes even more severe when combined with proxy contracts, delegatecalls, or reentrant pathways. If an attacker can call into a separate contract (e.g., a plugin or delegate) that, in turn, invokes multiple interfaces of the original contract, the boundaries between functions blur, allowing tightly coupled state logic to be exploited within a modular or upgradable architecture. This threat is commonly associated with vulnerabilities such as Reentrancy, Variable Shadowing, No Restricted Write, and broken access control.
- **Infinite or Early Termination of Logic:** Infinite or early termination of logic is a threat where a contract's execution flow is either trapped in an unresolvable

loop or prematurely terminated due to logic corruption, allowing attackers to bypass important conditions or disrupt contract functionality [5].

Ethereum imposes a block-level gas limit on transaction execution, thereby creating an implicit upper bound on the amount of computation a contract can perform. If a contract contains loops that scale with dynamic data structures, such as arrays of users, validators, or token holders, then as these structures grow, the gas required to complete the loop increases. When the cost exceeds the block gas limit, the transaction fails. Attackers can exploit this by intentionally inflating data structures (e.g., registering thousands of addresses), causing loops to become uncallable and disabling core contract features such as reward distribution or governance voting.
Conversely, underflows in counters or premature logic exits can cause early termination. For example, if a loop is based on a counter that silently wraps to zero due to arithmetic underflow, it may exit immediately, skipping critical validations or allowing unauthorized access. Such flaws may also emerge in time-sensitive contracts, where miscalculated timeouts or block intervals allow actions to complete before intended preconditions are met.
In governance, DeFi, or auction systems, where deterministic progression is essential, disruption of loop behavior can halt participation, create unfair advantages, or render the contract inoperative. These threats are particularly dangerous in autonomous contracts that lack administrative override mechanisms. This threat is commonly associated with vulnerabilities such as: Integer Overflow/Underflow, Block Gas Limit Dependent Loops, Timestamp Dependence, and Logic Misconfiguration.

7.1.2 Control Flow Manipulation

Unauthorized Access and Privilege Escalation refer to a class of threats where an attacker gains the ability to perform actions that should be restricted to trusted entities, such as contract owners, administrators, or privileged roles. In the decentralized environment of smart contracts, where code is the sole gatekeeper of permissions, a single misconfiguration can allow attackers to seize administrative control, hijack upgrade mechanisms, or manipulate funds and contract behavior [5, 6]. These threats are especially severe because they do not always require traditional exploits; instead, they emerge from flawed assumptions about identity, trust boundaries, or visibility of sensitive functions. Once an attacker escalates privileges, they can typically bypass all other layers of security, making this category among the most dangerous in smart contract systems.

- **Access Control Bypass via Misused Identifiers:** Access control bypass via misused identifiers occurs when a smart contract uses improper identity checks, such as relying on tx.origin instead of msg.sender, thereby enabling attackers to manipulate the call context and gain unauthorized access to privileged functionality.

This threat arises from a misunderstanding of how Ethereum's transaction propagation works. While msg.sender correctly identifies the immediate caller of a function, tx.origin refers to the externally owned account (EOA) that originated the entire transaction chain. Developers may mistakenly use tx.origin for authorization checks, assuming it reflects the user's identity interacting with the contract. Any intermediary contract invoked in the transaction path can relay calls while preserving tx.origin, allowing attackers to insert themselves in the middle and impersonate trusted accounts.

A common attack scenario involves deploying a malicious contract that invokes the vulnerable contract on the target user's behalf. If the victim is tricked into initiating a transaction, perhaps by interacting with a malicious dApp front-end, the attacker's contract can relay this call to the vulnerable contract. Because tx.origin remains the victim's address, the vulnerable contract assumes the call is trustworthy and permits execution of privileged functions such as fund transfers, ownership changes, or configuration updates. This is effectively a form of on-chain phishing, where the attack succeeds without any flaws in the function logic, only in the identity check mechanism.

The threat is magnified in systems with composable or upgradable architectures. If one module uses tx.origin for authentication, attackers can chain multiple calls through proxies, libraries, or plugins to manipulate access checks. The resulting escalation may allow an attacker to operate across a complex dApp environment under the guise of a legitimate user, bypassing even correctly designed access modifiers in other modules. This threat is commonly associated with vulnerabilities such as: Broken Access Control (Use of tx.origin), Misconfiguration via External Input, and Insecure Authentication Logic.

- **Public Exposure of Administrative Functions:** Public exposure of administrative functions is a threat where functions intended for internal or privileged use, such as initialization, upgrade, or configuration routines, are left publicly accessible, enabling anyone to invoke them and seize control over the contract [6].

  In Solidity, if a developer fails to explicitly specify a function's visibility, it defaults too public. Similarly, if a function lacks a proper access control modifier (such as onlyOwner), it becomes callable by any user on the network. These mistakes frequently affect deployment-time setup functions like initOwner() or configureSystem(), which are meant to be executed once and only by the deployer. If left exposed, attackers monitoring the blockchain can immediately invoke these functions upon deployment, often faster than the legitimate owner, granting themselves administrative privileges before the intended initialization occurs.

  Even more insidiously, public exposure of helpers or utility functions can indirectly allow attackers to bypass access controls. For example, a function that updates a whitelist, sets token emission rates, or changes oracle endpoints may not appear critical in isolation. But if such a function influences the behavior of privileged operations or financial flows, its exposure becomes a vector for control. Once an attacker takes over these functions, they can manipulate reward mechanisms, redirect funds, or introduce systemic logic changes to facilitate future exploitation.

In upgradable contracts or modular systems, exposed administrative functions can lead to catastrophic consequences. If an upgrade proxy's logic contract exposes upgradeTo() or setImplementation() without proper gating, attackers can point the proxy to a malicious contract, effectively hijacking all calls and funds passing through it. The ability to rewire the contract's behavior without touching the proxy interface makes such takeovers difficult to detect and nearly impossible to recover from. This threat is commonly associated with vulnerabilities such as: Default Visibility, No Restricted Write, Uninitialized State Variables, and Improper Initialization Logic.

- **Misconfiguration via External Input:** Misconfiguration via external input is a threat in which a smart contract accepts user-provided parameters, such as addresses, roles, or references to other contracts, without proper validation, allowing attackers to inject malicious or unintended logic into the system.

  Modern smart contracts often rely on user-supplied parameters to define modular behavior. For instance, contracts may allow users to register new strategy modules, plugin addresses, or governance delegates. While this flexibility is essential for composability and extensibility, it introduces significant risk when the inputs are not strictly validated. A malicious user can supply addresses that point to rogue contracts designed to hijack execution, intercept funds, or rewrite logic via delegatecall.

  One common example is the use of unverified contract addresses for delegated logic. If a system allows users to specify a contract to be executed via delegatecall, and that contract has not been vetted or interface-checked, the call will execute in the caller contract's storage context. An attacker can create a malicious contract that, when called, overwrites critical variables, such as ownership, balances, or configuration flags. If the input is unchecked, this results in a complete compromise of the calling contract.

  Misconfiguration can also occur when parameters control economic logic, such as interest rates, thresholds, or reward calculations. Without bounds checking, users may supply arbitrarily large or small values to manipulate protocol behavior. For example, setting an emission rate to an excessively high value could drain contract reserves, while lowering the threshold might grant access to functions prematurely or to unauthorized parties.

  In more subtle cases, misconfiguration arises from failing to enforce uniqueness, mutability, or proper sequencing in user-supplied data. If a system allows repeated overwriting of configuration entries or fails to lock critical parameters after initialization, attackers can iteratively manipulate state, gradually gaining leverage within the system. This threat is commonly associated with vulnerabilities such as: No Restricted Write, Unchecked External Call, Broken Access Control, and Delegatecall Misuse.

7.1.3 State Corruption and Inconsistencies

Smart contracts operate with immutable logic but mutable storage, and the correctness of that storage is fundamental to their reliability. The category of State Corruption and Inconsistencies encompasses threats that compromise the internal storage layout, disrupt data integrity, or cause contradictions in the contract's logic due to unexpected writes, uninitialized variables, or silent failures. These threats typically arise from improper assumptions about memory safety, variable isolation, or call behavior. While not always exploitable in isolation, state corruption is often the underlying enabler of more serious attacks, making it especially insidious. Since blockchain-based contracts cannot easily roll back or reset corrupted state, even a single incident of inconsistency can cause permanent contract dysfunction, economic imbalance, or governance failure.

- **Storage Collisions in Upgradeable Systems:** Storage collisions in upgradeable systems occur when different versions of a contract, or modules sharing execution context, accidentally map variables to the same storage slot, causing one variable's data to overwrite another's [2].
  In Ethereum, smart contract storage is a flat key-value store indexed by slot numbers determined at compile time. Upgradeable contracts separate logic and storage across two or more components, often using a proxy pattern in which the proxy holds storage and delegates logic to an implementation contract. For this delegation to function correctly, the logic contract must assume the exact same variable layout as the proxy. If the order or type of variables is changed in the implementation, such as inserting a new variable at the top or rearranging existing ones, this can lead to storage collisions: different variables occupying the same slot and unintentionally overwriting each other.
  This corruption is particularly dangerous because it rarely causes immediate reverts or visible errors. Instead, contracts begin behaving unpredictably, ownership might disappear, boolean flags might change, balances might reset or overflow, and access control gates might silently open or close. These issues are especially hard to trace because the deployed bytecode may appear intact, and function calls may return to being plausible but incorrect results. In more severe cases, a single collision during an upgrade can permanently disable an entire protocol, misdirect funds, or allow privilege escalation through corrupted roles.
  The problem becomes more complex in systems that use multiple inheritance, especially in older versions of Solidity. The compiler uses a deterministic but non-obvious ordering strategy (C3 linearization) to allocate storage for inherited contracts. If a developer unknowingly reuses variable names across inheritance branches or introduces new state variables in later versions, collisions become likely, especially if the upgrade path is not explicitly tracked with storage layout tooling. This threat is commonly associated with vulnerabilities such as: Storage Overlap/Collision, Delegatecall Misuse, and Uninitialized State Variables.
- **Invalid State Transitions due to Silent Failures:** Invalid state transitions due to silent failures occur when a contract continues execution based on the false

assumption that an external call or operation succeeded, resulting in a state that diverges from the intended logic.

In Solidity, certain low-level functions, such as call, send, and delegatecall, return a boolean indicating success but do not revert automatically. If a developer fails to check this return value, the contract may proceed as if the operation succeeded, even though it failed. This creates a dangerous mismatch between the perceived and actual contract state. For example, a payment function might attempt to send Ether to a recipient, fail due to out-of-gas in the recipient's fallback, but still mark the user as "paid." The result is loss of funds, broken accounting, or unfulfilled contractual obligations.

Such silent failures also occur in multi-step operations or workflows where intermediate steps can fail but are not explicitly handled. For instance, a contract that distributes rewards to a list of users via a loop may fail to transfer rewards to a single recipient. If that failure is ignored, the remaining recipients might receive incorrect amounts, or the total distributed value might diverge from expectations. These inconsistencies can cascade into further miscalculations in staking systems, DAOs, or voting mechanisms, especially when relying on automated scripts or oracles.

A more subtle manifestation of this threat occurs when exceptions are thrown in fallback functions, delegate calls, or external plugins. If the calling contract does not catch the failure, it may continue with corrupted data or skip essential security logic. In complex systems with upgradeable or modular components, unhandled exceptions in one module can cause incorrect outcomes in another, particularly when error handling relies on specific revert patterns or return values. This threat is commonly associated with vulnerabilities such as: Unchecked External Call, Unhandled Exceptions, Fallback Function Misuse, and Delegatecall Misuse.

- **Corruption of Critical Variables:** Corruption of critical variables is a threat where contract state is altered incorrectly, either through misused local storage references, uninitialized variables, or logic errors, causing unintended overwrites of important contract data.

  Solidity distinguishes between memory and storage, and mistakes in referencing one instead of the other can lead to serious data corruption. A common error is declaring a storage reference (e.g., SomeStruct storage data) without properly assigning it. This causes the variable to default to storage slot 0, where the most sensitive variables (e.g., owner, balances, or configuration flags) are often stored. Operations on such a reference then overwrite legitimate data in those slots, effectively destroying the original contract state.

  Similarly, variables that are declared but not initialized can behave unexpectedly. In Solidity, uninitialized state variables default to zero, false, or address(0). If a developer forgets to explicitly assign ownership or access control roles at deployment, these roles may remain unset. If an attacker invokes an exposed initialization function before the rightful owner does, they can gain full control over the

contract. This kind of takeover can be executed silently, often without triggering any alarms or errors.
Variable corruption can also arise from incorrect scoping, such as variable shadowing, where a local variable masks a state variable of the same name. The local variable is updated during execution, while the actual state remains unchanged. This results in logic that appears correct during function execution but fails to persist, breaking contract invariants and creating opportunities for exploitation.
In proxy contracts and upgradable systems, corruption may occur when delegatecalls are made to contracts with different assumptions about the storage layout. Any variable mismatch can overwrite access roles, token balances, or system flags, undermining the entire contract's security model. This threat is commonly associated with vulnerabilities such as: Variable Shadowing, Uninitialized State Variables, No Restricted Write, and Storage Overlap/Collision.

7.1.4 Financial Exploits and Asset Loss

Financial Exploits and Asset Loss represent a critical category of threats in which adversaries exfiltrate, redirect, or irreversibly lock funds controlled by a smart contract. These threats strike at the economic integrity of decentralized systems, often with immediate and devastating consequences. Unlike traditional software bugs, failures in financial logic on the blockchain cannot be patched after the fact or reversed through centralized intervention. As a result, even a small logic flaw, if exploitable, can result in the complete depletion of a contract's assets, disruption of token economies, or loss of user trust. This category includes both active exploits, such as draining funds via logic abuse, and passive flaws, such as those that permanently freeze or destroy assets due to misconfiguration.

- **Unauthorized Fund Transfer or Minting:** Unauthorized fund transfer or minting occurs when a contract allows unprivileged users to issue, transfer, or claim assets without appropriate authorization checks or arithmetic safeguards.
  This threat often stems from overlooked arithmetic flaws such as integer overflows or underflows, particularly in Solidity versions prior to 0.8.0, where arithmetic operations did not automatically revert. For example, if a user's balance is stored as a uint256 and a subtraction operation underflows due to insufficient balance, the result wraps around to an extremely large number. This may allow the user to send or approve tokens they do not possess, effectively fabricating funds.
  Similarly, flawed minting logic, especially in custom token contracts, may calculate the amount to mint based on unsafe or user-controlled input. Without bound checks or validation of the caller's role, an attacker can exploit this to mint excessive tokens and dump them on the market, causing inflation, devaluation, or disruption of collateral ratios in DeFi ecosystems.

Other manifestations include incorrect or missing role checks around administrative functions. For instance, if the mint() or transferFrom() function lacks proper onlyOwner, onlyMinter, or ERC20 allowance logic, anyone may invoke it freely. Additionally, in batch operations, failure to validate input arrays or enforce aggregate limits can result in the contract processing of unintended transfers of massive scale.

This threat has a long history of real-world impact, from early ERC20 implementation bugs to recent DeFi protocols losing millions due to unchecked mint functions, faulty decimals configuration, or reward miscalculations. Even contracts audited for logical correctness can succumb to subtle fund-creation errors if assumptions about integer arithmetic, authorization, or safe math behavior are violated. This threat is commonly associated with vulnerabilities such as: Integer Overflow/Underflow, No Restricted Write, Default Visibility, and Broken Access Control.

- **Draining via Multiple Withdrawals:** Draining via multiple withdrawals is a threat in which an attacker exploits repeated access to a withdrawal function, typically through recursive logic or race conditions, to extract more funds than they are entitled to.

  This threat is most famously associated with reentrancy attacks. A vulnerable contract may transfer Ether or tokens to the caller before updating internal records of their balance or state. If the recipient is a contract with an active fallback function, it can recursively call back into the withdrawal function before its balance is updated, allowing multiple withdrawals in a single transaction loop. Each recursive call is based on stale state, leading to repeated disbursements until the contract's funds are depleted.

  Beyond reentrancy, multiple withdrawals may occur due to double-spend race conditions or inadequate replay protection. For instance, a poorly designed rewards function may issue tokens based on a user's current balance without recording that rewards have already been claimed. If no timestamp, claim counter, or nonce is stored, the user may call the function repeatedly to accrue rewards indefinitely.

  In some cases, the issue may be triggered by multi-block logic, where a contract updates user balances across multiple blocks but fails to finalize intermediate states. This allows an attacker to observe transitional states and exploit the timing window to double-dip into assets.

  The consequences of this threat are typically catastrophic: contracts lose their Ether or token reserves, attackers exit with profit, and even if patched, the stolen funds remain unrecoverable due to blockchain immutability. This threat is commonly associated with vulnerabilities such as: Reentrancy, Unchecked External Call, Uninitialized State Variables, and Fallback Function Misuse.
- **Locked Ether (Permanent Fund Inaccessibility):** Locked Ether refers to a condition in which Ether held by a contract becomes permanently inaccessible due to missing or unreachable withdrawal logic, broken access controls, or destruction of required execution paths.

This threat does not involve an active attacker in most cases but arises from architectural oversight or logic omission. A contract may be marked as payable, enabling it to receive Ether, but lack any withdraw(), transfer(), or external call function to release those funds. Alternatively, the withdrawal function may be present but contain a logic flaw or a guard condition that is never satisfied, for instance, by requiring a specific address or timestamp that is unreachable due to prior state corruption or misconfiguration.

A notorious case of this was the 2017 Parity multisig wallet incident, in which a shared library was accidentally self-destructed, rendering all dependent wallets unusable. Although the wallets still held Ether, they had no logic left to execute a withdrawal, making the funds permanently locked.

Inheritance issues can also cause Ether to be locked if a child contract overrides a valid withdrawal function from a parent contract but leaves it empty or inoperable. Likewise, misuse of access control can render withdrawals impossible if the only authorized address is lost or if the contract requires permission from a self-destructed contract.

This threat is especially serious because it causes irreversible loss even without external exploitation. Users may continue to send Ether to the contract, unaware that it is unrecoverable. Moreover, locked funds inflate the perceived total supply of usable assets, causing market imbalances, governance problems, or unfair reward distributions in ecosystem-wide protocols. This threat is commonly associated with vulnerabilities such as: Locked Ether, Unprotected Self-destruct, Uninitialized State Variables, and Access Control Misconfiguration.

- **Self-Destruction for Theft or Griefing:** Self-destruction for theft or griefing is a threat where a contract is permanently removed from the blockchain via the selfdestruct opcode, either to steal funds by redirecting residual balances or to sabotage contract logic and availability.

  Solidity provides the selfdestruct(address) function as a low-level way to remove contract bytecode from the blockchain and, optionally, forward any remaining Ether to a specified address. If this function is exposed without strict access control, any user may call it, thereby terminating the contract's existence. Once self-destructed, the contract becomes a hollow shell: its storage is preserved, but all logic is erased, making all function calls revert.

  In financially motivated cases, an attacker may exploit this by destroying the contract and specifying their own address as the Ether recipient. In other cases, the destruction is carried out solely to disrupt service or disable functionality. This is especially dangerous in shared library systems, where one contract provides logic to many dependent contracts via delegatecall. If the library is destroyed, all dependent contracts lose access to that logic and become unusable, even if their individual security is intact.

  Such an incident occurred in the Parity wallet example mentioned earlier, where an unauthorized user's deletion of a shared logic contract disabled over $150 million in assets across all linked multisig wallets.

Griefing variants of this attack are even more pernicious in DAO settings or adversarial environments, where users destroy contracts not for personal gain, but to cause reputational or economic harm to a competing protocol. Test contracts accidentally deployed to mainnet with exposed selfdestruct() functions are frequent targets for such attacks. This threat is commonly associated with vulnerabilities such as: Unprotected Self-destruct, No Restricted Write, Delegatecall Misuse, and Initialization Errors.

7.1.5 Execution Environment and EVM-Level Exploits

Execution Environment and EVM-Level Exploits refer to threats arising from the nuanced behavior of the Ethereum Virtual Machine (EVM), low-level data encoding standards, and inter-contract execution [8]. Unlike traditional logic flaws, these threats are not always visible in high-level Solidity code; they emerge at the bytecode, ABI, or delegatecall layers, where attackers can exploit improper assumptions about memory layout, function interfaces, or execution context. These exploits are often subtle, deeply technical, and difficult to detect in static analysis. However, when triggered, they can result in total compromise of storage, control flow, or contract logic. This category underscores the importance of understanding the EVM's internal workings when designing and auditing smart contracts.

- **Short Address Encoding Exploit:** The short address encoding exploit occurs when a smart contract misinterprets improperly padded input data due to Ethereum ABI misalignment, leading to unintended manipulation of function parameters, especially in transfer and approval functions.
  The Ethereum Application Binary Interface (ABI) expects all function arguments to be padded to 32-byte slots. For example, an address parameter should be encoded as 32 bytes, with the first 12 bytes as zero padding, followed by the 20-byte address. However, if an attacker submits a transaction with a "short" address, say 19 or 20 bytes instead of the full 32, the contract may parse subsequent arguments incorrectly. The function selector remains valid, but the offsets of all subsequent arguments shift, causing the next parameter (often a token amount) to be read from the wrong positions in calldata.
  In a typical transfer(address to, uint256 amount) function, if the address is truncated by even one byte, the most significant byte of the amount field is interpreted as part of the to address, and the remaining bytes are shifted left. This could transform a small transfer (e.g., 1 token) into an enormous one (e.g., 2^248 tokens), depending on how the ABI decodes the data. If the contract does not perform length checks or input validation, the attack succeeds without violating any Solidity-level assumptions.
  While many modern clients and libraries (e.g., Web3.js, Ethers.js, and Solidity itself) perform input-length validation by default, this vulnerability persists in custom interfaces, low-level calls, or hand-crafted calldata, especially in early-stage or forked networks that reuse legacy contract code. Moreover, contracts

using assembly or calldata parsing logic are particularly vulnerable if they do not explicitly enforce argument lengths.
The short-address exploit reveals the fragility of low-level trust assumptions in EVM-based systems: even minor deviations in input formatting can lead to disproportionate and dangerous behavior. This threat is commonly associated with vulnerabilities such as: Short Address, ABI Misinterpretation, and Unchecked External Input.

- **Delegatecall-Based Hijacking:** Delegatecall-based hijacking occurs when a smart contract executes external logic using delegatecall to a user-controlled or malicious contract, resulting in unauthorized modification of the caller's storage.

  The delegatecall opcode is used in Solidity to execute code from another contract while preserving the calling contract's storage context. This is a foundational mechanism in upgradeable proxy patterns, in which the proxy delegates execution to an implementation contract while retaining its own data. However, if the contract being called is not fully trusted or its address is modifiable, delegatecall becomes a powerful attack vector.
  For example, a contract may allow users or administrators to specify which logic module to execute. If the address is not validated, an attacker can deploy a malicious contract with logic that, when executed via delegatecall, modifies variables in the caller's storage, such as overwriting the owner, resetting balances, enabling unauthorized withdrawals, or disabling safeties. Since the attacker's contract's storage layout can be tailored to align with sensitive storage slots in the victim, the damage is deterministic and targeted.
  Delegate-call-based attacks are especially dangerous in proxy systems, since a malicious upgrade can silently replace trusted logic with compromised bytecode. In some designs, even a single exposed upgradeTo() or configuration setter without role checks is enough for attackers to permanently take over the proxy. Once hijacked, the proxy can be configured to point to malicious code that operates identically to the original interface, thereby masking the takeover.
  Additionally, if the logic contract itself is deleted or replaced with malformed code, the proxy's behavior becomes undefined, often breaking the entire system. Because delegatecall executes in the caller's context, the boundaries between contracts disappear, and the full trust surface shifts to the integrity of the delegate target. This threat is commonly associated with vulnerabilities such as: Delegatecall Misuse, No Restricted Write, Storage Overlap/Collision, and Public Exposure of Administrative Functions.

7.1.6 *Timing and Miner Influence Attacks*

Timing and Miner Influence Attacks exploit the fact that miners, or block producers in general, have partial control over when and how transactions are executed [9]. These threats leverage block-level parameters, such as timestamps, block numbers, and transaction ordering, to manipulate contract logic to the attacker's benefit. Smart contracts often rely on on-chain timing or assume fair transaction sequencing, but the reality of decentralized networks is that miners (or validators) can influence these factors to varying degrees. When contracts depend on these manipulable values for critical decisions, such as random number generation, auction deadlines, or price feeds, they become vulnerable to attacks that can skew outcomes, extract unfair profits, or front-run users. This category highlights the importance of designing smart contracts that are resilient to the nondeterministic and adversarial timing environment of blockchain execution.

- **Timestamp Manipulation:** Timestamp manipulation is a threat where miners or validators adjust the block timestamp to influence the outcome of smart contracts that rely on block.timestamp for time-sensitive logic.
  The block.timestamp variable provides the time declared by the block producer; while it must be close to the actual time, this is not strictly enforced. Ethereum allows the timestamp to be manipulated within a ~15-s window of expected block time, and even larger deviations are possible in low-activity networks or during reorgs. Contracts that depend on exact timing, such as lotteries, bidding phases, interest accrual, or reward unlocks, are vulnerable if they use block.timestamp for logic enforcement.
  For example, consider a contract that uses block.timestamp as a seed for pseudo-random number generation. A miner observing the mempool can delay or reorder blocks slightly to ensure a favorable result. Similarly, in auctions that close at a specific timestamp, a miner might insert a late bid by artificially setting the block time slightly earlier, accepting a bid that should have expired. Conversely, miners can *prematurely* close auctions or investment rounds by incrementing the timestamp just enough to meet a contract's timeout condition, effectively excluding legitimate participants.
  In staking systems or vesting schedules, timestamp manipulation can alter when rewards are unlocked or when slashing conditions apply. Malicious actors can force premature reward harvesting or delay penalties by exploiting block time drift. While block.timestamp remains a widely used primitive for tracking time in Solidity, developers must be cautious when using it in critical branches of logic. Alternatives such as block.number (for approximate time tracking) or off-chain verification are sometimes preferred, depending on the threat model. This threat is commonly associated with vulnerabilities such as Timestamp Dependence, Block Gas Limit Dependent Loops, and Randomness Misuse.
- **Front-Running and Transaction Reordering:** Front-running and transaction reordering are threats where a miner or a well-positioned network observer anticipates a profitable transaction and inserts their own transaction before it in the block, changing the outcome in their favor.

  Ethereum transactions are visible in the mempool before they are mined. This transparency enables any observer, including miners, bots, or MEV (Miner Extractable Value) agents, to analyze pending transactions and exploit the order in which they are executed. Front-running typically involves observing a transac-

tion that will move the market state, such as a large token swap on a DEX, and submitting a competing transaction with higher gas fees to be executed first. This allows the attacker to buy a token at a lower price before the target transaction increases its price, or to sell before a large dump drives it down.
In a more advanced variant, known as a sandwich attack, the attacker placed two transactions: one before and one after the victims. The first raises the price (buy), the victim buys at the inflated price, and the attacker then sells at the now even higher price. The victim receives fewer tokens for their trade, while the attacker profits from the price spread. Miners, due to their power to determine transaction order within a block, can perform such strategies without racing in the mempool. They can also censor or delay specific transactions, especially in bribe-based or private relayer systems, ensuring only their arbitrage transaction is executed.
The impact of front-running is especially severe in financial primitives such as AMMs, lending pools, limit order books, and oracle update systems. It undermines fairness, erodes user trust, and leads to extractive behavior that drains value from users. Transaction reordering also affects governance votes, DAO execution queues, and timed events where call order determines outcomes. This threat is commonly associated with vulnerabilities such as: Transaction Order Dependence (Front-Running), Absence of Commit-Reveal Schemes, and Miner Extractable Value (MEV) Exploits.

7.1.7 Cross-Chain and Off-Chain Signature Replay

Cross-Chain and Off-Chain Signature Replay encompasses threats in which signed messages intended for one context, such as a specific chain, contract, or execution session, are maliciously reused in another. These exploits stem from weak or missing contextual binding in cryptographic signatures, allowing attackers to repurpose legitimate authorizations in unintended environments. As smart contract ecosystems increasingly rely on off-chain signatures for gasless interactions, meta-transactions, cross-chain bridges, and delegated approvals, this class of threats has grown in significance. Without strict domain separation and inclusion of contextual data (e.g., chain ID, nonce, contract address), signed messages can become portable tokens of authority, open to abuse across systems or networks. This category highlights the vital importance of binding signatures to the specific environment in which they are intended to operate.

- **Signature Replay on Multiple Chains:** Signature replay on multiple chains occurs when a valid off-chain signature generated for a transaction on one blockchain is reused on a different blockchain where the same contract (or one with compatible logic) also exists, enabling unauthorized execution.
  In Ethereum-based systems, off-chain signatures are frequently used to approve operations without incurring gas costs, such as through permit() functions (as in EIP-2612), meta-transactions, or multisig coordination. These signatures typi-

cally cover the operation being authorized and include metadata like nonces and deadlines. However, unless the message explicitly includes the chainId or is domain-separated via mechanisms like EIP-712, the same signature can be valid on any chain where the verifying contract exists at the same address or operates with similar logic.

For instance, if a user signs a permit() message to authorize a token spend on Ethereum mainnet, and the same token contract exists on a testnet or Layer-2 network (deployed to the same address and using the same domain parameters), an attacker can replay the signature to authorize a spend there as well. This is especially dangerous when assets are bridged across chains and the contracts on either side are intended to act independently. A legitimate signature on one network may unintentionally unlock funds on another, creating cross-chain leakage of authority.

Replay attacks can also occur when a contract is cloned or forked with the same interface but with different ownership logic. If the verifying code does not bind the signature to a specific deployment environment, any valid signature becomes reusable across deployments. Attackers can exploit this to drain wallets, mint tokens, or access privileged functions under the guise of valid authorization.

Defenses require explicit domain separation: the signature should include the chainId, the verifyingContract address, and, optionally, additional metadata that ties it to a particular use case. Standards such as EIP-712 and EIP-4337 address these concerns, but custom implementations often omit such protections, leaving them vulnerable. This threat is commonly associated with vulnerabilities such as: Absence of Chain-Specific Data in Signed Messages, Weak Meta-Transaction Verification, and Signature Replay Across Domains.

7.1.8 Deceptive Contract Behavior

Deceptive Contract Behavior refers to threats where a smart contract is intentionally designed to mislead users, auditors, or automated tools by presenting benign-looking logic while hiding malicious or trap-laden functionality [10]. Unlike bugs or oversights, these threats are deliberately engineered to exploit user trust or expectations. Such contracts often pass static and formal analysis by embedding subtle divergences between what the code appears to do and what it does under certain conditions. These behaviors are most often employed in scams, rug pulls, or bait-and-switch schemes and are especially dangerous because they exploit not only code vulnerabilities but also human psychology and interface assumptions. In decentralized environments where contracts are permissionless and pseudonymous, deceptive behaviors have become increasingly sophisticated, requiring scrutiny and behavior-based analysis.

- **Honeypot Contracts:** Honeypot contracts are deceptive smart contracts that appear exploitable, often by mimicking a known vulnerability, but include hidden logic that traps or penalizes anyone attempting to exploit them.
  These contracts are crafted to appear vulnerable, typically to bugs like unrestricted withdrawals, reentrancy, or unchecked permissions. An attacker analyzing the bytecode or interface may conclude that funds can be stolen or that privileges can be escalated. Encouraged by the seemingly open attack surface, the attacker deploys an exploit transaction, but instead of succeeding, they trigger a trap. The contract may immediately revert, blacklist the sender, consume excessive gas, or even execute logic that confiscates the attacker's own tokens or sends them to the contract creator.
  A common honeypot pattern is a withdraw() function that checks for a specific condition that appears unmet but, under execution (e.g., via an obfuscated internal call or assembly logic), always causes a revert unless the call originates from a whitelisted address. Another trick involves dynamic storage modifications: the contract appears to update balances or permissions but uses custom modifiers or hooks that undo the change at the last moment. Honeypots can also exploit quirks in EVM behavior, such as non-standard return values, misleading event emissions, or runtime code that differs from creation code. In some cases, contracts emit logs indicating success even though funds are never actually transferred, misleading bots or traders who rely on event monitoring.
  The goal of honeypots is typically to lure malicious actors, especially bots and front-runners, into revealing themselves or sacrificing capital. While ethically ambiguous, some honeypots are used for white-hat purposes (e.g., research or bot deterrence), while others are used maliciously to trick retail users into believing they're participating in a high-return opportunity. Because honeypots exploit human expectations and tool limitations, they pose a unique threat: even expert reviewers may overlook embedded deception if the contract passes basic interface checks or if the behavior is encoded through indirect logic paths. This threat is commonly associated with vulnerabilities such as Broken Access Control, Unchecked External Call, Default Visibility, and Logic Bombs Hidden in Obfuscated Code.
  The taxonomy of smart contract threats outlined in Fig. 7.1 provides a comprehensive, structured lens for understanding the diverse, evolving risks in decentralized systems. By organizing threats into categories, such as Control Flow Manipulation, Unauthorized Access and Privilege Escalation, State Corruption and Inconsistencies, Financial Exploits and Asset Loss, Execution Environment and EVM-Level Exploits, Timing and Miner Influence Attacks, Cross-Chain and Off-Chain Signature Replay, and Deceptive Contract Behavior, we uncover not only the individual vectors of exploitation but also the broader design weaknesses and systemic patterns they reflect [1, 4]. Each threat, while distinct in its mechanics, ultimately stems from assumptions about trust, determinism, and isolation in a permissionless execution model. Together, these threats reveal the multidimensional nature of smart contract insecurity, in which logic flaws, interface misuse, low-level encoding errors, and adversarial timing all intersect. A

Fig. 7.1 Smart contracts threats

robust security posture in smart contract development thus demands not only code correctness but architectural foresight, adversarial modeling, and a nuanced understanding of blockchain execution dynamics. As the ecosystem matures, threat models evolve to anticipate and mitigate both technical exploits and behavioral deception embedded in smart contract logic.

7.2 Comparative Analysis

This section provides a comparative analysis of smart contract threats by distinguishing between those most encountered in practice and those most dangerous in terms of potential impact. While certain threats arise across many contracts due to ingrained development patterns or systemic oversights, others, though less frequent, can cause irreversible failures and catastrophic losses. By analyzing these threats through the dual lenses of prevalence and severity, we can better understand where the greatest risks lie and how to prioritize security efforts. This analysis draws on the taxonomy established in earlier sections and synthesizes observations from both historical exploits and patterns seen in modern decentralized systems.

7.2.1 Most Common Threats

Among the most observed threats in smart contract ecosystems are Reentrant Withdrawals, Cross-Function Reentrancy, and Unchecked External Calls. These threats persist across generations of codebases and contract types, in part because they arise from intuitive yet unsafe development practices and are difficult to detect with surface-level testing alone.

Reentrant Withdrawals remain a widespread threat because developers frequently rely on external calls to transfer assets. This threat arises when a contract sends funds to an external address before properly updating its own internal state. The infamous DAO attack in 2016 exemplified this vulnerability, allowing an attacker to repeatedly re-enter the withdrawal function and drain millions of Ethers. Since then, the same pattern has reappeared in countless DeFi protocols, especially in staking systems, escrow contracts, and yield aggregators. Developers often assume that once a transfer is initiated, execution continues linearly, but in Ethereum, external calls serve as entry points that enable attackers to regain control mid-function unless carefully guarded.

Cross-Function Reentrancy builds on this same principle but involves more subtle interactions between functions. In modular contract designs, multiple externally callable functions often share state. If reentry occurs during one function and leads to a second function operating on the same data without checks, critical invariants can be broken. This pattern frequently surfaces in token contracts and DAOs, where administrative or financial actions are split across multiple functions that fail to coordinate access. Despite the increasing use of mutexes and ReentrancyGuard patterns, developers still underestimate how external execution paths can weave through supposedly independent code segments.

Unchecked External Calls are another pervasive source of security issues. When contracts use low-level functions such as call, send, or delegatecall and fail to check the return value, they create conditions in which failures are silently ignored. Developers often assume these calls will revert to error, but many simply return false without throwing an exception. This can lead to scenarios where the contract believes a transfer succeeded and continues execution, updating the state based on a false assumption. This vulnerability is especially common in reward distribution systems, plugin architectures, and fallback routing contracts, where third-party calls are made dynamically. Its frequency is reinforced by the deceptive simplicity of using "call" for flexibility, without recognizing the ambiguity in execution it introduces.

These threats are prevalent because they are rooted in Solidity's design trade-offs, offering flexibility at the cost of safety, and are often introduced through copy-pasted code, outdated tutorials, or rapid development practices. Even experienced developers occasionally overlook the subtle differences between safe and unsafe constructs, especially under the pressure of product deadlines. As such, they form the backbone of many real-world exploits and continue to demand careful auditing and robust design patterns to mitigate.

7.2.2 Most Dangerous Threats

While frequency is important, it does not necessarily align with severity. The most dangerous threats, those with the potential to cause irreversible contract failure or ecosystem-wide disruption, include Unprotected Self-Destruct, Storage Overlap and Collision, and Delegated Reentrancy via Delegatecall. These threats may be less frequently triggered, but when exploited, they lead to total loss of control, permanent fund inaccessibility, or systemic corruption of logic.

Unprotected Self-Destruct is perhaps the most absolute in its consequences. When a contract exposes a selfdestruct() function without proper access control, it allows an attacker to permanently erase the contract's bytecode from the blockchain. All functionalities are lost, future calls revert, and any funds or contract references become irretrievable. The 2017 Parity multisig incident is a stark example: a user unintentionally gained ownership of a critical library and invoked selfdestruct, bricking every wallet dependent on it. The impact exceeded $150 million in losses and affected thousands of users, illustrating how a single overlooked authorization could cascade into protocol-wide paralysis. The finality of this threat, its irreversible nature, and total deactivation of contract functionality mark it as one of the most catastrophic risks in decentralized systems.

Storage Overlap and Collision represent another class of silent but devastating threats, particularly in upgradeable contracts that rely on the proxy-delegatecall architecture. In such systems, logic contracts are executed in the storage context of proxies. If variable order, inheritance, or layout changes are misaligned between versions, a delegatecall can overwrite critical state variables such as ownership fields or configuration settings. This storage corruption may not cause immediate failure, but it fundamentally compromises trust and correctness. In many cases, it leads to privilege escalation, incorrect logic execution, or permanent loss of governance functionality. Because these bugs do not manifest under normal testing and often require formal verification or fuzzing to detect, they are especially insidious and can propagate unnoticed across large codebases. Their danger lies in the subtlety of their cause and the systemic scale of their effect.

Delegated Reentrancy, a more advanced variant of the reentrancy threat, arises when contracts combine delegatecall with unguarded function entry points. Unlike traditional reentrancy, which loops back into the same function, delegated reentrancy allows an attacker to inject logic into the caller's context, thereby manipulating state directly during reentry. This can bypass mutexes, evade reentrancy guards, and exploit privileged state changes in the originating contract. The combination of delegatecall's context-switching behavior with external reentry makes this threat exceptionally difficult to model and contain. Its capacity to span multiple layers of contract architecture and corrupt internal logic without leaving clear traces makes it one of the most technically severe and strategically dangerous attack vectors known in smart contract security.

Compared to threats like variable shadowing or floating pragma versions, which, while real, often result in edge-case behavior or non-critical bugs, these three threats strike at the operational and economic core of a protocol. They do not merely undermine logic; they destroy trust, lock or vaporize assets, and paralyze systems, sometimes irreversibly.

Taken together, this comparative analysis reveals that the most serious threats to smart contract security are not necessarily the most technically complex, but often the most overlooked during development and auditing. Reentrant Withdrawals and Unchecked External Calls appear again and again due to common coding practices and intuitive but risky design patterns. At the same time, threats like Unprotected Self-Destruct and Storage Collisions demonstrate that a single misconfiguration can render entire protocols inoperable, even if such threats are rarely executed in practice. True resilience in smart contract security requires addressing both axes of risk, frequency, and impact, with equal rigor. Developers and auditors must move beyond checking for the common and adopt a mindset that also anticipates the catastrophe. Only by evaluating the full risk surface, where technical flaws, architectural design, and real-world incentives intersect, can decentralized applications be built to endure the adversarial and evolving conditions of blockchain ecosystems.

7.3 Chapter Summary

This chapter presented a systematic analysis of smart contract threats by examining their structural origins, behavioral manifestations, and real-world consequences. Building upon a thematic taxonomy, we explored how different classes of threats, such as reentrant withdrawals, unchecked external calls, unprotected self-destruct mechanisms, and storage collisions, arise from both low-level vulnerabilities and broader architectural patterns. By analyzing each threat in terms of its prevalence and potential severity, we revealed a critical insight: the most frequently encountered threats are not always the most dangerous, and vice versa. Common threats often stem from habitual development practices and language-level pitfalls, while less frequent but more catastrophic threats can lead to irreversible outcomes such as contract destruction, privilege escalation, or total fund loss. This comparative approach underscores the need for a holistic security mindset, one that combines defensive coding techniques, rigorous auditing, and a deep understanding of adversarial execution contexts. Ultimately, robust smart contract security demands not just vulnerability identification but also structured threat modeling that accounts for both the likelihood of an exploit and the potential damage it can cause.

References

1. Ivanov, N., et al.: Security threat mitigation for smart contracts: a comprehensive survey. ACM Comput. Surv. **55**(14s), 1–37 (2023)
2. Khan, S.N., et al.: Blockchain smart contracts: applications, challenges, and future trends. Peer Peer Netw Appl. **14**, 2901–2925 (2021)
3. Peng, K., et al.: Security challenges and opportunities for smart contracts in internet of things: a survey. IEEE Internet Things J. **8**(15), 12004–12020 (2021)
4. Kaur, G., et al.: Smart contracts and defi security and threats. In: Understanding Cybersecurity Management in Decentralized Finance: Challenges, Strategies, and Trends, pp. 91–111. Springer International Publishing, Cham (2023)
5. Vivar, A.L., et al.: An analysis of smart contracts security threats alongside existing solutions. Entropy. **22**(2), 203 (2020)
6. Sayeed, S., Marco-Gisbert, H., Caira, T.: Smart contract: attacks and protections. IEEE Access. **8**, 24416–24427 (2020)
7. He, D., et al.: Unknown threats detection methods of smart contracts. IEEE Internet Things J. **11**(3), 4430–4441 (2023)
8. Sato, T., Imamura, M., Omote, K.: Threat analysis of poisoning attack against ethereum blockchain. In: IFIP International Conference on Information Security Theory and Practice. Springer International Publishing, Cham (2019)
9. Ruf, P., Stodt, J., Reich, C.: Security threats of a blockchain-based platform for industry ecosystems in the cloud. In: 2021 Fifth World Conference on Smart Trends in Systems Security and Sustainability (WorldS4). IEEE (2021)
10. Froehlich, M., Hulm, P., Alt, F.: Under pressure. A user-centered threat model for cryptocurrency owners. In: Proceedings of the 2021 4th International Conference on Blockchain Technology and Applications (2021)

Chapter 8
Attacks on Smart Contracts

Abstract This chapter delves into real-world smart contract attacks, highlighting how design flaws, developer oversights, and systemic assumptions combine to produce catastrophic exploits. It categorizes attacks from an attacker-oriented perspective, including execution flow manipulation, state corruption, access control subversion, economic exploitation, and user manipulation. Through detailed case studies, the DAO reentrancy hack, Rubixi constructor misnaming, BeautyChain integer underflow, GovernMental unchecked send(), Parity multisig wallet destruction, replay attacks across Ethereum and Ethereum Classic, BZX flash loan exploits, FairWin timestamp dependence, front-running sandwich attacks, and deceptive honeypot contracts, this chapter shows how both code-level errors and protocol-level gaps can be weaponized. The analysis distinguishes between the most common attacks, such as front-running, timestamp dependence, and honeypots, which recur frequently due to structural openness or developer misconceptions, and the most dangerous attacks, such as DAO reentrancy, Parity multisig, flash loan exploits, and replay attacks, which cause irreversible financial or systemic damage. Together, these cases emphasize that while frequent vulnerabilities erode user trust incrementally, rare but severe exploits can dismantle entire protocols in seconds. Finally, it concludes that robust smart contract security requires not only secure coding and auditing but also an architectural understanding of blockchain semantics and adversarial behaviors.

Smart contracts, while pivotal to the automation and decentralization of blockchain-based systems, have repeatedly demonstrated critical security vulnerabilities in adversarial environments [1, 2]. This chapter investigates a series of real-world smart contract attacks to dissect their root causes, technical execution, and broader implications [3]. By examining high-impact cases, including reentrancy in DAOs, arithmetic manipulation in token contracts, the unsafe use of self-destruct functions in Parity Wallets, and transaction-order dependence in decentralized finance protocols, we reveal how seemingly minor coding decisions can lead to substantial vulnerabilities [4, 5]. Beyond the mechanics of each exploit, the chapter identifies recurring design flaws and systemic weaknesses that transcend individual contracts, offering a structured perspective on why these failures occur and how they reflect deeper challenges in smart contract security [6, 7].

S. HajiHosseinKhani et al., *Understanding Cybersecurity for Smart Contracts*,
https://doi.org/10.1007/978-3-032-28863-9_8

8.1 Examination of Potential Attacks Stemming from Vulnerabilities

The evolution of Ethereum and decentralized finance has been driven not only by groundbreaking innovation but also by vulnerabilities exposed by early smart contracts. Real-world attacks provide essential insights into how theoretical weaknesses translate into practical exploits, highlighting how adversaries exploit the deterministic and composable nature of blockchain systems [8, 9]. This subsection provides a detailed analysis of major smart contract attacks, ranging from logic flaws such as reentrancy and arithmetic errors to deeper architectural oversights and transaction-flow manipulations [10]. The attacks are categorized from an attacker-oriented perspective, based on the strategic intent and execution path employed by adversaries [9, 11]. Each category reflects a distinct mode of adversarial behavior, defined by how an attacker engages with contract logic, state transitions, control structures, or systemic assumptions. The taxonomy ensures mutual exclusivity, assigning each attack to a single class based on its primary exploit logic.

8.1.1 Execution Flow Manipulation

This category encompasses attacks that deliberately distort the intended execution path of smart contracts to gain unauthorized control or extract value. The attacker's strategy centers on hijacking or redirecting execution through mechanisms such as reentrancy, misused fallback functions, or constructor misidentification [12]. These attacks typically operate within the boundaries of correct syntax and permissions, but subvert execution sequencing, allowing them to bypass logical or transactional safeguards.

- **DAO (Decentralized Autonomous Organization)**: The DAO Attack is a high-impact reentrancy exploit wherein an attacker manipulates the execution flow of a smart contract by recursively re-entering a vulnerable function before its internal state is updated, enabling unauthorized and repeated fund withdrawals. In June 2016, the Ethereum ecosystem faced an unprecedented crisis with the exploitation of The DAO (Decentralized Autonomous Organization), an autonomous investment fund governed entirely by smart contracts and collective token-holder voting. Conceptualized as a decentralized venture capital platform, The DAO represented a radical experiment in governance and pooled capital allocation. Within weeks of deployment, it garnered over 11 million ETH, approximately 14% of all Ether in circulation at the time, signifying enormous public trust in both its mission and the robustness of Ethereum's smart contract infrastructure [2, 4, 5].

  At the heart of the DAO's operational logic was a splitting mechanism that allowed users to exit the organization by creating a "child DAO." This function was designed to equitably return the user's share of ETH while updating the DAO's internal records to reflect changes in holdings and governance. However, a critical sequencing flaw was embedded within the code: it transferred Ether to the user before updating the contract's internal token balance and withdrawal records. This error created a reentrancy vulnerability, an opening that allowed an attacker to recursively invoke the withdrawal function before the initial transaction's state finalized [2, 10].

The exploit leveraged Ethereum's composability, the ability for contracts to interact programmatically. If the withdrawing party was a contract with a fallback function, that function could be designed to re-invoke the vulnerable DAO function during execution. Since the original balance update had not yet occurred, each reentrant call would be treated as an independent, legitimate withdrawal. This resulted in multiple transfers of the same funds.

To clarify the mechanics of vulnerability, consider the following simplified smart contract:

```
contract VulnerableFund {
 mapping(address => uint) public balances;

 function deposit() public payable {
   balances[msg.sender] += msg.value;
 }

 function withdraw() public {
   require(balances[msg.sender] > 0, "Nothing to withdraw");

   (bool success, ) = msg.sender.call{value: balances[msg.
sender]}("");
   require(success, "Transfer failed");

   balances[msg.sender] = 0;
 }

 function getBalance() public view returns (uint) {
   return address(this).balance;
 }
}
```

In this implementation, the user's balance is not reset until *the Ether has been* transferred. If the msg.sender is a contract, the contract's fallback function is executed during the low-level call. If this fallback function includes logic to recursively invoke withdraw(), the contract can repeatedly drain the vulnerable fund.

The attacker's contract, designed to exploit this logic, would resemble the following:

```
contract ReentrancyAttacker {
 VulnerableFund public vulnerable;
 address public owner;

 constructor(address _vulnerable) {
   vulnerable = VulnerableFund(_vulnerable);
   owner = msg.sender;
 }

 function attack() external payable {
   require(msg.value >= 1 ether, "Send at least 1 ETH to
initiate attack");
   vulnerable.deposit{value: 1 ether}();
   vulnerable.withdraw();
 }

 fallback() external payable {
   if (address(vulnerable).balance >= 1 ether) {
      vulnerable.withdraw();
   }
 }

 function withdrawFunds() external {
   require(msg.sender == owner, "Not owner");
   payable(owner).transfer(address(this).balance);
 }
}
```

In practice, the attacker deposits 1 ETH and initiates a withdrawal. The withdraw() function calls msg.sender, triggering the fallback function. Since the vulnerable contract has not yet updated the user's balance, the fallback re-invokes withdraw() successfully. This recursive loop continues until the contract's balance falls below the withdrawal threshold. After the exploit completes, the attacker uses withdrawFunds() to retrieve the stolen ETH.

The consequences were profound. Over 3.6 million ETH, worth tens of millions of dollars, was siphoned from the DAO, sending shockwaves through the Ethereum community. In an extraordinary governance move, the Ethereum network underwent a contentious hard fork to reverse the exploit's impact and return funds to users, leading to a schism and the creation of two separate chains: Ethereum (ETH) and Ethereum Classic (ETC). The incident raised existential

questions about the principles of decentralization, immutability, and trust in code-based governance systems.
The DAO attack is widely recognized as the archetype of reentrancy-based exploits. It forced a reevaluation of contract design principles and inspired the "checks-effects-interactions" pattern, which mandates that contracts update internal state before interacting with external addresses to prevent similar vulnerabilities. This attack stems from the threat of *Control Flow Manipulation*, specifically arising due to the vulnerability of *Reentrancy*.

- **Rubixi:** The Rubixi Attack is a constructor misnaming exploit in which a function intended to serve as a contract's constructor is mistakenly left as a public function due to a naming mismatch, allowing unauthorized users to assume ownership and execute destructive operations such as selfdestruct [9, 10].

The Rubixi smart contract, originally launched under the name *DynamicPyramid*, illustrates how a simple naming oversight can lead to a catastrophic security breach. Deployed in the early days of Ethereum, Rubixi operated as a classic pyramid scheme, offering disproportionate returns to early participants, funded by contributions from later investors. While its economic model was inherently unsustainable, the technical vulnerability that enabled its eventual demise was both subtle and deeply instructive.
Before Solidity version 0.4.22, constructors were defined by naming a function that matched the contract name. This naming convention, though straightforward in appearance, introduced fragility into the compilation and execution model. If a developer renamed the contract but failed to rename the constructor function accordingly, the function was not interpreted as a constructor. Instead, it was compiled as a publicly accessible function, callable by any address after deployment. This is precisely what happened in Rubixi. Though the contract was redeployed under the name Rubixi, the constructor remained named DynamicPyramid, the name of its earlier version. Solidity did not treat DynamicPyramid() as a constructor, and thus the function remained exposed post-deployment.
The consequences of this naming mismatch were profound. The DynamicPyramid() function's sole purpose was to set the contract's owner variable. Once the contract was deployed, any address could invoke this function and assign itself as the contract owner. This transformed what should have been a one-time initialization step into a persistent backdoor. Multiple opportunistic users competed to exploit this flaw, each calling DynamicPyramid() to override the owner value. Eventually, one succeeded in acting before the others, using their newly acquired privileges to invoke the contract's terminate() function.
A simplified reconstruction of the vulnerable contract is as follows:

```
contract Rubixi {
 address public owner;

 // Misnamed constructor - still called DynamicPyramid after
renaming
 function DynamicPyramid() public {
   owner = msg.sender;
 }

 modifier ownerOnly() {
  require(msg.sender == owner);
  _;
 }

       function collectAllFees() ownerOnly public {
           msg.sender.transfer(this.balance);
       }

 function terminate() ownerOnly public {
   selfdestruct(owner);
 }
}
```

The core issue lies in the misnamed constructor. When the contract is deployed as Rubixi, the DynamicPyramid() function is treated as a regular public function. Any external account may call it, and upon doing so, they become the contract's owner. Once in control, the attacker can call the terminate() function, which executes selfdestruct(owner), removing the contract's bytecode from the blockchain and transferring all remaining funds to the attacker's address.

The Rubixi attack did not require an elaborate attacker contract or sophisticated exploit logic. It was carried out using standard Ethereum transaction tools, possibly even from web interfaces such as MyEtherWallet or Etherscan. The exploit's simplicity and the ease with which ownership could be reassigned repeatedly made it a race condition among attackers, each attempting to become the final controller before the contract was destroyed.

While the ether lost in the Rubixi attack was modest by later standards, the incident's broader implications were substantial. It exposed the brittleness of early Solidity contract patterns and revealed the dangers of assuming immutability safeguards where none existed. More importantly, the Rubixi case prompted critical reflection within the Ethereum developer community. It catalyzed the deprecation of constructor-by-name declarations, leading to the introduction of the constructor keyword in Solidity 0.4.22, which provided syntactic clarity and compiler enforcement against such misconfigurations.

Rubixi is now remembered as one of the earliest warnings that the smallest errors, especially those made during contract initialization, can produce irreversible and wide-reaching effects. It remains a foundational case study in smart contract security pedagogy, particularly in relation to constructor logic, privilege assignment, and the potentially devastating consequences of unguarded selfdestruct operations. This attack stems from the threat of *Unauthorized Access and Code Lifecycle Manipulation*, specifically arising due to the vulnerability of *Constructor Misnaming and Unprotected Self-Destruct.*

8.1.2 State Corruption and Desynchronization

Attacks in this category exploit flaws that lead to unintended or inconsistent changes in contract state. Rather than altering the execution order, these adversaries target mechanisms in which the state is misrepresented, unvalidated, or misaligned across contract instances [11]. The goal is to force the system into accepting false assumptions about balances, permissions, or values.

- **BeautyChain Token:** The BeautyChain Underflow Attack is an arithmetic manipulation exploit in which an attacker leverages the lack of bounds checking on unsigned integer operations to induce an underflow, thereby generating artificially inflated token balances that violate the contract's intended supply constraints.
  The April 2018 exploit of the BeautyChain (BEC) token starkly revealed how unchecked arithmetic operations in Solidity could undermine the integrity of an entire token economy. At the time, Solidity, specifically versions prior to 0.8.0, performed arithmetic using unchecked modular arithmetic. In such a context, unsigned integers (e.g., uint256) did not throw exceptions upon overflow or underflow. Instead, values exceeding their range would wrap around within the finite bounds of 256-bit integers. This behavior, though mathematically consistent, proved hazardous in financial systems where accuracy in balances is paramount.
  The BEC contract, like many early ERC-20 implementations, relied on raw arithmetic operations without enforcing any safety checks on token transfers. Within the transfer() function, token balances were debited from the sender and credited to the recipient without validating that the sender held a sufficient balance. When a subtraction operation was attempted on a zero balance, the result was not a runtime error but rather an underflow, producing a new balance of 2^256–1, the maximum possible value of a uint256. This logical flaw enabled an attacker to forge a massive token balance out of thin air.
  A simplified abstraction of the vulnerable BEC token contract highlights this fatal oversight:

```
contract VulnerableToken {
 mapping(address => uint256) public balanceOf;

 function transfer(address _to, uint256 _value) public
returns (bool) {
   balanceOf[msg.sender] -= _value;
   balanceOf[_to] += _value;
   return true;
 }

 function mint(uint256 amount) public {
   balanceOf[msg.sender] = amount;
 }
}
```

In this contract, there is no validation to ensure that balanceOf[msg.sender] > = _value prior to performing the subtraction. If an address with a zero balance invokes transfer() with _value = 1, the subtraction operation causes balanceOf[msg.sender] to wrap around from 0 to 2^256–1. This arithmetic anomaly grants the caller an astronomical token balance. The recipient of the transfer receives 1 token as expected, but the attacker retains a balance equivalent to the upper limit of a 256-bit unsigned integer. With such a balance, the attacker can make successive transfers, effectively injecting forged tokens into the market.
The corresponding attacker contract required no complex logic. It merely needed to call the vulnerable transfer() function under the right preconditions:

```
contract UnderflowAttacker {
 VulnerableToken public token;

 constructor(address _token) {
   token = VulnerableToken(_token);
 }

 function executeAttack() public {
   token.transfer(address(0xdead), 1);
 }
}
```

Assuming the attacker's balance was initially zero, this contract successfully induced an underflow, inflating the attacker's balance to near-infinite levels. In the real-world incident, blockchain records revealed that the attacker's address abruptly showed a balance that was an order of magnitude larger than the total

declared supply of BEC. The attacker proceeded to transfer and sell these forged tokens, overwhelming decentralized exchanges with fraudulent volume and rapidly destabilizing the token's economy.
The aftermath was swift and unforgiving. The perceived value of BEC collapsed under the weight of the artificially injected tokens, and trust in the project evaporated overnight. The exploit did not stem from malicious intent embedded in the contract but from an elementary misunderstanding of Solidity's arithmetic model. It exposed a critical flaw in the assumptions of early token design: that simple operations such as subtraction are safe by default. The incident galvanized the community, leading to the widespread adoption of the SafeMath library and ultimately to the Solidity compiler's shift to safe arithmetic defaults in version 0.8.0.
The BEC exploit serves as a definitive example of how foundational arithmetic vulnerabilities can render complex security assumptions meaningless [9, 12]. In immutable environments where deployed code cannot be patched or rolled back, failing to anticipate edge-case behavior in basic operations can permanently jeopardize a project's viability. This attack stems from the threat of *State Corruption*, specifically arising due to the vulnerability of *Integer Underflow*.

- **GovernMental**: The GovernMental failure is an exception-handling vulnerability in which a contract uses send() to transfer Ether without checking its return value, leading to silent transfer failures that desynchronize internal state and irreversibly disrupt contract logic.

  The GovernMental contract, deployed in Ethereum's early developmental era, epitomizes how subtle mismanagement of low-level operations, specifically the unchecked return value of the send() function, can paralyze a contract's entire operational model. GovernMental was essentially a high-yield Ponzi scheme that promised users double returns on their Ether deposits. Participants would send ETH, join an internal queue, and, upon reaching the front, be repaid twice their original contribution, funded by subsequent investors. The mechanism's success relied entirely on the continuous and accurate execution of payouts.
  Central to this logic was a function that disbursed Ether to the first participant in line. However, the payout was executed using the low-level send() function, which sends exactly 2300 gas and returns a Boolean indicating success or failure. Critically, the contract ignored this return value. Thus, if the transfer failed silently because the recipient was a contract with a gas-heavy fallback function or explicit reversion, the system would nonetheless assume the payout succeeded and move to the next user in the queue.
  The following simplified contract reconstructs this logic:

```
contract GovernMental {
 struct Participant {
    address payable addr;
    uint amount;
 }
```

```
  Participant[] public queue;
  uint public payoutIndex;

  function invest() public payable {
    require(msg.value >= 1 ether);
    queue.push(Participant(payable(msg.sender), msg.value));
    payOut();
  }

  function payOut() internal {
    while (address(this).balance >= queue[payoutIndex].
amount * 2) {
      // Vulnerability: unchecked return value from send()
      queue[payoutIndex].addr.send(queue[payoutIndex].
amount * 2);
      payoutIndex++;
    }
  }

  function queueLength() public view returns (uint) {
    return queue.length - payoutIndex;
  }

  function contractBalance() public view returns (uint) {
    return address(this).balance;
  }
}
```

This implementation lacks a mechanism to verify whether the send() call succeeded. If the recipient is a contract address with a fallback function that rejects Ether or consumes more gas than the fixed 2300 gas stipend, the send() operation fails. Since the result is never checked, the contract increments the payoutIndex and continues its queue-advancement logic as though the payment were successful.

An attacker, or even an unwitting participant, could use a contract like the following to exploit the system:

```
contract RejectEther {
 fallback() external payable {
   // Consumes more than 2300 gas or reverts
   revert("Do not accept Ether");
 }
}
```

Once this contract address is added to the queue, GovernMental treats it like any other participant. When the payOut() function reaches this address, it attempts to send the required ETH. The send() fails silently, but the contract, unaware of the failure, increments the payout index. The queued contract receives no Ether, but the system has marked it as paid. This desynchronization means that all subsequent balance calculations and payout conditions become misaligned. The contract believes it has fulfilled a payment that, in fact, never occurred.

The consequence is catastrophic. Because the total balance appears insufficient to pay the next participant, even though it may contain enough funds, the payOut() logic stalls. All subsequent investments become trapped. The queue can no longer advance, and the promise of double returns is forever broken. Participants continue depositing Ether under the assumption that the system will eventually pay out, but the payout mechanism is irrevocably blocked. The contract has not halted or been destroyed; it continues to accept funds and report its balance, but its core logic is inert. The Ether is locked permanently, not through theft or malicious intent, but due to a failure to handle an external call's potential failure.

This vulnerability is emblematic of a broader class of failures in early smart contract design: misplaced trust in external calls to behave as expected. GovernMental did not incorporate fallback protection, recovery mechanisms, or even a simple conditional check on the success of send(). The lack of these safety measures doomed the contract to fail at the first unexpected edge case.

Unlike attacks that drain funds or rewrite ownership records, GovernMental's demise occurred quietly and passively. It was not so much exploited as broken by design. The contract's architecture made it impossible to detect or recover from transfer failures, and once its queue became misaligned, there was no recourse. This incident remains a seminal case study in smart contract development, highlighting the importance of comprehensive error handling, especially when interacting with potentially adversarial or unknown addresses on the blockchain. This attack stems from the threat of *State Corruption*, specifically arising from the vulnerability of Unhandled Exceptions in *Low-Level Calls*.

8.1.3 Access Control Subversion

This category includes attacks where the adversary circumvents, misuses, or misinterprets access control mechanisms to gain privileged functionality. Rather than corrupting execution flow or state directly, the attacker's focus is on bypassing or assuming roles reserved for trusted agents.

- **Parity Multi-Sig Wallet**: The Parity Multi-Sig Wallet incident is an access control and code lifecycle failure in which a publicly callable initialization function and an unprotected selfdestruct operation on a shared contract library allowed an unauthorized user to delete critical code, thereby permanently disabling all dependent proxy contracts.
  In November 2017, Ethereum suffered one of its most paralyzing incidents when the Parity Multi-Signature Wallet infrastructure was disabled. The failure did not stem from a malicious actor's sophisticated code injection or from a zero-day vulnerability. Rather, it emerged from a convergence of two seemingly benign design oversights: a shared WalletLibrary contract that had never been initialized and publicly accessible functions, including one to set contract ownership and another to invoke selfdestruct. These oversights combined to produce an irreversible outcome: over 500,000 ETH, valued at more than $150 million at the time, became immutably locked, inaccessible to their rightful owners, yet never technically "stolen."
  Parity's multi-signature wallet architecture was modular and efficient, relying on lightweight proxy contracts that executed their core logic via delegatecall to a shared WalletLibrary contract. Each proxy wallet stored a minimal state and relied on the shared library for all behavioral functionality, including transaction execution, owner management, and governance routines. However, the WalletLibrary itself was not deployed as a Solidity library, a keyword that would have disabled certain stateful behaviors and barred the inclusion of selfdestruct, but rather as a standard contract. As such, it included modifiable storage and publicly callable methods, including a fatal combination of initWallet() and kill().
  The initWallet() function was designed to initialize wallet parameters, such as ownership and the number of required confirmations, during proxy deployment via delegatecall. However, it was never invoked on the WalletLibrary itself during deployment, leaving it uninitialized and open to future calls. Since the function lacked access restrictions, any Ethereum address could call initWallet() on the library contract directly and overwrite its internal storage, including assigning ownership rights.
  This vulnerability was compounded by the presence of a second public function: kill(). This function issued a selfdestruct operation, deleting the contract's bytecode from the blockchain and transferring any remaining Ether to a recipient of the caller's choice. Because the contract lacked ownership verification or execution guards, anyone who first called initWallet() to assume control could immediately follow up with kill() to erase the contract.
  A simplified version of the vulnerable WalletLibrary contract illustrates the issue:

```
contract WalletLibrary {
 address[] public owners;
 uint public required;

 function initWallet(address[] memory _owners, uint _
required) public {
   owners = _owners;
   required = _required;
 }

 function kill() public {
   selfdestruct(payable(msg.sender));
 }
}
```

In this contract, the absence of any modifiers or conditional logic allows any caller to overwrite owner data via initWallet() and invoke contract deletion via kill(). The fatal exploit unfolded when a user, reportedly acting without malicious intent, interacted directly with the WalletLibrary contract. First, they called initWallet() and assigned themselves as the sole owner. Then, unaware of the broader consequences, they called kill(), invoking selfdestruct() and irreversibly erasing the WalletLibrary's code from Ethereum's global state.

Because every Parity multi-sig wallet proxy relied on this now-absent library via delegatecall, all wallet functions became non-functional immediately. Proxy wallets still held ETH and other assets in their local storage, but their operational logic, transaction submission, confirmation, and withdrawal were irretrievably gone. Because delegatecall requires the callee to have executable code, every subsequent call from the proxies failed silently. The funds remained technically present but permanently inaccessible.

Unlike prior attacks that illicitly transferred funds, this incident caused a form of functional annihilation. There was no malicious contract, no token laundering, and no direct profit for the user involved. Instead, the issue was rooted in architectural fragility and unguarded access control. Moreover, the tools used to carry out the exploit, Etherscan's contract interface or standard Ethereum clients, demonstrated that the attack vector was not only simple but available to any user with minimal technical sophistication.

The fallout from the Parity incident was swift and intense. While Parity Technologies confirmed that the event resulted from an accidental trigger by a curious user, the implications for decentralized finance were systemic. Trust in Parity's multi-sig infrastructure evaporated, legal discussions emerged around responsibility and compensation, and security paradigms for shared code libraries were reevaluated across the Ethereum development community.

This event remains one of the most cited cautionary tales in smart contract engineering. It underscored the need for secure initialization, robust access controls, restricted use of selfdestruct, and the perils of over-reliance on mutable shared components. It taught developers that immutability applies not just to individual contracts, but also to the architectural relationships between them, and that errors in this structure can propagate catastrophically across entire ecosystems. *This attack stems from the threats of Unauthorized Access and Code Lifecycle Manipulation, specifically arising from the vulnerabilities of Unprotected Initialization and Unrestricted Self-Destruct.*

- **Replay Attacks:** A Replay Attack is a cross-chain exploit in which a valid transaction from one blockchain (e.g., Ethereum) is maliciously rebroadcast on another compatible chain (e.g., Ethereum Classic), resulting in unauthorized but technically valid execution due to the absence of chain-specific data in the original transaction signature.

  Replay attacks exploit a critical gap in transaction authentication, specifically, the assumption that digital signatures are uniquely bound to a single blockchain context. In the early history of Ethereum, particularly during and after the DAO hard fork in 2016, this assumption proved dangerously flawed. The Ethereum and Ethereum Classic chains shared an identical history up to the fork, and post-fork, both retained identical contract addresses, balances, and transaction logic. However, because the pre-fork signature schema did not encode the *chain ID* into the signing process, a transaction authorized on one chain remained valid on the other.

  At the heart of Ethereum's transaction signature are the v, r, and s parameters, derived from elliptic-curve cryptography. Before the adoption of EIP-155, these values were calculated without any chain-specific metadata. Consequently, the same signed transaction byte string could be submitted to both Ethereum and Ethereum Classic and be considered valid by both networks, provided the account from which the transaction originated existed and had sufficient balance on both.

  To illustrate, consider a simple ERC20-style contract that performs token transfers:

```
contract ReplayableToken {
 mapping(address => uint256) public balances;

 constructor() {
   balances[msg.sender] = 1000;
 }

 function transfer(address to, uint256 value) public {
   require(balances[msg.sender] >= value, "Insufficient
balance");
```

```
        balances[msg.sender] -= value;
        balances[to] += value;
    }

    function balanceOf(address account) public view returns
  (uint256) {
        return balances[account];
    }
  }
```

This contract contains no flaw in its logic. It authorizes token transfers based on the standard msg.sender and balance conditions. However, if this contract were deployed on both Ethereum and Ethereum Classic under the same address, any transaction invoking transfer() on one chain, signed by the holder of a private key, could be extracted and reused on the other chain. The contract would have no mechanism to determine whether the transaction originated on a different network. Its execution would be indistinguishable from an intended call.

The attack vector requires no additional smart contract logic. An adversary simply monitors the Ethereum mempool or block explorers for signed transactions, extracts the raw bytes, and broadcasts them to Ethereum Classic. If the original sender held a balance or token equivalent on the second chain, the transaction would succeed on that chain as well. This created conditions in which users unknowingly duplicated economic actions, such as sending tokens to an Ethereum address and inadvertently doing the same on Ethereum Classic, thereby exposing assets to unauthorized transfers or double execution.

This vulnerability became a tangible threat in the wake of the DAO hard fork, when many users held mirrored balances on both chains. Without replay protection, adversaries could, and did, exploit these duplicated assets by simply resubmitting transactions across chains. Exchanges were forced to suspend deposits and withdrawals, wallets had to issue warnings, and dApps were compelled to re-engineer signing logic to account for this multi-chain risk.

The security flaw was not in the smart contracts, which correctly enforced balance logic and access control, but in the signature protocol itself. Ethereum's early design failed to encode the identity of the executing chain, resulting in a cryptographically valid, but semantically ambiguous, signature format. Only with the implementation of EIP-155, which added the chain ID to the signed transaction hash, did Ethereum resolve this vulnerability. From that point onward, a transaction signed for Ethereum would no longer be valid on Ethereum Classic, and vice versa.

Replay attacks serve as a textbook example of how cryptographic mechanisms, while technically sound, must incorporate contextual boundaries to be secure in a multi-chain environment. Without encoding that context, the authenticity of a signature extends beyond its intended scope, allowing attackers to reflect, reuse, and resubmit actions that were never meant to leave their native execution environment. This attack is a form of *Cross-Chain Execution Exploitation*, made possible by the vulnerability of *Missing Chain Context in Signature Schemes Prior to EIP-155*.

8.1.4 Economic Manipulation and Exploitation

This class of attacks involves adversaries who exploit economic assumptions, pricing formulas, or execution ordering to extract value without directly violating contract logic. These attacks often rely on sophisticated observations of how market-facing contracts behave under changing conditions and use those insights to profit at the expense of unsuspecting users or protocols.

- **ERC20 token manipulation on exchanges:** The Short Address Attack is a calldata manipulation vulnerability in which incomplete or improperly padded input data causes misalignment in parameter decoding, allowing attackers to subvert ERC20 token transfers on exchange platforms and manipulate trade outcomes.
  The Short Address Attack, which emerged during Ethereum's formative years, exemplifies how discrepancies between high-level function expectations and low-level data encoding can be exploited to disrupt otherwise secure token transfers. Unlike vulnerabilities stemming from flawed contract logic, this exploit originated from the assumptions made by off-chain platforms, primarily exchanges, about the correctness of transaction calldata submitted by users. It highlighted the dangers of unvalidated, user-supplied input data and demonstrated how Ethereum's strict yet low-level ABI encoding model can be turned against unwitting systems.
  In the Ethereum Virtual Machine, function arguments are encoded according to the Application Binary Interface (ABI), in which each parameter is expected to occupy exactly 32 bytes. For ERC20 tokens, the transfer(address,uint256) function requires 32 bytes for the address parameter and 32 bytes for the uint256 amount. When encoded correctly, either through Solidity interfaces or verified web tools, each parameter is properly aligned and padded to meet these requirements. However, if a platform accepts raw transaction input without enforcing strict padding rules, an attacker can deliberately craft malformed calldata to exploit this alignment expectation.
  Consider a simplified ERC20 token contract:

```
contract SimpleToken {
 mapping(address => uint256) public balances;

 constructor() {
   balances[msg.sender] = 1000000 * (10 ** 18);
 }
```

```
  function transfer(address to, uint256 amount) public
returns (bool) {
    require(balances[msg.sender] >= amount, "Insufficient
balance");
    balances[msg.sender] -= amount;
    balances[to] += amount;
    return true;
  }

  function balanceOf(address account) public view returns
(uint256) {
    return balances[account];
  }
}
```

The transfer() function assumes it receives well-formed calldata. However, when exchanges allowed users to submit transactions through interfaces that did not enforce ABI padding, such as raw RPC calls or customized Web3 clients, they unintentionally opened themselves to exploitation. If an attacker provided only 20 bytes for the address field (rather than the expected 32), the Ethereum Virtual Machine would automatically right-pad the remaining bytes with zeros during decoding. As a result, the subsequent amount field was shifted, and the value decoded by the EVM no longer matched the originally intended or displayed value on the platform. For example, a transaction crafted to appear as a transfer of 1 token could, due to this shift, be interpreted by the smart contract as a transfer of merely 1 wei, a minuscule fraction of a token. Yet the exchange's front-end or accounting layer, which may have parsed the original input rather than the decoded EVM parameters, would treat it as a full token transfer. The contract, seeing no logical or authorization violation, would proceed to move the minimal amount, while the exchange misrecorded the transaction, awarding the attacker disproportionate value.

The Short Address Attack did not require an accompanying smart contract. Attackers used custom scripting tools or manipulated client libraries to generate malformed transactions. These transactions passed through the exchange's transaction routing infrastructure undetected. Once processed, they allowed the attacker to perform trades that appeared legitimate on the surface but were fundamentally skewed by underlying data misalignment.

The effects were wide-reaching. Multiple decentralized trading platforms experienced financial discrepancies, with token balances manipulated or drained due to misinterpreted transfers. Notably, the tokens themselves and their transfer() logic remained compliant with ERC20 standards. The vulnerability lay entirely in the gap between user-supplied calldata and the system's assumptions about its structure. This case illuminated a broader issue in smart contract ecosystems: the security of on-chain logic is only as strong as the correctness and validation of the data fed into it.

In response, Ethereum development tools, exchanges, and wallet providers began enforcing stricter input validation, including length checks on calldata, enforcing the ABI at the interface layer, and increasing use of typed transaction-encoding libraries. The incident became a case study in the subtle dangers of assumptions about data integrity and emphasized the importance of treating all external input as potentially adversarial, regardless of how standardized or routine it may appear. This attack stems from the threat of *State Manipulation via Input Misalignment*, specifically arising due to the vulnerability of *Malformed Calldata Exploitation in ABI-decoded Function Parameters*.

- **The BZX Flash Loan Exploit:** The BZX Flash Loan Exploit refers to a series of sophisticated economic attacks executed in early 2020 that leveraged flash loans to manipulate on-chain asset prices and extract profit from decentralized finance (DeFi) lending protocols. This exploit is classified as an *economic exploitation attack* facilitated by atomic, zero-collateral borrowing, allowing attackers to orchestrate multi-step arbitrage strategies within a single transaction [8, 9].

  The BZX protocol, a DeFi lending and margin trading platform, was targeted twice in February 2020 by attackers who used flash loans, unsecured loans that must be borrowed and repaid within the same transaction, to manipulate oracle-fed price data and extract asymmetric profits. These flash loans were obtained from DyDx and Aave, allowing the attackers to momentarily control significant capital without owning it, thereby enabling precise, high-impact trades across multiple DeFi protocols in rapid succession.

  In the first attack, the adversary initiated a 10,000 ETH flash loan from DyDx and, in the same transaction, split the proceeds across several DeFi actions. They used a portion of the borrowed ETH to purchase WBTC on Uniswap, significantly raising its price on the AMM-based exchange. BZX relied on the manipulated Uniswap price as a price oracle to determine collateral values. The attacker then opened a leveraged short position on WBTC using BZX's Fulcrum platform, borrowing against ETH collateral. Because the WBTC price was artificially inflated at that moment, BZX overvalued the attacker's position, allowing them to withdraw more ETH than they should have been permitted to.

  Once the transaction was completed, the flash loan was repaid, but the attacker retained a profit extracted through the pricing discrepancy created by their own manipulated trades. The exploit depended entirely on the ability to execute all operations atomically, within a single block, before the market could react or correct itself.

  To illustrate the mechanics, consider a simplified representation of the pricing dependency between BZX and Uniswap:

```
contract SimplifiedLending {
 IUniswap uniswap;
 IERC20 wbtc;
 mapping(address => uint256) public deposits;

 function openPosition(uint256 ethAmount) public {
   uint256 wbtcPrice = uniswap.getPrice(wbtc);
   uint256 collateralValue = ethAmount * wbtcPrice;
   require(collateralValue > threshold, "Insufficient
collateral");
   deposits[msg.sender] += ethAmount;
   // Further lending logic...
 }
}
```

In this model, the protocol accepts ETH as collateral and calculates its value using the WBTC price fetched from Uniswap. If the attacker manipulates this price just before invoking openPosition(), they can exploit the inflated valuation to withdraw more than what their ETH deposit justifies.

The second BZX exploit followed a similar pattern but used Aave's flash loans and manipulated Synthetix-based oracles. In both cases, the key enabler was the atomic nature of flash loans, which allowed attackers to borrow large amounts of capital, use that capital to distort on-chain market conditions, and then unwind the trade before the borrowed capital had to be returned, all within a single transaction.

These attacks did not rely on logic errors within the BZX smart contracts. Instead, they exposed systemic vulnerabilities at the intersection of composability, oracle design, and price discovery mechanisms in DeFi. The transparency and atomicity of blockchain transactions meant that attackers could simulate and execute complex strategies that traditional financial systems, with their inherent latency and separation of concerns, would have naturally prevented.

The real-world impact of the BZX exploits was immediate and material. Together, the two attacks extracted nearly $1 million in ETH from the protocol and prompted a broader reassessment of oracle design, the potential for flash loan abuse, and inter-protocol dependencies across the DeFi landscape. BZX temporarily suspended operations and restructured several of its components, while other platforms began to rethink the reliance on manipulable on-chain pricing sources.

The BZX Flash Loan Exploit demonstrated that economic attacks do not always stem from flawed code. Rather, they may exploit architectural assumptions about market integrity, liquidity stability, and the trustworthiness of oracles. It underscored the need for robust oracle protections, limits on flash loan usage, and greater resistance to manipulation in composable financial systems. This attack stems from the threat of *economic exploitation*, specifically arising from the vulnerability to oracle manipulation via *unprotected price sources and unrestricted flash loan usage*.

- **Front-Running:** The Front-Running Exploit is a transaction ordering manipulation in which an adversary observes pending transactions in the public mempool and strategically inserts their own transactions, often with higher gas fees, to execute before the victim's, thereby extracting value by preemptively influencing contract state transitions.

  Among the most enduring and pervasive forms of exploitation in Ethereum's decentralized finance (DeFi) landscape is front-running: an opportunistic manipulation that exploits the transparent nature of the Ethereum mempool and the deterministic execution of smart contracts. Unlike vulnerabilities that arise from flaws in code logic or improper access control, front-running capitalizes on the assumption that transaction execution is fair and time-neutral. In reality, Ethereum's open transaction pool, where pending transactions are visible to all, and its gas-based prioritization of inclusion provide a fertile environment for adversarial actors to rearrange execution order to their advantage.

  At the core of front-running lies the fact that Ethereum miners and validators construct blocks by selecting transactions from the mempool based on incentives, typically favoring those with higher gas prices. Sophisticated adversaries, including MEV (Maximal Extractable Value) bots and miners themselves, exploit this mechanism by preemptively submitting transactions that will be mined before the victim's, thereby manipulating contract state in ways that diminish the victim's outcome and enhance their own. The effects are particularly pronounced in protocols with state-sensitive pricing models, such as automated market makers (AMMs) like Uniswap.

  To illustrate, consider a minimal AMM-style decentralized exchange contract that uses the constant product formula to determine token output:

```
contract MiniDEX {
 uint public ethReserve;
 uint public tokenReserve;
 mapping(address => uint) public tokenBalances;

 constructor() {
   ethReserve = 100 ether;
   tokenReserve = 1000000;
 }

 function swapETHForTokens() public payable {
   uint tokensOut = getTokenAmount(msg.value);
   require(tokenReserve >= tokensOut, "Insufficient token
liquidity");
   ethReserve += msg.value;
```

```
        tokenReserve -= tokensOut;
        tokenBalances[msg.sender] += tokensOut;
    }

    function getTokenAmount(uint ethIn) public view returns
(uint) {
        return (ethIn * tokenReserve) / (ethReserve + ethIn);
    }
}
```

In this system, the number of tokens received is a function of current reserves. A large incoming swap increases the ETH reserve and reduces the token reserve, thereby raising the price for subsequent buyers. If a frontrunner detects a large pending swap in the mempool, they can submit a buy transaction at the current, lower price, ensuring it is mined first by paying a higher gas fee. Once the victim's transaction executes and unfavorably updates the reserves, the frontrunner completes the loop by selling the tokens back at a profit, extracting value from the victim's trade in a pattern known as a sandwich attack.
A simplified attacker contract might be structured as follows:

```
contract SandwichAttacker {
    MiniDEX public dex;
    address public owner;

    constructor(address _dex) {
        dex = MiniDEX(_dex);
        owner = msg.sender;
    }

    function executeFrontRun() public payable {
        dex.swapETHForTokens{value: msg.value}();
    }

    function executeBackRun() public {
        uint tokenBalance = dex.tokenBalances(address(this));
        // Simulate token sale logic for illustrative purposes
        dex.tokenReserve() += tokenBalance;
        dex.ethReserve() -= (tokenBalance * dex.ethReserve()) /
dex.tokenReserve();
        payable(owner).transfer(address(this).balance);
    }

    receive() external payable {}
}
```

While simplified, this contract captures the strategic bracketing of the victim's trade: a purchase before and a sale after, thereby "sandwiching" the victim. In reality, MEV bots automate this behavior across multiple blocks and exchanges, leveraging highly optimized mempool scanning, priority gas auctions, and atomic transaction bundles.

The critical feature of this exploit is that it does not stem from any flaw in the MiniDEX contract itself. The code executes exactly as intended, computing prices based on the current state. The vulnerability lies in transaction-order dependence, a structural property of Ethereum's public block production model. Since the mempool is visible and ordering is economically driven, adversaries with sufficient speed and capital can systematically front-run vulnerable transactions.

The real-world impact of front-running is systemic. In DeFi protocols, users attempting swaps, providing liquidity, liquidating loans, or minting NFTs often find themselves outmaneuvered by bots that extract profits from their actions before they can complete. Victims suffer increased slippage, failed trades, or loss of arbitrage opportunities. Meanwhile, front-runners extract risk-free profit through microseconds of strategic advantage.

Efforts to mitigate this behavior include transaction batching, private mempools, commit-reveal schemes, and adoption of MEV-aware systems like Flashbots. However, the phenomenon remains deeply embedded in Ethereum's economic model and continues to shape how protocols are designed and deployed. The front-running attack is no longer a rare event but a structural element of blockchain-based markets, and understanding its mechanics is essential for any participant operating within DeFi. This attack stems from the threat of *Execution Manipulation*, specifically from the vulnerability of *Transaction Ordering Dependence in Transparent Mempool Environments*.

- **FairWin:** The FairWin Timestamp Dependence Exploit is a manipulation vulnerability in which contracts rely on block.timestamp (or now) for logic-critical decisions, enabling miners to bias execution outcomes by subtly altering the block timestamp within permitted consensus limits.

  The FairWin contract, which operated as a pseudo-gambling and investment application during its brief and controversial tenure in September 2019, exemplifies how dependence on miner-controlled variables, particularly block.timestamp, can undermine fairness and determinism in smart contract execution. FairWin was, at one point, among the most gas-consuming contracts on the Ethereum network, drawing attention not only for its speculative, pyramid-like structure but also for its flawed use of temporal variables to govern bonuses, queue logic, and reward eligibility.

  In Solidity, the block.timestamp global variable provides the timestamp of the current block, ostensibly representing the moment at which the block was mined. However, this value is not a fixed or externally verified quantity; it is set by the block miner and must only satisfy minimal constraints: it must be greater than the previous block's timestamp and within an allowable drift, generally capped at around 900 s. Within this window, miners may arbitrarily forward or delay the timestamp, creating an avenue for strategic exploitation if smart contracts incorporate this value into logic that determines bonuses, state changes, or conditional behaviors.

FairWin's code incorporated timestamp-based features into its gamification and reward mechanics. For example, users could receive bonuses if they deposited Ether when the current timestamp met certain conditions. In a simplified illustration of this logic, consider the following Solidity contract:

```
contract TimeBasedBonus {
 mapping(address => uint256) public balances;

 function deposit() public payable {
   if (block.timestamp % 15 == 0) {
      balances[msg.sender] += msg.value * 2;
   } else {
      balances[msg.sender] += msg.value;
   }
 }

 function withdraw(uint256 amount) public {
   require(balances[msg.sender] >= amount, "Insufficient
balance");
   balances[msg.sender] -= amount;
   payable(msg.sender).transfer(amount);
 }

 function getTime() public view returns (uint) {
   return block.timestamp;
 }

 receive() external payable {}
}
```

This contract rewards a depositor with double the amount sent if block. The timestamp modulo 15 equals zero when the transaction is processed. Superficially, this may appear as a form of on-chain randomness or a creative engagement mechanism. In practice, however, it grants block producers, the miners, the ability to rig the outcome. If a miner submits a deposit transaction and mines the block that includes it, they can slightly adjust the timestamp to satisfy the modulus condition, thereby triggering the bonus. The bonus appears fair, but it is achieved through asymmetric access to the mechanism governing eligibility: the block timestamp itself.

Such manipulation does not violate Ethereum's consensus rules, as the timestamp is valid as long as it falls within the acceptable bounds. The result is indistinguishable on the chain from a naturally aligned timestamp, making the exploit undetectable in isolation. Manipulation remains silent but effective, granting miners an unfair economic advantage in contracts that interpret time as a condition for reward or priority.

The real FairWin contract contained numerous interdependencies between user actions, time-sensitive reward calculations, and queue advancement. Timestamp checks determined whether a user was eligible for an immediate payout, whether they could re-enter the reward pool, and, in some cases, whether they could withdraw at all. A miner or validator with sufficient insight into the contract's state and timing logic could delay or expedite block production to manipulate outcomes. For example, by timing a transaction to execute precisely when block. timestamp triggered a favorable bonus or when a queue cutoff could be bypassed, an attacker could optimize their returns at the expense of fair participation.

Importantly, this attack did not require specialized contracts or deep EVM manipulation. A coordinated miner, or a user colluding with one, could conduct the exploit by simply mining their own transactions and adjusting timestamps to meet the criteria embedded in the contract logic. As FairWin drew massive user engagement and capital flow, such manipulations, even if subtle, had outsized consequences. Participants interacting with the system without this strategic capability were disadvantaged in a game that appeared randomized or time neutral.

The broader implications of the FairWin incident go beyond its specific contract. It exposed a dangerous assumption in many early Ethereum contracts: that block. timestamp is a reliable and impartial variable. While suitable for approximate timekeeping, it is fundamentally unsuitable for randomness, critical timing gates, or any logic that assumes miner neutrality. The FairWin case thus serves as a definitive example of how adversaries with control over block production can weaponize timestamp dependence to violate fairness in decentralized protocols without violating protocol rules. This attack stems from the threat of *Execution Manipulation*, specifically from the vulnerabilities of *Timestamp Dependence and Miner-controlled Temporal Logic*.

8.1.5 User Manipulation

Distinct from technical manipulation, this category encompasses attacks that rely on social engineering, behavioral assumptions, or the presentation of adversarial code. These attacks target the human elements of smart contract interaction, greed, overconfidence, or trust in interfaces, by creating scenarios that bait attackers themselves into becoming victims.

- **Honeypot Attack:** A Honeypot Attack is a defensive deception technique in which a smart contract is deliberately designed to appear vulnerable to exploitation, typically by simulating common flaws such as unrestricted withdrawals or reentrancy bugs, while in fact containing logic that traps malicious users and causes them to forfeit their funds upon attempted exploitation.
  Honeypot contracts invert the traditional dynamics of vulnerability exploitation. Rather than being exploited, they exploited. These contracts are deliberately engineered to lure malicious actors by simulating exploitable conditions, unguarded Ether transfers, public access to privileged functions, or apparent logic oversights, while embedding subtle mechanics that ensure only the original deployer or a carefully controlled execution path can successfully retrieve any funds. For all other users, particularly those interacting with attacker contracts, the exploit either fails silently, reverts, or traps the attacker's funds.
  This attack class gained notoriety during Ethereum's formative years, as developers and white-hat engineers deployed honeypots to punish opportunists using scanning tools or mempool watchers to identify seemingly weak contracts. The sophistication of honeypot design lies in its use of obscure Solidity behaviors, such as the quirks of msg.sender.call, insufficient gas stipends for fallback functions, or EOA-only behavior logic, to mislead attackers without ever violating contract correctness. The honeypot thus transforms the attacker's own assumptions into liabilities.
  Consider a seemingly straightforward contract that claims to reward users who guess a preset number:

```
contract Honeypot {
 uint public luckyNumber = 7;

 function claimReward(uint guess) public {
   if (guess == luckyNumber) {
      (bool success, ) = msg.sender.call{value:
address(this).balance}("");
      require(success, "Transfer failed");
   }
 }

 receive() external payable {}
}
```

At a glance, this contract appears vulnerable. The number is publicly visible, and calling claimReward(7) seems to transfer all ETH to the caller. An attacker, believing they've discovered an exploitable logic flaw, might construct a contract to automate the withdrawal and receive the transferred funds:

```
contract Attacker {
 Honeypot public target;
 address public owner;

 constructor(address _target) {
   target = Honeypot(_target);
   owner = msg.sender;
 }

 function attack() external payable {
   require(msg.value >= 1 ether, "Need ETH to bait reward");
   payable(address(target)).transfer(msg.value);
   target.claimReward(7);
 }

 receive() external payable {
   payable(owner).transfer(address(this).balance);
 }
}
```

In this setup, the attacker's contract deposits Ether into the honeypot and then calls the reward function. However, the trap is embedded within the msg.sender. call logic. In Solidity, when a contract receives Ether via a call, the default gas stipend is 2300 units, which is insufficient for complex fallback logic or even for some simple operations. If the attacker's contract attempts to perform actions during this callback or inadvertently reverts (e.g., due to a fallback gas failure or explicit revert), the call fails. The require (success) condition then triggers a revert, nullifying the transfer and preserving the contract balance.

Even more advanced honeypots embed EOA-only success conditions or deliberately manipulate internal state so that only the deployer, using an externally owned account (EOA), can successfully pass through the reward logic. These contracts might appear to function during static analysis or pass superficial audits, but are coded to fail during dynamic interaction unless the exact gas, call type, and sender identity align with the original deployer's context.

The genius of the honeypot lies not just in technical misdirection but in psychological manipulation. The attacker is led to believe they have uncovered a genuine weakness, reinforced by the transparency of Solidity source code and public state variables. The moment they act, whether by submitting funds, invoking a crafted exploit, or launching a malicious contract, they fall into the trap. Their ETH is accepted, their contract reverts or stalls, and the honeypot contract survives untouched, often indefinitely, collecting the remains of failed exploit attempts.

While honeypots are not widespread due to ethical concerns and potential legal ambiguity, they represent one of the most compelling illustrations of adversarial thinking in Ethereum. They exploit not the contract's vulnerabilities, but the attacker's overconfidence, greed, and flawed assumptions. The effectiveness of a honeypot does not rest on its ability to enforce access control, but on its mastery of smart contract semantics and its deep understanding of how attackers operate. This attack is categorized as a Behavioral Deception Exploit, enabled by the *Intentional Misrepresentation of Contract Logic and Dynamic Execution Constraints*.

- **Phishing-style exploits:** The tx.origin exploit is a phishing-based authorization vulnerability in which a contract uses tx.origin, rather than msg.sender, to verify permissions, allowing attackers to hijack access by luring the rightful user into executing a malicious intermediary call.

Phishing-style exploits that abuse the tx.origin variable for access control are among the most insidious classes of attacks in Ethereum's history. These attacks do not require vulnerabilities in arithmetic, logic, or storage. Rather, they exploit developer misunderstanding of Ethereum's transaction call stack, particularly the semantic distinction between tx.origin and msg.sender. The former always refers to the original externally owned account (EOA) that initiated the transaction, even across multiple nested call layers. The latter reflects the immediate caller of the current function. When developers mistakenly authorize sensitive operations based on tx.origin, they unwittingly expose their contracts to social-engineering attacks that exploit the chain of trust.

The canonical form of this vulnerability appears in contracts that protect privileged operations, such as transferring funds, by verifying that tx.origin == owner. On the surface, this appears sufficient, as only the owner's address can pass the check. However, if the owner is tricked into interacting with a malicious contract that forwards the call, the check is bypassed. The originating address (tx.origin) remains the owner, but the current caller (msg.sender) is now untrusted attacker-controlled code.

Consider the following simplified implementation of such a vulnerable contract:

```
contract TokenVault {
 address public owner;

 constructor() {
   owner = msg.sender;
 }

 function transferTo(address payable _to, uint amount)
public {
   require(tx.origin == owner, "Not authorized");
   _to.transfer(amount);
 }
```

```
  receive() external payable {}
}
```

This contract's transferTo() function authorizes Ether transfers if tx.origin equals the owner address. The developer intends to restrict fund movements to the owner's direct actions. However, this logic breaks down if the owner is manipulated into indirectly initiating the call.

An attacker can exploit this by deploying a malicious contract that contains a function which, when invoked, forwards a call to transferTo() on the victim's vault. This call encodes a transfer to the attacker's own address, wrapped within a function that the attacker asks the vault owner to call. The attacker's contract may present itself as a harmless interface, a rewards claim, a token airdrop, or a decentralized application front-end, to lure the victim.

Here is a simplified version of such an attacker contract:

```
contract PhishingAttack {
  address payable public vault;

  constructor(address payable _vault) {
    vault = _vault;
  }

  function trigger() public {
    vault.call(abi.encodeWithSignature("transferTo(address,u
int256)", msg.sender, 10 ether));
  }

  receive() external payable {}
}
```

The attack hinges on social engineering. The attacker shares the PhishingAttack contract with the victim and entices them, perhaps through a UI or a persuasive message, to call trigger(). Once executed, the call chain is initiated from the victim's EOA, satisfying the tx.origin == owner condition in the vault. However, because msg.sender within the vault is now the attacker contract, the actual logic being executed is under the control of a third party.

The vault's transferTo() function then transfers funds as instructed, assuming the action is initiated by the owner. But the destination address and parameters have been provided by the attacker's contract. By the time the owner realizes the true nature of the transaction, the Ether has already been transferred, and the exploit is complete. On chain, the transaction appears legitimate, signed by the owner, with no apparent irregularities, leaving the attacker with plausible deniability and the victim with irreversible loss.

The sophistication of this exploit lies in its simplicity. No complex attack vector is required beyond a misused global variable and a plausible lure. The vulnerable contract performs its logic exactly as programmed. The error lies in its blind trust in tx.origin as a basis for authorization, ignoring that tx.origin spans the entire external call chain, not just the immediate caller.

These attacks have persisted in various forms across decentralized applications, especially in systems where contract calls are abstracted through interfaces or where users are encouraged to interact with contracts via third-party tools. The lesson is foundational: authorization checks must rely on msg.sender, not tx.origin, and should be implemented with tightly scoped access-control mechanisms, such as role-based permissions or ownership modifiers. This attack stems from the threat of *Unauthorized Access*, specifically arising due to the vulnerability of *Broken Authorization via Misuse of tx.origin.*

As Fig. 8.1 presents, the attacker-centric taxonomy not only clarifies the strategic dimensions of smart contract exploitation but also underscores the multifaceted nature of threats in decentralized systems. By focusing on how each exploit is executed, rather than on which vulnerability it targets, this classification enables security analysts, developers, and auditors to anticipate adversarial behaviors and design countermeasures grounded in attacker intent. As smart contract complexity increases, so too does the need to interpret security through the adversary's lens.

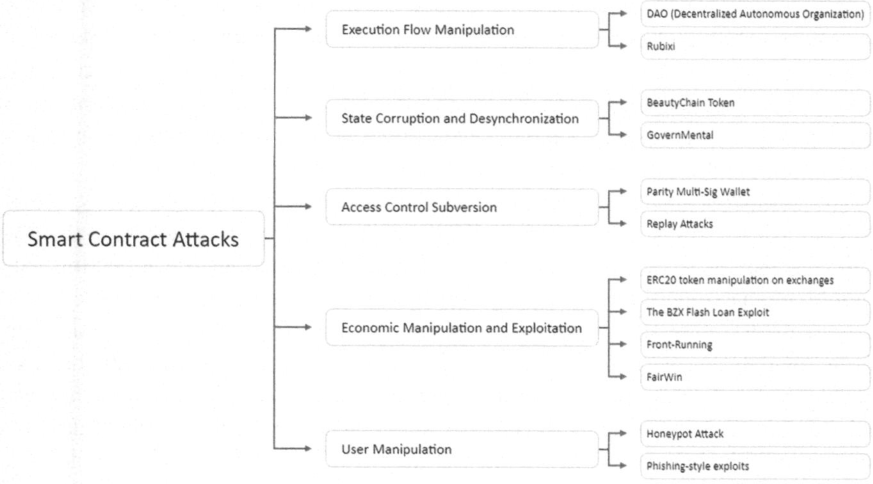

Fig. 8.1 Smart contracts attacks

8.2 Comparative Analysis

This subsection provides a comparative analysis of the vulnerabilities discussed in Sects. 8.1.1, 8.1.2, 8.1.3, 8.1.4, and 8.1.5. While each case presents a unique mode of exploitation, broader patterns emerge when we examine them through the lens of prevalence and impact. Here, we distinguish between the most *common* attacks, which have recurred across many contracts or ecosystems, and the *most dangerous* ones, which have caused irreversible financial or systemic damage. This comparative lens allows readers to understand not only how these attacks occur but also why certain vulnerabilities persist in smart contract development and which types of vulnerabilities pose the greatest risk to decentralized infrastructure.

8.2.1 Most Common Attacks

Among the broad landscape of smart contract vulnerabilities, certain attacks recur with striking frequency due to underlying flaws in contract architecture, developer misconceptions, or unresolved protocol design patterns. One of the most pervasive is the Front-Running attack. Its prevalence stems not from faulty contract logic, but from an inherent structural openness of the Ethereum network itself. By exploiting the transparency of the mempool and the deterministic execution order of transactions, adversaries, often automated MEV bots, can monitor, intercept, and reorder pending trades, particularly in automated market maker protocols such as Uniswap. The ease with which this attack can be automated, coupled with the predictability of token pricing mechanisms, has made it one of the most routine forms of extractive behavior in decentralized finance. Its recurrence is rooted in transaction-order dependence and the assumption that execution order will mirror submission order, a design assumption frequently violated in practice.

The Honeypot Contracts represent another widespread class of attacks, albeit with an inverted adversarial dynamic. While not perpetrated by attackers in the traditional sense, these deceptive contracts bait would-be exploiters by appearing vulnerable, often to reentrancy or unguarded balance transfers, but are constructed such that any exploitation attempt triggers the loss of funds. Their ubiquity is tied to the public availability of smart contracts and the proliferation of scanners that detect low-hanging vulnerabilities. Honeypots capitalize on predictable attacker behaviors and the superficial analysis performed by automated tools. Their repeated deployment across blockchain explorers and test networks highlights how psychological deception, not just code logic, drives many interactions in permissionless environments.

A third commonly observed case is the FairWin—Timestamp Dependence vulnerability. Contracts like FairWin relied heavily on block timestamps to trigger game logic or calculating bonuses. Such design introduces a subtle yet exploitable vector, since miners have limited but effective control over the block timestamp field. As a result, any logic tied to now or block.timestamp becomes susceptible to manipulation. The widespread misunderstanding of Ethereum's block production mechanics among developers has led to repeated misuses of time-based conditions, making this vulnerability a recurring theme across lottery, betting, and scheduling applications.

These attacks are united not just by their technical vectors but by their frequency in real deployments. They expose the persistent gap between perceived and actual contract behavior, fueled by developer assumptions, inadequate audits, and overreliance on superficially secure patterns. The recurring nature of these vulnerabilities, transaction ordering, perceived openness, and block metadata misuse, illustrates a systemic pattern in which ease of development and perceived determinism create fertile ground for exploitation.

8.2.2 Most Dangerous Attacks

In contrast to common attacks that exploit visible or surface-level patterns, some smart contract exploits manifest with devastating consequences despite their relative rarity. The DAO Attack remains the most iconic and destructive instance in Ethereum's history. Through a reentrancy vulnerability embedded within the DAO's withdrawal logic, the attacker was able to recursively drain a significant portion of the contract's holdings before its internal balance was correctly updated. The subtlety of the logic flaw, buried within inter-contract calls, coupled with the magnitude of the funds at stake, created a scenario in which nearly $60 million in Ether was siphoned off within hours. The fallout included not just financial loss, but an ideological split and the subsequent creation of Ethereum Classic. The attack's catastrophic impact underscores how recursive control-flow manipulation, particularly when triggered during value-transfer operations, can undermine even high-profile, thoroughly audited projects.

Similarly, the Parity Multisig Wallet Hack, especially its second iteration, illustrates how vulnerabilities in contract initialization and upgradeability can lead to irreversible system-wide collapse. A publicly callable initWallet function, left exposed in the library contract, allowed a user to gain ownership and then accidentally self-destruct the contract. This permanently disabled all dependent multisig wallets and froze over half a million Ether. The destructiveness of this attack was not in its complexity but in the absolute finality of its consequences: assets became inaccessible forever. The danger lay in the system-level interdependence on a single contract and the silent, misunderstood power of initialization logic.

The BZX Flash Loan Exploit typifies a newer class of economically motivated, high-speed, composable attacks. Flash loans themselves are not vulnerable, but when paired with poorly isolated logic in DeFi protocols, they allow an attacker to manipulate price oracles, lending positions, or liquidity pools, all within a single atomic transaction. The BZX exploits demonstrated how chain composability and instantaneous liquidity could be orchestrated to extract large profits by momentarily distorting protocol state. What makes this class of attack exceptionally dangerous is the combination of speed, invisibility to traditional audit logic, and the systemic shockwave it sends through interlinked financial primitives. The attacker holds no funds, takes no long-term risk, and walks away with manipulated gains while leaving the system intact but drained.

Finally, Replay Attacks, while mitigated in modern Ethereum through EIP-155, represent a foundational cryptographic failure. By allowing signed transactions to execute identically across divergent chains (Ethereum and Ethereum Classic), early replay attacks enabled attackers to duplicate actions, causing unauthorized transfers or repeated contract interactions. The flaw was not in the contract code, but in the signing mechanism's omission of chain-specific context. As such, these attacks highlight how protocol-layer design oversights can expose users to systemic cross-chain risks that traditional auditing methods cannot detect.

These most dangerous attacks share a common theme: irreversibility. Whether through recursive depletion, permanent destruction, cross-chain duplication, or instantaneous state collapse, their impact transcends individual contracts and calls into question the integrity of the broader ecosystem. Each reflects a deeper architectural flaw in which a single overlooked assumption cascades into catastrophic failure.

The contrast between the most common and the most dangerous smart contract attacks reveals an essential tension in decentralized systems. Frequency does not equate to severity, and severity is often masked by rarity. Attacks such as front-running and timestamp manipulation occur regularly but typically yield only incremental value extraction. In contrast, reentrancy, unguarded initialization, and flash loan composability, though less frequently encountered, can dismantle entire protocols in seconds. A mature security posture must therefore consider both vectors: the habitual patterns that erode user trust through continual exploitation, and the latent threats that, if triggered, can obliterate trust in a single event. Robust smart contract design demands not only protection against what often occurs, but also resilience against what must never occur at all.

8.3 Chapter Summary

This chapter examined the anatomy and consequences of major real-world smart contract attacks, revealing how design flaws, coding missteps, and misplaced assumptions about the blockchain environment converge to produce critical vulnerabilities. By analyzing exploit mechanisms such as reentrancy, arithmetic underflows, unprotected self-destruction, and transaction-order dependence, we traced the technical pathways through which adversaries compromise contract integrity and extract value. The case studies illustrated that while many attacks originate from recurring developer oversights, such as improper state synchronization or unsafe external calls, others exploit deeper infrastructural traits, including delegatecall misuse, mempool transparency, and the mutability of shared components. The comparative lens applied throughout the chapter revealed a striking contrast: frequent but preventable flaws continue to erode surface-level security, while rarer attacks often stem from systemic vulnerabilities that can lead to catastrophic failure. Collectively, these insights highlight that securing smart contracts requires not only disciplined programming and thorough auditing, but also a structural understanding of blockchain execution semantics. Effective defense demands anticipating both what can go wrong in code and how adversaries may weaponize the very properties of the decentralized environment itself.

References

1. Sayeed, S., Marco-Gisbert, H., Caira, T.: Smart contract: attacks and protections. IEEE Access. **8**, 24416–24427 (2020)
2. Atzei, N., Bartoletti, M., Cimoli, T.: A survey of attacks on ethereum smart contracts (sok). In: International Conference on Principles of Security and Trust. Springer Berlin Heidelberg, Berlin, Heidelberg (2017)
3. Liu, C., et al.: Reguard: finding reentrancy bugs in smart contracts. In: Proceedings of the 40th International Conference on Software Engineering: Companion Proceedings (2018)
4. Rodler, M., et al.: Sereum: protecting existing smart contracts against re-entrancy attacks. arXiv preprint https://arxiv.org/abs/1812.05934 (2018)
5. Luu, L., et al.: Making smart contracts smarter. In: Proceedings of the 2016 ACM SIGSAC Conference on Computer and Communications Security (2016)
6. Singh, A., et al.: Blockchain smart contracts formalization: approaches and challenges to address vulnerabilities. Comput. Secur. **88**, 101654 (2020)
7. Kemmoe, V.Y., et al.: Recent advances in smart contracts: a technical overview and state of the art. IEEE Access. **8**, 117782–117801 (2020)
8. Jiao, T., et al.: A survey of ethereum smart contract security: attacks and detection. Distrib. Ledger Technol.: Res. Pract. **3**(3), 1–28 (2024)
9. Wu, G., et al.: A comprehensive survey of smart contract security: state of the art and research directions. J. Netw. Comput. Appl., 103882 (2024)
10. Destefanis, G., et al.: Smart contracts vulnerabilities: a call for blockchain software engineering? In: 2018 International Workshop on Blockchain Oriented Software Engineering (IWBOSE). IEEE (2018)
11. Alaba, F.A., et al.: Smart contracts security application and challenges: a review. Cloud Comput. Data Sci., 15–41 (2024)
12. Mense, A., Flatscher, M.: Security vulnerabilities in ethereum smart contracts. In: Proceedings of the 20th International Conference on Information Integration and Web-Based Applications & Services (2018)

Chapter 9
Analyzers and Detection Tools for Smart Contracts

Abstract This chapter provides a comprehensive exploration of analyzers and detection tools for smart contracts, highlighting their pivotal role in safeguarding decentralized applications as they scale across financial and computational ecosystems. It systematically classifies tools by methodology, including symbolic execution, abstract interpretation, formal verification, fuzzing, AI-based detection, code instrumentation, control flow analysis, and disassembly analysis, while also distinguishing between academic and industrial solutions. Within each category, it examines representative tools, emphasizing how they detect or identify vulnerabilities such as reentrancy, arithmetic errors, transaction-order dependence, gas inefficiencies, and access control flaws. Special attention is given to the rise of AI-driven frameworks, which combine machine learning, graph neural networks, and multimodal approaches to expand detection coverage and adaptability, though often at the cost of interpretability and computational overhead. Furthermore, this chapter compares the strengths and limitations of traditional methods, which provide formal guarantees and explainability, with modern approaches that excel in scalability and generalization but face challenges with interpretability and data requirements. Also, it stresses the importance of integrating these tools into broader auditing workflows, where they complement manual reviews and formal practices to ensure resilient smart contract development lifecycles. Ultimately, this chapter concludes that the future of vulnerability detection lies in hybrid systems that merge formal rigor with AI adaptability, offering more comprehensive, precise, and efficient security analysis for increasingly complex decentralized ecosystems.

Smart contract security has emerged as a critical focus area as decentralized applications continue to expand across financial and computational ecosystems [1]. This chapter explores the evolving landscape of analyzers and detection tools for identifying vulnerabilities in smart contracts, underscoring their pivotal role in ensuring trust, correctness, and operational robustness. The tools examined span both academic and industrial domains and are systematically organized according to core analytical methodologies, including symbolic execution, formal verification, abstract interpretation, and fuzz testing [2, 3]. Within each methodological category, tools are further classified as either academic or industrial, reflecting their origin,

S. HajiHosseinKhani et al., *Understanding Cybersecurity for Smart Contracts*,
https://doi.org/10.1007/978-3-032-28863-9_9

intended application, and level of deployment maturity. This dual-layered structure enables a comprehensive overview of contemporary detection capabilities, followed by a comparative evaluation of tool performance, strengths, and limitations across both domains. The chapter concludes by addressing the integration of these tools into smart contract auditing practices, emphasizing best practices and key challenges in maintaining security throughout the development and deployment lifecycle [4–6].

9.1 Overview of Tools for Detecting Vulnerabilities

Smart contract security has become a vital focus in both academic research and industry practice, leading to the development of numerous tools to detect and identify vulnerabilities in deployed and in-development contracts [1]. These tools vary significantly in their design goals, detection capabilities, and underlying methodologies, which range from symbolic execution and formal verification to machine learning, fuzz testing, static analysis, and taint tracking [2]. To provide a structured understanding of this landscape, we categorize existing tools based on their core detection methodology [7, 8]. Within each methodological category, tools are further subdivided into academic and industrial solutions, reflecting their origin, intended use case, and deployment maturity level [4]. This organization enables a comparative view that highlights both research-driven innovation and real-world applicability. Each tool is briefly described to convey its key mechanisms, strengths, and limitations.

9.1.1 Abstract Interpretation Tools

Abstract interpretation-based tools analyze smart contracts by constructing mathematical abstractions of program behavior, allowing them to reason about all possible execution paths without executing the code [5, 7, 9]. This formal method enables early detection and identification of subtle or edge-case vulnerabilities, such as gas inefficiencies, unhandled exceptions, or unintended control flows, that might elude conventional testing [6, 10, 11]. By simulating over-approximate program states, these tools provide provable guarantees about contract safety or flag paths that could lead to resource exhaustion or logic violations [12–14]. The following tools exemplify the utility of abstract interpretation in both detection and identification contexts.

- **Academic tools**
  Asparagus—Detector [15]
  Asparagus is an abstract interpretation-based tool that analyzes gas consumption behavior in Ethereum smart contracts. It synthesizes parametric upper bounds on gas consumption using polyhedral and real algebraic geometry techniques to

model and predict gas usage across all possible execution paths. Asparagus outperforms earlier tools like Gastap in both applicability and bound tightness, making it more effective at detecting vulnerabilities such as gas-limit underestimation, out-of-gas exceptions, and excessive gas use within loops [13, 15]. By offering fine-grained upper bounds with mathematical rigor, Asparagus enhances the precision of gas-aware auditing and mitigates risks associated with unpredictable execution failures. However, its specialized focus on gas behavior means it does not cover logic-related vulnerabilities, and its reliance on complex symbolic models may limit scalability for large contracts with intricate control flows [15].

MichelsonLiSA—Detector [16]

MichelsonLiSA extends abstract interpretation techniques to the Tezos blockchain ecosystem by applying the LiSA (Library for Static Analysis) framework to analyze Michelson smart contracts, Tezos's stack-based low-level language. The tool translates Michelson bytecode into a high-level intermediate representation (IR), enabling semantic analysis via control-flow graphs (CFGs), taint tracking, and data-flow analysis. Its main strength lies in its ability to detect untrusted cross-contract invocations and improper state transitions, which are especially relevant in Tezos applications. MichelsonLiSA's layered abstraction pipeline bridges the gap between low-level execution semantics and high-level vulnerability analysis [16]. However, its effectiveness is closely tied to the accuracy of the IR translation and may require additional configuration to handle Michelson code with non-standard stack manipulation patterns or unconventional branching logic.

Gastap—Identifier [13]

Gastap is one of the earliest tools to apply abstract interpretation for gas-aware analysis in Ethereum smart contracts. It automatically infers upper bounds on gas consumption for public functions by combining control-flow graph construction with size analysis and gas-equation generation. Accepting both Solidity source code and EVM bytecode, Gastap provides precise annotations that help identify functions susceptible to out-of-gas exceptions [13]. Its outputs are particularly useful for contract verification, debugging, and gas-efficiency certification. The tool's web interface and automated annotations enhance accessibility for developers. However, while effective at profiling gas usage, Gastap does not detect logic vulnerabilities or cross-function interactions, and its analysis can be overly conservative in contracts with complex loops or recursion, potentially generating loose bounds that reduce practical utility [13].

Abstract interpretation provides a mathematically grounded approach to vulnerability analysis, enabling detection and identification of issues arising from unbounded execution paths, gas inefficiencies, and unverified inter-contract operations [7, 9, 17]. Tools such as Asparagus, MichelsonLiSA, and Gastap demonstrate the versatility of this approach across blockchain environments, from Ethereum to Tezos, and highlight its potential to enhance smart contract reliability. While powerful for formal reasoning and resource estimation, these tools often face challenges with scalability, over-approximation, and limited coverage of logic-based vulnerabilities, underscoring the need for complementary analysis techniques for comprehensive security auditing [18–20].

9.1.2 AI-Based Methods

AI-based tools represent a modern and highly scalable approach to smart contract vulnerability analysis. These tools apply advanced machine learning (ML) and deep learning (DL) algorithms to automatically extract patterns from contract code and transactional behavior. By training models on labeled data, they can identify both known and previously unseen vulnerabilities with high precision. Unlike rule-based systems, AI-driven tools can generalize across different coding styles and contract structures, making them especially effective in detecting semantic flaws, logic bugs, and abnormal behaviors. This category is divided into tools designed for vulnerability detection and those aimed at vulnerability identification, often distinguished by the granularity of analysis or application phase. Below is a selection of AI-based tools that illustrate the evolving role of artificial intelligence in smart contract security.

- **Academic tools**
  Block-Gram—Detector [21]
  Block-Gram employs an innovative approach by extracting low-dimensional, semantically rich features directly from Ethereum bytecode. The process involves converting bytecode into opcode sequences, segmenting these into functional blocks, and then mining both structural and attribute-level information. What distinguishes Block-Gram is its integration of Shapley Additive Explanations (SHAP), which enhances interpretability by highlighting which features most influence detection outcomes. Released in 2023, this model effectively detects vulnerabilities such as integer overflow/underflow, transaction-ordering dependence (TOD), call-stack-depth attacks, timestamp dependencies, and reentrancy issues. Its architecture not only accelerates detection latency but also facilitates a transparent understanding of the model's decisions.
  Cross-Modality Mutual Learning Vulnerability Detector—Detector [22]
  The Cross-Modality Mutual Learning Vulnerability Detector introduces a dual-network paradigm in which a teacher network, trained on both source code and bytecode, informs a student network that operates solely on bytecode. This cross-modal transfer significantly improves the student model's detection capability by leveraging richer semantic alignment during training. Published in 2023, the tool is particularly adept at identifying reentrancy, delegatecall misuse, timestamp dependence, and arithmetic overflows/underflows. The model's robustness across different smart contract representations exemplifies the advantages of mutual learning strategies in AI-based security analysis.
  CodeNet—Detector [23]

CodeNet proposes a novel representation strategy by transforming smart contracts into two-dimensional images while preserving the structural semantics of the original code. This transformation enables CodeNet's convolutional neural network (CNN) to process smart contracts in a manner similar to how it processes visual data, allowing it to learn abstract syntactic and semantic features efficiently. Introduced in 2022, the system can detect a range of vulnerabilities, including unchecked low-level calls, tx.origin misuse, timestamp dependencies, and reentrancy attacks. By shifting vulnerability detection into the domain of image recognition, CodeNet demonstrates the potential of cross-disciplinary techniques in smart contract analysis.

ContractArmor–detector [24]

ContractArmor combines symbolic analysis with generative AI by integrating a rule-based static analysis engine with ChatGPT's natural language processing capabilities. The tool constructs potential attack surfaces by identifying critical variables, suspicious numeric patterns, and high-risk logic constructs, and then verifies them using contextual queries against the GPT model. Released in 2024, ContractArmor provides a hybrid methodology that combines expert rules with AI-driven evaluation, enhancing the precision of vulnerability detection for integer manipulation, insecure calls, and reentrancy logic. Its dual analysis approach is particularly useful for auditing complex contract behaviors.

Deep Learning-Based Malicious Smart Contracts Detection Scheme—Detector [25]

Deep Learning-Based Malicious Smart Contracts Detection Scheme leverages a combination of deep recurrent neural architectures, specifically LSTM, GRU, and ANN models, to classify smart contracts as malicious or benign. By transforming bytecode into opcode sequences and encoding them into high-dimensional vectors using one-hot representations, the system captures behavioral patterns indicative of threats. Released in 2022, this framework focuses on identifying malicious contract behavior rather than targeting specific vulnerability types, making it especially valuable for filtering out high-risk contracts during deployment or transaction validation.

Deep Learning-Based Vulnerability Detection Framework—Detector [26]

It is proposed in 2023 by Narayana and Sathiyamurthy. This framework leverages deep learning models, such as artificial neural networks (ANNs), autoencoders, and multi-label classifiers, to detect critical smart contract vulnerabilities, including reentrancy, Denial of Service (DoS), and transaction-origin misuse. The approach extracts syntactic and semantic features from the Abstract Syntax Trees (ASTs) of Solidity contracts, transforming them into structured representations suitable for neural processing. By applying multi-label classification, it can simultaneously detect multiple vulnerabilities, improving analysis efficiency. Its key advantage lies in its ability to learn complex, non-linear patterns from code representations without relying heavily on handcrafted rules. However, it requires a large, labeled training dataset to perform effectively, and, like many deep learning models, it may face interpretability challenges.

Deep Learning and Expert Rules-Based Vulnerability Detection Mechanism—Detector [27]

Deep Learning and Expert Rules-Based Vulnerability Detection Mechanism is a hybrid mechanism that integrates the strengths of deep learning and domain-specific expert rules for vulnerability detection in Ethereum smart contracts. The system first uses Graph Neural Networks (GNNs) to analyze the contract's dependency graphs and structural relationships, flagging potential vulnerabilities such as reentrancy, timestamp dependency, hardcoded gas usage, and code injections. The flagged results are then verified using predefined expert rules at the EVM level, providing a secondary validation layer that enhances precision and reduces false positives. This two-stage design combines the adaptability of machine learning with the precision of formal methods. The approach benefits from increased robustness and explainability, although its performance can be constrained by the quality of rule definitions and the need for significant computational resources during training and graph processing.

DeepInfer—Detector [28]

DeepInfer is a deep learning-based framework introduced for inferring function signatures and return types from Ethereum Virtual Machine (EVM) bytecode. It lifts bytecode into an intermediate representation (IR) that preserves semantic information and applies Graph Neural Networks (GNNs) to extract type-related features from the resulting structure. This enables accurate inference of contract behavior even in the absence of source code. DeepInfer is particularly effective for reverse engineering and auditing opaque contracts, though its performance may be limited when applied to heavily obfuscated or non-standard contract architectures.

DistilBERT-MLP/LSTM Reentrancy Detector—Detector [29]

DistilBERT-MLP/LSTM Reentrancy Detector detects reentrancy vulnerabilities in Solidity smart contracts using a three-stage deep learning pipeline. The process begins with custom tokenization of Solidity code, followed by masked language model pre-training using DistilBERT to capture contextual semantics. Finally, the model is fine-tuned using a binary classifier that combines Multilayer Perceptrons (MLPs) and Long Short-Term Memory (LSTMs). This approach leverages the advantages of both contextual and sequential modeling to improve vulnerability-detection accuracy. However, it requires significant computational resources and is specialized for reentrancy, which limits its scope.

Dynamit—Detector [30]

Dynamit is a machine-learning-based detector that identifies reentrancy vulnerabilities by analyzing transaction behavior without relying on source code. It monitors runtime transaction metadata such as gas usage and balance differences and uses a random forest classifier to distinguish between benign and malicious activity. The primary advantage of Dynamit lies in its independence from static analysis or instrumentation, making it suitable for real-time application. However, its lightweight feature set may not capture more complex reentrancy logic or indirect exploit vectors.

EA-RGCN—Detector [31]

EA-RGCN is a graph convolutional network model for detecting vulnerabilities in smart contracts. It constructs semantic graphs for contract functions and uses residual GCN layers and edge-attention mechanisms to extract both structural and contextual features. This enables detection of diverse vulnerabilities such as arithmetic bugs, reentrancy, timestamp dependence, and unchecked low calls. EA-RGCN excels at capturing fine-grained interactions within contract logic, though it may require substantial computational power and model tuning to generalize across different contract families.

Ensemble Models-Based Digital Forensic Framework—Detector [32]

Ensemble Models-Based Digital Forensic Framework combines natural language processing techniques with ensemble machine learning for vulnerability classification. It extracts text-based features using Term Frequency-Inverse Document Frequency (TF-IDF), Continuous Bag-of-Words (CBOW), and Skip-Gram models, and balances the dataset using the Synthetic Minority Oversampling Technique (SMOTE). These features are fed into multiple classifiers to detect vulnerabilities such as DoS attacks, access control flaws, reentrancy, and poor randomness. This ensemble approach improves classification accuracy and reduces false positives but may struggle to capture deeper semantic patterns that are not reflected in textual data alone.

Extended Multimodal AI Framework—Detector [33]

Extended Multimodal AI Framework, developed by Jie et al. in 2023, leverages multiple input sources, Solidity source code, build outputs, and bytecode, to provide a comprehensive vulnerability detection platform. The framework integrates bi-LSTM with self-attention, textCNN, and random forest classifiers to analyze and fuse features across different modalities. It supports contracts regardless of whether source code is available and excels in flexibility and adaptability. However, the use of diverse models and input types increases system complexity, which can hinder deployment efficiency and interpretability.

HGAT—Detector [34]

HGAT (Hierarchical Graph Attention Network) leverages hierarchical graph attention mechanisms to detect vulnerabilities in smart contracts by abstracting contract functions into code graphs from Abstract Syntax Trees (ASTs) and Control Flow Graphs (CFGs). Node features are extracted using graph attention layers, and the resulting vector representations are concatenated to improve vulnerability classification. HGAT can detect vulnerabilities such as reentrancy, timestamp dependencies, and integer overflow and underflow. Its strength lies in capturing both syntactic and control-flow semantics through layered attention, though scalability may be a concern for large contract sets.

Integrated DL-Based Vulnerability Detector—Detector [35]

Integrated DL-Based Vulnerability Detector employs a two-step deep learning approach to enhance smart contract vulnerability detection. In the first step, a transformer model captures opcode relationships while a Bidirectional Gated Recurrent Unit (BiGRU) aggregates sequential features. In the second step, a Text-CNN with spatial attention focuses on locally salient and semantically meaningful information. This hierarchical framework detects 13 different vulnerability types, including reentrancy, access control errors, arithmetic overflows/underflows, unchecked low-level call returns, DoS, bad randomness, TOCTOU (front-running), time manipulation, short address attacks, call stack exhaustion, mishandled exceptions, transaction-ordering dependence, and insecure self-destruct usage. The multi-layered design enhances detection granularity but increases model complexity, which may hinder real-time analysis or deployment on resource-constrained environments.

ML-Based SCs Vulnerability Detector—Detector [32]

ML-Based SCs Vulnerability Detector applies classical machine learning techniques to distinguish between valid and invalid smart contracts based on transactional behavior. The tool employs k-Nearest Neighbors (KNN), Naive Bayes, Support Vector Machines (SVM), and Random Forest to identify vulnerabilities such as transaction-origin misuse, check-effects-interaction violations, reentrancy bugs, unsafe inline assembly, block-timestamp misuse, low-level call issues, block-hash reliance, and unsafe self-destruct commands. Its model variety provides interpretability and ease of deployment, although its detection precision depends heavily on feature quality and manual engineering, making it sensitive to noisy or incomplete input data.

MSgram—Detector [36]

MSgram (Multi-Semantic gram) enhances vulnerability detection by tokenizing smart contracts across three semantic dimensions, textual, structural, and hybrid sequences. It uses an N-gram language model to extract contextual meaning from each semantic space and integrates results through Intersection and Union strategies. MSgram can detect reentrancy, timestamp dependency, integer overflows/underflows, unchecked low-level calls, improper self-destruct usage, call stack depth misuse, and tx.origin-based vulnerabilities. By offering multi-perspective analysis, it improves vulnerability coverage but may introduce redundancy in analysis and increase computational cost, especially when scaling to large contract corpora.

Multimodal Decision Fusion Model—Detector [37]

Multimodal Decision Fusion Model employs deep learning and decision-level fusion techniques to detect smart contract vulnerabilities. It extracts and integrates features from Solidity source code, opcodes, and control-flow graphs (CFGs) using separate neural components, then fuses their predictions via a learned decision mechanism. The tool targets vulnerabilities such as arithmetic bugs, reentrancy, transaction-ordering dependence (TOD), and locked Ether issues. Its multimodal architecture improves detection robustness across diverse contract forms but can introduce overhead for preprocessing and coordinating multiple model outputs, potentially increasing latency and resource consumption.

SC-Defender—Detector [38]

SC-Defender focuses on vulnerability detection in IoT-enabled smart contracts by leveraging Solidity ASTs and a Tree-Based Convolutional Neural Network (TBCNN). It employs an AST-pruning technique to eliminate irrelevant nodes, thereby enhancing the focus and efficiency of the vulnerability detection process.

SC-Defender is particularly effective at identifying reentrancy flaws, especially in lightweight IoT deployments. While the tailored design improves efficiency, its applicability to general-purpose smart contracts may be limited by its IoT-specific assumptions and limited vulnerability scope.

S-HGTNs—Detector [39]

S-HGTNs (Spatial Heterogeneous Graph Transformer Networks) targets fraud detection in Ethereum smart contracts. It constructs a Heterogeneous Information Network (HIN) to represent diverse contract entities and employs transformer-based architectures to automatically generate meta-paths. These paths capture patterns associated with illicit behavior, enabling the detection of anomalies such as financial fraud, illegal fundraising, and money laundering. S-HGTNs bring novel utility to financial crime prevention in blockchain ecosystems, though their focus is more on transactional anomalies than on traditional code-level vulnerabilities, limiting their applicability to developers seeking to detect programming flaws in smart contract logic.

Semantic ML-Based Reentrancy Detector—Detector [40]

Semantic ML-Based Reentrancy Detector utilizes machine learning to detect reentrancy vulnerabilities in smart contracts by analyzing their semantic structure. It combines information extracted from Abstract Syntax Trees (ASTs) with machine learning models to identify vulnerabilities and provide corrective feedback. The model's semantic focus allows it to understand the structural context of code segments, enhancing its ability to detect complex reentrancy patterns with interpretability and precision. However, it is limited in scope, as it primarily targets reentrancy and may not generalize well to other vulnerability classes.

SG-EA-RGCN Vulnerability Detector—Detector [31]

SG-EA-RGCN Vulnerability Detector (Signed Graph Entity Alignment Relational Graph Convolutional Network) is a graph-based smart contract vulnerability detection tool that constructs semantic graphs of contract code and employs residual GCNs with edge-attention mechanisms. It identifies vulnerabilities including reentrancy, timestamp dependence, tx.origin usage, unchecked send, unhandled exceptions, arithmetic overflows and underflows, and transaction-ordering dependence (TOD). By analyzing interdependencies and dataflow paths in the contract code, the tool achieves accurate and explainable detection outcomes through relationship-driven insights. Its graph-based architecture, however, demands significant preprocessing and computational overhead, which may affect scalability on large datasets.

SVScanner—Detector [41]

SVScanner (Smart Vulnerability Scanner) uses deep learning to detect vulnerabilities in Ethereum smart contracts by combining tokenized code sequences and AST-derived features. It applies a TextCNN model for classification, allowing it to capture both syntactic and structural patterns. SVScanner effectively identifies reentrancy issues, integer-related bugs, and timestamp dependency vulnerabilities. Its architecture balances model simplicity and vulnerability coverage, offering a lightweight yet effective detection solution. Nonetheless, it struggles to detect logic-dependent vulnerabilities that require inter-function context or data-flow reasoning beyond surface-level patterns.

Transaction-based Analysis with LSTM Network—Detector [39]

Transaction-based analysis using an LSTM network detects malicious smart contracts by analyzing behavioral patterns in their transaction histories. It extracts features such as balance changes, ether flows, and transaction timing to train an LSTM model to recognize behavioral signatures. This tool is particularly effective at detecting high-risk contracts, such as Ponzi schemes and gambling platforms, by emphasizing runtime behavior over static code analysis. However, its reliance on historical transaction data makes it unsuitable for detecting vulnerabilities in newly deployed or inactive contracts with limited on-chain activity.

ABCNN—Identifier [42]

ABCNN (Attention-Based Convolutional Neural Network) combines the strengths of CNN architectures with self-attention mechanisms to detect vulnerabilities in smart contracts. By preprocessing opcode sequences and applying layered attention to highlight significant instructions, ABCNN improves detection speed and accuracy. It identifies vulnerabilities such as reentrancy, arithmetic errors, and time manipulation, offering robust performance in diverse contract scenarios. One limitation is its dependence on opcode sequences alone, which may hinder its ability to interpret structural nuances or semantic dependencies that reside outside linear instruction flows.

ASSBert—Identifier [43]

ASSBert integrates Active and Semi-Supervised learning with the transformer-based BERT architecture to detect vulnerabilities in smart contracts. It uses active learning to minimize the amount of labeled data required and semi-supervised learning to boost model generalization. ASSBert detects vulnerabilities such as timestamp dependence, reentrancy, call-depth issues, transaction-ordering dependence, arithmetic errors, and misuse of tx.origin. The model excels in data efficiency and performance, particularly in low-resource settings. However, its performance may degrade when exposed to contracts exhibiting highly novel structures not reflected in its training data, limiting its ability to generalize beyond familiar patterns.

AWD-LSTM—Identifier [32]

AWD-LSTM (Average Stochastic Gradient Descent Weight-Dropped LSTM) uses a language-model-inspired encoder to classify smart contracts into categories such as suicidal, prodigal, greedy, and normal. It analyzes opcode sequences and identifies invocation-depth vulnerabilities using learned sequence patterns. The model's robustness in handling sequential opcode data provides a reliable method for coarse-grained vulnerability categorization and risk profiling. Nevertheless, its coarse classification granularity restricts its applicability for detecting fine-grained or multi-label vulnerabilities.

AMEVulDetector—Identifier [44]

AMEVulDetector (Attentive Multi-Encoder Vulnerability Detector) combines deep learning with expert-defined patterns to detect vulnerabilities in smart contracts, including reentrancy, block timestamp dependence, and infinite loops. It constructs a semantic graph of the smart contract and uses an attentive multi-encoder network to fuse structural features and domain knowledge. The tool assigns interpretability weights to different inputs, aiding both detection and explanation of identified vulnerabilities through transparent attention-based mechanisms. A key limitation is its reliance on predefined expert patterns, which may reduce adaptability to emerging or complex vulnerabilities not covered by existing rules.

BiGAS Detection Model—Identifier [45]

BiGAS Detection Model combines a bidirectional gated recurrent unit (BiGRU) with an attention mechanism and a support vector machine (SVM) to detect reentrancy vulnerabilities in smart contracts. It tokenizes the contract code and uses a functional model to extract semantic and syntactic features for classification. The hybrid architecture allows it to capture sequential context while focusing on the most relevant code patterns through attention weighting. However, its vulnerability-specific design limits its utility for detecting other security issues beyond reentrancy.

Bi-GRU with Attention Vulnerability Detector—Identifier [46]

The Bi-GRU with Attention Vulnerability Detector uses a BiGRU network combined with an attention mechanism to detect reentrancy and timestamp-dependency vulnerabilities in Ethereum smart contracts. It processes opcode sequences into vector representations, emphasizing the most significant parts of the sequence to improve contextual awareness and precision in identifying vulnerable segments. The model, however, may incur high computational costs during training, especially when trained on large datasets or complex opcode sequences.

Blass—Identifier [47]

Blass applies a Bi-LSTM model with attention to classify smart contract vulnerabilities, including reentrancy, integer overflow, timestamp dependence, and dangerous delegatecall. It constructs program slices enriched with semantic code structure features, enabling the model to learn deeper contextual associations within the contract logic. Its design leads to superior performance compared to traditional detection techniques. A limitation of Blass is its sensitivity to slicing accuracy; poorly generated slices can reduce detection reliability and interpretability.

CBGRU—Identifier [48]

CBGRU (Convolutional Bidirectional Gated Recurrent Unit) integrates CNN and BiGRU architectures, enhanced with Word2Vec and FastText embeddings, to detect vulnerabilities in smart contracts. It targets vulnerabilities such as infinite loops, reentrancy, timestamp dependencies, call-stack-depth attacks, and integer overflows and underflows. The hybrid model enhances both local feature recognition through CNNs and long-range sequence understanding via BiGRU. Despite its robustness, the complexity of its multi-component architecture can lead to longer inference times and increased training overhead.

CGE—Identifier [49]

CGE (Contract Graph Embedding) uses graph neural networks (GNNs) combined with expert knowledge to detect vulnerabilities in smart contracts. It builds control- and data-flow graphs to encode contract semantics, applying normalization and temporal message propagation to highlight critical nodes. The model effectively detects reentrancy, timestamp dependence, and infinite loop vulnerabilities through its structured representation of execution paths. However, its reliance on precise graph construction can reduce accuracy when handling contracts with obfuscated or incomplete graph structures.

ContractWard—Identifier [50]

ContractWard employs machine learning techniques, including XGBoost, to detect six types of vulnerabilities in smart contracts: integer overflow, integer underflow, transaction-ordering dependence (TOD), call stack depth attacks, timestamp dependencies, and reentrancy. It extracts bigram features from simplified opcodes to train models that can recognize rapid batching and other attack signatures. One limitation is that its reliance on opcode-level features may overlook higher-level semantic patterns or logic errors present in the source code.

Deep Learning-Based Vulnerability Detector—Identifier [25]

Deep Learning-Based Vulnerability Detector combines CNNs, LSTMs, CNN-BiLSTM, and residual networks to identify vulnerabilities in smart contracts. It focuses on reentrancy, integer overflow and underflow, call stack depth attacks, TOD, and timestamp dependencies. The model uses unigram and bigram extraction methods, optimized with modified TF-IDF scoring, to enhance vulnerability classification performance. Despite its comprehensive architecture, the model requires substantial training data and may overfit if the dataset lacks diversity in vulnerability contexts.

DeeSCVHunter—Identifier [51]

DeeSCVHunter (Deep SCs Vulnerability Hunter) is a deep learning-based framework developed in 2021 to detect reentrancy and time-dependence vulnerabilities in smart contracts. DeeSCVHunter uses a technique called Vulnerability Candidate Slice (VCS) to enhance detection by incorporating both data and control dependencies. The framework applies CNNs and RNNs to learn vulnerability patterns from code slices. It is supported by publicly available code and datasets, promoting transparency and reproducibility. Nevertheless, its specialization in only a subset of vulnerabilities limits its applicability for comprehensive smart contract auditing.

DL4SC—Identifier [52]

DL4SC is a deep learning-based framework introduced in 2024 that detects vulnerabilities in smart contracts using a combination of transformer encoders and CNNs. DL4SC processes opcode sequences and detects issues such as reentrancy, arithmetic vulnerabilities, and timestamp dependence. It employs the Sparrow Search Algorithm (SSA) to optimize hyperparameters and is publicly released with its corresponding dataset. A potential drawback is its computational intensity, which may hinder scalability for large-scale contract analysis or real-time auditing.

DR-GCN and TMP—Identifier [49, 53]

DR-GCN and TMP are two graph-based vulnerability detection models for smart contracts introduced in 2020. DR-GCN applies degree-free graph convolutional networks on contract graphs, while TMP uses temporal message propagation to retain sequence-sensitive context. These tools represent contracts as semantic and syntactic graphs and can detect vulnerabilities such as reentrancy, timestamp dependence, and infinite loops. However, both models may struggle to generalize across contracts with highly dynamic or unconventional execution paths, requiring frequent retraining or tuning for different datasets.

ESCORT—Identifier [35]

ESCORT (Efficient SCs Optimization and Risk Tool), launched in 2023, is a deep learning-based framework that provides comprehensive vulnerability detection for Ethereum smart contracts. ESCORT features a unified feature extractor and multiple analysis branches, allowing it to simultaneously detect various vulnerabilities, including reentrancy, integer overflow/underflow, callstack depth attacks, timestamp dependencies, unchecked sends, tx.origin misuse, assertion violations, accessible self-destructs, and arbitrary jumps. It supports bytecode analysis and is optimized for transfer learning, allowing rapid extension to new vulnerability types. However, the framework's complexity and reliance on deep learning models may increase training time and computational requirements, limiting its accessibility for lightweight or real-time analysis.

Eth2Vec—Identifier [54]

Eth2Vec (Ethereum Bytecode to Vectors) is a static analysis tool introduced in 2020 that detects smart contract vulnerabilities by analyzing code similarity. Eth2Vec automatically learns latent features from EVM bytecodes using neural language modeling techniques, which makes it resilient to code rewriting and obfuscation. It improves vulnerability detection by translating low-level bytecode into vector representations that preserve semantic meaning. Nonetheless, its effectiveness can be constrained when facing contracts with highly irregular or novel structures, where similarity-based inference may fail to capture functional risks accurately.

HAM—Identifier [46]

HAM (Hybrid Attention Mechanism) is a smart contract vulnerability detection tool proposed in 2023 that combines single-head and multi-head attention mechanisms. HAM extracts code fragments centered on known vulnerability patterns, improving detection accuracy for reentrancy, arithmetic flaws, unchecked return values, timestamp dependencies, and tx.origin issues. It is validated using publicly available datasets and demonstrates strong accuracy and adaptability. A key limitation, however, is its dependence on predefined patterns, which may reduce its effectiveness in detecting previously unseen or novel vulnerabilities.

Machine Learning-Based Vulnerability Detection Scheme—Identifier [32]

Machine Learning-Based Vulnerability Detection Scheme is a 2020 framework designed to detect specific Ethereum smart contract vulnerabilities, such as has-short-address, has-flows, and is-greedy. It uses a slicing matrix approach to extract relevant features and trains various machine learning models, including neural networks and random forests, to identify these vulnerabilities. The model has been validated using public GitHub datasets. However, its narrow focus on a limited set of vulnerabilities and reliance on manually curated datasets may hinder its generalizability to broader or evolving threat landscapes.

MANDO-GURU—Identifier [55]

MANDO-GURU is an open-source vulnerability detection framework introduced in 2022 that analyzes smart contracts through heterogeneous graph embeddings derived from control-flow and call graphs. MANDO-GURU detects a broad spectrum of vulnerabilities including reentrancy, front running, arithmetic bugs, control and call graph issues, symbolic execution flaws, and data flow vulnerabilities. It operates at both the line-level and contract-level granularity, making it a comprehensive analysis solution. Despite its thoroughness, MANDO-GURU's reliance on graph construction and embedding techniques can lead to scalability issues when analyzing extremely large or complex contracts.

MODNN—Identifier [48]

MODNN (Multiple-Objective Detection Neural Network) is a machine learning-based framework developed in 2022 for vulnerability detection in smart contracts. It employs Crucial Operation Sequence (COS) features to capture both explicit and implicit vulnerability indicators, enabling parallel detection of multiple vulnerabilities, including integer overflow and underflow, callstack depth attacks, transaction-ordering dependence (TOD), timestamp dependency, reentrancy, unchecked sends, tx.origin misuse, and assert failures. While MODNN improves scalability and reduces training overhead, its performance may degrade when encountering obfuscated or highly optimized bytecode.

Multi-Task Learning Vulnerability Detection Model—Identifier [48]

Multi-Task Learning Vulnerability Detection Model is a 2022 framework that employs a multi-task learning architecture for analyzing smart contracts. It features a shared semantic layer and task-specific CNN-based layers for detecting and classifying issues such as arithmetic errors, reentrancy, and unknown addresses. Despite its improved task adaptability, the model struggles to detect rarely occurring or previously unseen vulnerability types due to bias in the training datasets.

RLRep—Identifier [52]

RLRep is a reinforcement learning-based tool introduced in 2024 that provides repair suggestions for smart contract vulnerabilities. It uses an encoder–decoder architecture and policy-gradient algorithms to provide automated fixes for vulnerabilities such as exception disorder, integer overflow, reentrancy, TOD, and tx.origin misuse. Although RLRep minimizes the need for labeled data and supports flexible repair generation, its recommendations are sometimes overly generic and may require manual refinement to preserve complex business logic.

S-gram—Identifier [36]

S-gram is a semantic-aware security auditing tool for Ethereum smart contracts, introduced in 2020. It uses a custom S-gram model to analyze token sequences and rank vulnerability patterns, including reentrancy, integer overflow/underflow, timestamp dependency, and unchecked low-level calls. While S-gram improves detection accuracy by focusing on semantic patterns, it can produce false positives when semantic representations are overly abstract or misaligned with actual control flow.

SCLMF—Identifier [56]

SCLMF (Semantic Classification and Meta-Learning Framework) is a 2023 framework that transforms bytecode into RGB images and applies few-shot learning through CNNs and Model-Agnostic Meta-Learning (MAML). It accurately identifies vulnerabilities in low-data settings using a learner–meta-learner structure. However, the image-based transformation increases computational overhead and may lose fine-grained syntactic cues important for certain types of vulnerabilities.

SCVDIE—Identifier [33]

SCVDIE (Smart Contract Vulnerability Detection with Integrated Ensembles) is a machine learning-based tool introduced in 2022 that uses an ensemble of CNN, RNN, and transformer models to detect vulnerabilities such as integer underflow and overflow, call stack depth attacks, TOD, timestamp dependencies, and reentrancy. While ensemble learning boosts robustness and accuracy, it also increases training time and requires more computational resources compared to single-model approaches.

SecBERT—Identifier [57]

SecBERT (Security-enhanced Bidirectional Encoder Representations from Transformers), introduced in 2023, is a BERT-based architecture for multi-label vulnerability detection in bytecode. It extracts rich contextual features using transformers and applies a multilayer perceptron for final classification. While SecBERT performs well across multiple vulnerability types, its reliance on pre-trained language models can make it less interpretable and resource-intensive during inference.

sGuard+—Identifier [58]

sGuard+, introduced in 2020, is a machine learning-guided automated repair tool for smart contract vulnerabilities. It detects issues at the function level using features from source code and bytecode, offering refined repair strategies that preserve business logic and reduce gas overhead. Although sGuard+ enhances code maintainability and efficiency, it may fail to fully address vulnerabilities when the contract logic deviates from common coding patterns it was trained on.

SmartConDetect—Identifier [59]

SmartConDetect is a static analysis tool for detecting security vulnerabilities in Solidity smart contracts. Released in 2023, it employs a pre-trained BERT model to analyze code fragments and identify susceptible code patterns. This tool can detect twenty-three vulnerabilities, including gas exhaustion, unchecked function calls, misuse of view and pure functions, incorrect return types, locked ether, and various misuse patterns across ERC-20 functions and Solidity syntax. Its extensive vulnerability coverage enhances detection precision across multiple categories. However, SmartConDetect's reliance on pre-trained models may limit its ability to adapt to newly emerging vulnerabilities or evolving coding practices without retraining.

SmartEmbed—Identifier [60]
SmartEmbed is a tool designed for clone and bug detection in smart contracts through structural code embedding. Launched in 2019, it uses deep learning and similarity-checking techniques to efficiently and accurately identify code clones and clone-related bugs. By generating code embedding vectors that capture semantic and syntactic structures, SmartEmbed facilitates similarity-based vulnerability detection. Nevertheless, its detection capabilities are largely restricted to clone-related bugs and may not generalize well to diverse vulnerability types outside the clone spectrum.
SmartMixModel—Identifier [61]
SmartMixModel is a machine learning-based vulnerability detection model for Solidity smart contracts. Released in 2022, it integrates high-level syntactic features with low-level bytecode representations to improve the accuracy of vulnerability detection. It identifies issues such as unsafe array length manipulation, costly loops, locked ether, tx.origin misuse, redundant fallback functions, and hardcoded addresses. The model's hybrid feature design strengthens detection of both logical and structural flaws. However, its dependence on hand-engineered features may limit scalability to more complex or obfuscated contract logic.
Sliced-JGNN—Identifier [62]
Sliced Joint Graph Neural Network (Sliced-JGNN) is a graph-based model for smart contract vulnerability detection introduced in 2023. It constructs and integrates abstract syntax trees (ASTs), control flow graphs (CFGs), and program dependency graphs (PDGs), and applies program slicing to eliminate irrelevant components. Sliced-JGNN accurately identifies vulnerabilities such as reentrancy, suicide contracts, short address attacks, unchecked return values, and timestamp dependencies. While the slicing mechanism improves relevance, the multi-graph construction process introduces computational overhead and may hinder scalability to large datasets.
TP-Detect—Identifier [56]
Trigram Pixel-Detect (TP-Detect) is a machine learning-based tool introduced in 2023 for detecting smart contract vulnerabilities using trigram and pixel-level feature extraction. It converts contract code into numerical representations and employs classifiers like Naive Bayes and Random Forest to identify vulnerabilities such as integer overflows/underflows, call stack depth attacks, reentrancy, and transaction-ordering dependencies. Its simplicity of features enables fast model training and evaluation. However, TP-Detect's basic representation of code patterns may limit its performance on complex or non-trigram vulnerabilities.
VulDeeSmartContract—Identifier [63]
VulDeeSmartContract is a deep learning-based tool introduced in 2020 that detects reentrancy vulnerabilities in Ethereum smart contracts. It uses a BiLSTM model augmented with attention mechanisms to capture both semantic and control-flow information from contract snippets. The framework focuses specifically on reentrancy by learning contextual patterns from code sequences. While

highly effective in detecting reentrancy, VulDeeSmartContract lacks support for identifying other types of vulnerabilities, limiting its applicability as a general-purpose analysis tool.

- **Industrial tools**

  MAIAN—Detector [64]
  MAIAN uses symbolic execution to detect three classes of vulnerabilities in Ethereum smart contracts: suicidal contracts (those that can be killed arbitrarily), prodigal contracts (those that leak Ether to arbitrary users), and greedy contracts (those that lock Ether indefinitely). Published in 2018, MAIAN executes a symbolic analysis of contract behaviors over a set of input constraints, tracing paths to identify states where critical operations may be executed unsafely. As an industrial tool, MAIAN is recognized for its precision in isolating behavioral flaws that could compromise asset security. However, it can suffer from path explosions in large or complex contracts, hindering scalability and potentially leading to incomplete analysis.
  Cider—Identifier [65]
  Cider applies reinforcement learning to infer invariants for arithmetic safety verification in smart contracts. It frames invariant generation as a Markov Decision Process (MDP) and uses a neural policy network to predict meaningful invariants. This approach reduces the reliance on runtime assertions and improves the detection of arithmetic overflow vulnerabilities. Despite its innovation, Cider's effectiveness depends heavily on the quality of training data and reward shaping, which may limit its ability to generalize to unseen contract structures.

The comprehensive review of these 57 AI-driven tools for smart contract vulnerability detection reveals the growing sophistication and diversity of methodologies for securing decentralized applications [18, 20, 66]. From early rule-based detectors and symbolic analyzers to advanced deep learning architectures and graph-based models, each tool offers a distinct approach to identifying critical security flaws, including reentrancy, arithmetic bugs, and access control issues [53, 67–69]. While traditional tools prioritize formal guarantees and explainability, modern learning-based models excel in adaptability and scalability across large, evolving codebases [7, 9, 33, 57] However, important limitations remain, as many models face trade-offs between interpretability and detection accuracy, struggle to generalize to novel vulnerabilities, or depend heavily on high-quality labeled data and precise code parsing [37, 43, 44, 70]. As smart contract ecosystems become increasingly complex, the future of vulnerability detection will likely hinge on hybrid systems that integrate formal analysis, graph reasoning, and pretrained language models to balance precision, coverage, and efficiency [14, 22, 31, 49, 55]. Together, these tools form the foundation of an evolving AI-assisted security landscape, pushing the boundaries of what automated analysis can achieve in blockchain safety [19, 20, 71].

9.1.3 Code Instrumentation

Code instrumentation tools enhance the security and observability of smart contracts by injecting additional logic into the source code or bytecode for monitoring, enforcement, or correction purposes [4, 72, 73]. This method enables dynamic tracking of execution behavior, enforces runtime policies, and allows for automated bug rectification without altering the contract's core semantics [58, 74, 75]. These tools are particularly effective at addressing vulnerabilities that manifest at runtime or that rely on external call behavior, gas dynamics, or complex control flows [4, 58, 72]. Instrumentation-based methods serve both preventive and corrective purposes, often bridging static and dynamic analysis in a hybrid security framework [58, 73, 75].

- **Academic tools**

  HermHD—Detector [76]

  Hermes High-Density (HermHD) is a bytecode-level obfuscation tool that aims to enhance the security of Ethereum smart contracts by complicating their static analysis surface. It applies six obfuscation patterns, such as control-flow flattening, opaque predicates, and instruction reordering, to transform the bytecode into semantically equivalent yet structurally opaque forms. By obscuring contract logic without affecting functionality, HermHD impedes reverse-engineering attempts and reduces the risk of exploit identification by automated scanners. Its core advantage lies in proactively shielding contracts from adversarial analysis while preserving runtime correctness. However, HermHD does not detect or repair vulnerabilities directly and may inadvertently increase gas consumption or interfere with legitimate debugging and auditing efforts due to the decreased transparency of obfuscated code.

  SmartShield—Detector [58]

  SMARTSHIELD is an automated bytecode rectification framework designed to patch critical vulnerabilities in Ethereum smart contracts post-compilation. By analyzing EVM bytecode and applying targeted transformations, it mitigates three prevalent flaws: state changes after external calls, unchecked arithmetic operations, and unverified success of external calls. The system rewrites vulnerable bytecode segments while maintaining semantic equivalence and optimizing gas efficiency, enabling secure contract deployment without source-level edits. SMARTSHIELD's key strength is its ability to automatically harden deployed or legacy contracts, closing known vulnerability windows before exploitation occurs. However, it is limited to predefined vulnerability patterns and may not generalize well to newer or more complex exploit vectors not captured by its internal rule set.

  SolAnalyser—Detector [4]

  SolAnalyser integrates static and dynamic analysis techniques through source code instrumentation to detect a wide range of vulnerabilities in Solidity smart contracts. It inserts runtime assertions into contract code, generates relevant test inputs, and monitors execution traces to uncover vulnerabilities such as integer overflows, division by zero, timestamp dependency, and transaction origin misuse. It also includes a fault-seeding mechanism to evaluate the effectiveness of its detection routines. SolAnalyser's hybrid approach enables thorough coverage across both syntactic and behavioral flaws, making it particularly effective in revealing bugs that manifest under specific input conditions. Nevertheless, the instrumentation and execution phases introduce performance overhead, and the tool's dependency on automated input generation may limit its effectiveness in uncovering deeply nested or context-dependent vulnerabilities.

Code instrumentation offers a flexible and practical approach to enhancing smart contract security, particularly in scenarios where runtime behavior, gas dynamics, or post-deployment vulnerabilities are critical concerns [4, 58, 74, 75]. The tools in this category, ranging from obfuscation-based hardening in HermHD, to bytecode patching in SMARTSHIELD, to hybrid dynamic detection in SolAnalyser, illustrate how instrumentation can serve both defensive and diagnostic roles [4, 58]. While this technique excels in augmenting contract behavior and detecting runtime anomalies, it may introduce performance trade-offs, increased gas usage, or reduced code clarity, especially in heavily instrumented or obfuscated outputs [4, 58, 73]. Nonetheless, it remains a valuable strategy for reinforcing smart contract reliability and resilience [58, 74, 75].

9.1.4 Control Flow Analysis

Control Flow Analysis (CFA) enables the detection of smart contract vulnerabilities by examining the paths through which program execution may flow [77–79]. By constructing control flow graphs (CFGs), these tools analyze branching structures, loop behaviors, and data dependencies, enabling them to identify risks that often depend on the structure or order of execution [77, 78, 80]. This methodology is particularly effective for uncovering logic flaws, gas-related inefficiencies, and privilege escalations, as it can highlight paths that lead to unsafe states or unintended interactions [14, 81, 82]. The tools in this category leverage CFA to statically analyze smart contracts, often at the bytecode level, to detect critical vulnerabilities with high structural fidelity [2, 78, 80].

- **Academic tools**
  MadMax—Detector [83]
  MadMax is a static analyzer that uses control-flow analysis and declarative pattern matching to identify gas-related vulnerabilities in Ethereum smart contracts. Built around a custom decompiler, MadMax reconstructs control-flow graphs from EVM bytecode and uses high-level semantic abstractions to capture constructs such as dynamically sized arrays, nested loops, and resumable function segments. Its primary focus is on detecting vulnerabilities that could lead to excessive gas consumption, including unbounded mass operations, wallet griefing attacks, and loop overflows. By expressing vulnerability patterns in a declar-

ative language, MadMax enables extensibility and precise, rule-based detection. Its core strength lies in its scalability to large contracts and its specialization in gas-focused logic flows. However, it is limited to specific vulnerability classes and may not capture semantic issues unrelated to control structure or gas estimation.

WaLi—Detector [84]

WaLi is a control-flow-based vulnerability detection tool tailored for WebAssembly (Wasm) smart contracts. It constructs control-flow graphs directly from Wasm bytecode and simulates execution in a Wasm virtual machine to trace potential security flaws along critical execution paths. WaLi identifies access control vulnerabilities by applying pattern-based analysis to the paths where unauthorized actions or privilege escalations could occur. Its ability to operate on Wasm contracts broadens its applicability beyond Ethereum, addressing a growing ecosystem of smart contracts written for alternative blockchains. WaLi's runtime simulation enhances detection accuracy by capturing execution-dependent behaviors, particularly in access-sensitive contexts. However, its reliance on predefined patterns and Wasm-specific execution semantics may constrain its flexibility and limit its ability to detect novel or cross-cutting vulnerabilities.

Control Flow Analysis offers a structurally rich approach to detecting vulnerabilities, emphasizing the execution flow over isolated code constructs [2, 77–80]. Tools like MadMax and WaLi demonstrate how CFG construction and path analysis can reveal critical security risks, especially those tied to gas usage, loop structures, and access privileges [77, 81, 85]. While MadMax excels at detecting Ethereum gas inefficiencies through high-level semantic abstraction, WaLi introduces runtime-aware CFA for Wasm smart contracts. These tools collectively illustrate the power of CFA in analyzing execution order and interaction patterns. However, their effectiveness is often bounded by the granularity of control flow representations and the specificity of the vulnerabilities they are configured to detect [17, 18, 20].

9.1.5 Disassembly Analysis

Disassembly analysis tools enhance smart contract security by transforming low-level bytecode into more intelligible representations, allowing for more effective vulnerability inspection and behavioral reasoning [2, 80, 86]. By deconstructing compiled logic into control-flow graphs or intermediate forms such as Static Single Assignment (SSA), these tools facilitate semantic inspection and uncover hidden or emergent behaviors [2, 86, 87]. This approach is particularly valuable when the source code is unavailable or incomplete, enabling both detection and identification of vulnerabilities directly from compiled smart contracts [28, 80, 88]. The tools in this category apply disassembly to support static analysis, symbolic execution, and multi-contract behavior tracing [2, 80, 86, 88].

- **Academic tools**

  Porosity—Detector [87]

  Porosity is an early yet influential EVM bytecode decompiler that translates compiled contracts into Solidity-like syntax, enabling source-level inspection of contracts when the original code is unavailable. It supports static and dynamic analysis by reconstructing control flow and enabling vulnerability detection through a familiar syntax interface. Porosity helps uncover critical issues such as reentrancy, call stack depth problems, and timestamp dependencies by generating human-readable representations of opaque bytecode. Its accessibility and clarity make it a valuable tool for forensic analysis and reverse engineering. However, since it relies on pattern-based reconstruction, the output may not fully capture original logic structures or variable semantics, and its utility is diminished in heavily optimized or obfuscated contracts.

  EtherProv—Identifier [89]

  EtherProv is a provenance-aware analysis tool that combines disassembly with static and dynamic techniques to identify vulnerabilities across Ethereum smart contracts and transaction histories. It employs control-flow graph (CFG) instrumentation and leverages Datalog queries to trace asset flows, detect reentrancy, and assess improper write permissions, such as restricted storage modifications. EtherProv extends traditional bytecode analysis by contextualizing vulnerabilities within multi-contract deployments and historical execution traces, providing real-time insights into the behavior of deployed systems. Its standout capability is the integration of provenance reasoning, which enables the identification of vulnerabilities that span multiple interactions. However, the complexity of cross-contract analysis and reliance on external transaction data may limit performance in high-throughput environments or when access to historical logs is restricted.
- **Industrial tools**

  Octopus—Detector [90]

  Octopus is an open-source security analysis framework that applies disassembly and control flow analysis to smart contracts and WebAssembly modules across multiple platforms, including Ethereum, Bitcoin, EOS, and NEO. By decompiling bytecode into a Static Single Assignment (SSA) representation and generating control- and call-flow graphs, Octopus enables detailed vulnerability analysis and symbolic execution. Its modular framework supports cross-platform auditing, making it highly versatile for blockchain ecosystems with different bytecode semantics. Octopus's strength lies in its ability to translate low-level logic into analyzable high-level formats, thereby aiding in the detection of complex flaws such as unreachable code, unintended paths, and opaque calls. However, its broad applicability may introduce platform-specific abstractions that reduce precision, and its symbolic execution component may encounter scalability issues on large or deeply nested contracts.

Disassembly analysis plays a crucial role in smart contract security by bridging the gap between low-level bytecode and high-level semantic reasoning [2, 80, 86–88].

Tools like Octopus, Porosity, and EtherProv showcase the strength of this approach in uncovering vulnerabilities when source code is missing, ambiguous, or intentionally hidden [87, 89] By generating readable representations and control flow graphs, these tools empower auditors, researchers, and developers to trace logic errors and detect unsafe patterns across both isolated and interconnected contracts [2, 86, 88, 89]. Nonetheless, challenges remain in scalability, reconstruction fidelity, and multi-platform abstraction, underscoring the importance of combining disassembly with complementary static and dynamic techniques for comprehensive security assurance [17, 18, 20].

9.1.6 Formal Verification

Formal verification tools bring mathematical rigor to smart contract analysis by translating contract logic into formal specifications and verifying them against predefined properties [6, 13, 77]. These tools use theorem proving, symbolic model checking, and satisfiability modulo theories (SMT) to guarantee contract correctness and detect vulnerabilities [77, 79, 85]. This category is divided into tools for vulnerability detection and vulnerability identification [6, 77, 79].

- **Academic tools**
  Celestial—Detector [91]
  Celestial is a formal verification framework for Solidity smart contracts, translating them into the F* proof-oriented programming language. Designed to be both rigorous and developer-friendly, Celestial verifies contracts against blockchain-specific semantics and then erases the proof-specific annotations to regenerate deployable Solidity code. Its main strength lies in its automation capabilities, which lower the barrier to entry for developers unfamiliar with formal verification. Celestial guarantees functional correctness by leveraging formal semantics throughout the verification process. However, its dependency on F* introduces a steep learning curve for users seeking deeper customization, and the abstraction may oversimplify certain dynamic behaviors inherent in complex contracts.
  ConCert—Detector [92]
  ConCert is a formal verification framework that utilizes the Coq proof assistant to verify smart contracts written in CameLIGO and similar high-level languages. The tool emphasizes functional correctness, safety, and sound reasoning about inter-contract interactions. By extracting Coq-verified contracts to executable blockchain code, ConCert bridges the gap between formal logic and practical deployment. It is particularly suited for complex decentralized applications requiring modular and compositional verification. The major advantage of ConCert is its alignment with Coq's powerful proof ecosystem, enabling expressive logic modeling. Nonetheless, its reliance on deep Coq expertise limits its accessibility to mainstream developers, and the verification process can be time-consuming for large-scale contracts.
  FEther—Detector [93]

FEther, short for Formal Ether, is a definitional interpreter built in Coq for verifying Ethereum smart contracts. It merges symbolic execution with higher-order logic theorem proving to check the semantic alignment between Solidity contracts and their formal models. FEther features automation strategies for both execution and proof synthesis, enabling consistent validation of functional correctness. Its integration with Coq enables fine-grained formal reasoning. However, its extensibility requires familiarity with Coq's logic frameworks, and the overhead of symbolic interpretation may become computationally intensive when applied to deeply nested contract logic or high-complexity state transitions.

HoRStify—Detector [14]

HoRStify (Hostile-Resistant Static Analysis) is a sound static analysis tool for Ethereum smart contracts, built on a formal proof framework that integrates program slicing, dependency analysis, and Datalog-based logical encoding. It is designed to verify security properties such as timestamp dependency and single-entrancy by analyzing data flows and control-flow dependencies in control-flow graphs. The advantage of HoRStify lies in its formal static slicing approach, which isolates relevant program fragments to simplify vulnerability detection. However, while its declarative logic improves precision, the technique may overlook certain runtime-specific behaviors that cannot be captured statically or modeled accurately through Datalog abstractions.

NuSMV Model-Checking Framework—Detector [94]

This framework adapts the NuSMV symbolic model checker to the domain of Ethereum smart contracts by translating Solidity code into NuSMV's input language and using Computation Tree Logic (CTL) to specify contract properties. Through exhaustive model checking, it evaluates all possible state transitions to detect property violations, including unreachability, liveness failures, and behavioral inconsistencies. Its strength lies in formal expressiveness and the systematic analysis of all execution paths. However, the translation process can be error-prone for complex contracts, and scalability becomes a concern as the state space grows due to nested control structures or dynamic contract behavior.

PROMELA and SPIN Model-Checking Framework—Detector [94]

This model-checking framework leverages SPIN (Simple PROMELA Interpreter) to formally verify smart contract correctness by translating Solidity source code into PROMELA, a formal modeling language. Using assertions, deadlock detection, and Linear Temporal Logic (LTL), the framework inspects contract behaviors and validates compliance with desired safety and liveness properties. The approach enables exhaustive path checking and is well-suited for verifying concurrency-related properties, particularly in multi-function interactions. Its key advantage is the SPIN environment's maturity and robustness, which support nuanced verification tasks. However, the need to manually translate contracts and specify temporal properties can make the tool less accessible for developers without prior formal methods experience, and scalability can become a bottleneck for large contracts with intricate logic.

SAFEVM—Detector [6]

SAFEVM is a formal verification tool tailored for Ethereum bytecode, translating EVM programs into equivalent C code embedded with verification annotations compatible with established C verifiers such as CPAchecker, SeaHorn, and VeryMax. This transformation enables the reuse of mature verification techniques from the C programming ecosystem to assess smart contract safety properties, including array bounds checking and general assertion validation. SAFEVM's advantage lies in its portability and its ability to leverage established C verification toolchains for EVM analysis, enhancing reliability and reusability. Nevertheless, the translation process is inherently lossy, and maintaining semantic equivalence between EVM bytecode and its C counterpart can be challenging, especially for contracts employing unconventional bytecode structures or low-level opcodes.

VeriMove—Detector [95]

VeriMove is a model-checking framework for Move smart contracts, extending the VeriSolid platform to address Move-specific semantics. The tool enables formal verification of global properties across multiple function executions, targeting critical issues such as reentrancy and integer overflow/underflow. It systematically models contract behaviors and state transitions to detect logic violations using model checking and abstraction techniques. VeriMove's key strength is its adaptability to the Move language, making it valuable in ecosystems such as Diem and Aptos. However, its applicability remains limited to Move-based environments, and its effectiveness in handling highly dynamic or data-driven smart contracts has yet to be comprehensively evaluated in real-world settings.

2Vyper—Identifier [96]

2Vyper is an SMT-based automated formal verification tool built specifically for Vyper smart contracts. It introduces a tailored specification methodology that supports reasoning even in the presence of unverified or partially specified code. The tool is particularly effective in addressing reentrancy and resource-based vulnerabilities by providing domain-specific specifications for state transitions and value flows. It supports modular reasoning, allowing compositional analysis of contract systems. The precision and soundness of 2Vyper offer strong guarantees of safety. However, the tool's limitations are its limited support for Solidity contracts and its reliance on detailed specifications, which can be labor-intensive to write and may hinder adoption by developers unfamiliar with SMT solvers.

EtherTrust—Identifier [97]

EtherTrust is a static analysis tool that focuses on Ethereum bytecode and applies Horn-clause-based reachability analysis to verify smart contract correctness. It analyzes control flow and call graphs to identify security-critical issues such as reentrancy and transaction-environment dependencies. EtherTrust offers a sound, logic-grounded framework that operates at the bytecode level, making it suitable for analyzing compiled contracts even without access to source code. Its primary strength lies in its formal rigor and precision. However, as a low-level analysis tool, it may struggle with scalability when applied to complex contracts or those relying heavily on dynamic runtime behavior, and its usability is limited for non-expert users lacking formal methods background.

eThor—Identifier [14]

eThor is a sound, automated static analyzer for Ethereum smart contracts that uses Horn-clause-based reachability analysis to formally detect and verify security properties. It translates EVM bytecode into logical formulas and constructs control flow representations to determine whether specific program states can be reached, effectively identifying vulnerabilities such as single-entrancy. Designed for scalability and precision, eThor performs well on large-scale datasets and provides formal correctness guarantees. Its core strength lies in offering a rigorous and automation-friendly pipeline for bytecode-level contract analysis. However, eThor may face limitations in analyzing highly dynamic behavior or user-defined patterns that fall outside its predefined property specifications, and its use requires familiarity with formal semantics.

ESBMC-Solidity—Identifier [98]

ESBMC-Solidity is a model checker tailored for Solidity contracts, using symbolic execution and satisfiability modulo theories (SMT) to detect security vulnerabilities. The tool introduces a custom frontend that translates Solidity's JSON Abstract Syntax Tree (AST) into an intermediate representation for symbolic analysis. It supports verification of critical issues such as integer overflows, out-of-bounds accesses, and misuse of tx.origin, and generates counterexamples for each discovered vulnerability. ESBMC-Solidity is notable for its precision in exploring execution paths and its strong diagnostic capabilities through concrete counterexamples. However, its reliance on complete contract specifications and computational intensity can pose scalability challenges when applied to large or highly interdependent contract systems.

FSPVM-E—Identifier [99]

FSPVM-E (Formal Symbolic Process Virtual Machine for Ethereum) is a hybrid formal verification framework implemented in Coq that combines symbolic execution with higher-order logic theorem proving. It introduces a formal memory model, an intermediate programming language (Lolisa), and a verified interpreter (FEther) to reason about Ethereum smart contracts with mathematical rigor. FSPVM-E allows detection of a wide range of vulnerabilities, including integer overflows, unchecked sends, stack overflows, and divide-by-zero errors. Its integration with Coq enables trusted, modular verification and supports formal modeling at multiple abstraction levels. However, the learning curve for both Coq and Lolisa is steep, and the tool requires significant manual effort for specification and proof development, which can limit adoption among practitioners.

F^* Verification—Identifier [91]

The F^* verification approach translates Solidity code and EVM bytecode into the F^* functional programming language, enabling formal reasoning about runtime safety and functional correctness. Using dependent types and relational reasoning, developers can specify and verify critical properties of smart contracts, ensuring that programs behave securely across all execution scenarios. The key advantage of F^* lies in its expressive type system and tight integration with formal proof techniques, which enable deep verification of contract logic. However, its use requires advanced expertise in functional programming and formal specification, and the lack of out-of-the-box integration with popular development environments can hinder widespread adoption in the Ethereum ecosystem.

Predicate Abstraction-Based Validation Framework—Identifier [5]

This framework applies predicate abstraction to validate smart contracts by constructing finite labeled transition systems from the source code. It enables auditors to analyze contract behavior by identifying function-call sequences and verifying conformance with expected requirements using predicates based on state variables and domain-specific logic. This tool is especially valuable in detecting logical defects and deviations from contractual obligations. Its strength lies in its ability to bridge the gap between specification and implementation through abstract modeling, helping auditors identify overlooked inconsistencies. However, it depends heavily on well-formed predicates and accurate modeling assumptions. Poorly defined abstractions can lead to false positives or overlook complex runtime behaviors, limiting its reliability without domain expertise.

SmartFast—Identifier [100]

SmartFast is a formal analysis tool designed for Ethereum smart contracts that introduces a specialized intermediate representation called SmartIR. This representation captures contract semantics while enabling precise taint analysis and rule-based vulnerability detection across 15 categories, including reentrancy, logic flaws, authorization issues, and mathematical errors. SmartFast distinguishes itself through its modular design and integration of static analysis with formal verification to improve both recall and precision. Its major advantage lies in its ability to detect a broad spectrum of vulnerabilities through customized rule sets. However, as with many taint-tracking tools, SmartFast may produce false positives in complex control flows, and its effectiveness depends on the coverage of its predefined rules.

Solc-verify—Identifier [96]

Solc-verify is a source-level formal verification tool for Ethereum smart contracts that uses SMT solvers and modular program analysis to reason about Solidity code annotated with formal specifications. Built directly into the Solidity compiler pipeline, it allows developers to write verification conditions alongside their code and verify properties such as reentrancy resistance, arithmetic correctness, and assertion validity. Its tight integration with Solidity tooling makes it accessible and practical for contract developers aiming to formally validate their code during development. However, solc-verify's verification capabilities are currently limited by the expressiveness of the supported annotations and may struggle to verify contracts that exhibit complex interprocedural behaviors or depend on external interactions.

Solicitous—Identifier [101]

Solicitous is a formal verification tool integrated with the official Solidity compiler that leverages constrained Horn clauses (CHCs) to analyze smart contract behavior. It enables fully automated reasoning over contract logic using theorem provers, focusing on proving unbounded safety properties and generating counterexamples when violations are found. Its strength lies in its native integration with Solidity's compilation flow, which simplifies its adoption and ensures compatibility with modern contract codebases. Solicitous is particularly effective in analyzing general safety invariants and reasoning about infinite execution paths. However, it may face limitations in verifying liveness properties or reasoning about runtime data dependencies, and its performance can degrade with increasingly large or complex contracts.

Solidifier—Identifier [8]

Solidifier is a bounded model checking tool that verifies Solidity smart contracts by translating them into Boogie, an intermediate verification language, and encoding Ethereum-specific semantics for formal reasoning. It models memory precisely and introduces lazy contract deployment mechanisms to reduce verification complexity. Solidifier excels at exploring semantic correctness beyond pattern matching, detecting nuanced vulnerabilities such as improper state manipulation or logic inconsistencies. The advantage of this approach is its focus on semantic-level correctness, making it well-suited for high-assurance contract verification. However, being a bounded verifier, Solidifier may miss bugs that manifest beyond its exploration depth, and its dependence on precise memory modeling can pose scalability challenges.

Vandal—Identifier [80]

Vandal is a logic-driven analysis framework that translates EVM bytecode into semantic logic relations to facilitate vulnerability detection in Ethereum smart contracts. It performs static analysis by converting low-level bytecode into a Datalog-compatible intermediate representation, allowing security properties to be defined and queried as logic rules. This declarative approach supports easy customization and rapid prototyping of new vulnerability checks, making Vandal highly adaptable. Its strengths lie in its extensibility and ability to uncover vulnerabilities such as unchecked send operations, unsecured balances, reentrancy, and misuse of the tx.origin opcode. However, Vandal's reliance on Datalog specifications can be a barrier for developers unfamiliar with logic programming, and it may struggle to model contracts with highly dynamic control flow or inter-contract dependencies accurately.

VERISMART—Identifier [11]

VERISMART is a domain-specific formal verifier focused on ensuring arithmetic safety in Ethereum smart contracts. It automatically discovers transaction invariants using a symbolic execution engine and verifies properties such as integer overflows and underflows. The tool is designed to scale without compromising precision, using a novel algorithm that captures transaction effects over multiple execution paths. Its standout feature is exhaustive verification of arithmetic correctness while maintaining a low false positive rate. However, VERISMART's domain-specific nature limits its applicability to arithmetic and numeric safety checks, and it may not detect broader categories of logical or semantic vulnerabilities beyond its specialized focus.

VERISOL—Identifier [102]

VERISOL is a formal verification framework developed for verifying smart contracts used in Microsoft's Azure Blockchain Workbench. It translates Solidity programs into the Boogie intermediate verification language and applies semantic conformance checking using the Boogie verification engine. VERISOL is capable of identifying logic errors and functional inconsistencies, providing proofs or counterexamples to confirm contract correctness. It has successfully uncovered previously unknown bugs in production smart contracts, demonstrating its effectiveness in practical settings. Nonetheless, VERISOL's verification relies heavily on manual annotations and preconditions, which can introduce a steep learning curve and limit automation for unfamiliar developers with formal methods.

VeriSolid—Identifier [103]

VeriSolid is a model-based verification framework that enables developers to formally specify and verify smart contract logic using a high-level transition-system abstraction. It defines contract behavior using operational semantics and then automatically generates correct-by-design Solidity code from the verified model. VeriSolid excels at verifying properties like reentrancy safety, deadlock freedom, and access control correctness, making it suitable for mission-critical contract development. Its intuitive modeling approach enables structured reasoning about complex logic. However, the abstraction level used by VeriSolid may oversimplify certain low-level behaviors, and developers need to invest effort in learning the modeling language and accurately translating informal specifications into formal states and transitions.

ZEUS—Identifier [104]

ZEUS is a comprehensive formal verification framework that combines abstract interpretation and symbolic model checking to evaluate smart contracts for both safety and semantic correctness. It accepts Solidity source code and automatically checks for adherence to secure programming practices, such as avoiding reentrancy, unchecked call results, transaction-state dependencies, and integer-arithmetic issues. ZEUS supports property specification and generates counterexamples when violations are found, contributing to a rigorous validation process. Its integration of multiple formal techniques makes it powerful and flexible. However, its analysis can be computationally intensive for large contracts, and the complexity of its backend may make customization difficult without deep expertise in formal methods.

- **Industrial tools**

  Securify—Identifier [69]

  Securify is a scalable static analysis tool for Ethereum smart contracts that identifies security violations by applying compliance and violation patterns to a symbolic representation of the contract's dependency graph. The tool parses Solidity code or EVM bytecode, constructs semantic fact graphs, and evaluates patterns that represent secure and insecure behaviors, such as reentrancy, unguarded writes to storage, transaction order dependence (TOD), and unchecked return values. Securify's strength lies in its rule-based engine, which enables both precision and scalability, allowing it to analyze thousands of real-world contracts with minimal false positives. However, its reliance on predefined patterns can limit its ability to detect novel or context-specific vulnerabilities, and the abstraction it uses may overlook subtle data-dependent bugs not captured by the symbolic facts.

Formal verification tools are among the most rigorous approaches to ensuring the correctness and security of smart contracts [9, 91, 96, 105]. By leveraging theorem proving, model checking, and symbolic reasoning, these tools provide mathematical guarantees about contract behavior and systematically eliminate classes of vulnerabilities that may go undetected through conventional testing [6, 8, 94, 98]. The tools reviewed in this section, ranging from theorem-proving environments like Coq and F* to model checkers based on Boogie and SMT solvers, highlight the depth and breadth of formal methods applied in the blockchain space [91, 97, 103, 106]. While these approaches offer unmatched precision and reliability, they also have limitations, including steep learning curves, scalability challenges, and a need for expertise in formal specification [7, 9, 107]. Nonetheless, integrating formal verification into the smart contract development lifecycle is a critical step toward building provably secure decentralized systems [10, 69, 103]. As these tools continue to evolve, they are likely to play an increasingly central role in safeguarding the integrity of smart contract ecosystems [18, 20, 108].

9.1.7 Fuzzing

Fuzzing, or fuzz testing, is a dynamic security analysis technique that involves feeding smart contracts random, invalid, or unexpected inputs to uncover vulnerabilities that might not be detectable by static analysis [109–112]. This approach is particularly effective in testing how contracts respond to edge cases, incorrect inputs, or malicious sequences of operations [113–116]. Fuzzing tools often integrate symbolic execution, taint analysis, differential testing, or reinforcement learning to improve coverage and guide test case generation [109, 114, 117, 118]. These tools aim to expose vulnerabilities such as reentrancy, integer overflows, denial-of-service conditions, and logic errors by simulating real-world attack scenarios [109–111, 119]. While fuzzing provides broad exposure to runtime issues and helps evaluate robustness under stress, it also demands substantial computational resources and may not guarantee complete exploration of code paths [18, 20, 120].

- **Academic tools**
  ConFuzzius—Detector [110]
  ConFuzzius is a hybrid fuzzing tool introduced in 2021 for analyzing smart contracts by combining symbolic execution with evolutionary fuzzing. It intelligently generates meaningful transaction sequences through constraint solving and dynamic data dependency analysis, increasing its coverage of complex contract

behaviors. The tool can detect a broad range of vulnerabilities, including assertion failures, reentrancy, unsafe delegate calls, and time-dependent logic. Its hybrid approach enhances the depth and accuracy of vulnerability discovery across various execution paths. However, ConFuzzius may face scalability challenges in large or highly state-dependent contracts due to the overhead of symbolic constraint solving and the complexity of exploring the input space.

CrossFuzz—Detector [111]

CrossFuzz, released in 2024, is a fuzzing framework designed to identify vulnerabilities across interacting smart contracts. It leverages cross-contract data flow and constructor parameter tracing to effectively generate and mutate transaction sequences. This data-centric mutation strategy enhances the tool's ability to uncover reentrancy bugs, assertion failures, and inter-contract inconsistencies. Its inter-contract reasoning makes it well-suited to analyzing complex decentralized applications. Despite its advanced modeling, the complexity of inter-contract behavior poses challenges for mutation optimization and path prioritization, potentially affecting performance and completeness.

EF CF—Detector [112]

EF CF is a high-performance fuzzer introduced in 2023 that transforms EVM bytecode into native C++ code for efficient execution and fuzzing. It uses structure-aware mutation strategies and ABI-guided input generation to accurately simulate transaction sequences. EF CF excels in detecting vulnerabilities related to access control, compositional reentrancy, and delegatecall misuse due to its optimized modeling of complex smart contract interactions. While its performance is impressive, the translation process and ABI dependency may introduce compatibility issues for non-standard contracts or those with unconventional behaviors.

EtherDiffer—Detector [115]

EtherDiffer, published in 2023, adopts a differential testing approach to uncover inconsistencies in Ethereum's Remote Procedure Call (RPC) interfaces. By generating concurrent transactions and simulating propagation delays, the tool identifies bugs such as gas estimation discrepancies, uncle block access issues, and malformed return values. Its unique design provides insight into low-level node behavior and client-specific implementation bugs. However, EtherDiffer's focus on node-level discrepancies makes it less effective at detecting high-level contract logic vulnerabilities and requires controlled environments for accurate deviation detection.

EthPloit—Detector [113]

EthPloit is an exploit generation tool introduced in 2020 that combines fuzzing with static taint analysis to create targeted attack inputs for Ethereum smart contracts. It employs a dynamic seed selection strategy and uses an instrumented EVM to account for blockchain-specific behaviors and constraints. By analyzing tainted paths and selectively mutating transaction parameters, EthPloit uncovers vulnerabilities such as crash bugs, denial-of-service (DoS) conditions, and incorrect gas estimation. Its strength lies in generating exploit-ready inputs, making it valuable for red-teaming and penetration testing scenarios. However, the reliance on accurate taint tracking and symbolic behavior emulation increases analysis overhead and may lead to false positives if path constraints are misinterpreted.

EVMFuzzer—Detector [119]

EVMFuzzer, released in 2019, is a differential fuzzing tool designed to test the correctness and security of EVM implementations across different clients. It generates and mutates seed contracts, executes them across multiple EVM environments, and identifies discrepancies in execution results. Using dynamic priority scheduling and benchmark-driven oracles, it detects vulnerabilities such as illegal stack operations, segmentation faults, and DoS bugs. EVMFuzzer is particularly useful for identifying consensus failures and virtual machine inconsistencies. However, its focus on VM-level rather than contract-level vulnerabilities may lead it to overlook higher-level logic flaws within individual smart contracts.

FuzzDelSol—Detector [116]

FuzzDelSol is a binary-only, coverage-guided fuzzing framework developed in 2023 for Solana smart contracts. It models Solana's execution environment and smart contract interactions to generate transactions that effectively uncover vulnerabilities. FuzzDelSol can detect critical issues such as missing signer or owner checks, arbitrary cross-program invocation, and integer errors, such as overflows. Its ability to operate without source code makes it suitable for black-box testing and deployed contract auditing. However, the complexity of modeling Solana's parallel execution semantics and runtime constraints can limit the tool's accuracy and increase the difficulty of configuration.

GasFuzzer—Detector [109]

GasFuzzer, introduced in 2020, is a specialized fuzzing tool targeting gas-related vulnerabilities in Ethereum smart contracts. It employs a two-phase fuzzing strategy: a gas-greedy phase that prioritizes high-gas-consumption paths and a gas-leveling phase that manipulates gas inputs to expose exception-based vulnerabilities. GasFuzzer detects issues such as exceptions disorder and out-of-gas conditions, making it particularly effective in optimizing and stress-testing gas-sensitive functions. While its targeted approach yields high accuracy for gas-related bugs, it is limited in scope and does not address broader security vulnerabilities, such as logic flaws or unauthorized state changes.

HFContractFuzzer—Detector [114]

HFContractFuzzer is a fuzzing tool developed in 2021 for smart contracts written in Go on the Hyperledger Fabric platform. It integrates the go-fuzz framework with a MockStub-based simulation of blockchain state to test contract behaviors. The tool improves fuzzing efficiency by enhancing the initial corpus and customizing mutation algorithms, enabling detection of logic loopholes, type conversion errors, and integer overflows. HFContractFuzzer supports unit testing-like workflows for enterprise-grade contracts. However, its reliance on Go-based contracts and a Fabric-specific architecture limits its generalizability to other blockchain platforms or languages.

Hydra—Detector [120]

Hydra, introduced in 2019, is a framework that automates bug-bounty processes for Ethereum smart contracts using principled differential analysis. It leverages

N-version programming by running multiple compiled versions of a contract in parallel to detect behavioral inconsistencies and trigger automatic bug reporting. A coordinating metaprogram ensures secure handling of discrepancies and manages bounty payouts to incentivize responsible disclosure. Hydra is particularly effective in identifying logic errors and reentrancy issues by exploiting divergence in execution paths. Its innovation lies in linking security testing to economic incentives, though its success depends on the availability of diverse contract variants and may not generalize well to all smart contract types.

IcyChecker—Detector [117]

IcyChecker is a fuzzing-based detection framework introduced in 2023 to uncover state-inconsistency bugs in Ethereum smart contracts. It begins by replaying historical on-chain transactions to capture real-world execution context, then generates and mutates new transaction sequences to detect inconsistencies in the resulting states. IcyChecker excels at detecting bugs arising from environmental assumptions or multi-transaction dependencies, such as reentrancy, front-running, bad randomness, and access control violations. Its strength lies in its real-context replay engine, but the reliance on complete and accurate historical data can make it less effective for newly deployed or rarely used contracts.

Invariant-Based Scarcity Defect Detector—Detector [118]

Published in 2022, this tool employs invariant checking to detect scarcity-related defects in blockchain assets. It defines transfer and swap invariants as test oracles and uses the ConFuzzius fuzzing engine to generate relevant inputs. By ensuring that asset supply and balance logic remain consistent across various transaction patterns, this detector reveals scarcity defects, such as token loss due to incorrect minting/burning logic. Its advantage lies in formally encoding economic correctness as invariants, providing a domain-specific safeguard. However, the method is narrowly focused on scarcity issues and may miss other categories of vulnerabilities unrelated to token economics.

ILF—Detector [109]

The Imitation Learning-based Fuzzer (ILF), released in 2019, combines symbolic execution with imitation learning to improve the effectiveness of fuzzing for Ethereum smart contracts. It uses a symbolic execution engine as an expert to generate ideal input sequences, then trains a neural policy to mimic and extend these behaviors for broader coverage. ILF efficiently detects vulnerabilities such as leaking ether, unhandled exceptions, suicidal contracts, and delegatecall misuse. It is particularly powerful for contracts requiring complex state exploration. However, its reliance on accurate symbolic paths and training data introduces overhead, and performance may degrade if symbolic analysis fails or generalization is poor.

ItyFuzz—Detector [111]

ItyFuzz, introduced in 2023, is a snapshot-based fuzzing framework that enhances efficiency by replacing repeated execution with direct state snapshots. It uses dataflow and comparison-based waypoints to identify promising states and prioritizes their mutation. This enables efficient detection of vulnerabilities such as reentrancy, timestamp dependence, integer overflow, out-of-gas conditions, unhandled exceptions, and short address attacks. By focusing on state snapshots, ItyFuzz significantly reduces fuzzing time and computational costs. However, maintaining accurate and restorable state snapshots across multiple interdependent transactions is technically challenging and may introduce fidelity trade-offs in some cases.

Language-Agnostic Fuzzing Framework—Detector [121]

This framework, introduced in 2022, enables fuzz testing of smart contracts written in multiple programming languages by converting them into LLVM Intermediate Representation (IR). It integrates existing fuzzing engines such as AFL++, Honggfuzz, and libFuzzer to perform coverage-guided fuzzing at the IR level, enabling uniform handling of Solidity, Rust, Go, and other contract languages. The tool is particularly beneficial for enterprise-level DevOps environments, where heterogeneous smart contract codebases are common. Its primary strength lies in scalability and maintainability. However, since it operates at an abstracted IR level, it may miss language-specific behaviors or vulnerabilities tied to high-level constructs.

MagicMirror—Detector [113]

MagicMirror, developed in 2023, is a high-coverage fuzzing tool that combines dynamic symbolic execution and traditional fuzzing techniques. It employs dynamic taint analysis to track data flow through smart contracts, allowing it to prioritize critical paths and ensure deeper coverage. The tool detects a broad range of vulnerabilities, including integer overflows, timestamp dependencies, reentrancy, unhandled exceptions, out-of-bounds conditions, and short address attacks. MagicMirror is especially useful in uncovering deeply embedded logic errors that require contextual understanding of input propagation. Despite its thoroughness, the complexity of integrating taint analysis and symbolic execution increases overhead and can hinder performance on large-scale contracts.

ReDefender—Detector [122]

ReDefender is a fully automated fuzzing tool introduced in 2022 for detecting reentrancy vulnerabilities in Ethereum smart contracts. It preprocesses target contracts to extract candidate reentrant functions, then generates fuzzing inputs specifically designed to simulate recursive invocations. Execution logs are then analyzed to confirm exploitability. ReDefender streamlines the reentrancy testing pipeline, offering a focused, low-false-positive solution. However, while effective at its specialization, its scope is limited; it is not designed to detect broader classes of bugs such as gas-related exceptions or logic errors.

SeqFuzz—Detector [123]

SeqFuzz, released in 2023, is a guided mutation-based fuzzer that generates realistic transaction sequences using two key techniques: Dynamic Dependency Learning (DDL) and Dynamic Variable Analysis (DVA). DDL maps dependencies between contract state variables, while DVA identifies relationships between external inputs and contract behavior. SeqFuzz applies this knowledge to prioritize mutations that affect critical paths. The tool can detect a wide array of vulnerabilities, including arbitrary writes, ether leaks, control hijacking, suicidal contracts, mishandled exceptions, and transaction origin misuse. Its precision in generating semantically meaningful sequences is a major advantage, though its guided analysis introduces complexity that may not scale easily to massive multi-contract systems.

SynTest-Solidity—Detector [124]

SynTest-Solidity, developed in 2022, is a fuzzing and automated test case generation framework tailored for Solidity smart contracts. It supports multiple metaheuristic search algorithms, including random search, NSGA-II, and DynaMOSA, to optimize test suite diversity and code coverage. The tool provides both command-line and web-based interfaces for accessibility and integrates with Solidity development pipelines. SynTest-Solidity stands out for its emphasis on optimizing mutation strategies and multi-objective test generation, making it ideal for developers focused on systematic security testing. While highly customizable, the learning curve associated with tuning search algorithms may pose a barrier for less experienced users.

ContractFuzzer—Identifier [125]

ContractFuzzer, introduced in 2018, applies fuzzing techniques to test Ethereum smart contracts for security vulnerabilities by generating random inputs and executing transactions under various conditions. It operates using a predefined vulnerability detection oracle to identify common issues such as reentrancy, timestamp dependence, integer overflows, unchecked external calls, exception disorder, and out-of-gas errors. This approach allows ContractFuzzer to simulate real-world attack scenarios, making it a valuable tool for exposing latent bugs. While it remains one of the earliest and most widely referenced fuzzing tools, its rule-based detection system may not readily adapt to emerging or complex multi-contract attack surfaces.

Etherolic—Identifier [126]

Etherolic, released in 2020, is a robust fuzzing and exploit generation tool for Ethereum smart contracts. It combines concolic testing and dynamic taint analysis to evaluate contracts even when source code is unavailable. Etherolic performs bytecode-level analysis and can detect a wide range of issues, including integer overflows and underflows, race conditions, reentrancy, locked ether, unhandled exceptions, and denial-of-service vulnerabilities. It also identifies zero-day bugs with high precision by integrating protection recognition logic to reduce false positives. Despite its strengths, Etherolic's reliance on bytecode instrumentation and concolic execution makes it resource-intensive and slower than lightweight fuzzers.

GFuzzer—Identifier [127]

GFuzzer, introduced in 2022, is a grey-box fuzzing tool designed for EOSIO smart contracts. It utilizes execution feedback, particularly branch coverage data, to guide mutation strategies and enhance path exploration. By applying a distance-based mutation technique, GFuzzer efficiently generates inputs that traverse hard-to-reach code branches, enabling it to detect vulnerabilities such as fake EOS transfers, forged notification events, and block information dependency issues. GFuzzer's grey-box approach strikes a balance between coverage and performance; however, its applicability is limited to EOSIO contracts and may require adaptation for use on Ethereum-based platforms.

NeoDiff—Identifier [128]

NeoDiff, developed in 2021, is a differential fuzzing framework for smart contract virtual machines across various blockchain platforms, including Ethereum and Neo. It applies coverage-guided and state-guided fuzzing strategies to discover discrepancies and critical security issues, such as memory corruption and behavioral inconsistencies, across virtual machine implementations. NeoDiff excels in detecting VM-level flaws by using multi-platform testing to compare semantic differences. While it supports portability across smart contract ecosystems, its focus on VM-layer bugs rather than application-level vulnerabilities limits its usefulness in contract logic testing.

ReGuard—Identifier [129]

ReGuard, released in 2018, is a fuzzing-based analyzer designed to detect reentrancy bugs in Ethereum smart contracts. It translates Solidity code into C++ and then uses fuzz testing to generate a wide range of random and diverse transaction sequences. By dynamically analyzing execution traces during these fuzzing runs, ReGuard can identify runtime conditions that lead to reentrancy vulnerabilities. Its strength lies in its ability to simulate and detect real-world reentrancy scenarios with high precision. However, its scope is narrowly focused on reentrancy and does not generalize to broader categories of vulnerabilities, limiting its versatility.

RLF (Reinforcement Learning Fuzzer)—Identifier [118]

RLF, introduced in 2022, is a reinforcement learning–guided fuzzing tool designed to discover complex vulnerabilities in Ethereum smart contracts by modeling the fuzzing process as a Markov Decision Process (MDP). It learns to generate vulnerable transaction sequences by optimizing for both vulnerability discovery and code coverage. RLF is particularly adept at identifying multi-step vulnerabilities such as ether leaks, suicidal contracts, delegatecall misuse, and exception handling errors. This learning-based strategy enables RLF to explore sophisticated contract behaviors, but the model training can be computationally expensive and may require significant time to converge on optimal policies.

SMARTIAN—Identifier [109]

SMARTIAN (Symbolic Model Analysis Reasoning Tool for IoT and Applications in Networks), published in 2021, is a hybrid fuzzer that enhances vulnerability discovery through both static and dynamic data-flow analysis. It systematically generates critical transaction sequences by analyzing dependencies across smart contract variables and operations. SMARTIAN can detect a wide range of vulnerabilities, including reentrancy, ether leakage, assertion failures, control-flow hijacking, integer bugs, and suicidal behavior in contracts. Its dual approach significantly improves code coverage and vulnerability detection. However, this added depth introduces runtime overhead and complexity in setting up the analysis environment.

sFuzz—Identifier [110]
sFuzz, released in 2020, is an adaptive fuzzing framework for Ethereum smart contracts written in Solidity. It combines AFL-style fuzzing with a lightweight adaptive mutation strategy, using runtime feedback to dynamically refine its input generation. By executing a large number of randomized test cases, sFuzz identifies issues such as reentrancy, gasless sends, exception disorders, integer overflows and underflows, timestamp and block number dependencies, and freezing. Its design ensures high code coverage with minimal configuration. Although sFuzz is highly effective at discovering a wide spectrum of vulnerabilities, it may not provide as fine-grained diagnostic insights as hybrid or concolic approaches.
WASAIUP—Identifier [130]
WASAIUP, introduced in 2023, is a hybrid concolic fuzzing tool developed for EOSIO smart contracts. It integrates symbolic execution and concrete execution in a demand-driven manner to improve efficiency and precision. WASAIUP is tailored to detect specific vulnerabilities, including fake EOS transfers, fake notification attacks, missing authorization checks, rollback flaws, and blockinfo dependency issues. Its hybrid execution model ensures broader path coverage and precise bug localization. However, the tool's design is tightly coupled with the EOSIO architecture, which may reduce its transferability to Ethereum or other blockchain platforms without significant adaptation.

- **Industrial tools**

  Echidna—Detector [131]
  Echidna is a widely used fuzzing tool introduced in 2020 for Ethereum smart contracts. It relies on property-based testing and random input generation to detect issues such as reentrancy, assertion violations, and gas-related exceptions. Integrated with Slither, Echidna benefits from static pre-analysis to guide its fuzzing campaign. It supports a variety of frameworks and offers ease of use with minimal configuration, making it highly accessible for developers. Nonetheless, its random fuzzing strategy may result in low path coverage for contracts with deeply nested logic or specific transaction sequences, potentially overlooking subtle vulnerabilities.
  Harvey—Identifier [112]
  Harvey, released in 2020, is a grey-box fuzzer designed to improve the effectiveness of fuzz testing in smart contracts. It predicts which inputs are most likely to explore new execution paths or reveal vulnerabilities by learning from historical execution traces. Unlike simpler fuzzers, Harvey also mutates entire transaction sequences to examine complex state transitions, thereby increasing the likelihood of exposing vulnerabilities such as assertion violations and memory access errors. Its integration with public datasets enables benchmarking and reproducibility. Although powerful, its predictive input model introduces training complexity and may exhibit diminishing returns in smaller or simpler contracts.

The fuzzing-based tools discussed in this category collectively underscore the power and versatility of fuzz testing as a dynamic approach to vulnerability detection and identification for smart contracts [109–112]. These tools exploit techniques ranging from adaptive mutation strategies and symbolic execution to reinforcement learning and concolic analysis to generate diverse, often unexpected inputs that can trigger subtle and complex vulnerabilities [113–115, 117, 118]. Whether designed for Ethereum, EOSIO, Solana, or Hyperledger Fabric, fuzzers such as ConFuzzius, sFuzz, RLF, and WASAIUP can uncover issues including reentrancy, integer bugs, block-state dependencies, and transaction-sequence exploits across different blockchain environments [114, 116, 122, 127, 130]. Although challenges remain in achieving full path coverage and minimizing performance overhead, fuzzing continues to evolve as an indispensable method in the smart contract security landscape, offering a scalable, automated, and context-aware means to stress-test contracts under adversarial and edge-case conditions [18, 20, 120].

9.1.8 Model-Based Testing

The eighth category, Model-Based Testing, focuses on constructing abstract representations of smart contract behavior, often in the form of finite-state machines, control-flow graphs, or formal logic models, to guide systematic testing and vulnerability analysis [103, 132–134]. By simulating state transitions and user interactions, this approach generates meaningful test cases tailored to uncover hidden flaws in contract logic, access control, and transactional flow [4, 132, 135]. Model-based testing provides an environment for verifying that a contract behaves as intended across diverse execution paths and adversarial scenarios, helping reveal vulnerabilities that are otherwise difficult to detect through conventional testing [94, 133, 134]. The tools in this category harness various modeling strategies, including abstract interpretation, symbolic analysis, genetic algorithms, and hybrid orchestration of third-party tools, to achieve both vulnerability detection and identification across a range of platforms and contract types [4, 91, 135, 136].

- **Academic tools**
  ADF-GA—Detector [135]
  ADF-GA is a model-based testing framework introduced in 2020 that utilizes genetic algorithms to automatically generate test cases for Solidity smart contracts. By constructing control flow graphs and applying data flow analysis to identify variable usages, ADF-GA systematically explores execution paths and optimizes input generation through an enhanced fitness function. This approach facilitates the detection of vulnerabilities such as reentrancy bugs, incorrect state transitions, and integer overflow or underflow, enabling thorough validation of contract behavior without exhaustive manual effort.
  FSolidM—Detector [134]
  FSolidM, developed in 2018, provides a framework for modeling secure Ethereum smart contracts using Finite State Machines (FSMs). It features a graphical editor for specifying contract states and transitions, along with a Solidity code generator and modular plugins that implement common security

mechanisms, such as access control and reentrancy protection. While FSolidM supports secure contract development from the outset, it is not designed for post-deployment vulnerability detection and is thus excluded from analytical evaluations in this survey. Nonetheless, it offers substantial value in formalizing contract logic and promoting best practices during the design phase.

ModCon—Detector [132]

ModCon is a versatile model-based testing platform launched in 2020 that supports both permissioned and permissionless blockchain environments. It enables users to define custom state-transition models, specify pre- and post-conditions, and generate oracle-guided test cases. ModCon's web-based interface facilitates contract testing by capturing complex behavioral patterns and enabling tailored analysis workflows. The platform is particularly effective at detecting vulnerabilities related to functional correctness, improper state transitions, and contract logic flaws in intricate smart contract systems.

SCs Modeling and Behavior Verification—Detector [5]

The SCs Modeling and Behavior Verification Tool, introduced in 2018, applies formal modeling through behavior interaction priorities to simulate and verify smart contract behavior under diverse scenarios. By modeling interactions among contracts, users, and the blockchain, it performs statistical model checking to identify potential vulnerabilities, including transaction reordering, pending-transaction leakage, and network eavesdropping. Through simulating adversarial behaviors, this approach uncovers design flaws and strengthens the resilience of contract logic prior to deployment.

SmartInspect—Detector [137]

SmartInspect, released in 2018, is a Solidity smart contract inspector that applies decompilation techniques to reconstruct source-level representations of deployed contracts. Its mirror-based architecture interprets contract state directly from EVM bytecode, enabling state inspection without modifying or redeploying the contract. This facilitates post-deployment analysis and validation of contract logic, particularly when source code is unavailable, and supports debugging by mapping binary structures back to their original abstractions.

Elysium—Identifier [138]

Elysium is a bytecode-level vulnerability patching tool introduced in 2022, designed to automatically fix security flaws in smart contracts. It integrates detection capabilities from established tools such as Osiris, Oyente, and Mythril and applies patching techniques informed by control flow graphs (CFGs) and taint analysis. By analyzing Ethereum bytecode, Elysium identifies and addresses a wide range of critical vulnerabilities, including same-function and cross-function reentrancy, misuse of delegatecall, create-based reentrancy, transaction origin misuse, suicidal contracts, and both integer overflows and underflows. Its bytecode-level intervention enables direct patching without access to the source code, making it highly practical for deployed contracts. While Elysium is effective in automating the patching process and is openly available via GitHub, it inherits the limitations of its integrated tools and may struggle with deeply obfuscated or non-standard bytecode structures.

ESAF—Identifier [139]
The Ethereum Security Analysis Framework (ESAF), introduced in 2021, offers a unified environment for smart contract vulnerability analysis by integrating multiple established tools into a single containerized framework. ESAF enhances the efficiency of smart contract assessment by managing tool dependencies and harmonizing output formats, enabling consistent, reproducible results across a wide range of contracts. It supports persistent monitoring and facilitates both individual and batch vulnerability assessments by leveraging the combined capabilities of tools such as Oyente, Mythril, and Securify. ESAF's modular and scalable architecture simplifies workflow automation and supports integration into CI/CD pipelines. Despite its strengths, ESAF's effectiveness is contingent on the detection scope of the tools it aggregates, which may result in blind spots if none of the underlying analyzers cover certain vulnerability classes.
SecSEC—Identifier [140]
Securing Smart Ethereum Contracts (SecSEC), introduced in 2024, is a hybrid identifier that enhances vulnerability detection using a machine-learning-based ensemble approach. It integrates multiple existing smart contract analysis tools and applies logistic regression to synthesize their outputs, improving the overall detection performance. By training on a large dataset of real-world contracts labeled with known vulnerabilities, SecSEC learns to assign weights to different tool outputs, effectively balancing precision and recall. This approach allows SecSEC to reduce false positives and capture vulnerabilities that might be missed by any single tool. However, its reliance on labeled datasets and pre-integrated tools introduces dependency risks, both in terms of generalizability to novel vulnerability patterns and continued tool compatibility as ecosystems evolve.
SmartBugs—Identifier [120]
SmartBugs, introduced in 2020, is an extensible execution framework designed to support reproducible and comprehensive vulnerability detection in Solidity smart contracts. It enables batch execution of multiple security analysis tools, such as HoneyBadger, Maian, and Mythril, within a Docker-based containerized infrastructure. Through a unified command-line interface and customizable configurations, SmartBugs facilitates large-scale evaluations and comparative studies by providing structured reports on a range of vulnerability types, including reentrancy, integer overflows/underflows, unchecked sends, timestamp dependence, uninitialized storage pointers, and denial-of-service. Its architecture promotes tool interoperability and dataset management, making it suitable for both researchers and practitioners. The main limitation of SmartBugs lies in its passive role as a wrapper: its detection capabilities are inherently limited to the strengths and scopes of the tools it encapsulates.
SmartBugs 2.0—Identifier [141]
Released in 2023, SmartBugs 2.0 builds on the foundation of its predecessor by expanding tool integration and improving standardization. It supports the analysis of both Solidity source code and EVM bytecode, incorporating 19 distinct vulnerability detection tools to provide wide coverage across various security categories. SmartBugs 2.0 detects complex issues such as arithmetic overflows,

access control violations, unchecked low-level calls, unsafe delegate calls, gas-consumption inefficiencies, short address attacks, and suicidal contracts. The framework maps all vulnerability findings to the Smart Contract Weakness Classification (SWC) taxonomy, ensuring consistency and enabling benchmarking. Its strengths lie in scalability, tool diversity, and automated output harmonization. However, its reliance on third-party tools means its detection efficacy depends on the quality and update status of those integrated analyzers.
SoliAudit—Identifier [142]
SoliAudit, introduced in 2019, is a machine learning and fuzzing-based smart contract vulnerability assessment tool. It combines static classification using features extracted from Solidity bytecode with dynamic fuzz testing to validate findings through simulated execution. SoliAudit identifies 13 types of vulnerabilities, including reentrancy, arithmetic overflows, denial-of-service, timestamp manipulation, and transaction-origin misuse, without relying on predefined rules or expert knowledge. Its hybrid design enables both broad detection and behavioral verification. However, SoliAudit's performance is sensitive to the quality of the training data and the scope of the feature engineering process. Additionally, like other ML-based systems, it may struggle to detect novel attack vectors that deviate from learned patterns.

Model-based testing tools introduce a structured, systematic approach to smart contract security by leveraging abstract models, control-flow representations, and formal behavior specifications [4, 103, 132–134]. These tools excel at uncovering subtle and complex issues by simulating various execution scenarios, validating state transitions, and identifying deviations from intended contract behavior [5, 91, 94, 132, 135]. Approaches such as genetic algorithms, finite-state machines, and formal verification enable high test coverage and the detection of logic flaws, state inconsistencies, and critical vulnerabilities [103, 134–136]. Moreover, identifier tools in this category enhance security auditing by integrating multiple analyzers, patching frameworks, and machine-learning-based ensemble methods [120, 140, 142]. Despite their thoroughness, model-based tools often require significant upfront effort to construct accurate models or prepare training datasets, and their effectiveness can be bounded by the capabilities of the integrated tools or the assumptions made during modeling [17–20]. Nevertheless, this category significantly advances smart contract reliability and safety by combining rigorous analysis with scalable automation [19, 20, 71].

9.1.9 Mutation Testing

This category leverages mutation testing, a technique that introduces small, deliberate changes, known as mutations, into smart contract source code to simulate realistic errors [39, 50, 143]. These altered contracts, referred to as mutants, are executed to assess whether existing test suites can detect and appropriately respond to such injected faults [39, 143]. This method provides insight into the robustness and fault-detection capabilities of the test suites, helping to identify deficiencies and improve overall test adequacy [50, 144]. The tools below employ mutation testing, with the first three categorized as detectors and the remaining two as identifiers [39, 50, 143].

- **Academic tools**
  RegularMutator—Detector [145]
  RegularMutator is a mutation testing tool introduced in 2020 for Solidity smart contracts. It employs regular expressions to systematically generate mutants by inserting common syntactic and semantic errors into the source code. The tool assesses the effectiveness of test suites by examining whether they can detect and fail these mutated contracts. Compared to traditional line coverage metrics, RegularMutator demonstrated greater accuracy in identifying weak spots within the testing logic and improving test coverage quality.
  ReSuMo—Detector [146]
  ReSuMo, short for Regression Suite Mutation, is a mutation testing tool designed for large-scale regression analysis in evolving Solidity smart contracts. Published in 2023, it introduces a static, file-level selection mechanism that mutates only the relevant portions of code and re-executes a targeted subset of associated test files. This incremental update strategy, which leverages historical test results, significantly accelerates mutation testing within continuous integration workflows and enables efficient assessment of regression test adequacy.
  SuMo—Detector [147]
  SuMo is a comprehensive mutation testing framework released in 2022 for Solidity-based smart contracts. It offers both a command-line interface and a web-based RESTful API, facilitating seamless integration into development environments. SuMo supports 44 distinct mutation operators that simulate a wide range of coding errors. It integrates with Truffle and Ganache to compile and test contracts, and provides users with detailed mutation score reports, enhancing test-suite validation through automation and traceability.
  MuRE—Identifier [148]
  MuRE (Mutation Testing Approach to Reentrancy Detection Tools Evaluation) was introduced in 2023 as a targeted mutation testing framework for evaluating the effectiveness of reentrancy detection tools. It uses symbolic execution to identify vulnerable reentrancy paths, then applies a custom mutation strategy to generate categorized reentrancy variants. These classified mutants serve as benchmarks for assessing detection tools, enabling MuRE to systematically compare the performance and limitations of existing reentrancy analyzers.
  MuSC—Identifier [149]
  MuSC, or Mutation Testing Tool for Ethereum Smart Contracts, was released in 2019 to evaluate the robustness of test suites through controlled code modifications. It applies specialized mutation operators tailored to Solidity, generating a broad array of mutants that reflect typical fault patterns. MuSC supports automated deployment and execution within testnets and evaluates whether the test

suite can detect injected anomalies, thus quantifying the depth and reliability of contract testing.

In summary, mutation testing tools provide a systematic and empirical approach to assessing the effectiveness of test suites in detecting subtle faults within smart contracts [147–149]. By introducing realistic code mutations and monitoring whether tests catch the injected errors, these tools identify coverage blind spots and promote stronger, more secure testing practices [147, 149]. The tools reviewed in this section demonstrate the maturity and utility of mutation-based analysis in both detection and identification tasks for Solidity-based smart contracts [147–149].

9.1.10 Pattern Matching and Syntactical Analysis

Pattern matching and syntactic analysis are foundational approaches to detecting and identifying vulnerabilities in smart contracts by examining the structural and syntactic elements of the source code [3, 67, 150, 151]. These tools rely on predefined vulnerability signatures, syntactic features, and matching rules to uncover coding inconsistencies, logic flaws, and compliance violations [3, 150, 152, 153]. By leveraging abstract syntax trees (ASTs), intermediate representations, or regular expressions, these methods facilitate efficient detection of both common and subtle errors across large codebases [38, 67, 151, 154]. While they may lack the semantic depth of symbolic or formal methods, their speed, rule extensibility, and compatibility with development environments make them integral components of automated smart contract auditing [17–20]. In this section, we review 35 tools that use this methodology: 14 designed primarily for detection and 21 for vulnerability identification [17, 18, 20].

- **Academic tools**
  DeFiRanger—Detector [130]
  DeFiRanger is a detection tool introduced in 2023 to identify price-manipulation attacks in DeFi applications. The tool constructs a Cash Flow Tree (CFT) from raw transaction data, lifting low-level semantics into a higher-level representation. It then applies a library of predefined semantic patterns to identify traces indicative of price manipulation, offering precise insight into economic vulnerabilities. DeFiRanger excels at capturing complex manipulations across contract interactions, but it remains primarily focused on price-based attack patterns, which limits its broader vulnerability coverage.
  Horus—Detector [155]
  Horus is a logic- and graph-driven tool designed to automate the detection and analysis of attacks on Ethereum smart contracts. It utilizes Datalog queries to identify attack patterns from execution traces and employs graph database techniques to trace stolen assets. Developed in Python, Horus stands out for its dual capability in detection and forensics, providing detailed insights into both the attack vector and the associated asset flows. However, its reliance on post-

execution traces makes it better suited to forensic analysis than to pre-deployment vulnerability detection.

MSmart—Detector [152]

MSmart builds upon the widely used SmartCheck static analyzer by expanding its rule set and enhancing existing checks to cover additional vulnerabilities in Solidity contracts. Released in 2023, MSmart detects issues such as integer overflows, timestamp dependencies, self-destruct vulnerabilities, delegatecall misuse, and denial-of-service (DoS) risks. It supports batch detection, making it well-suited for efficiently auditing large volumes of contracts. Nonetheless, MSmart's effectiveness is tied to the specificity of its rule definitions, which may overlook vulnerabilities outside its predefined scope.

Naga—Detector [144]

Naga is a detection tool that targets centralized security risks in decentralized ecosystems, with a particular focus on Ethereum wallets and smart contracts. Introduced in 2023, it uses intermediate representations (IRs) to perform data dependency analysis and detect centralized risk patterns that undermine decentralization principles. Naga is notable for addressing an underexplored class of vulnerabilities, centralization in ostensibly decentralized systems. Its main limitation is the narrow focus on centralization risks, which may not generalize to broader categories of smart contract vulnerabilities.

SafelyAdministrated—Detector [156]

SafelyAdministrated, introduced in 2021, is a pattern-recognition tool designed to identify ERC-20 tokens that have been administered on the Ethereum mainnet. It operates by analyzing nine syntactic features associated with administrative control, such as the presence of self-destruction mechanisms, upgradability via changes to addresses or parameters, and minting or burning capabilities. By classifying tokens based on these traits, the tool highlights the prevalence of administrated designs and the potential risks they pose to token holders. Its primary advantage lies in its ability to reveal hidden centralization in widely used token contracts. However, its static approach may overlook administrative logic implemented through unconventional or obfuscated patterns.

SCGraphs—Detector [157]

SCGraphs is a vulnerability detection tool that employs semantic contract graphs and approximate graph matching based on the Weisfeiler-Lehman kernel. Introduced in 2023, the tool constructs semantic representations (SCGraphs) of contracts and compares them against a curated vulnerability graph library derived from manually audited contracts. This graph-based approach enables SCGraphs to detect subtle vulnerabilities such as reentrancy, timestamp dependency, delegatecall misuse, and integer overflows by capturing structural and semantic similarities. While the method improves detection generalization, it may incur computational overhead and reduce precision when code variants superficially resemble known vulnerable patterns.

SIF—Detector [73]

The Solidity Instrumentation Framework (SIF), published in 2019, is a framework for analyzing and modifying Solidity contracts through abstract syntax trees (ASTs). It provides utilities for generating call and control flow graphs, seeding faults, and instrumenting code, allowing developers to explore the internal structure and behavior of contracts in depth. SIF supports analysis for vulnerabilities such as division by zero, overflows, and underflows, serving both academic and security auditing contexts. While highly extensible, its utility is best suited for research and experimentation, as it requires manual configuration and lacks built-in automation for large-scale auditing.

SolChecker—Detector [158]

SolChecker is a static analysis tool developed in 2022 that identifies security vulnerabilities in Solidity smart contracts by analyzing their abstract syntax trees. It inspects both control and data flow to flag over a dozen known vulnerability types, including reentrancy, unchecked calls, and abuse of tx.origin. By evaluating a dataset of over 47,000 real-world contracts, SolChecker demonstrates high effectiveness in detecting practical vulnerabilities. Its structured AST-based approach ensures accurate identification of code-level risks, though it is limited by the predefined nature of its rule set and may not detect more complex or emergent vulnerabilities.

SolGuard—Detector [159]

SolGuard is a security analysis plugin that extends the Solhint linter with three additional rules specifically designed to identify issues related to external calls in Solidity smart contracts. Introduced in 2021, it checks for the correct ordering of state variable declarations, warns against using address parameters in constructors, and ensures the inclusion of fallback functions. These targeted checks help address common patterns leading to vulnerable fallback behaviors or incorrect constructor configurations. SolGuard's strength lies in its simplicity and ease of integration with existing linters; however, its limited rule set restricts its scope to vulnerability detection and may not capture complex or obfuscated external-call issues.

TokenScope—Detector [160]

TokenScope, developed in 2019, is a detection tool that identifies behavioral inconsistencies in Ethereum-based cryptocurrency tokens. It analyzes how tokens interact with users and third-party services by comparing observed behaviors against standards derived from core data structures, standard interfaces, and event patterns. In a large-scale analysis of 7472 tokens and over 3 million transactions, TokenScope identified anomalies such as integer overflows, fake deposits, and incorrect balance updates. Its comprehensive dataset-driven approach makes it valuable for uncovering systemic issues in token implementations, but it may be less effective at analyzing bespoke token logic or newer token standards not covered by its rule set.

UBF-ChaincodeScan—Detector [161]

UBF-ChaincodeScan, released in 2023, is a two-phase static analysis tool designed for detecting vulnerabilities in Node.js-based smart contracts for Hyperledger Fabric. In the validation phase, it verifies syntax, script commands, and contract language; the scanning phase performs a detailed security analysis and produces a JSON report. The tool identifies a wide range of issues including misuse of global variables, insecure random number generation, system command execution, and unchecked error handling. Its broad detection capability and tailored focus on Hyperledger Fabric fill a gap in non-Ethereum ecosystems. However, the tool's dependency on JavaScript-based contracts and its niche scope may limit its adoption in more diverse smart contract environments.

Vulpedia—Detector [162]

Vulpedia, introduced in 2022, is a static analysis tool that uses abstract vulnerability signatures to detect critical security flaws in Ethereum smart contracts. By compiling a library of vulnerable and benign code signatures, it formulates detection rules for issues such as reentrancy, tx.origin misuse, unexpected reverts, and self-destruct abuse. Its signature-based pattern matching enhances accuracy in identifying known exploit types. The strength of Vulpedia lies in its precision and ease of use for recurring vulnerability patterns, but like other signature-based tools, it may struggle to detect novel vulnerabilities or variants not covered in its predefined rulebase.

AChecker—Identifier [163]

AChecker, released in 2023, is a static analysis tool tailored to detect access control vulnerabilities in smart contracts. Unlike conventional pattern-matching tools, AChecker uses static data-flow analysis to infer intended access control policies and then applies symbolic analysis to detect inconsistencies between expected and actual access paths. This technique enables it to uncover subtle logic flaws in authorization mechanisms that pattern-based methods might miss. AChecker's innovative approach increases detection robustness, particularly for access control violations, though it can be computationally intensive and requires well-structured source code to function effectively.

CloudAudit—Identifier [163]

CloudAudit, introduced in 2020, leverages XPath-based static analysis to detect integer overflow vulnerabilities in Solidity smart contracts. The tool defines 83 specific XPath patterns spanning 11 categories of overflow behaviors, including arithmetic operations such as addition, subtraction, and multiplication. By matching these patterns against the abstract syntax tree (AST) of smart contracts, CloudAudit identifies precise code locations where overflows might occur. Its targeted approach ensures high accuracy in detecting well-known integer arithmetic bugs. However, the effectiveness of CloudAudit depends on the completeness of its predefined patterns, which may limit its adaptability to evolving coding practices or novel overflow scenarios.

EOSIOAnalyzer—Identifier [164]

EOSIOAnalyzer is a static analysis framework tailored for smart contracts on the EOSIO platform, released in 2022. It translates Wasm bytecode into a high-level intermediate representation to enable precise control and data-flow tracking. The tool uses a context-sensitive data-flow algorithm to detect EOSIO-specific vulnerabilities, such as fake EOS transfers, forged transfer notifications, and reliance on block-level information. EOSIOAnalyzer fills a critical gap in smart contract analysis beyond Ethereum and provides fine-grained insights into Wasm contracts. However, its platform-specific focus and dependency on accurate bytecode translation can limit its generalizability to other blockchain ecosystems.

Graph Embedding-Based Bytecode Matching Tool—Identifier [54]

Introduced in 2021, this tool applies graph embedding and bytecode matching to detect vulnerabilities in Ethereum smart contracts. It slices and normalizes bytecode, then performs graph-based similarity comparisons against a known set of vulnerable patterns. By encoding structural features into embeddings, it accurately identifies threats such as reentrancy, unprotected ownership, mishandled exceptions, integer overflows, and weak randomness. Its primary advantage lies in detecting semantic similarity rather than surface-level patterns, making it more resilient to code obfuscation. Nonetheless, the method's reliance on training data and graph construction can introduce computational overhead and may struggle with previously unseen attack structures.

Matching Rules-Based SCs Audit Tool—Identifier [153]

This 2020 auditing tool utilizes rule-based pattern matching to evaluate the security posture of Ethereum smart contracts. It assigns threat levels, high, medium, or low, by comparing feature vectors of detected vulnerabilities against predefined rule sets. The system detects various issues, including reentrancy, integer overflows, timestamp dependencies, and permission theft, and produces an extensible audit report that developers can modify to incorporate emerging threat types. Its flexibility and rule-based extensibility make it adaptable to evolving standards. However, its accuracy is bounded by the specificity and completeness of its rules, and it may underperform in identifying compound or novel vulnerabilities.

NeuCheck—Identifier [133]

NeuCheck, launched in 2019, uses a syntax tree-based representation to transform smart contract source code into an intermediate form while preserving semantic structure. This avoids the abstraction loss typical in some static analysis techniques. It applies to detect vulnerabilities such as access control flaws, hash collisions, integer overflows, reliance on predictable variables, and reentrancy. NeuCheck emphasizes cross-platform analysis and improved performance over tools like Mythril and Securify. Its key strength lies in preserving semantic richness to achieve higher detection accuracy; however, the method requires well-structured, clean source code to ensure effective parsing and may not scale efficiently with deeply nested or obfuscated contracts.

Remix Solidity Static Analysis Plugin—Identifier [59]

The Remix Solidity Static Analysis Plugin is a built-in tool within the Remix IDE, designed to enhance the security and reliability of Solidity smart contracts through real-time static analysis. Introduced in 2023, it supports 21 analysis modules that span categories such as security, gas efficiency, and economic vulnerabilities. The plugin detects issues, including access control violations, arithmetic bugs, denial-of-service attacks, front-running risks, and unchecked low-level calls. Its graphical user interface makes it accessible even to novice developers, providing instant feedback during contract development. While it offers broad coverage and ease of use, the plugin's rule-based approach may miss nuanced or context-specific vulnerabilities, particularly those requiring dynamic analysis or deeper semantic reasoning.

SafeCheck—Identifier [154]

SafeCheck, released in 2024, is a static analysis tool designed to identify six critical vulnerabilities in Ethereum smart contracts: reentrancy, timestamp dependency, dangerous use of delegatecall, denial-of-service (DoS), self-destruction, and transaction-order dependence (TOD). It translates smart contract bytecode into an intermediate representation and applies Datalog-based rules to extract semantic patterns associated with these vulnerabilities. SafeCheck's strength lies in combining deep semantic extraction with a formal rule engine, enabling it to identify subtle issues that simpler tools often miss. However, as with other rule-based systems, its performance depends on the quality and scope of the ruleset, and it may require regular updates to remain effective against emerging attack strategies.

SmartAnvil—Identifier [165]

SmartAnvil is an open-source platform designed for comprehensive analysis of Solidity smart contracts through a combination of static analysis, inspection of deployed contracts, and blockchain navigation. Introduced in 2019, it includes key components such as SmaccSol for parsing contract syntax, SmartGraph for semantic flow analysis, and SmartInspect for inspecting live contract states. This modular architecture enables SmartAnvil to detect semantic bugs and operational anomalies across both source and deployed contracts. Its holistic view and ability to inspect deployed code provide deeper insights than source-only tools. However, the platform's complexity and broader scope may pose a steeper learning curve for users unfamiliar with semantic analysis frameworks.

SmartDagger—Identifier [166]

SmartDagger is a bytecode-level static analysis tool designed to detect cross-contract vulnerabilities in Ethereum smart contracts. Released in 2022, it introduces innovative mechanisms to recover contract attribute information directly from bytecode, which is crucial when source code is unavailable. The tool selectively analyzes a subset of functions that participate in inter-contract communication, using partial dataflow reuse to improve analysis efficiency. SmartDagger excels at identifying vulnerabilities arising from cross-contract interactions, such as unprotected access via delegatecall or external calls between contracts, and offers high accuracy even in complex call-chain scenarios. Its main limitation is its reliance on bytecode, which may complicate vulnerability interpretation and debugging compared to source-level tools.

Smartmuv—Identifier [167]

Smartmuv is a source code-based static analysis tool developed in 2022 to extract and analyze the storage state of Ethereum smart contracts. It leverages abstract syntax trees (ASTs) and control flow graphs (CFGs) to track the structure and behavior of state variables, including complex mapping types across inheritance hierarchies. This capability allows Smartmuv to facilitate smooth contract upgrades and migrations by providing an accurate representation of a persistent state. It is particularly valuable for developers maintaining evolving contract systems or transitioning to proxy-based upgradable architectures. However, Smartmuv's focus on storage state may limit its ability to identify functional or control-flow vulnerabilities that are unrelated to storage variables.

SoliDetector—Identifier [168]

SoliDetector is a comprehensive static defect detection tool for Solidity smart contracts, introduced in 2023. It employs a knowledge graph to model syntactic and logical relationships in the code, supporting the detection of 20 distinct defect types, including reentrancy, unsafe type inference, locked funds, and token API violations. By using SPARQL queries, SoliDetector can infer complex semantic relationships and localize vulnerabilities with high precision. This approach enables the tool to identify both simple syntax flaws and subtle logical errors that arise from non-obvious dependencies. While powerful, the use of knowledge graphs and query languages may entail a steeper learning curve when integrating into existing development workflows.

SolidityCheck—Identifier [151]

SolidityCheck is a lightweight static analysis tool introduced in 2019 that uses regular expressions to identify a wide range of issues in Solidity smart contracts. Capable of detecting 20 different vulnerabilities, including reentrancy, integer overflow, and other frequent coding mistakes, it provides rapid feedback by matching known error patterns directly in the source code. SolidityCheck also supports instrumentation techniques to efficiently locate and report problematic statements. Its main advantages are its speed and simplicity, making it suitable for initial code reviews or integration in CI/CD pipelines. However, its reliance on regular expressions may limit its effectiveness in detecting more complex or nested vulnerabilities that require semantic understanding.

SPCon—Identifier [169]

SPCon (Security Policy Conformance), introduced in 2023, is a smart contract analysis tool designed to detect permission bugs by validating conformance to access control policies. It reconstructs likely access control models by mining historical transaction data and then validates them against predefined information flow policies. SPCon can identify unauthorized access, incorrect role assignments, and access control violations that deviate from expected policy behavior. This role-mining approach allows it to uncover vulnerabilities that may go unnoticed in code-centric analysis. Its main limitation is its dependency on rich transaction history, making it less effective for newly deployed contracts or those with limited usage data.

Static Analysis-Based Vulnerability Detection Approach—Identifier [154]

This tool, introduced in 2022, focuses on expanding the boundaries of smart contract vulnerability detection using static analysis without relying strictly on predefined rules or patterns. It addresses blind spots of conventional static analyzers, especially for vulnerabilities such as gas-related inefficiencies and access control misconfigurations. By employing a more flexible and dynamic set of heuristics, this approach enhances detection capabilities and adapts to novel vulnerabilities. However, due to its less rigid structure, the tool may suffer from

reduced precision or increased false positives, particularly when analyzing syntactically unconventional contracts.
Static Analyzer for Price Gouging TOD Vulnerabilities—Identifier [170]
This prototype analyzer, developed in 2022, aims to detect and correct price-gouging vulnerabilities in time-of-deposit (TOD) contracts. It uses static analysis techniques to extract data dependencies related to pricing logic and automatically modifies vulnerable contract sections. Built on top of the Slither analysis engine, the tool emphasizes semantic correctness while providing actionable insights for developers. While specialized in scope, its effectiveness in mitigating pricing-related TOD flaws highlights its utility in DeFi applications. However, its narrow focus and experimental status may limit its adoption beyond price-related contexts.
SWAT—Identifier [171]
SWAT (SWC-based Analysis Tool) is a static analysis framework that categorizes smart contract vulnerabilities according to the Smart Contract Weakness Classification (SWC) standard. Introduced in 2022, it uses pattern matching in Solidity code to detect a wide range of issues, such as outdated compiler versions, deprecated functions, and type errors. By aligning with the SWC taxonomy, SWAT standardizes vulnerability detection and reporting, making it easier to integrate with auditing workflows. The tool is valuable for its comprehensive rule coverage, though like other rule-based systems, it may miss vulnerabilities not yet formalized in the SWC registry.
VULTRON—Identifier [172]
VULTRON is a vulnerability detection framework introduced in 2019 that focuses on identifying irregular transaction behavior in smart contracts. It detects mismatches between internal bookkeeping and actual transfers, capturing issues such as reentrancy, exception disorder, gasless sends, and arithmetic anomalies. VULTRON uses a generalized model to represent transaction logic and track abnormal behaviors across different execution paths, offering cross-platform adaptability. While its generality broadens its scope, it may struggle to achieve precision in contracts exhibiting highly custom logic or nonstandard flow patterns.

- **Industrial tools**
  Solidity Vulnerability Scanner—Identifier [173]
  The Solidity Vulnerability Scanner, released in 2022, is a parsing- and pattern-matching-based tool for identifying and categorizing security issues in Solidity smart contracts. It detects vulnerabilities such as reentrancy, integer overflow and underflow, denial of service, and floating pragmas. The tool stands out for providing line-by-line mitigation suggestions, making it especially user-friendly for developers new to smart contract security. Its comprehensiveness and developer-oriented design make it a strong choice for education and secure development practices. However, like many pattern-based tools, its detection capabilities are bound by its predefined rule set, requiring updates to remain effective against new exploit patterns.

SmartCheck—Identifier [150]
SmartCheck, launched in 2018, is a static analysis tool that transforms Solidity code into an XML-based intermediate representation and applies XPath pattern-matching rules to detect a wide array of vulnerabilities. The tool supports over 20 detection rules, targeting issues such as reentrancy, unchecked external calls, integer division, use of tx.origin, redundant fallback functions, locked funds, and unsafe type inference. It provides categorized reports with severity levels and code snippets to assist developers in remediation. SmartCheck is valued for its detailed pattern coverage and compatibility with legacy contracts. However, its reliance on syntactic patterns may result in false positives or overlook complex logic vulnerabilities that require more contextual analysis.

SASC—Identifier [174]
Static Analysis for Smart Contracts (SASC), developed in 2018, applies topological analysis and logic risk modeling to identify security issues in Ethereum smart contracts. It focuses on a wide range of vulnerabilities, including call stack depth limits, transaction order dependence, reentrancy, timestamp misuse, reliance on tx.origin, and division by zero errors. SASC generates detailed HTML reports that help developers visualize and address identified risks. Its strength lies in offering both structural and semantic inspection across multiple vulnerability types. However, due to its earlier development date, it may not fully support newer Solidity features or the more recent best practices introduced in evolving smart contract standards.

Solhint—Detector [24]
Solhint, initially released in 2017 and maintained by Protofire, is a Solidity linting tool that combines style enforcement with basic security checks. It uses a configuration-driven ruleset to ensure coding consistency while identifying common issues such as unsafe type usage, outdated compiler versions, and misused visibility specifiers. Solhint supports automatic fixing for many detected issues and integrates seamlessly with developer workflows. Although not designed for deep vulnerability detection, it plays a crucial role in early-stage contract development by promoting best practices and reducing the likelihood of basic mistakes.

Ethlint—Detector [175]
Originally released as Solium in 2016 and later renamed Ethlint, this tool is a JavaScript-based static analyzer that enforces coding standards and identifies stylistic and security issues in Solidity smart contracts. Ethlint integrates smoothly with organizational build systems and offers a command-line interface that supports multiple output formats and automated code corrections. While its emphasis is more on standardization and developer hygiene, its detection of misused constructs contributes to foundational code security, though it lacks the depth to analyze semantic vulnerabilities.

The tools in the Pattern Matching and Syntactical Analysis category offer a diverse and powerful set of approaches for detecting vulnerabilities in smart contracts by examining structural code patterns and syntactic features [133, 150–154, 158].

These tools leverage static rules, abstract syntax trees, regular expressions, knowledge graphs, and formal query languages to uncover a wide spectrum of issues ranging from reentrancy and access control flaws to style inconsistencies and unsafe coding practices [24, 73, 150, 164, 175]. While rule-based detection provides efficiency and interpretability, it also presents inherent limitations in identifying novel or obfuscated vulnerabilities [17–20]. Despite these constraints, syntactic and pattern-based tools remain foundational in smart contract analysis, especially when integrated with broader toolchains or used alongside semantic, symbolic, or formal verification methods [67, 69, 108]. Their adaptability across different contract languages and platforms further reinforces their significance in securing the smart contract ecosystem [20, 159, 164, 165].

9.1.11 Runtime Verification

The Runtime Verification category comprises tools that dynamically observe the execution of smart contracts (SCs) to ensure they comply with specified behavioral properties [11, 23, 103]. Unlike static analysis, which inspects code prior to deployment, runtime verification monitors smart contract interactions during actual execution [11, 23]. These tools are particularly effective at detecting violations, attacks, or inconsistencies in real time, enabling timely intervention and remediation [11, 103]. Through techniques such as code instrumentation, event logging, anomaly detection, and dynamic taint analysis, runtime verification tools enforce correctness, safety, and liveness properties [23, 103]. While runtime verification can be computationally expensive and may introduce overhead into execution, it remains critical for identifying emergent behaviors that static analysis alone might miss, especially in dynamic, adversarial blockchain environments [11, 23]. The tools in this category demonstrate the application of runtime verification to a wide array of security risks, including access violations, gas depletion, and reentrancy attacks [11, 23, 103].

- **Academic tools**
  ContractLarva—Detector [176]
  ContractLarva is a runtime verification framework for Ethereum smart contracts that enables monitoring of contract behavior based on formally defined specifications. Introduced in 2018, the tool instruments Solidity code with additional monitoring logic, allowing it to observe and react to control-flow and data-flow events during execution. ContractLarva supports user-defined reparation strategies, enabling real-time enforcement of safety properties and immediate corrective actions upon detecting violations such as unauthorized access, improper function execution, and data corruption. Its use of formal property specifications makes it particularly suitable for precise behavioral monitoring. However, a major limitation of ContractLarva is the added execution overhead from code instrumentation, which can degrade performance and increase gas costs on the Ethereum Virtual Machine (EVM).

DappGuard—Detector [74]

DappGuard is a real-time monitoring and defense system introduced in 2017 to protect Solidity-based smart contracts against a broad set of vulnerabilities. It continuously inspects blockchain transactions for abnormal behavior, leveraging a rule-based engine to detect known patterns such as excessive gas usage or repeated exceptions. DappGuard can mitigate numerous vulnerabilities at runtime, including reentrancy, exception disorder, unauthorized state access, and timestamp dependence. It supports comprehensive coverage through a predefined ruleset addressing both functional and structural vulnerabilities. One of its key advantages is its capacity to actively block and respond to detected exploits in real time. However, DappGuard's reliance on predefined patterns limits its adaptability to novel or complex, previously unseen attack behaviors, potentially resulting in undetected threats or false positives.

ECFChecker—Detector [177]

ECFChecker is a specialized runtime tool designed to verify the Effectively Callback Free (ECF) property of Ethereum smart contracts during execution. Developed in 2017, ECFChecker integrates directly with the EVM and applies an efficient, polynomial-time online algorithm to detect and prevent non-ECF executions that may lead to dangerous behaviors such as reentrancy, particularly those responsible for the DAO exploit. By ensuring that contracts are not reentered by unauthorized external calls, ECFChecker enforces a secure execution paradigm. Its integration at the EVM level ensures minimal intrusion into smart contract development processes. Nevertheless, its scope is narrowly focused on enforcing ECF properties, limiting its utility in detecting a wider spectrum of vulnerabilities beyond reentrance-related issues.

EVM—Detector [178]

The EVM-detector is a modified Ethereum Virtual Machine introduced in 2019 to prevent malicious transactions in real time. It enhances the default EVM by integrating monitoring hooks and enforcing strict checks on opcode structures and execution paths. The tool aims to intercept and reject transactions that may trigger vulnerabilities such as arithmetic overflows or timestamp-based manipulation, thus acting as a defensive shield at the EVM execution level. Its embedded nature enables seamless, efficient enforcement without requiring changes to the smart contracts themselves. However, this benefit comes at the cost of compatibility and deployability, as modifying the core EVM requires systemic changes to the blockchain infrastructure, making it impractical for decentralized deployment in current Ethereum networks.

EVM-Shield—Detector [179]

EVM-Shield, released in 2024, is an advanced runtime verification tool that enforces fine-grained access control over Ethereum smart contract storage. It employs a hybrid storage analyzer to dynamically identify sensitive variables and integrates a multi-stage cache-based filtering mechanism to monitor and block unauthorized access attempts. This allows EVM-Shield to proactively detect and prevent attacks such as reentrancy, integer overflows, and unauthorized Ether transfers. One of its core strengths is its high precision and minimal false positives, enabled by its contextual understanding of storage access patterns. Despite its robustness, EVM-Shield introduces runtime overhead and may incur additional gas costs, making it more suitable for high-stakes contracts where security takes precedence over performance.

Xscope—Detector [180]

Xscope, introduced in 2023, is a runtime verification tool aimed at enhancing the security of cross-chain bridges, an increasingly critical component in decentralized finance. Unlike traditional tools that focus solely on Ethereum contracts, Xscope addresses the emerging landscape of inter-blockchain communication. It monitors cross-chain transactions in real time and performs offline analysis to identify novel security threats. Specifically, it detects three newly observed bug classes: unrestricted deposit emitting, inconsistent event parsing, and unauthorized unlocking. By formalizing these behaviors into runtime checkers, Xscope improves the reliability and trustworthiness of cross-chain bridge interactions. However, its effectiveness is currently specialized to cross-chain bridge vulnerabilities, making it less generalizable to standard Ethereum smart contracts.

ÆGIS—Identifier [181]

ÆGIS is a dynamic vulnerability identification framework developed in 2020 that operates by monitoring Ethereum smart contracts for known exploit patterns during execution. It utilizes domain-specific language to encode attack behaviors and applies these patterns to detect and revert malicious transactions in real time. ÆGIS is particularly effective at identifying various types of reentrancy vulnerabilities, including same-function, cross-function, delegated, and create-based reentrancy, as well as high-profile exploits like the Parity Wallet hacks. Additionally, it supports community-driven security updates through a smart contract-based voting mechanism, enabling decentralized evolution of its detection logic. While ÆGIS offers powerful runtime defense, its detection capability is bounded by the specificity of predefined attack patterns, limiting its responsiveness to unforeseen exploit strategies.

ContractGuard—Identifier [75]

ContractGuard is an anomaly-based Intrusion Detection System (IDS) introduced in 2020 to provide post-deployment protection for Ethereum smart contracts. It profiles legitimate contract-execution behavior using context-tagged acyclic paths and detects deviations from that behavior to identify anomalies. ContractGuard targets a wide array of vulnerabilities, including reentrancy, unsafe delegate calls, arithmetic bugs, and logic errors. It enhances contract resilience by rolling back transactions when deviations are detected. Its ability to detect unknown attacks through behavioral anomalies is a significant advantage over rule-based tools. However, building and maintaining accurate behavioral profiles is challenging and may lead to false positives if contract usage evolves beyond initial training scenarios.

Gas Gauge—Identifier [182]

Gas Gauge, released in 2023, is a hybrid vulnerability-identification tool that focuses on detecting Out-of-Gas (OOG) denial-of-service vulnerabilities in Ethereum smart contracts. It integrates static analysis, white box fuzzing, and

runtime verification to identify potentially dangerous loop constructs. The tool analyzes contract bytecode to locate looping patterns, generates triggering inputs via fuzzing, and then performs runtime tests to confirm exploitability. By simulating loop execution and gas consumption, Gas Gauge provides developers with actionable repair suggestions. Although its loop-focused specialization is valuable for mitigating a common class of DoS attacks, its scope does not extend to other vulnerability types, thus limiting its utility in broader security assessments.
SODA—Identifier [72]
SODA, introduced in 2020, is a general-purpose runtime framework for online vulnerability detection in EVM-compatible smart contracts. It separates the monitoring and detection processes by collecting contract execution traces and analyzing them through external applications. SODA identifies a range of critical vulnerabilities, including reentrancy, improper authorization checks, missing event logs, and time-based dependencies. Its modular design allows developers to rapidly prototype and deploy new detection modules for emerging vulnerabilities, making it highly adaptable to evolving security threats. While SODA's flexibility is a major strength, its dependence on external detection logic can introduce delays between observation and response, which may be critical in high-frequency attack scenarios.
Solitor—Identifier [183]
Solitor, developed in 2018, is a runtime verification tool for Ethereum smart contracts that enables the specification and enforcement of contract properties using in-code annotations. Developers can define preconditions, postconditions, and invariants within the Solidity code itself, which Solitor then monitors during execution. This tight integration between specification and runtime checking helps ensure that contracts behave as expected in deployed environments. By embedding formal behavioral expectations directly into the codebase, Solitor facilitates early bug detection and contract self-validation. However, the effectiveness of Solitor depends heavily on the completeness and accuracy of developer-provided annotations. Inadequate or incorrect specifications can lead to undetected violations or false assurances of correctness.
TaintGuard—Identifier [184]
TaintGuard, introduced in 2023, is a hybrid static-runtime verification tool focused on preventing implicit privilege leakage in Solidity smart contracts. It leverages taint tracking at the Abstract Syntax Tree (AST) level to identify sensitive variables and cross-contract delegate calls that may compromise contract privileges. By instrumenting the source code with monitoring logic, TaintGuard observes contract behavior at runtime to detect unauthorized state changes resulting from indirect call flows. Its layered analysis allows developers to secure inter-contract communication and mitigate the risk of privilege escalation. Despite its strengths, TaintGuard's reliance on accurate taint propagation paths and runtime instrumentation may incur overhead and lead to incomplete coverage in complex contract architectures.
Runtime verification tools serve as a crucial layer of defense in the operational lifecycle of smart contracts by providing continuous monitoring and real-time

enforcement of expected behaviors [72, 74, 176, 183]. Unlike static analysis techniques that inspect code prior to deployment, these tools actively oversee contract execution to catch violations as they occur, offering a dynamic and responsive security mechanism [75, 176, 179, 184]. The tools reviewed in this category exemplify a diverse range of approaches, from instrumentation-based monitors such as ContractLarva and Solitor to anomaly-detection frameworks such as ContractGuard and EVM-level defenses such as EVM-Shield [75, 176, 179, 183]. While runtime verification introduces additional computational costs and may require complex integration, its ability to detect context-specific and evolving vulnerabilities makes it indispensable for maintaining secure smart contract systems in production environments [11, 23, 75, 184]. Collectively, these tools highlight how runtime verification not only strengthens post-deployment resilience but also facilitates rapid response to emerging threats, bridging the gap between preventive design and adaptive security [72, 74, 180, 182].

9.1.12 Symbolic Execution

Symbolic execution is a powerful methodology for smart contract analysis that systematically explores program paths using symbolic inputs rather than concrete values [52, 113, 185]. By simulating contract execution and tracking variable constraints, symbolic execution engines can detect vulnerabilities across multiple execution paths without requiring actual transaction data [52, 113]. This approach enables comprehensive discovery of logic errors, security flaws, and unintended behaviors by analyzing multiple feasible execution branches [52, 185]. Tools that use symbolic execution typically integrate constraint solvers and predefined vulnerability specifications, making them highly effective for automated vulnerability detection and pre-deployment auditing of smart contracts [52, 113, 185].

- **Academic tools**
  Abbe—Detector [130]
  Abbe (Abnormal BEhavior detection in Ethereum), proposed by Nguyen et al. in 2019, is a symbolic execution–based tool designed to detect attack vectors in Ethereum smart contracts by analyzing abnormal transaction behavior. The tool decompiles smart contract bytecode and combines symbolic execution with heuristic rules to trace critical vulnerabilities, including reentrancy, gasless send, force-sending Ether via selfdestruct, integer and array overflows, uninitialized storage pointers, and delegatecall-based overrides. By analyzing symbolic traces of transaction executions, Abbe identifies patterns that deviate from normal contract behavior, enabling simultaneous detection of multiple vulnerability classes. Its strength lies in its breadth of coverage and the use of symbolic abstractions to generalize across execution paths. However, its precision depends heavily on

handcrafted heuristic rules and may miss edge-case vulnerabilities that these rules do not adequately represent.

ConSym-OSIRIS—Detector [49]

Introduced by Yin et al. in 2022, ConSym-OSIRIS integrates symbolic execution with mutation testing to improve vulnerability detection in smart contracts. The framework symbolically executes program paths while simultaneously introducing systematic code mutations to expose latent or mutation-sensitive faults. This combined analysis reveals hidden vulnerabilities such as integer overflows and underflows, reentrancy, arithmetic inconsistencies, and incorrect state updates. The primary contribution of ConSym-OSIRIS lies in its hybrid analysis pipeline, which increases both coverage and fault localization accuracy. However, incorporating mutation testing significantly increases computational overhead and analysis time, making the tool less suitable for large-scale contract datasets or rapid auditing scenarios.

CESC—Detector [186]

CESC (Concurrency Exploit Smart Contracts), proposed by Li in 2019, targets concurrency-related vulnerabilities in Ethereum smart contracts using symbolic execution. It analyzes interactions with shared storage and traces control flows to detect transaction-order dependence (TOD), unauthorized Ether transfers, storage pollution, and contract self-destruction vulnerabilities. By merging symbolic execution traces with storage-access analysis, CESC can pinpoint concurrency-induced security flaws that are often overlooked by conventional analyzers. Its precise modeling of storage interactions helps reduce false positives. Nevertheless, its specialization in concurrency issues may limit its effectiveness in detecting purely logical or control-flow vulnerabilities unrelated to concurrent interactions.

EtherSolve—Detector [100]

EtherSolve, introduced by Pasqua et al. in 2023, focuses on reconstructing control flow graphs (CFGs) from Ethereum bytecode using symbolic execution. The tool symbolically evaluates stack operations to resolve dynamic jump targets, thereby improving CFG reconstruction for contracts with complex or obfuscated control flows. This enhanced CFG construction enables more precise detection of vulnerabilities such as reentrancy and tx.origin misuse. EtherSolve significantly improves CFG completeness compared to traditional bytecode analyzers, facilitating deeper program analysis. However, the symbolic evaluation of stack states introduces scalability challenges when processing large collections of contracts.

EthChecker—Detector [187]

Developed by Han et al. in 2024, EthChecker employs a hybrid approach that combines symbolic execution and fuzz testing, guided by a genetic programming algorithm. The system generates targeted inputs while symbolically exploring potential execution paths to maximize code coverage. EthChecker detects vulnerabilities including reentrancy, timestamp dependency, arithmetic overflow and underflow, and unhandled exceptions. Its key innovation is the context-guided evolutionary strategy that directs exploration toward unexplored or suspicious regions of code. Although the integration of fuzzing improves vulnerability discovery, it also increases system complexity and may introduce redundant exploration when genetic parameters are poorly tuned.

Ethainter—Detector [188]

Ethainter, introduced by Brent et al. in 2020, is a symbolic execution tool designed to detect composite information-flow violations in Ethereum smart contracts. The tool performs taint analysis to track how sensitive inputs propagate through control-flow decisions and across multiple transactions. By examining guard conditions and tracking tainted storage states, Ethainter identifies vulnerabilities such as tainted delegatecall invocations, unchecked selfdestruct calls, and unsafe static calls. Its inter-transactional analysis enables the detection of complex vulnerability chains spanning multiple execution contexts. However, its focus on taint-based vulnerabilities means that purely logical flaws may remain undetected, and the depth of analysis increases computational overhead.

EthRacer—Detector [55]

EthRacer, developed by Kolluri et al. in 2019, uses symbolic execution combined with happens-before (HB) analysis to detect event-ordering bugs in Ethereum smart contracts. The tool explores different execution schedules by reordering events and transactions, identifying inconsistencies in contract state or output behavior. EthRacer combines fuzzing with symbolic execution to mitigate path explosion and focuses specifically on concurrency vulnerabilities arising from nondeterministic transaction ordering. It effectively detects issues such as transaction-order dependence and multi-call interference. However, its concurrency-focused design means it may overlook vulnerabilities unrelated to scheduling or ordering effects.

EXGEN—Detector [16]

EXGEN (Exploit Generation), introduced by Jin et al. in 2023, is a cross-platform vulnerability analysis framework that targets both Ethereum and EOS smart contracts. It translates contracts into a unified intermediate representation and uses symbolic execution to synthesize exploit contracts that can trigger vulnerabilities. EXGEN can detect issues such as reentrancy, arithmetic overflows and underflows, call injection, suicidal contracts, and unauthorized value transfers. Its distinctive feature is automated exploit synthesis, which demonstrates the practical exploitability of discovered vulnerabilities. However, generating exploit contracts increases the complexity of symbolic analysis and computational resource consumption.

FSFC—Detector [189]

FSFC (Filter-based Secure Framework for Ethereum Smart Contracts), introduced by Wang et al. in 2020, combines fuzz testing and symbolic execution in a two-phase vulnerability-detection pipeline. The framework first generates diverse inputs via fuzzing and then uses symbolic execution to explore complex or state-dependent execution paths in depth. FSFC can detect vulnerabilities including reentrancy, arithmetic errors, access control violations, self-destruct vulnerabilities, and denial-of-service conditions. The synergy between stochastic input exploration and deterministic symbolic reasoning improves coverage and accuracy. However, coordinating both phases introduces additional runtime overhead and may lead to redundant path exploration if not carefully optimized.

GasChecker—Detector [190]

GasChecker, developed by Chen et al. in 2021, is a symbolic execution–based analyzer designed to identify gas inefficiencies in Ethereum smart contracts. It detects patterns such as dead code, expensive loop operations, redundant computations, and inefficient storage accesses that increase gas consumption. GasChecker employs a parallel MapReduce architecture and feedback-driven load balancing to scale symbolic exploration across large datasets. While its primary objective is gas optimization, identifying such inefficiencies can also reveal potential denial-of-service risks. Nevertheless, the tool's focus on resource consumption may lead it to overlook broader logical or security vulnerabilities.

GASPER—Detector [95]

GASPER, introduced by Chen et al. in 2017, is one of the earliest symbolic execution tools designed to detect gas-costly patterns in Ethereum smart contract bytecode. It identifies inefficiencies such as dead code, opaque predicates, and redundant loop operations that unnecessarily increase gas usage. GASPER analyzes loop behaviors and constant conditions through symbolic evaluation to flag constructs that do not meaningfully contribute to contract logic. Its strength lies in helping developers optimize contract performance and reduce operational costs. However, its narrow focus on gas consumption limits its ability to detect broader security vulnerabilities or logical flaws within smart contracts.

HoneyBadger—Detector [191]

HoneyBadger, developed by Torres et al. in 2019, targets the detection of honeypot contracts, deceptive smart contracts that lure users into transferring funds under false pretenses. The tool combines symbolic execution with control-flow and cash-flow analysis to identify misleading code paths and execution traps. It analyzes EVM bytecode to uncover inconsistencies between advertised behavior and actual logic, flagging contracts that prevent withdrawal despite appearing secure. HoneyBadger is notable for pioneering automated detection of this class of social-engineering-based smart contract attacks. While effective in uncovering honeypots, its reliance on heuristics can lead to false positives, and it is less comprehensive for general-purpose vulnerability detection.

Jyane—Detector [192]

Jyane, introduced by Fang et al. in 2021, specializes in detecting reentrancy vulnerabilities using an enhanced path profiling approach. It reconstructs control flow graphs from EVM bytecode and applies a refined Ball-Larus Path Profiling algorithm to assign unique IDs to execution paths. Using Deterministic Finite Automata (DFA), Jyane detects suspicious call sequences indicative of reentrancy flaws. Its key innovation is combining path-sensitive analysis with symbolic execution to increase detection precision without relying solely on source code. While Jyane performs well in identifying reentrancy risks with low false positives, it may not capture other types of vulnerabilities that fall outside its path profiling model.

NPChecker—Detector [193]
NPChecker, proposed by Wang et al. in 2019, addresses nondeterministic behaviors in Ethereum smart contracts, particularly those arising from transaction-order dependence and unpredictable external interactions. It integrates symbolic execution with model checking and information flow tracking to identify vulnerabilities such as failed external calls, reliance on system properties, and nondeterministic payment logic. NPChecker systematically explores how variability in transaction sequencing can affect contract behavior, making it a powerful tool for detecting elusive bugs linked to scheduling and state inconsistencies. Its thorough analysis of temporal and external dependencies sets it apart, though its focus on nondeterminism may overlook more deterministic flaws.
Pluto—Detector [194]
Pluto, introduced by Ma et al. in 2022, enhances symbolic execution by extending analysis to inter-contract relationships. It constructs an Inter-contract Control Flow Graph (ICFG) and derives Inter-Contract Path Constraints (ICPC) to explore cross-contract execution paths. Pluto is particularly effective in identifying vulnerabilities that emerge from interactions between multiple contracts, including reentrancy, timestamp dependency, and integer overflow. Its precise modeling of contract interdependencies strengthens its accuracy in complex deployment scenarios. However, the complexity of ICFG generation may lead to performance trade-offs when scaling large contract systems.
ReDetect—Detector [63]
ReDetect, proposed by Yu et al. in 2021, is a symbolic execution-based framework for reentrancy vulnerability detection at the EVM bytecode level. It preprocesses source files into assembly code, constructs control flow graphs, and analyzes potential reentrancy paths using symbolic exploration. A notable strength of ReDetect is its five-path filtering strategy, which significantly reduces false positives. Its low-level focus and careful pruning mechanisms make it well-suited for large-scale automated analysis. However, the tool is specifically tailored for reentrancy issues and may require integration with complementary tools to detect a broader range of vulnerabilities.
Reentrancy Vulnerability Identification Framework—Detector [40]
Developed by Fatima Samreen and Alalfi in 2020, this framework combines static code parsing and dynamic attacker simulation to detect reentrancy vulnerabilities. It uses Tree Transformation Language (TXL) to parse Solidity code and leverages ABI specifications to automatically generate attacker contracts. These are used to simulate reentrancy scenarios and identify exploitable contract behaviors. By blending symbolic and concrete execution elements, the framework achieves high detection fidelity. Its dynamic simulation of attacks provides insight into practical exploitability, though the approach is resource-intensive and primarily focused on a single class of vulnerability.
SAILFISH—Detector [195]
SAILFISH, introduced by Bose et al. in 2022, is a scalable analysis framework targeting state-inconsistency bugs in Ethereum smart contracts. It employs a two-phase approach: an initial lightweight exploration to identify suspicious paths, fol-

lowed by a precise symbolic evaluation using a novel value-summary analysis technique. This hybrid strategy enhances performance without compromising accuracy. SAILFISH efficiently detects vulnerabilities like transaction-order dependence and reentrancy, especially in contracts with intricate state transitions. While its incremental refinement minimizes redundant path exploration, its performance may still degrade with deeply nested or highly recursive contract logic.

Sereum—Detector [196]

Developed by Rodler et al. in 2018, Sereum is a runtime protection system designed to defend deployed smart contracts against reentrancy attacks. It leverages dynamic taint tracking to monitor information flows between storage variables and control-flow decisions during execution. By intervening at runtime, Sereum blocks suspicious reentrant calls before state inconsistencies can occur. Its real-time protection with negligible overheads makes it particularly suited for operational environments. However, because it operates post-deployment, Sereum is a mitigation rather than detection tool and may not catch vulnerabilities that do not manifest during observed executions.

Seraph—Detector [197]

Seraph, introduced by Yang et al. in 2020, supports cross-platform symbolic execution for Ethereum and WebAssembly smart contracts. It models smart contract behavior using symbolic semantic graphs (SSGs) that capture critical dependency structures. This enables Seraph to detect a broad range of vulnerabilities including insecure message calls, PRNG misuse, and integer overflows. The tool's connector APIs abstract low-level interactions, facilitating analysis across virtual machines. Seraph's cross-platform capability and deep semantic modeling broaden its applicability, although the complexity of maintaining accurate semantic graphs across runtimes may pose scalability challenges.

SMARTEST—Detector [198]

SMARTEST, created by Wu et al. in 2023, integrates deep learning models with symbolic execution to improve smart contract vulnerability detection. It leverages Transformer, GRU, and RNN architectures to learn patterns from known vulnerabilities, guiding symbolic execution toward high-risk paths. This synergy enhances vulnerability coverage for issues like division by zero, ERC20 standard violations, and assertion failures. By combining machine learning's efficiency with symbolic execution's thoroughness, SMARTEST achieves a balance between speed and precision. Nevertheless, the model's dependence on training data introduces a risk of missing novel or unlearned vulnerability patterns.

Static Analyzer for Solidity Vulnerability Detection—Detector [23]

Developed by Hwang and Ryu in 2020, this tool combines symbolic execution with static data flow analysis to detect a wide array of security flaws in Solidity-based smart contracts. It identifies vulnerabilities such as reentrancy, integer overflows and underflows, timestamp dependence, unprotected self-destructs, unchecked call return values, denial-of-service vectors, and transaction-ordering dependence. By analyzing control and data flow patterns within the code, it generates detailed vulnerability reports and suggests mitigation strategies. The tool enhances contract security pre-deployment, although its static nature may lead to conservative approximations and false positives in dynamic contexts.

Symbolic Execution-Based Vulnerability Detector—Detector [199]

Yao et al. proposed this enhanced symbolic execution framework in 2022 by integrating an optimized pruning algorithm to accelerate Mythril's analysis engine. The tool also introduces a novel detection algorithm supported by an LSTM-based machine learning model for early vulnerability prediction. It detects critical issues such as unchecked call returns, reentrancy, TOD, tx.origin misuse, and time-based logic vulnerabilities. This hybrid system combines the speed of machine learning with the depth of symbolic execution, improving both detection rate and accuracy. However, the additional training phase introduces complexity and may limit generalizability without continual model updates.

Teether—Detector [200]

Teether, introduced by Krupp and Rossow in 2018, focuses on the automated generation of exploits using symbolic execution. Rather than merely detecting vulnerabilities, Teether identifies execution paths leading to exploitable instructions such as CALL, DELEGATECALL, and SELFDESTRUCT, and resolves constraints to generate concrete exploits. This proof-generating capability provides strong evidence of the severity of vulnerability. Teether targets issues such as arbitrary code execution and unauthorized code execution. While effective at confirming the exploitability of contracts, its emphasis on generating exploits rather than broad vulnerability coverage limits its use as a general-purpose detection tool.

TransRacer—Detector [201]

Developed by Ma et al. in 2023, TransRacer is designed to detect transaction race vulnerabilities in Ethereum smart contracts. It employs symbolic execution to analyze function dependencies and identify races arising from the nondeterministic ordering of transactions. By pruning function pairs with no read/write conflicts and validating results through concrete execution, TransRacer accurately identifies race conditions with minimal overhead. Its focus on temporal execution dynamics adds a valuable layer to vulnerability detection. However, its specialized scope may mean it overlooks other classes of logical or semantic bugs beyond race conditions.

VerX—Detector [10]

VerX, introduced by Permenev et al. in 2020, is an advanced verifier for Ethereum smart contracts that proves functional properties and verifies temporal safety conditions using symbolic execution and delayed predicate abstraction. It reduces the verification of temporal logic to reachability analysis, enabling precise modeling of unbounded interactions and transaction sequences. VerX is particularly suited for formally verifying properties in contracts involving external interactions and complex state transitions. Its thoroughness and ability to handle real-world contracts make it powerful for high-assurance verification, though it demands significant computational resources and expertise in specifying formal properties.

Annotary—Identifier [202]

Introduced by Weiss and Schütte in 2019, Annotary is a concolic execution framework that enhances vulnerability detection by allowing developers to annotate Solidity source code directly. These annotations guide symbolic execution across inter-transactional and inter-contract control flows. Annotary combines symbolic execution on EVM bytecode with concrete value resolution from the Ethereum blockchain, improving analysis precision. It detects issues such as reentrancy, arithmetic overflows, unchecked send returns, uninitialized state variables, and visibility modifier misconfigurations. While powerful for capturing context-sensitive behaviors, Annotary requires developers to supply annotations, which may limit automation and scalability.

Conkas—Identifier [185]

Conkas, presented in 2024 by Veloso, is a modular static analysis tool designed for EVM bytecode. It uses symbolic execution powered by the Z3 SMT solver and leverages a modified Rattle intermediate representation to improve analysis accuracy. Conkas identifies vulnerabilities including arithmetic issues, reentrancy, time manipulation, transaction ordering dependence, and unchecked low-level calls. Its modular architecture allows flexibility and integration with other tools. However, as part of a master's thesis, its adoption and long-term support may be limited without continued development and community involvement.

DefectChecker—Identifier [203]

Introduced by Chen et al. in 2022, DefectChecker performs symbolic execution on EVM bytecode to identify a wide range of vulnerabilities. It detects issues such as transaction-state dependencies, denial-of-service attacks from external influences, strict balance-equality constraints, nested calls, unchecked external calls, greedy behavior, and reliance on block information. The tool's public dataset and code make it accessible for benchmarking and further research. Although its bytecode-level focus enhances universality, it may sacrifice some high-level semantic insights compared to source-level analyzers.

ETHBMC—Identifier [204]

ETHBMC (Ethereum Bounded Model Checker), proposed by Frank et al. in 2020, employs symbolic execution within a bounded model-checking framework to validate smart contracts. It models Ethereum's semantics, including inter-contract communication, memory management, and hash functions like keccak256. ETHBMC generates concrete counterexamples for vulnerabilities such as arbitrary ether extraction, suicidal contract logic, control flow hijacking, and memory handling issues. Its precision and formal rigor make it well-suited for critical contract verification. However, its bound nature may overlook behaviors that manifest beyond the chosen execution depth.

GASOL—Identifier [12]

GASOL, released in 2020 by Albert et al., focuses on optimizing gas consumption in Ethereum contracts through a hybrid of static analysis and symbolic execution. It identifies gas-related inefficiencies such as redundant storage access, under-optimized loop constructs, and expensive arithmetic operations. GASOL not only flags issues but also suggests improvements, contributing to cost-effective and efficient contract deployment. Its optimization-centric design complements security-focused tools but does not directly address logical vulnerabilities unless they relate to gas inefficiencies.

HFCCT—Identifier [205]

Developed in 2022 by Li et al., the Hyperledger Fabric Contract Code Tester (HFCCT) targets smart contracts written for the Hyperledger Fabric platform. It integrates dynamic symbolic execution with static abstract syntax tree (AST) analysis to detect a wide range of vulnerabilities. These include misuse of global variables, weak randomness, reliance on system timestamps, unsafe iteration over map structures, unhandled errors, and cross-channel invocation issues. HFCCT also checks for improper use of external libraries and unsafe system commands. Its platform-specific design provides in-depth analysis for Fabric-based contracts, but its applicability to Ethereum and other blockchains is limited.

Honeytoken-Detector—Identifier [206]

Introduced by Liu and Cai in 2023, this symbolic-execution-based tool is designed to identify honeypot tokens in Ethereum smart contracts. It targets deceptive behaviors including transfer inconsistencies, transfer restrictions, fake event logs, infinite minting, balance manipulation, and proxy token misuse. The tool performs bytecode parsing, control flow graph construction, and symbolic path exploration to detect such traps. Its focus on malicious tokens enhances the security of the Ethereum ecosystem, though its specialization limits its use cases to token-based contracts rather than general vulnerability detection.

Improved Symbolic Execution-Based Vulnerability Detector—Identifier [199]

This enhanced version of Mythril, introduced in 2022 by Yao et al., combines symbolic execution with a machine learning model based on long short-term memory (LSTM) networks. The tool supports both source code and bytecode analysis and is designed to detect vulnerabilities such as integer overflows and underflows, unchecked call return values, transaction-ordering dependence, authorization via tx.origin, and misuse of block values. The ML model enables rapid identification of potential issues, while symbolic execution provides accurate localization. Its hybrid approach balances efficiency and depth, though reliance on pretrained models may limit interpretability or necessitate retraining as vulnerability types evolve.

KEVM—Identifier [207]

KEVM, developed in 2017 by Hildenbrandt et al., provides a complete formal semantics of the Ethereum Virtual Machine using the K framework. It enables symbolic execution and formal verification of smart contracts against their specifications and has passed the official EVM test suite. KEVM can detect low-level issues such as stack overflows, out-of-gas conditions, division by zero, invalid opcodes, and access to nonexistent accounts. Its strength lies in its formal rigor and applicability to mission-critical contract validation. However, the complexity of the K framework may pose a learning curve for non-specialist developers.

KEVM Verifier—Identifier [97]

Developed by Park et al. in 2018, the KEVM Verifier extends KEVM to provide comprehensive formal verification capabilities for Ethereum contracts. It allows the verification of functional correctness and security properties for high-stakes contracts such as those used in Ethereum Casper and MakerDAO. The verifier supports formal specification of behaviors and proves correctness using symbolic execution within the K framework. This makes it suitable for projects that demand strong guarantees. Nevertheless, writing formal specifications requires expertise in formal methods, which may limit its adoption in broader developer communities.

MAIAN—Identifier [64]

Introduced by Nikolić et al. in 2018, MAIAN is a symbolic-execution-based tool that analyzes smart-contract execution traces to detect vulnerabilities in contract states and behaviors. Specifically, it identifies greedy, prodigal, and suicidal contracts, those that lock funds indefinitely, leak Ether to arbitrary users, or allow self-destruction under unsafe conditions. MAIAN operates on EVM bytecode using a customized symbolic engine, enabling it to reveal deeply rooted execution flaws. It is effective at discovering critical vulnerabilities before deployment, although it may struggle with highly obfuscated contracts or those requiring complex inter-contract analysis.

MOPS—Identifier [208]

MOPS, or Multi-Objective Oriented Path Search, was developed by Fu et al. in 2019 to improve the efficiency of vulnerability detection. It combines static analysis with dynamic symbolic execution, using taint analysis to focus on Ether transfer paths. By emphasizing critical execution paths, MOPS detects reentrancy, transaction-ordering dependence, delegatecall misuse, suicidal contracts, and unhandled exceptions. It balances precision and speed, making it suitable for large-scale contract screening. However, its reliance on Ether-related paths may underrepresent non-financial vulnerabilities.

NFTGuard—Identifier [209]

Developed by Yang et al. in 2023, NFTGuard is a symbolic execution-based analysis tool tailored specifically for NFT smart contracts. It detects five major defect types including Risky Mutable Proxy, ERC-721 Reentrancy, Unlimited Minting, Missing Requirements, and Public Burn. NFTGuard leverages both source code and bytecode representations to enhance detection accuracy. Integrating symbolic execution with domain-specific rules for NFTs delivers targeted insights into common security flaws. While highly effective for NFT-specific vulnerabilities, it may not generalize as well to contracts outside the NFT domain.

Osiris—Identifier [210]

Osiris, introduced by Torres et al. in 2018, is a symbolic execution and taint analysis tool focused on identifying integer-related vulnerabilities in Ethereum smart contracts. It detects issues like arithmetic overflow, truncation errors, and signedness bugs at the bytecode level. Osiris constructs control- and data-flow dependencies to perform fine-grained vulnerability detection. It is particularly effective for contracts with complex arithmetic logic, though its focus on integer bugs limits its ability to detect other types of vulnerabilities.

Oyente—Identifier [68]
Launched by Luu et al. in 2016, Oyente is one of the earliest symbolic execution tools for Ethereum bytecode analysis. It identifies common security vulnerabilities such as transaction-ordering dependence, timestamp dependence, mishandled exceptions, and reentrancy. Oyente translates bytecode into an intermediate representation and symbolically executes it to explore multiple execution paths. Despite its historical importance and influence, Oyente has limitations in handling newer Solidity features and often produces a high number of false positives due to lack of path pruning and concrete execution validation.
Park—Identifier [211]
Proposed by Zheng et al. in 2022, Park introduces a parallel-fork symbolic execution model to enhance the efficiency of vulnerability detection in smart contracts. By distributing execution across multiple CPU cores and integrating dynamic forking and adaptive process restriction, Park accelerates symbolic path exploration. It supports detection of vulnerabilities such as transaction-ordering dependence, timestamp dependence, mishandled exceptions, and reentrancy. Park integrates with tools like Oyente and Mythril, enhancing their speed and coverage. While powerful, it requires significant computational resources and may be challenging to configure for novice users.
RA—Identifier [188]
Re-entrancy Analyzer (RA), developed by Chinen et al. in 2020, is a static analysis tool leveraging symbolic execution and SMT solving to detect reentrancy vulnerabilities in Ethereum smart contracts. It operates directly on EVM bytecode and does not depend on predefined attack patterns. RA models inter-contract behavior, enabling it to analyze cross-functional interactions and misuse of fallback functions. It is particularly useful for detecting complex reentrancy scenarios but may face limitations in symbolic path explosion when scaling to large contract systems.
sCompile—Identifier [77]
sCompile, introduced by Chang et al. in 2019, is a vulnerability detection tool that analyzes critical program paths in smart contracts. By combining control flow graph construction with symbolic execution, sCompile focuses on paths involving monetary transactions and safety properties. It flags potentially dangerous conditions like sending Ether to nonexistent addresses, self-destruct calls, and irreversible fund transfers. Its prioritization of paths by severity improves efficiency, though the scope of vulnerabilities it detects is limited to transactional integrity and may not encompass the full spectrum of logic bugs.
SolSEE—Identifier [212]
SolSEE, proposed by Lin et al. in 2022, is a source-level symbolic execution engine for Solidity contracts. Unlike tools that work on bytecode, SolSEE preserves high-level semantic information, supports advanced Solidity constructs, and offers a web-based interface for visualization and debugging. It detects vulnerabilities such as integer overflows and underflows, as well as assertion violations, with greater clarity. Its ability to analyze source code improves interpretability and educational value, though it may not detect low-level bytecode issues introduced during compilation.

Solar—Identifier [213]
Solar, introduced by Feng et al. in 2020, is a symbolic execution system that synthesizes adversarial contracts capable of exploiting vulnerabilities in target smart contracts. It encodes known vulnerability patterns, such as reentrancy, time manipulation, access control bypass, and batch overflow, and symbolically evaluates contracts to identify exploitable paths. By focusing on automatic exploit generation, Solar reveals not only the existence of vulnerabilities but also their severity and exploitability. Its precision makes it valuable for red teaming and penetration testing, though its effectiveness is bounded by its predefined exploit templates.
Symvalic—Identifier [79]
Symvalic, developed by Smaragdakis et al. in 2021, combines symbolic expressions with concrete execution values to create a hybrid static analysis framework for Ethereum contracts. It achieves a high level of semantic modeling through the interplay between fixpoint computations and symbolic solvers. Symvalic is particularly adept at modeling complex financial logic, making it suitable for auditing high-value contracts. It identifies vulnerabilities such as reentrancy and overflow with low false positives. However, the sophistication of its analysis engine may introduce computational overhead during large-scale analysis.
WANA—Identifier [214]
WebAssembly ANalysis (WANA), introduced by Jiang et al. in 2021, is a symbolic execution engine designed for detecting vulnerabilities in smart contracts compiled to WebAssembly (Wasm), particularly on platforms like EOSIO. WANA supports the full Wasm instruction set, enabling precise analysis of smart contracts using symbolic execution. It effectively detects vulnerabilities such as fake token transfers, forged notification events, block-information dependencies, reentrancy issues, mishandled exceptions, and dangerous delegatecall usage. WANA's extensibility to Ethereum and other blockchain platforms underscores its versatility, although its Wasm-specific design may limit its direct applicability to purely EVM-based environments.

- **Industrial tools**
  MPro—Detector [87]
  MPro, developed by Zhang et al. in 2019, is a hybrid analysis tool that combines static detection techniques with symbolic execution to improve the scalability and depth of vulnerability exploration in smart contracts. Static analysis is first used to identify potentially vulnerable sites, followed by symbolic execution to generate targeted test inputs for those locations. MPro excels at detecting depth-n vulnerabilities that manifest only through specific sequences of function calls, such as reentrancy and unrestricted contract self-destruction. Its layered approach balances performance with analytical precision. However, because symbolic exploration is guided by patterns identified during the static phase, the tool may overlook emergent vulnerabilities that do not correspond to those initial patterns.

Mythril—Identifier [57]
Created by ConsenSys in 2018, Mythril is one of the most widely adopted symbolic execution tools for analyzing Ethereum smart contracts. It operates directly on EVM bytecode and leverages SMT solving, taint tracking, and control-flow analysis to detect vulnerabilities such as reentrancy, integer overflows, unrestricted Ether flows, unprotected self-destruct operations, and misuse of tx.origin. Mythril supports both on-chain and off-chain analysis and integrates with development environments including Truffle and Remix, making it a standard component of many security auditing pipelines. Despite its extensive coverage and flexibility, the broad scope of its detection mechanisms can occasionally lead to false positives without additional contextual filtering.
Mythril Extension for Gasless Send Issue Detection—Detector [215]
This extension, introduced in 2019, enhances the Mythril analysis engine to specifically model gas consumption during symbolic execution. It detects contracts vulnerable to gasless-send issues, where fallback functions fail due to exceeding the 2300-gas stipend limit for send operations. By simulating EVM gas behavior, the extension identifies scenarios in which Ether transfers silently fail, potentially causing denial-of-service conditions. The precise gas modeling enables developers to better understand low-level execution constraints. However, the extension focuses narrowly on gasless-send vulnerabilities and does not extend Mythril's broader vulnerability-detection capabilities.
Rattle—Detector [45]
Rattle, developed by Trail of Bits in 2019, converts Ethereum bytecode into Static Single Assignment (SSA) form to facilitate deeper symbolic and static analysis. This intermediate representation simplifies the tracking of control flow and data dependencies, enabling detection of vulnerabilities such as storage access anomalies, control-flow hijacking, and unsafe external calls. Rattle's modular architecture and SSA transformation make it suitable for integration into advanced analysis pipelines and formal verification workflows. Nevertheless, because it operates primarily at the bytecode abstraction level, certain context-dependent behaviors visible in source-level code may not be fully captured.
SoMo—Detector [48]
SoMo, developed by Fang et al. in 2023, focuses on detecting insecure modifier usage in Ethereum smart contracts. It constructs a Modifier Dependency Graph (MDG) to capture relationships between function modifiers and contract logic. Symbolic execution is then applied to explore execution paths that may bypass or misuse these modifiers. Through this analysis, SoMo identifies subtle logic flaws in access control enforcement, offering insights into how modifiers influence the execution flow. While this specialized approach addresses a previously underexplored source of vulnerability, its effectiveness is limited for contracts that rely minimally on modifiers.
Manticore—Identifier [216]
Developed by Mossberg et al. in 2019, Manticore is a general-purpose symbolic execution framework that supports both Ethereum smart contracts and native

binaries. It enables systematic exploration of program states without relying on predefined vulnerability signatures, allowing it to uncover issues such as reentrancy, integer overflows, assertion violations, and memory safety errors. Manticore provides flexible APIs that allow analysts to create custom analyses and test cases, making it particularly valuable for research and advanced auditing scenarios. However, because it is designed as a general symbolic execution engine rather than a specialized smart contract analyzer, effective use often requires manual configuration and expertise.

MythX—Identifier [135]

Released in 2020 by Mueller, MythX is a commercial security analysis platform that integrates symbolic execution, fuzzing, and static analysis to assess Ethereum and EVM-compatible smart contracts. It detects vulnerabilities including timestamp dependence, unsafe Ether withdrawals, weak randomness, and unchecked assertions. Designed with scalability in mind, MythX provides cloud-based APIs and integrates with CI/CD pipelines and development environments. Its automated workflow simplifies large-scale security analysis for developers. However, the reliance on a cloud infrastructure raises potential concerns regarding code privacy and vendor dependency for enterprise users.

Pakala—Identifier [217]

Pakala, developed by Keoleian in 2024, is an open-source, Python-implemented symbolic execution tool for the Ethereum Virtual Machine. It uses the Z3 SMT solver and includes a custom SHA-3 module to perform cryptographic hash operations during analysis. Pakala follows a two-phase workflow in which symbolic execution first enumerates potential execution outcomes, and the results are then analyzed to identify vulnerabilities such as unsafe suicide() calls or excessive Ether transfers. Its transparent architecture makes it suitable for educational and experimental use. However, compared with more mature analysis frameworks, Pakala currently offers a more limited feature set and scalability.

Symbolic execution has emerged as one of the most powerful methodologies for vulnerability detection and identification in smart contracts. By simulating contract execution with symbolic inputs rather than concrete values, these tools systematically explore execution paths and reason about potential program states. The tools reviewed in this category demonstrate the broad applicability of symbolic execution, from identifying access control violations and detecting gas inefficiencies to verifying temporal safety properties and modeling complex inter-contract interactions. Although symbolic execution offers high analytical precision, it also introduces challenges such as path explosion, scalability limitations, and the need for carefully defined constraints. Despite these limitations, symbolic execution remains a cornerstone technique in smart contract security analysis, enabling deep inspection of program logic and uncovering vulnerabilities that may remain hidden under conventional testing methods.

9.1.13 Taint Analysis

The thirteenth tool category focuses on Taint Analysis, a methodology that monitors the propagation of potentially dangerous or "tainted" data through the execution paths of smart contracts. In Ethereum and Solidity-based systems, taint analysis enables security tools to trace how untrusted or sensitive input data influences contract behavior, potentially leading to vulnerabilities such as reentrancy, arithmetic overflow, unvalidated randomness, and denial-of-service conditions. By tracking data flows from sources (e.g., user inputs) to sinks (e.g., critical state updates or external calls), taint analysis exposes implicit dependencies and hidden propagation paths that traditional static analysis may overlook. Tools in this category primarily focus on vulnerability identification through taint-tracking techniques, often integrating symbolic execution and control-flow analysis to provide deeper, more precise security inspections.

- **Academic tools**

  Clairvoyance—Identifier [218]

  Clairvoyance is a cross-contract taint analysis tool introduced in 2020 to detect reentrancy vulnerabilities with high accuracy. The tool addresses limitations in prior work by introducing Path Protection Techniques (PPTs), which summarize contract-specific control paths critical to reentrancy safety. Clairvoyance statically analyzes Solidity contracts, tracing tainted inputs across function boundaries and inter-contract calls. By combining lightweight symbolic execution with taint propagation, it distinguishes between genuine reentrancy risks and false positives caused by benign call sequences. While Clairvoyance enhances detection precision and reduces analysis time, it may still struggle in environments with dynamic contract creation or obfuscated control flow.

  DoSChecker—Identifier [219]

  DoSChecker, introduced in 2023, is a taint-driven static analysis tool designed to detect four specific patterns of Denial-of-Service (DoS) vulnerabilities in Ethereum smart contracts. These include Loops with Exceptional Instructions (LWEI), Unbounded Batch High Gas Instructions (UBHGI), Transfer Procedures with Non-Payable Fallback Functions (TPWNPFF), and Strict Balance Equality (SBE). By applying symbolic execution and bytecode-level taint tracking, DoSChecker identifies execution paths where untrusted inputs could trigger gas exhaustion or execution halts. It offers a modular vulnerability detection engine that supports configurable gas cost thresholds and contract heuristics. However, its performance may degrade when analyzing large or deeply nested control flow graphs.

  EASYFLOW—Identifier [220]

  EASYFLOW, introduced in 2019, is a taint analysis-based tool for detecting integer overflow and underflow vulnerabilities in Ethereum smart contracts. It dynamically extends the EVM interpreter to trace data propagation during transaction execution, classifying overflows into three categories: manifested, protected, and potential. EASYFLOW also generates targeted transactions to provoke vulnerable code paths and validate actual exploitability. By combining taint tracking and transaction simulation, it improves the precision of vulnerability localization and minimizes false alarms. However, the overhead of EVM extension and input generation may limit scalability when applied to large-scale or gas-intensive contracts.

RNVulDet—Identifier [221]

RNVulDet, short for Randomness Vulnerability Detection, is a taint-based analysis tool introduced in 2023 to identify bad randomness vulnerabilities in Ethereum smart contracts. It simulates a realistic EVM runtime environment and examines contract execution using stack state analysis, memory segmentation, and storage key-value comparisons. By replaying transactions and analyzing how entropy sources like block.timestamp, blockhash, or msg.sender are used in randomness generation, RNVulDet reveals insecure implementations vulnerable to prediction or manipulation. The tool is particularly valuable for detecting vulnerabilities in lottery or game contracts. While its runtime emulation improves precision, the accuracy of its transaction replay may depend on the availability of blockchain state.

SESCon—Identifier [3]

SESCon is a static taint analysis tool that employs XPath-like queries to detect security vulnerabilities in Solidity smart contracts. Introduced in 2021, SESCon uses a rule-based engine to interpret Ethereum community-defined vulnerability patterns, such as reentrancy, time-of-dependence (TOD), tx.origin misuse, block.timestamp abuse, and unsafe use of the selfdestruct instruction. It constructs an abstract syntax tree (AST) of the contract and tracks tainted values as they move through control and data paths. The use of XPath queries makes it extensible for custom pattern definitions, but SESCon's reliance on static patterns may miss unconventional or obfuscated vulnerability expressions.

SIGUARD—Identifier [222]

SIGUARD is a 2023 taint analysis tool tailored for identifying signature-related vulnerabilities in Ethereum contracts. It focuses on issues arising from incorrect signature verification and insecure handling of external calls. SIGUARD constructs control-flow graphs from EVM bytecode and simulates execution paths using symbolic and taint analyses to track signature-dependent logic. It detects bugs such as stateless signature verification, where contracts fail to bind signatures to specific domains, and unseparated signing-domain vulnerabilities, which allow attackers to reuse valid signatures across contexts. The tool enhances detection accuracy for contracts that implement off-chain authentication schemes, but may require manual validation of edge cases.

SmartScan—Identifier [223]

SmartScan, developed in 2021, is a hybrid vulnerability detection tool that integrates static and dynamic taint analysis to detect Denial-of-Service (DoS) vulnerabilities in Ethereum smart contracts. It initially scans contract code for known vulnerability patterns and then validates their exploitability through dynamic contract execution. SmartScan specifically targets DoS vulnerabilities caused by unexpected reverts that may be missed by static analyzers alone. By interacting with the contract at runtime, it verifies whether untrusted data can influence failure conditions. While the hybrid model enhances detection coverage, it requires a testable deployment environment and sufficient input generation to simulate all execution paths.

Taint analysis has proven to be an effective technique for uncovering a wide range of vulnerabilities in smart contracts by tracing how untrusted or sensitive data propagates through control and data flows [3, 184, 222, 223]. The tools in this category demonstrate how marking and monitoring tainted values at various stages, such as during external calls, random number generation, or state updates, can reveal vulnerabilities that might otherwise evade traditional static or symbolic analysis [3, 219, 221, 222]. From detecting reentrancy and denial-of-service issues to uncovering flawed randomness and signature misuse, taint analysis offers both breadth and depth in security evaluation [219, 221–223]. While the precision of these tools can vary with the completeness of the taint propagation logic and execution context, their ability to reason about indirect flows makes them indispensable for safeguarding smart contract behavior [17, 18, 20]. Collectively, these tools highlight taint analysis as a valuable asset in the evolving landscape of smart contract security [20, 71, 108].

9.1.14 Visualization Analysis

The fourteenth category involves visualization analysis, a methodology that enhances the comprehension of smart contract (SC) logic and behavior by transforming code into graphical representations. By visually depicting control flow, function structure, execution traces, and contract architectures, these tools assist developers and auditors in interpreting complex SCs and identifying potential vulnerabilities. Visualization tools are especially useful for reverse engineering, invariant detection, and assessing data flow within contracts. The first six tools listed below focus on vulnerability detection, while the last tool focuses on vulnerability identification in SCs.

- **Academic tools**

  E-EVM—Detector [186]

  E-EVM is a visualization and emulation tool designed to illustrate the execution of Ethereum smart contracts on the EVM. Introduced in 2018, it provides detailed visualizations of control-flow graphs, stack states, and opcodes at each execution step. These visual depictions aid in interpreting low-level contract behavior, helping users detect issues such as invalid jump destinations and reentry vulnerabilities. E-EVM is especially useful for auditing contract execution flows, revealing hidden execution patterns, and identifying loops or inefficiencies within contract logic.

Erays—Detector [88]
Erays is a reverse-engineering tool developed in Python that decompiles Ethereum bytecode into high-level pseudocode. Published in 2018, Erays enhances understanding of closed-source contracts by partially recovering source code, identifying code reuse, and analyzing complexity. This pseudocode reconstruction aids in identifying potential vulnerabilities by providing developers with a readable abstraction of the bytecode, making it easier to detect logic flaws, especially in opaque or obfuscated contracts.
EthIR—Detector [2]
EthIR, or Ethereum Intermediate Representation, is a framework built to enable high-level semantic analysis of Ethereum bytecode. It uses control-flow graphs generated by Oyente and transforms them into a Rule-Based Representation (RBR), thereby making Ethereum bytecode more interpretable. EthIR assists in detecting gas inefficiencies, unbounded loops, and potential denial-of-service vulnerabilities by exposing high-level behavioral patterns through formal visual structures. Introduced in 2018, it enables formal reasoning over execution logic for security analysis.
InvCon—Detector [224]
InvCon is a dynamic invariant detection tool released in 2022 that uses historical transaction data to infer behavioral invariants in Ethereum contracts. It assists in reverse engineering and compliance verification by identifying deviations from expected behaviors. With a user-friendly web interface and a Python-Java backend, InvCon detects inconsistencies with standards such as ERC20 and highlights invariant violations that may signal logic bugs or non-compliance vulnerabilities. Its visualization of inferred patterns helps developers refine or audit contract logic.
Smart-Graph—Detector [60]
Smart-Graph is a web-based tool introduced in 2021 that generates enriched UML class diagrams for Solidity contracts. It incorporates Solidity-specific constructs, including fallback functions, modifiers, and access controls, into its visualizations. By transforming contract architecture into a familiar UML format, Smart-Graph helps developers spot architectural issues such as high code complexity or problematic interaction flows. The tool improves code maintainability and auditability by offering clear visual summaries of smart contract structures.

- **Industrial tools**
  SolGraph—Detector [225]
  SolGraph generates DOT-format control-flow graphs for Solidity functions, enhancing visibility into flow and function interactions within a contract. Introduced in 2018, it highlights potentially vulnerable points by using color-coded representations of various function types and operations, such as external calls and value transfers. SolGraph is particularly helpful for developers seeking to understand how functions interconnect and to identify suspicious control paths that could lead to vulnerabilities such as reentrancy or access mismanagement.
  Slither—Identifier [67]

Slither is a static analysis framework introduced in 2019 that also employs visualization as part of its feature set. It converts Solidity code into SlithIR, an SSA-based intermediate representation that facilitates precise taint analysis, dataflow analysis, and vulnerability detection. Slither offers detailed code insights through its visualization capabilities, allowing developers to identify vulnerabilities such as reentrancy, uninitialized variables, locked Ether, and unsafe self-destruction. Its modular design and broad vulnerability coverage make it one of the most widely adopted tools in Ethereum contract analysis.

Visualization analysis offers a powerful lens for interpreting, debugging, and securing smart contracts [2, 60, 67, 88, 186, 224, 225]. By converting complex codebases and execution flows into intuitive graphical representations, these tools bridge the gap between low-level semantics and high-level comprehension [60, 88, 186, 225]. The tools in this category demonstrate that visualizing execution logic, control flow, or contract architecture not only helps spot flaws early but also enhances audit efficiency and accuracy [2, 60, 67, 224]. As smart contracts grow more intricate, visualization techniques will continue to play an essential role in promoting code transparency, maintainability, and security assurance [17–20].

In conclusion, the growing ecosystem of vulnerability detection tools for smart contracts reflects the increasing demand for secure and reliable decentralized systems. By organizing these tools according to their underlying analytical methodologies, such as abstract interpretation, artificial intelligence, code instrumentation, control flow analysis, disassembly analysis, formal verification, and fuzz testing, this section offers a structured overview that facilitates both theoretical understanding and practical comparison. Within each methodological category, tools are further classified into academic and industrial subgroups, highlighting the balance between research-driven innovation and real-world applicability. Figure 9.1 presents a taxonomy of these tools, visually mapping their classification by technique and origin. This organization not only illustrates the diversity and depth of existing approaches but also sets the stage for the comparative evaluation that follows, enabling readers to assess tool performance, coverage, and utility across the smart contract security landscape.

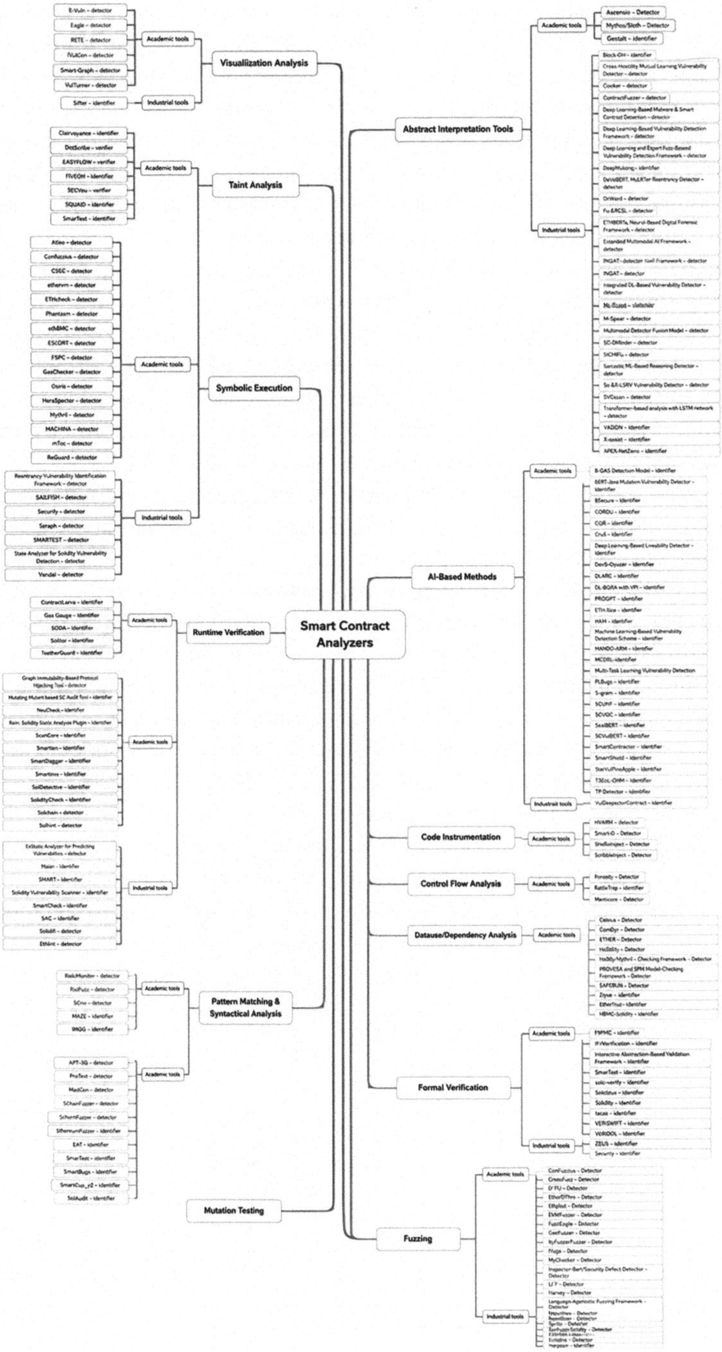

Fig. 9.1 Taxonomy of smart contract analyzers based on their underlying methodologies

9.2 Comparative Analysis

A comprehensive evaluation of smart contract vulnerability detection tools requires a structured and criterion-based approach to ensure relevance, accuracy, and practical applicability [17, 18, 66, 71, 120, 164]. This subchapter presents a detailed comparative analysis of both academic and industry tools, categorized into three core analytical types, static, dynamic, and hybrid, each assessed through tailored evaluation frameworks [18, 20, 71, 100, 120]. Recognizing the distinct objectives and operational contexts of academic and industrial domains, we developed domain-specific criteria that reflect their respective needs: research extensibility and reproducibility on one side, and usability, scalability, and integration on the other [17, 19, 71, 120].

For academic tools, the assessment emphasizes factors such as flexibility, automation, extensibility, and experimental reliability, key indicators of a tool's contribution to research innovation and reproducibility [18, 40, 120, 164]. In contrast, the evaluation of industry tools incorporates additional dimensions such as user experience, support, real-world deployment capacity, and vulnerability mitigation guidance, reflecting the performance-driven and application-focused nature of industry use cases [24, 67, 226, 227].

Each subsection provides a category-specific analysis, supported by comparison tables that evaluate the tools against defined criteria using a binary (Yes/No) scoring model. Tools are grouped and discussed based on their performance percentiles, top-tier, mid-tier, and bottom-tier, followed by actionable insights and development recommendations [18–20, 71, 100, 120].

9.2.1 Evaluating Academic Tools

Academic smart contract (SC) analysis tools are central to advancing research in blockchain security, as they enable the exploration of emerging vulnerabilities, support formal experimentation, and often serve as prototypes for future industry adoption. The evaluation of academic tools in this study is guided by seven criteria that capture their research utility, adaptability, and analytical depth. These criteria include flexibility, detailed documentation and publication, integration capabilities, automation, comprehensive vulnerability coverage, reliable testing with real-world data, and extensibility.

By assessing tools across these dimensions, we aim to identify not only which tools currently offer the most robust functionality but also where the broader landscape of academic tooling may benefit from targeted improvements. The tools are divided into static, dynamic, and hybrid analysis categories, each evaluated in dedicated subsections. For each category, the results are summarized in comparison tables (Tables 9.1, 9.2, and 9.3) based on a binary scoring model. Tools are sorted according to the number of criteria they meet, providing a transparent and structured basis for comparative discussion.

- **Static Analysis Tools**
  Static analysis tools examine SC code without executing it, enabling vulnerability detection early in the development cycle. These tools are particularly valuable

Table 9.1 Static analysis

Tool	Flexibility	Detailed documentation	Integration capabilities	Automation	Comprehensive coverage	Reliable testing and evaluation	Extensibility
ESCORT	Y	Y	Y	Y	Y	Y	Y
SoliDetector	N	Y	Y	Y	Y	Y	Y
SIF	N	Y	Y	Y	Y	Y	Y
Solc-Verify	N	Y	Y	Y	Y	Y	Y
Vandal	N	Y	Y	Y	Y	Y	Y
Predicate Abstraction-Based Validation Framework (Unnamed Tool)	N	Y	N	Y	Y	Y	Y
Eth2Vec	N	Y	N	Y	Y	Y	Y
Gastap	N	Y	Y	Y	Y	Y	N
sCompile	Y	Y	Y	N	Y	Y	N
SolGuard	N	Y	Y	Y	N	Y	Y
VeriSol	N	Y	Y	Y	Y	Y	N
Zeus	Y	Y	Y	Y	Y	N	N
Erays	N	Y	Y	Y	Y	Y	N
eThor	N	Y	Y	Y	Y	Y	N
Gasper	N	Y	N	Y	Y	Y	Y
MadMax	N	Y	N	Y	Y	Y	Y
Oyente	N	Y	N	Y	Y	Y	Y
VerX	N	Y	N	Y	Y	Y	Y
Conkas	N	Y	N	Y	Y	Y	Y
SAFEVM	N	Y	Y	Y	Y	Y	N
EthBMC	N	Y	Y	Y	Y	Y	N
Multi-Task Learning Vulnerability Detection Model (Unnamed Tool)	N	Y	N	Y	Y	Y	Y

CBGRU	N	Y	N	Y	Y	Y	Y
S-HGTNs	Y	Y	Y	Y	Y	N	N
sGuard+	N	Y	Y	Y	Y	Y	N
ESBMC-Solidity	N	Y	N	Y	Y	Y	Y
SmartDagger	N	Y	N	Y	Y	Y	Y
Symvalic	N	Y	N	Y	Y	Y	Y
Remix Solidity Static Analysis Plugin (Unnamed Tool)	N	Y	Y	Y	Y	Y	N
SecBERT	N	Y	N	Y	Y	Y	Y
SmartFast	N	Y	Y	Y	Y	Y	N
PROMELA and SPIN Model-Checking Framework (Unnamed Tool)	N	Y	N	Y	Y	Y	Y
NFTGuard	N	Y	N	Y	Y	Y	Y
Ethainter	N	Y	N	Y	Y	Y	N
SESCon	N	Y	N	Y	Y	Y	N
SmartAnvil	N	Y	Y	N	Y	Y	N
SmartEmbed	N	Y	N	Y	Y	Y	N
Solidifier	N	Y	N	Y	Y	Y	N
Soliditycheck	N	Y	N	Y	Y	Y	N
VeriSmart	N	Y	N	Y	Y	Y	N
VeriSolid	N	Y	N	Y	Y	Y	N
DefectChecker	N	Y	N	Y	Y	Y	N
S-GRAM	N	Y	N	Y	Y	Y	N
EtherTrust	N	Y	Y	Y	N	Y	N
EthIR	N	Y	Y	Y	N	Y	N

(continued)

Table 9.1 (continued)

Tool	Flexibility	Detailed documentation	Integration capabilities	Automation	Comprehensive coverage	Reliable testing and evaluation	Extensibility
GasChecker	N	Y	Y	Y	Y	N	N
Osiris	N	Y	N	Y	Y	Y	N
SmartShield	N	Y	N	Y	Y	Y	N
GASOL	N	Y	Y	Y	Y	N	N
MODNN	N	Y	N	Y	Y	Y	N
ContractWard	N	Y	N	Y	Y	Y	N
CGE	Y	Y	N	Y	Y	N	N
SWAT	N	Y	N	Y	Y	Y	N
CodeNet	N	Y	N	Y	Y	Y	N
SCVDIE	N	Y	N	Y	Y	Y	N
Deep Learning-Based Malicious SCs Detection Scheme (Unnamed Tool)	N	Y	N	Y	Y	Y	N
ABCNN	N	Y	N	Y	Y	Y	N
AWD-LSTM	N	Y	N	Y	Y	Y	N
Machine Learning-Based Vulnerability Detection Scheme (Unnamed Tool)	N	Y	N	Y	Y	Y	N
MSmart	N	Y	N	Y	Y	Y	N
Blass	N	Y	N	Y	Y	Y	N
SafeCheck	N	Y	N	Y	Y	Y	N
Sliced-JGNN	N	Y	N	Y	Y	Y	N
Extended Multimodal AI Framework (Unnamed Tool)	N	Y	N	Y	Y	Y	N
SVScanner	N	Y	N	Y	Y	Y	N
Multimodal Decision Fusion Model (Unnamed Tool)	N	Y	N	Y	Y	Y	N

Deep Learning-Based Vulnerability Detection Framework (Unnamed Tool)	N	Y	N	Y	Y	Y	N
Block-gram	N	Y	N	Y	Y	Y	N
Ensemble Models-Based Digital Forensic Framework (Unnamed Tool)	N	Y	N	Y	Y	Y	N
EtherSolve	N	Y	N	Y	Y	Y	N
TaintGuard	N	Y	N	Y	Y	Y	N
ContractArmor	N	Y	N	Y	Y	Y	N
CrossFuzz	N	Y	N	Y	Y	Y	N
EA-RGCN	N	Y	N	Y	Y	Y	N
SG-EA-RGCN Vulnerability Detector (Unnamed Tool)	N	Y	N	Y	Y	Y	N
Vulpedia	N	Y	N	Y	Y	Y	N
MichelsonLiSA	N	Y	N	Y	Y	Y	N
ExGen	N	Y	N	Y	Y	Y	N
Xscope	N	Y	N	Y	Y	Y	N
Naga	N	Y	N	Y	Y	Y	N
ConSym-OSIRIS	N	Y	N	Y	Y	Y	N
MANDO-GURU	N	Y	N	Y	Y	Y	N
SolSEE	N	Y	N	Y	Y	N	Y
SPCon	N	Y	N	Y	Y	Y	N
Matching Rules-Based SCs Audit Tool (Unnamed Tool)	N	Y	N	Y	Y	N	Y
Honeytoken-Detector	N	Y	N	Y	Y	Y	N

(continued)

Table 9.1 (continued)

Tool	Flexibility	Detailed documentation	Integration capabilities	Automation	Comprehensive coverage	Reliable testing and evaluation	Extensibility
Improved Symbolic Execution-Based Vulnerability Detector (Unnamed Tool)	N	Y	N	Y	Y	N	Y
EOSIOAnalyzer	N	Y	N	Y	Y	Y	N
SC-Defender	N	Y	N	Y	Y	Y	N
SolChecker	N	Y	N	Y	Y	Y	N
SCGraphs	N	Y	N	Y	N	Y	Y
VeriMove	N	Y	N	Y	Y	Y	N
UBF-ChaincodeScan	Y	Y	N	Y	Y	N	N
DL4SC	N	Y	N	Y	Y	Y	N
TP-Detect	N	Y	N	Y	Y	Y	N
WaLi	N	Y	N	Y	Y	Y	N
SmartConDetect	N	Y	N	Y	Y	Y	N
Clairvoyance	N	Y	N	Y	Y	Y	N
Graph Embedding-Based Bytecode Matching Tool (Unnamed Tool)	N	Y	N	Y	Y	Y	N
ConCert	Y	Y	N	N	Y	N	Y
F* Verification	N	Y	N	N	Y	Y	Y
DR-GCN and TMP	N	Y	N	Y	Y	Y	N
KEVM Verifier	N	Y	N	Y	Y	Y	N
NuSMV Model-Checking Framework (Unnamed Tool)	N	Y	N	Y	Y	Y	N
MSgram analysis	N	Y	N	Y	Y	Y	N
NPChecker	N	Y	N	Y	Y	Y	N
RegularMutator	N	Y	N	Y	Y	Y	N

Static Analyzer for Solidity Vulnerability Detection	N	Y	N	Y	Y	Y	N
SCs Modeling and Behavior Verification (Unnamed Tool)	N	Y	N	Y	Y	Y	N
Solicitous	N	Y	N	Y	Y	Y	N
VulDeeSmartContract	N	Y	N	Y	N	Y	Y
Siguard	N	Y	N	Y	Y	Y	N
Cross-Modality Mutual Learning Vulnerability Detector (Unnamed Tool)	N	Y	N	Y	N	Y	Y
Smart-Graph	N	Y	N	N	Y	Y	N
SmartInspect	N	Y	N	Y	N	N	Y
RA	N	Y	N	Y	N	Y	N
HermHD	N	Y	N	Y	N	Y	N
Static Analysis-Based Vulnerability Detection Approach (Unnamed Tool)	N	Y	N	N	Y	Y	N
TransRacer	N	Y	N	Y	N	Y	N
Smartmuv	N	Y	N	Y	N	Y	N
Asparagus	N	Y	N	Y	N	Y	N
Elysium	N	Y	N	Y	Y	N	N
2Vyper	N	Y	N	Y	Y	Y	N
DoSChecker	N	Y	N	Y	N	Y	N
MuRE	N	Y	N	Y	N	N	Y
SCLMF	N	Y	N	Y	Y	N	N
HoRStify	N	Y	N	Y	Y	N	N

(continued)

Table 9.1 (continued)

Tool	Flexibility	Detailed documentation	Integration capabilities	Automation	Comprehensive coverage	Reliable testing and evaluation	Extensibility
Static Analyzer for Price Gouging TOD Vulnerabilities (Unnamed Tool)	N	Y	N	Y	N	Y	N
Semantic ML-Based Reentrancy Detector (Unnamed Tool)	N	Y	N	Y	N	Y	N
Invariant-Based Scarcity Defect Detector (Unnamed Tool)	N	Y	N	Y	N	Y	N
ReDetect	N	Y	N	Y	N	Y	N
Transaction-based analysis with LSTM network	N	Y	N	Y	N	Y	N
SMARTEST	N	Y	N	Y	N	Y	N
AChecker	N	Y	N	N	N	Y	N
Porosity	N	Y	N	N	N	N	N

Table 9.2 Dynamic analysis

Tool	Flexibility	Detailed documentation	Integration capabilities	Automation	Comprehensive coverage	Reliable testing and evaluation	Extensibility
SODA	Y	Y	Y	Y	Y	Y	Y
ContractLarva	Y	Y	Y	Y	N	Y	Y
ModCon	Y	Y	Y	Y	Y	N	Y
sFuzz	N	Y	Y	Y	Y	Y	Y
ReGuard	N	Y	Y	Y	Y	Y	Y
GFuzzer	N	Y	Y	Y	Y	Y	Y
DappGuard	N	Y	Y	Y	Y	Y	Y
SynTest-Solidity	N	Y	Y	Y	Y	Y	N
Language-Agnostic Fuzzing Framework (Unnamed Tool)	N	Y	Y	Y	Y	N	Y
Bi-GRU with Attention Vulnerability Detector (Unnamed Tool)	N	Y	N	Y	Y	Y	Y
EVM-Shield	N	Y	N	Y	Y	Y	Y
EF CF	N	Y	N	Y	Y	Y	Y
AEGIS	N	Y	N	Y	Y	Y	Y
Hydra	N	Y	Y	Y	Y	Y	N
Solitor	N	Y	N	Y	N	Y	Y
ContractFuzzer	N	Y	N	Y	Y	Y	N
Etherolic	N	Y	N	Y	Y	Y	N
EVMFuzzer	N	Y	N	Y	Y	Y	N
Easyflow	N	Y	N	Y	Y	Y	N
ASSBert	N	Y	N	Y	Y	Y	N
RNVulDet	N	Y	N	Y	Y	Y	N
SuMo	N	Y	N	Y	Y	Y	N
RLRep	N	Y	N	Y	Y	Y	N

(continued)

Table 9.2 (continued)

Tool	Flexibility	Detailed documentation	Integration capabilities	Automation	Comprehensive coverage	Reliable testing and evaluation	Extensibility
InvCon	N	Y	N	Y	Y	Y	N
AMEVulDetector	N	Y	N	Y	Y	Y	N
FuzzDelSol	N	Y	N	Y	Y	Y	N
EtherDiffer	N	Y	N	Y	Y	Y	N
NeoDiff	N	Y	Y	Y	Y	N	N
SeqFuzz	N	Y	N	Y	Y	Y	N
MagicMirror	N	Y	N	Y	Y	Y	N
Ethchecker	N	Y	N	Y	Y	Y	N
HGAT	N	Y	N	Y	Y	Y	N
Symbolic Execution-Based Vulnerability Detector (Unnamed Tool)	N	Y	N	Y	Y	Y	N
Integrated DL-Based Vulnerability Detector (Unnamed Tool)	N	Y	N	Y	Y	Y	N
ABBE	N	Y	N	Y	Y	Y	N
ADF-GA	N	Y	N	Y	Y	Y	N
CESC	N	Y	N	Y	Y	Y	N
EthRacer	N	Y	N	Y	Y	Y	N
FSFC	N	Y	N	Y	Y	Y	N
Gasfuzzer	N	Y	N	Y	Y	Y	N
ILF	N	Y	N	Y	Y	Y	N
Mythril extension for ™gasless send™ issue detection	N	Y	N	Y	Y	Y	N
ItyFuzz	N	Y	N	Y	Y	Y	N
E-EVM	Y	Y	N	N	N	Y	N

Sereum	N	Y	N	Y	N	Y	N
Park	N	Y	N	N	Y	Y	N
BiGAS	N	Y	N	Y	N	Y	N
DistilBERT-MLP/LSTM Reentrancy Detector	N	Y	N	Y	N	Y	N
DeepInfer	N	Y	N	Y	N	Y	N
TokenScope	N	Y	N	Y	N	Y	N
DeFiRanger	N	Y	N	Y	N	Y	N
Horus	N	Y	N	Y	N	Y	N
IcyChecker	N	Y	N	Y	N	Y	N
HFContractFuzzer	N	Y	N	Y	Y	N	N
Dynamit	N	Y	N	Y	N	Y	N
ML-Based SCs Vulnerability Detector (Unnamed Tool)	N	Y	N	Y	N	Y	N
ReDefender	N	Y	N	Y	N	Y	N
Celestial	N	Y	N	Y	N	Y	N
ECFChecker	N	Y	N	Y	N	Y	N
EVM	N	Y	N	Y	N	Y	N
RLF	N	Y	N	N	N	Y	N

Table 9.3 Hybrid analysis

Tool	Flexibility	Detailed documentation	Integration capabilities	Automation	Comprehensive coverage	Reliable testing and evaluation	Extensibility
Seraph	Y	Y	Y	Y	Y	Y	Y
Vultron	Y	Y	Y	Y	Y	Y	Y
WANA	Y	Y	Y	Y	Y	Y	Y
KEVM	N	Y	Y	Y	Y	Y	Y
SmartBugs	N	Y	Y	Y	Y	Y	Y
FSPVM-E	Y	Y	Y	Y	Y	N	Y
MuSc	N	Y	Y	Y	Y	Y	Y
ConFuzzius	N	Y	Y	Y	Y	Y	Y
Deep Learning and Expert Rules-Based Vulnerability Detection (Unnamed Tool)	N	Y	Y	Y	Y	Y	Y
ESAF	N	Y	Y	Y	Y	Y	Y
SecSEC	N	Y	Y	Y	Y	Y	Y
Smartian	Y	Y	N	Y	Y	Y	Y
SmartBugs 2.0	N	Y	Y	Y	Y	Y	Y
WASAIUP	N	Y	Y	Y	Y	Y	Y
GasGauge	N	Y	Y	Y	Y	Y	N
NeuCheck	N	Y	Y	Y	Y	Y	N
HoneyBadger	N	Y	N	Y	Y	Y	Y
HFCCT	Y	Y	N	Y	Y	Y	N
SmartMixModel	N	Y	N	Y	Y	Y	Y
Solar	Y	Y	N	Y	Y	Y	N
FEther	N	Y	N	N	Y	Y	Y
SmartScan	N	N	Y	N	Y	Y	Y
EthPloit	N	Y	N	Y	Y	Y	N

TEEther	N	Y	N	Y	Y	Y	N
ContractGuard	N	Y	N	Y	Y	Y	N
MAIAN	N	Y	N	Y	Y	Y	N
SoliAudit	N	Y	N	Y	Y	Y	N
HAM	N	Y	N	Y	Y	Y	N
CloudAudit	N	Y	Y	Y	Y	N	N
Deep Learning-Based Vulnerability Detector (Unnamed Tool)	N	Y	N	Y	Y	Y	N
Pluto	N	Y	N	Y	Y	Y	N
ReSuMo	N	Y	N	Y	Y	Y	N
Mops	N	Y	N	Y	Y	Y	N
Reentrancy Vulnerability Identification Framework	N	Y	N	Y	Y	Y	N
SolAnalyser	Y	Y	N	N	N	N	Y
SafelyAdministrated	N	Y	N	Y	N	Y	N
SAILFISH	N	Y	N	Y	N	Y	N
EtherProv	N	Y	N	Y	N	Y	N
DeeSCVHunter	N	Y	N	Y	N	Y	N

in academic contexts for their efficiency, scalability, and capacity to support formal verification.
The top 20% of tools, such as ESCORT and SoliDetector, consistently meet most or all criteria. These tools demonstrate outstanding flexibility across SC platforms, provide extensive documentation, and offer seamless integration with research frameworks. They also support automated analysis and are extensible, making them adaptable to evolving research goals. Their performance reflects a high level of technical maturity and attention to user needs.
Mid-tier tools (60%), including sCompile and Zeus, excel in select areas, such as integration and documentation, but often fall short in extensibility and automation. This inconsistency suggests that while these tools are useful for specific scenarios, they may require further development to serve broader academic use cases effectively.
The bottom 20%, such as Porosity and AChecker, lack critical functionality in multiple areas. Their limited automation, sparse vulnerability coverage, and poor extensibility reduce their value for research. These tools highlight the need for more robust design principles and greater investment in development.
Overall, the evaluation reveals strong performance in documentation and integration but recurring weaknesses in automation and extensibility. This indicates that while many tools are user-friendly and well-documented, they may demand significant manual input and lack flexibility for future enhancement. Improving these aspects would significantly increase their utility in academic research.

- **Dynamic Analysis Tools**
  Dynamic tools execute smart contracts in controlled environments to uncover runtime behaviors and exploit conditions that static tools might overlook. They are particularly useful for evaluating real-world risk scenarios and simulating attacks.
  The top 25% of dynamic tools, such as ContractLarva, ModCon, and SODA, excel across nearly all evaluation criteria. These tools offer comprehensive vulnerability coverage, strong automation, detailed documentation, and the ability to integrate with research environments. Their use of real-world datasets for testing further enhances their reliability and relevance.
  Mid-tier tools like GFuzzer, DappGuard, and EVMFuzzer perform well in core detection tasks but often underperform in terms of extensibility and robustness testing. While they may serve practical short-term needs, they may not support longitudinal or comparative studies without additional engineering effort.
  The bottom 25%, such as RLRep, SeqFuzz, and EVM, show limitations in nearly every category. They tend to lack integration features, have minimal documentation, and rarely include real-world evaluation, significantly reducing their practical value in academic contexts.
  The recurring issue across dynamic tools is limited extensibility and inconsistent documentation. Enhancing these tools with modular architectures, well-maintained documentation, and support for evolving SC standards would improve their long-term research utility.
- **Hybrid Analysis Tools**
  Hybrid tools integrate static and dynamic methods to offer a more holistic approach to vulnerability detection. They are particularly promising in academic research due to their ability to detect both syntactic flaws and behavioral anomalies.

Leading hybrid tools, such as SmartBugs, KEVM, Vultron, WANA, and FSPVM-E, rank in the top 30% and meet nearly all criteria. They offer detailed documentation, extensive vulnerability coverage, and real-world testing capabilities. Their automation and integration strengths make them highly suitable for rigorous academic use.
Mid-tier tools like MuSc, ConFuzzius, and ESAF perform well in flexibility and documentation but fall short in extensibility and automation. This partial effectiveness suggests room for improvement, particularly in optimizing them for long-term research workflows.
Lower-tier tools, TEEther, SoliAudit, and HAM, lack core capabilities such as integration support, real-world testing, and automation. These shortcomings severely constrain their applicability for academic experimentation.
The hybrid category shows significant potential, but several tools still suffer from limited flexibility, incomplete documentation, and weak automation. As hybrid methods grow in importance, developing tools that combine high detection coverage with seamless usability will be essential.
Across all academic tools evaluated, some clear trends emerge. Documentation, automation, and vulnerability coverage are widely supported, with 237, 223, and 192 tools meeting those criteria, respectively. However, only 24 tools demonstrated flexibility across multiple platforms, and just 50 offered integration capabilities. Extensibility remains a challenge, with only 62 tools adequately supporting it.
This disparity suggests that academic tools often prioritize detection capabilities and documentation but fall short in offering the configurability and scalability needed for advanced or longitudinal research projects. Future development should focus on modular tool design, enhanced automation, and better integration to maximize both usability and research value.

9.2.2 Evaluating Industrial Tools

Beyond academic exploration, smart contract (SC) security tools are critical in real-world applications where financial assets, enterprise infrastructure, and end-user trust are at stake. Industry tools are designed with operational constraints in mind, such as speed, usability, scalability, and continuous support. Their evaluation must therefore extend beyond detection accuracy to encompass broader software engineering and usability factors.

To this end, we assess industry tools using fifteen criteria that reflect practical deployment needs. These criteria include flexibility, usability and user experience, scalability and performance, integration capabilities, support, maintenance and updates, documentation, automation, comprehensive vulnerability coverage, real-world testing, availability and licensing, detailed vulnerability reporting, and repair or mitigation suggestions, alongside extensibility. Each tool is evaluated on a binary (Yes/No) scale and grouped into static, dynamic, and hybrid categories. Tables 9.4, 9.5, and 9.6 summarize the comparison results, with tools ranked by the number of criteria they satisfy.

Table 9.4 Static analysis tools

Tool	Flexibility	Usability and user experience	Scalability and performance	Integration capabilities	Support	Maintenance and update	Detailed documentation	Automation	Comprehensive coverage	Reliable testing and evaluation	Availability and open source	Detailed vulnerability reporting	Repair/ Mitigation suggestion	Extensibility
Slither	N	N	Y	Y	Y	Y	Y	Y	Y	Y	Y	Y	N	Y
Securify	N	N	Y	Y	Y	Y	Y	Y	Y	Y	Y	Y	N	Y
SoMo	N	N	Y	Y	Y	Y	Y	Y	N	Y	Y	Y	N	Y
Solhint	N	Y	N	Y	Y	Y	Y	Y	Y	N	Y	N	Y	Y
Ethlint	N	Y	N	Y	Y	Y	Y	Y	Y	N	Y	N	Y	Y
SmartCheck	N	N	Y	Y	N	N	Y	Y	Y	Y	Y	Y	N	Y
Cider	N	N	Y	N	N	Y	Y	Y	Y	Y	N	Y	N	Y
Solidity Vulnerability Scanner	N	Y	N	N	N	N	N	Y	Y	Y	N	Y	Y	Y
Rattle	N	N	N	N	Y	Y	N	Y	Y	Y	Y	N	N	Y
SASC	N	N	Y	N	N	N	Y	Y	Y	Y	N	Y	N	N
Solgraph	N	Y	N	N	Y	N	N	Y	Y	N	Y	N	N	N

Table 9.5 Dynamic analysis tools

Tool	Flexibility	Usability and user experience	Scalability and performance	Integration capabilities	Support	Maintenance and update	Detailed documentation	Automation	Comprehensive coverage	Reliable testing and evaluation	Availability and open source	Detailed vulnerability reporting	Repair/Mitigation suggestion	Extensibility
Manticore	Y	Y	Y	Y	Y	Y	Y	Y	Y	Y	Y	Y	N	Y
Echidna	N	Y	Y	Y	Y	Y	Y	Y	Y	Y	Y	N	N	Y
Harvey	N	N	Y	Y	N	Y	Y	Y	Y	Y	N	N	N	Y
Pakala	N	Y	N	N	N	N	Y	Y	Y	N	Y	Y	N	N

Table 9.6 Hybrid analysis tools

Tool	Flexibility	Usability and user experience	Scalability and performance	Integration capabilities	Support	Maintenance and update	Detailed documentation	Automation	Comprehensive coverage	Reliable testing and evaluation	Availability and open source	Detailed vulnerability reporting	Repair/Mitigation suggestion	Extensibility
Mythril	Y	Y	Y	Y	Y	Y	N	Y	Y	Y	Y	Y	Y	Y
MPro	Y	N	Y	Y	Y	N	Y	Y	Y	Y	Y	N	N	Y
MythX	Y	Y	Y	Y	Y	Y	N	Y	Y	Y	N	N	N	Y
Octopus	Y	N	N	N	N	N	N	Y	Y	N	Y	N	N	Y

- **Static Industrial Tools**
  Static analysis tools in the industry are valued for their ability to detect vulnerabilities quickly and without executing code, making them efficient for early-stage audits and CI/CD pipelines. As shown in Table 9.4, leading tools such as Slither, SoMo, and SmartCheck demonstrate strong performance across critical categories, including documentation, automation, and comprehensive coverage. Their user support and regular updates further contribute to their reliability in production settings.
  However, the evaluation reveals several shortcomings in the broader set of static tools. Flexibility and integration capabilities remain limited across many tools, reducing their ability to adapt to diverse smart contract environments or fit seamlessly into enterprise workflows. While SmartCheck stands out for its integration support, most tools lack robust APIs or plugin mechanisms.
  Usability and performance also present challenges. Despite efforts by tools like Ethlint and Solhint to enhance user experience, many others lack intuitive interfaces, posing adoption barriers for non-expert users. Moreover, scalability is inadequately addressed: only SoMo explicitly supports large-scale analysis, which is essential for enterprise-grade applications.
  Support and maintenance also vary widely. While Rattle and Solhint maintain regular updates and offer accessible user support, others offer limited channels for issue resolution or documentation updates. Furthermore, few tools provide detailed vulnerability reporting or actionable remediation guidance, key features for real-time auditing and incident response.
  In summary, while some static industry tools offer strong detection and documentation capabilities, widespread gaps persist in flexibility, integration, usability, and extensibility. To improve adoption and utility, future development should prioritize user interface design, API integration, and detailed repair guidance alongside scalable architecture.
- **Dynamic Industrial Tools**
  Dynamic tools simulate smart contract execution to detect runtime vulnerabilities, including reentrancy, gas-related issues, and environment-specific bugs. As summarized in Table 9.5, leading tools such as Manticore, Echidna, and Harvey show comprehensive support for many key features. They excel in scalability, automation, extensibility, and real-world testing, making them highly suited for enterprise vulnerability assessments.
  All four dynamic tools evaluated, Manticore, Echidna, Harvey, and Pakala, are open-source and provide detailed documentation, promoting transparency and community-driven enhancements. Integration capabilities and regular updates are also consistent among the top performers, enabling sustainable adoption.
  However, several deficiencies are evident. None of the tools provides repair or mitigation suggestions, limiting their ability to directly support remediation workflows. Additionally, detailed vulnerability reporting is missing from tools like Echidna and Harvey, which limit their utility in professional auditing, where actionable outputs are essential.

Support services are inconsistent. While Manticore and Echidna offer community and documentation support, Harvey and Pakala provide little in the way of user assistance, potentially hindering onboarding and troubleshooting.
Flexibility is another concern. Tools like Harvey, Echidna, and Pakala are often optimized for specific execution contexts and do not generalize well across platforms, limiting their deployability in heterogeneous environments.
To enhance dynamic industry tools, future work should integrate robust reporting modules, support repair recommendation systems, and expand platform flexibility. Enhancing user support infrastructure and maintaining ease of integration will be crucial for broad adoption.

- **Hybrid Industrial Tools**
Hybrid tools combine static and dynamic analysis to provide a holistic view of smart contract security, capturing both code-level and runtime vulnerabilities. As shown in Table 9.6, the four industry-level hybrid tools evaluated exhibit notable strengths in automation, comprehensive coverage, extensibility, and flexibility. These attributes make them suitable for handling diverse vulnerabilities and adapting to evolving contract designs.
Three of the tools also demonstrate excellence in scalability, integration, and open-source availability, highlighting their potential for enterprise-scale deployment. These capabilities ensure that hybrid tools can efficiently process complex SCs and integrate into broader security pipelines. Despite these strengths, certain limitations persist. Some tools lack detailed documentation, making adoption and configuration difficult, especially for teams with less experience in smart contract security. Additionally, detailed vulnerability reports and repair recommendations are often missing, limiting security teams' ability to take timely, informed action on findings.
User experience design is another area of concern. Poor interface design or inadequate workflow support can lead to inefficiencies and reduce the tool's effectiveness, even when the underlying detection algorithms are robust. To improve the utility of hybrid industry tools, future development should focus on usability enhancements, enriched documentation, and actionable reporting. Integrating remediation suggestions will significantly enhance the tools' operational value.
The evaluation of industry tools across static, dynamic, and hybrid categories highlights several systemic patterns. Most tools perform well in automation (19 tools), detailed documentation (16 tools), and vulnerability coverage (15 tools), underscoring a commitment to detection performance and accessibility. However, critical gaps remain in areas essential for practical adoption: only 4 tools demonstrated cross-platform flexibility, 8 addressed usability and user experience, 8 offered repair guidance, and 8 supported extensibilities.
These findings suggest that while detection capability is often prioritized, aspects that influence operational deployment, such as platform adaptability, actionable

reporting, and integration with security workflows, remain underdeveloped. For industry use cases, especially in high-stakes DeFi, enterprise, and infrastructure environments, such limitations can reduce a tool's real-world impact.

Going forward, industry-grade SC tools should evolve beyond pure detection to offer a complete lifecycle solution, including enriched reporting, guided mitigation, and seamless user experiences. Emphasizing these factors will accelerate tool adoption, improve remediation timelines, and enhance the overall resilience of blockchain systems.

9.3 Auditing Smart Contracts Development and Use

The development and deployment of smart contract vulnerability detection tools require rigorous auditing and systematic evaluation to ensure their reliability, relevance, and security. These tools play a critical role in identifying and mitigating risks within decentralized applications (dApps), and their effectiveness directly influences the integrity of smart contract ecosystems. However, unlike evaluating smart contracts themselves, auditing a detection tool involves assessing the tool's quality, completeness, and operational behavior throughout its lifecycle, from initial development to real-world use.

This section outlines the essential parameters to consider when auditing the development and practical deployment of smart contract detection tools. Each parameter addresses a different aspect of tool quality, ranging from core detection capabilities to usability, maintainability, and ecosystem integration. Together, they form a framework for understanding the strengths and limitations of these tools and for guiding their continuous improvement.

Accuracy and Precision

At the heart of any vulnerability detection tool lies its capacity to deliver accurate results. Precision refers to the proportion of detected vulnerabilities that are true positives, while recall denotes the proportion of actual vulnerabilities that are correctly identified. High accuracy ensures that developers are not overwhelmed by false alarms, nor lulled into a false sense of security by undetected flaws. Inadequate accuracy can result in inefficient debugging, mistrust in the tool, and ultimately, the deployment of insecure contracts.

Coverage of Vulnerabilities

Comprehensive vulnerability coverage is essential to ensure the tool's utility across various use cases. The tool should be capable of identifying a broad spectrum of vulnerability types, including but not limited to reentrancy, integer overflow and underflow, timestamp and block hash misuse, transaction-ordering dependence (TOD), access control issues, denial-of-service (DoS), and unchecked low-level calls. Tools with limited coverage may be effective only in narrowly scoped environments and fail to detect novel or complex attack vectors. A well-audited tool must be benchmarked against known vulnerability taxonomies, such as the SWC Registry, or against datasets like SmartBugs.

Integration Capabilities

A key factor in the practical adoption of a detection tool is its ability to integrate into existing development workflows. This includes compatibility with widely used frameworks such as Remix, Truffle, and Hardhat, as well as support for continuous integration and deployment (CI/CD) pipelines. Tools that lack integration features require manual intervention and are more likely to be bypassed in agile environments. Well-integrated tools promote early detection vulnerability, enabling security to be addressed throughout the development lifecycle.

Usability and Developer Experience

A tool's effectiveness is not limited to its detection power but also extends to its ease of use. Auditing a detection tool involves examining its user interface (command-line or graphical), configuration complexity, output clarity, and accessibility of results. Tools that generate complex outputs or require extensive manual configuration may be difficult for non-expert developers to use. Enhanced usability fosters adoption and encourages developers to act upon the tool's findings promptly and effectively.

Scalability and Performance

Detection tools must be able to scale with the increasing size and complexity of modern smart contracts. Scalability refers to a tool's ability to analyze large codebases or efficiently handle high volumes of smart contracts. Performance includes runtime speed, memory efficiency, and the ability to perform under load or in distributed environments. Poorly optimized tools may lead to excessive analysis times, reduced responsiveness, and bottlenecks in automated testing environments.

Automation and Workflow Compatibility

Modern smart contract development increasingly relies on automation to improve reliability and efficiency. A well-audited tool should support batch processing, scheduled analyses, and hooks for triggering vulnerability scans during code commits or builds. Automation minimizes human error, supports continuous security practices, and ensures analysis is part of a larger DevSecOps strategy. Tools that cannot be automated introduce friction into development pipelines and may eventually be neglected.

Extensibility and Modularity

Security threats evolve over time, and a detection tool must be flexible enough to keep pace. Extensibility refers to the tool's ability to be expanded or customized, such as adding new detection modules, supporting additional smart contract languages (e.g., Vyper, Cairo), or integrating third-party plugins. Tools with modular architecture are more maintainable, adaptable, and sustainable over the long term. A lack of extensibility often results in obsolescence or narrow applicability.

Testing and Evaluation

Robust testing is fundamental to validating the reliability and security of any analysis tool. Auditing should involve evaluating the tool's performance against curated datasets of vulnerable and benign smart contracts. This includes benchmarks such as the SmartBugs dataset, EtherScan's verified contracts, and adversarial examples that reflect real-world attacks. Evaluation metrics such as precision, recall, F1-score, and false positive rate should be well-documented and reproducible. Tools without clear testing strategies risk delivering misleading results or being ineffective in practical use.

Formal Verification and Soundness

For tools that employ formal methods or claim logical guarantees (e.g., symbolic execution, SMT solvers, or formal semantics), their soundness and completeness should be clearly defined and tested. Soundness ensures that all reported vulnerabilities are real, while completeness ensures that all possible vulnerabilities are captured. In practice, trade-offs often exist between the two. Nevertheless, the assumptions, limitations, and scope of formal guarantees must be transparent to avoid misuse and misinterpretation.

Documentation and Transparency

A well-documented tool is not only easier to use but also more trustworthy. Comprehensive documentation should include architecture overviews, installation instructions, use-case examples, explanation of detection techniques, and caveats. Transparency in how the tool performs analysis, especially for AI-based tools, is essential for reproducibility, validation, and academic scrutiny. Tools lacking detailed documentation are harder to audit, maintain, and adopt, especially by larger teams.

Maintenance and Update Frequency

Security tooling must keep pace with rapid changes in the ecosystem, including updates to the Solidity compiler, the emergence of new vulnerability types, and evolving blockchain standards. A well-maintained tool reflects responsiveness to user feedback, bug fixes, and feature enhancements. Auditing should involve examining the release history, community involvement, and long-term maintenance strategy. Stagnant tools risk becoming incompatible or irrelevant.

Licensing and Accessibility

Whether a tool is open-source or commercially licensed affects its accessibility, transparency, and user community. Open-source tools often enjoy broader adoption, community-driven improvements, and easier audits. Commercial tools may offer dedicated support and proprietary features, but can pose challenges regarding cost, accessibility, and vendor lock-in. Licensing terms should align with the tool's intended audience and deployment context.

Security of the Tool Itself

A security tool must not introduce vulnerabilities of its own. Tools that process smart contracts, especially through web interfaces or cloud-based APIs, must be audited to ensure they do not leak sensitive data, permit injection attacks, or expose infrastructure weaknesses. Secure design principles should be enforced throughout the tool's development lifecycle, including secure input handling, sandboxed execution, and clear access control policies.

Legal and Ethical Compliance

Depending on the jurisdiction and application domain, smart contract analysis tools may be subject to legal regulations or industry standards. For instance, in regulated environments (e.g., DeFi or healthcare), tools must comply with data protection rules such as GDPR. Ethical considerations also apply in the use of detection results, especially in cases involving responsible disclosure or automated decision-making. A rigorous audit includes assessing compliance with relevant legal and ethical standards.

Output Interpretability and Actionability

Finally, the tool's output must be meaningful and actionable. Effective tools go beyond binary flags, providing detailed explanations, severity assessments, and suggested remediations. Interpretable output is especially important when results are consumed by developers, auditors, or legal teams who may not have deep technical backgrounds. Tools that fail to communicate findings clearly are unlikely to be trusted or used effectively.

In conclusion, auditing smart contract vulnerability detection tools requires a multidimensional evaluation framework that addresses not only their technical detection capabilities but also their usability, scalability, maintainability, and security. As these tools become integral to the secure development and deployment of decentralized applications, developers and auditors must carefully assess each parameter to ensure the tool's reliability, relevance, and long-term applicability. By prioritizing comprehensive vulnerability coverage, seamless integration, automation, extensibility, and transparent documentation, tool creators can better meet the evolving demands of both academic research and industry deployment. Ultimately, a rigorous auditing process ensures that these tools not only effectively identify vulnerabilities but also meaningfully contribute to advancing secure blockchain ecosystems.

9.4 Chapter Summary

This chapter dissected the landscape of smart contract vulnerability detection tools, distinguishing their methodologies, capabilities, and shortcomings across academic and industrial domains. By evaluating tools through the lens of static, dynamic, and hybrid analysis, we exposed not only the technical strengths of leading frameworks but also the recurring limitations that undermine reliability, scalability, and long-term utility. Academic tools frequently excel in innovation and detailed reporting but often fall short in extensibility, integration, and adaptability to diverse use cases. Conversely, industrial tools emphasize usability, automation, and deployment readiness, yet often lack transparency, extensibility, or meaningful repair guidance. Across both domains, comparative analysis revealed a fragmented ecosystem in which no single solution satisfies the full spectrum of evaluation criteria, and in which vulnerability coverage, update frequency, and practical integration remain unevenly addressed. These findings underscore that the development of robust detection tools must go beyond technical detection and embrace a holistic design approach, one that balances accuracy with usability, and research rigor with real-world applicability. Ensuring the future resilience of smart contracts requires tools that not only uncover vulnerabilities but evolve alongside the technologies they aim to protect.

References

1. Tharammal, R.R., Nitnaware, P.: Maximizing efficiency in smart contract execution costs techniques for cost optimization on blockchain networks. In: 2024 International Conference on Integration of Emerging Technologies for the Digital World (ICIETDW). IEEE (2024)
2. Albert, E., et al.: Ethir: a framework for high-level analysis of ethereum bytecode. In: International Symposium on Automated Technology for Verification and Analysis. Springer International Publishing, Cham (2018)
3. Ali, A., Abideen, Z.U., Ullah, K.: SESCon: secure Ethereum smart contracts by vulnerable patterns' detection. Secur. Commun. Netw. **2021**(1), 2897565 (2021)
4. Akca, S., Rajan, A., Peng, C.: Solanalyser: a framework for analysing and testing smart contracts. In: 2019 26th Asia-Pacific Software Engineering Conference (APSEC). IEEE (2019)
5. Abdellatif, T., Brousmiche, K.-L.: Formal verification of smart contracts based on users and blockchain behaviors models. In: 2018 9th IFIP International Conference on New Technologies, Mobility and Security (NTMS). IEEE (2018)
6. Albert, E., et al.: SAFEVM: a safety verifier for Ethereum smart contracts. In: Proceedings of the 28th ACM SIGSOFT International Symposium on Software Testing and Analysis (2019)
7. Almakhour, M., Sliman, L., Samhat, A.E., Mellouk, A.: Verification of smart contracts: a survey. Pervas. Mob. Comput. **67**, 101227 (2020)
8. Antonino, P., Roscoe, A.W.: Solidifier: bounded model checking solidity using lazy contract deployment and precise memory modelling. In: Proceedings of the 36th Annual ACM Symposium on Applied Computing (2021)
9. Tolmach, P., Li, Y., Lin, S.-W., Liu, Y., Li, Z.: A survey of smart contract formal specification and verification. ACM Comput. Surv. **54**(7), 1–38 (2021)

10. Permenev, A., Dimitrov, D., Tsankov, P., Drachsler-Cohen, D., Vechev, M.: VerX: safety verification of smart contracts. In: Proceedings of the 2020 IEEE Symposium on Security and Privacy (S&P), pp. 1661–1677 (2020)
11. So, S., Lee, M.-J., Park, J., Lee, H.-S., Oh, H.-G.: VERISMART: a highly precise safety verifier for ethereum smart contracts. In: Proceedings of the 2020 IEEE Symposium on Security and Privacy (S&P), pp. 1678–1694 (2020)
12. Albert, E., Correas, J., Gordillo, P., Román-Díez, G., Rubio, A.: Gasol: gas analysis and optimization for ethereum smart contracts. In: International Conference on Tools and Algorithms for the Construction and Analysis of Systems, pp. 118–125. Springer (2020)
13. Albert, E., Gordillo, P., Rubio, A., Sergey, I.: Running on fumes. In: Ganty, P., Kaâniche, M. (eds.) Verification and Evaluation of Computer and Communication Systems, pp. 63–78. Springer International Publishing, Cham (2019)
14. Schneidewind, C., Grishchenko, I., Scherer, M., Maffei, M.: EthOr: practical and provably sound static analysis of ethereum smart contracts. In: Proceedings of the 2020 ACM SIGSAC Conference on Computer and Communications Security (CCS), pp. 621–640 (2020)
15. Cai, Z., et al.: Asparagus: automated synthesis of parametric gas upper-bounds for smart contracts. In: Proceedings of the ACM on Programming Languages 7, OOPSLA2, pp. 882–911 (2023)
16. Olivieri, L., Negrini, L., Arceri, V., Jensen, T., Spoto, F.: Design and implementation of static analyses for tezos smart contracts. Distributed Ledger Technologies: Research and Practice (2024)
17. di Angelo, M., Salzer, G.: A survey of tools for analyzing ethereum smart contracts. In: Proceedings of the 2019 IEEE International Conference on Decentralized Applications and Infrastructures (DAPPCON), pp. 69–78 (2019)
18. Kushwaha, S.S., Joshi, S., Singh, D., Kaur, M., Lee, H.-N.: Ethereum smart contract analysis tools: a systematic review. IEEE Access. **10**, 57037–57062 (2022)
19. Vacca, A., Di Sorbo, A., Visaggio, C.A., Canfora, G.: A systematic literature review of blockchain and smart contract development: techniques, tools, and open challenges. J. Syst. Softw. **174**, 110891 (2021)
20. Wu, G., Wang, H., Lai, X., Wang, M., He, D., Chan, S.C.: A comprehensive survey of smart contract security: state of the art and research directions. J. Netw. Comput. Appl., 103882 (2024)
21. Xie, X., Wang, H., Jian, Z., Fang, Y., Wang, Z., Li, T.: Block-Gram: mining knowledgeable features for efficient smart contract vulnerability detection. Digit Commun Netw. (2023)
22. Qian, P., Liu, Z., Yin, Y., He, Q.: Cross-modality mutual learning for enhancing smart contract vulnerability detection on bytecode. In: Proceedings of the ACM Web Conference (WWW), pp. 2220–2229 (2023)
23. Hwang, S.-J., Choi, S.-H., Shin, J., Choi, Y.-H.: CodeNet: code-targeted convolutional neural network architecture for smart contract vulnerability detection. IEEE Access. **10**, 32595–32607 (2022)
24. Protofire. Solhint Documentation (2024). Accessed 10 June 2024
25. Wu, Z., Li, S., Wang, B., Liu, T., Zhu, Y., Zhu, C., Hu, M.: Detecting vulnerabilities in ethereum smart contracts with deep learning. In: Proceedings of the 2022 4th International Conference on Data Intelligence and Security (ICDIS), pp. 55–60 (2022)
26. Narayana, K.L., Sathiyamurthy, K.: Automation and smart materials in detecting smart contract vulnerabilities in blockchain using deep learning. Mater. Today Proc. **81**, 653–659 (2023)
27. Liu, Z., Jiang, M., Zhang, S., Zhang, J., Liu, Y.: A smart contract vulnerability detection mechanism based on deep learning and expert rules. IEEE Access. **11**, 77990–77999 (2023)
28. Zhao, K., Li, Z., Li, J., Ye, H., Luo, X., Chen, T.: DeepInfer: deep type inference from smart contract bytecode. In: Proceedings of the 31st ACM Joint European Software Engineering Conference and Symposium on the Foundations of Software Engineering (ESEC/FSE), pp. 745–757 (2023)

29. Lê Hông, B., Tịnh, L.Đ., Tân, Đ.M., Dũng, T.T., Duy, P.T., Hòa, P.V.: Contextual language model and transfer learning for reentrancy vulnerability detection in smart contracts. In: Proceedings of the 12th International Symposium on Information and Communication Technology, pp. 739–745 (2023)
30. Eshghie, M., Artho, C., Gurov, D.: Dynamic vulnerability detection on smart contracts using machine learning. In: Proceedings of the 25th International Conference on Evaluation and Assessment in Software Engineering, pp. 305–312 (2021)
31. Chen, D., Feng, L., Fan, Y., Shang, S., Wei, Z.: Smart contract vulnerability detection based on semantic graph and residual graph convolutional networks with edge attention. J. Syst. Softw. **202**, 111705 (2023)
32. Xing, C., Chen, Z., Chen, L., Guo, X., Zheng, Z., Li, J.: A new scheme of vulnerability analysis in smart contracts with machine learning. Wirel. Netw, 1–10 (2020)
33. Yuan, D., Wang, X., Li, Y., Zhang, T.: Optimizing smart contract vulnerability detection via multi-modality code and entropy embedding. J. Syst. Softw. **202**, 111699 (2023)
34. Ma, C., Liu, S., Guang, X.: HGAT: smart contract vulnerability detection method based on hierarchical graph attention network. J. Cloud Comput. **12**(1), 93 (2023)
35. Yang, Z., Zhu, W., Yu, M.: Improvement and optimization of vulnerability detection methods for ethereum smart contracts. IEEE Access. **11**, 78207–78223 (2023)
36. Liu, H., Liu, C., Zhao, W., Jiang, Y., Sun, J.: S-gram: towards semantic-aware security auditing for ethereum smart contracts. In: Proceedings of the 2018 33rd IEEE/ACM International Conference on Automated Software Engineering (ASE), pp. 814–819 (2018)
37. Deng, W., Wei, H., Huang, T., Cao, C., Peng, Y., Hu, X.: Smart contract vulnerability detection based on deep learning and multimodal decision fusion. Sensors. **23**(16), 7246 (2023)
38. Mittal, A., Widjaja, G., Pecho, R.D.C., Kiruba, R., Falcón Roque, J.M., Chandra, A.: Blockchain-based abstract syntax tree to detect vulnerability in IoT-enabled smart contracts. In: Proceedings of the 2023 Second International Conference on Smart Technologies for Smart Nation (SmartTechCon), pp. 270–275 (2023)
39. Liu, L., Tsai, W.-T., Bhuiyan, M.Z.A., Peng, H., Liu, M.: Blockchain-enabled fraud discovery through abnormal smart contract detection on ethereum. Futur. Gener. Comput. Syst. **128**, 158–166 (2022)
40. Fatima Samreen, N., Alalfi, M.H.: Reentrancy vulnerability identification in ethereum smart contracts. In: Proceedings of the 2020 IEEE International Workshop on Blockchain Oriented Software Engineering (IWBOSE), pp. 22–29 (2020)
41. Zhang, H., Zhang, W., Feng, Y., Liu, Y.: SVScanner: detecting smart contract vulnerabilities via deep semantic extraction. J. Inf. Secur. Appl. **75**, 103484 (2023)
42. Sun, Y., Li, G.: Attention-based machine learning model for smart contract vulnerability detection. J. Phys. Conf. Ser. **1820**(1), 012004 (2021)
43. Sun, X., Tu, L., Zhang, J., Cai, J., Li, B., Wang, Y.: ASSBert: active and semi-supervised BERT for smart contract vulnerability detection. J. Inf. Secur. Appl. **73**, 103423 (2023)
44. Liu, Z., Qian, P., Wang, X., Zhu, L., He, Q., Ji, S.: Smart contract vulnerability detection: from pure neural network to interpretable graph feature and expert pattern fusion. In: Proceedings of the 30th International Joint Conference on Artificial Intelligence (IJCAI), pp. 2751–2759 (2021)
45. Zhang, L., Li, Y., Guo, R., Wang, G., Qiu, J., Su, S., Liu, Y., Xu, G., Chen, H., Tian, Z.: A novel smart contract reentrancy vulnerability detection model based on BiGAS. J. Signal Process. Syst., 1–23 (2023)
46. Wu, H., Dong, H., He, Y., Duan, Q., Duan, Q.: Smart contract vulnerability detection based on hybrid attention mechanism model. Appl. Sci. **13**(2), 770 (2023)
47. Ren, X., Wu, Y., Li, J., Hao, D., Alam, M.: Smart contract vulnerability detection based on a semantic code structure and a self-designed neural network. Comput. Electr. Eng. **109**, 108766 (2023)
48. Zhang, L., Wang, J., Wang, W., Jin, Z., Yupeng, S., Chen, H.: Smart contract vulnerability detection combined with multi-objective detection. Comput. Netw. **217**, 109289 (2022)

49. Liu, Z., Qian, P., Wang, X., Zhuang, Y., Qiu, L., Wang, X.: Combining graph neural networks with expert knowledge for smart contract vulnerability detection. IEEE Trans. Knowl. Data Eng. **35**(2), 1296–1310 (2023)
50. Wang, W., Song, J., Xu, G., Li, Y., Wang, H., Su, C.: ContractWard: automated vulnerability detection models for ethereum smart contracts. IEEE Trans. Netw. Sci. Eng. **8**(2), 1133–1144 (2021)
51. Yu, X., Zhao, H., Hou, B., Ying, Z., Bowen, W.: DeeSCVHunter: A deep learning-based framework for smart contract vulnerability detection. In: Proceedings of the 2021 International Joint Conference on Neural Networks (IJCNN), pp. 1–8 (2021)
52. Liu, Y., Wang, C., Ma, Y.: DL4SC: a novel deep learning-based vulnerability detection framework for smart contracts. Autom. Softw. Eng. **31**(1), 24 (2024)
53. Zhuang, Y., Liu, Z., Qian, P., Liu, L., Wang, X., He, Q.: Smart contract vulnerability detection using graph neural network. In: Proceedings of the 29th International Joint Conference on Artificial Intelligence (IJCAI), pp. 3283–3290 (2020)
54. Ashizawa, N., et al.: Eth2vec: learning contract-wide code representations for vulnerability detection on ethereum smart contracts. In: Proceedings of the 3rd ACM International Symposium on Blockchain and Secure Critical Infrastructure (2021)
55. Nguyen, H.-H., Nguyen, N.-M., Doan, H.-P., Ahmadi, Z., Doan, T.-N., Lu, J.: MANDO-GURU: vulnerability detection for smart contract source code by heterogeneous graph embeddings. In: Proceedings of the 30th ACM Joint European Software Engineering Conference and Symposium on the Foundations of Software Engineering (ESEC/FSE), pp. 1736–1740 (2022)
56. Srinivasan, P., et al.: TP-Detect: trigram-pixel based vulnerability detection for ethereum smart contracts. Multimed. Tools Appl. **82**(23), 36379–36393 (2023)
57. Vu, D., Nguyen, T., Tong, V., Souihil, S.: Enhancing multi-label vulnerability detection of smart contracts using language models. In: Proceedings of the 2023 5th Conference on Blockchain Research & Applications for Innovative Networks and Services (BRAINS), pp. 1–4 (2023)
58. Zhang, Y., Ma, S., Li, J., Li, K., Nepal, S., Gu, D.: SmartShield: automatic smart contract protection made easy. In: Proceedings of the 2020 IEEE 27th International Conference on Software Analysis, Evolution and Reengineering (SANER), pp. 23–34 (2020)
59. Mohanty, D., Anand, D.: Evaluating the remix solidity static analysis plugin using SB curated dataset. In: Proceedings of the 2023 7th International Conference on Computing, Communication, Control and Automation (ICCUBEA), pp. 1–4 (2023)
60. Pierro, G.A.: Smart-Graph: graphical representations for smart contracts on the ethereum blockchain. In: Proceedings of the 2021 IEEE International Conference on Software Analysis, Evolution and Reengineering (SANER), pp. 708–714 (2021)
61. Shakya, S., Mukherjee, A., Halder, R., Maiti, A., Chaturvedi, A.: SmartMixModel: machine learning-based vulnerability detection of solidity smart contracts. In: Proceedings of the 2022 IEEE International Conference on Blockchain, pp. 37–44 (2022)
62. Cai, J., et al.: Combine sliced joint graph with graph neural networks for smart contract vulnerability detection. J. Syst. Softw. **195**, 111550 (2023)
63. Yu, R., Shu, J., Yan, D., Jia, X.: ReDectEct: reentrancy vulnerability detection in smart contracts with high accuracy. In: Proceedings of the 2021 17th International Conference on Mobility, Sensing and Networking (MSN), pp. 412–419 (2021)
64. Nikolic, I., Kolluri, A., Sergey, I., Saxena, P., Hobor, A.: MAIAN: Automatic Detection of Greedy, Prodigal, and Suicidal Contracts. GitHub (2018)., Accessed 14 June 2024
65. Liu, J., Chen, Y., Tan, B., Dillig, I., Feng, Y.: Learning contract invariants using reinforcement learning. In: Proceedings of the 37th IEEE/ACM International Conference on Automated Software Engineering (ASE), pp. 1–11 (2022)
66. Chu, H., et al.: A survey on smart contract vulnerabilities: data sources, detection and repair. Inf Softw Technol. **159**, 107221 (2023)

67. Feist, J., Grieco, G., Groce, A.: Slither: a static analysis framework for smart contracts. In: Proceedings of the 2019 IEEE/ACM 2nd International Workshop on Emerging Trends in Software Engineering for Blockchain (WETSEB), pp. 8–15 (2019)
68. Luu, L., Chu, D.-H., Olickel, H., Saxena, P., Hobor, A.: Making smart contracts smarter. In: Proceedings of the 2016 ACM SIGSAC Conference on Computer and Communications Security (CCS), pp. 254–269 (2016)
69. Tsankov, P., Dan, A., Drachsler-Cohen, D., Gervais, A., Buenzli, F., Vechev, M.: Securify: practical security analysis of smart contracts. In: Proceedings of the 2018 ACM SIGSAC Conference on Computer and Communications Security (CCS), pp. 67–82 (2018)
70. Sendner, C., Chen, H., Fereidooni, H., Petzi, L., König, J., Stang, J., Sadeghi, A.-R., Koushanfar, F.: Smarter Contracts: Detecting Vulnerabilities in Smart Contracts with Deep Transfer Learning. NDSS (2023)
71. Lashkari, B., Musilek, P.: Evaluation of smart contract vulnerability analysis tools: a domain-specific perspective. Information. **14**(10), 533 (2023)
72. Chen, T., et al.: SODA: a generic online detection framework for smart contracts. In: Proceedings of the 27th Network and Distributed System Security Symposium (NDSS), pp. 1–17 (2020)
73. Peng, C., Akça, S., Rajan, A.: SIF: a framework for solidity contract instrumentation and analysis. In: Proceedings of the 2019 26th Asia-Pacific Software Engineering Conference (APSEC), pp. 466–473 (2019)
74. Cook, T., Latham, A., Lee, J.-H.: DappGuard: active monitoring and defense for solidity smart contracts (2017)
75. Wang, X., He, J., Xie, Z., Zhao, G., Cheung, S.-C.: ContractGuard: defend ethereum smart contracts with embedded intrusion detection. IEEE Trans. Serv. Comput. **13**(2), 314–328 (2020)
76. Hou, Z., Dong, C., Shang, Y.: HermHD: enhancing smart contract security based on code obfuscation. In: Proceedings of the 2023 11th International Conference on Information Technology: IoT and Smart City (2023)
77. Chang, J., et al.: sCompile: critical path identification and analysis for smart contracts. In: Formal Methods and Software Engineering Lecture Notes in Computer Science, vol. 11852, pp. 286–304. ICFEM (2019)
78. Pasqua, M., Benini, A., Contro, F., Crosara, M., Preda, M.D., Ceccato, M.: Enhancing ethereum smart-contracts static analysis by computing a precise control-flow graph of ethereum bytecode. J. Syst. Softw. **200**, 111653 (2023)
79. Smaragdakis, Y., Grech, N., Lagouvardos, S., Triantafyllou, K., Tsatiris, I.: Symbolic value-flow static analysis: deep, precise, complete modeling of ethereum smart contracts. In: Proceedings of the ACM on Programming Languages 5, OOPSLA, pp. 1–30 (2021)
80. Brent, L., et al.: Vandal: a scalable security analysis framework for smart contracts. arXiv preprint arXiv:1809.03981 (2018)
81. Chen, T., Feng, Y., Li, Z., Zhou, H., Luo, X., Li, X., Xiao, X., Chen, J., Zhang, X.: GasChecker: scalable analysis for discovering gas-inefficient smart contracts. IEEE Trans. Emerg. Top. Comput. **9**(3), 1433–1448 (2021)
82. Chen, T., Li, X., Luo, X., Zhang, X.: Under-optimized smart contracts devour your money. In: Proceedings of the 2017 IEEE 24th International Conference on Software Analysis, Evolution and Reengineering (SANER), pp. 442–446 (2017)
83. Grech, N., et al.: Madmax: surviving out-of-gas conditions in ethereum smart contracts. In: Proceedings of the ACM on Programming Languages 2. OOPSLA, pp. 1–27 (2018)
84. Yang, S., Li, H., Zheng, Z.: WaLi: control-flow-based analysis of wasm smart contracts. International Conference on Blockchain and Trustworthy Systems, Springer Nature Singapore, Singapore (2022)
85. Özdemir Sönmez, F., Knottenbelt, W.J.: ContractArmor: attack surface generator for smart contracts. Proc. Comput. Sci. **231**, 8–15 (2024)
86. Crytic: Rattle: An EVM Binary Static Analysis Framework. GitHub (2024)

87. Suiche, M.: Porosity: A Decompiler for Blockchain-Based Smart Contracts Bytecode, vol. 25. DEF CON (2017)
88. Zhou, Y., Kumar, D., Bakshi, S., Mason, J.M., Miller, A., Bailey, M.: EraYs: reverse engineering ethereum's opaque smart contracts. In: Proceedings of the 27th USENIX Security Symposium (USENIX Security '18), pp. 1371–1385 (2018)
89. Linoy, S., Ray, S., Stakhanova, N.: EtherProv: provenance-aware detection, analysis, and mitigation of ethereum smart contract security issues. In: Proceedings of the 2021 IEEE International Conference on Blockchain, pp. 1–10 (2021)
90. FuzzingLabs: Octopus: a neural fuzzer for finding unique bugs in smart contracts. GitHub repository (2024) https://github.com/FuzzingLabs/octopus
91. Dharanikota, S., Mukherjee, S., Bhardwaj, C., Rastogi, A., Lal, A.: Celestial: a smart contracts verification framework. In: Proceedings of the 2021 Formal Methods in Computer Aided Design (FMCAD), pp. 133–142 (2021)
92. Nielsen, E.H., Annenkov, D., Spitters, B.: Formalising decentralised exchanges in Coq. In: Proceedings of the 12th ACM SIGPLAN International Conference on Certified Programs and Proofs (2023)
93. Yang, Z., Lei, H.: Fether: an extensible definitional interpreter for smart-contract verifications in coq. IEEE Access. **7**, 37770–37791 (2019)
94. Osterland, T., Rose, T.: Model checking smart contracts for ethereum. Pervas. Mob. Comput. **63**, 101129 (2020)
95. Keilty, E., Nelaturu, K., Wu, B., Veneris, A.: A model-checking framework for the verification of move smart contracts. In: Proceedings of ...
96. Bräm, C., et al.: Rich specifications for Ethereum smart contract verification. In: Proceedings of the ACM on Programming Languages 5, OOPSLA, pp. 1–30 (2021)
97. Park, D., Zhang, Y., Saxena, M., Daian, P., Roşu, G.: A formal verification tool for ethereum VM bytecode. In: Proceedings of the 2018 26th ACM Joint European Software Engineering Conference and Symposium on the Foundations of Software Engineering (ESEC/FSE), pp. 912–915 (2018)
98. Song, K., Matulevicius, N., de Lima Filho, E.B., Cordeiro, L.C.: ESBMC-solidity: an SMT-based model checker for solidity smart contracts. In: Proceedings of the ACM/IEEE 44th International Conference on Software Engineering: Companion Proceedings (ICSE Companion), pp. 65–69 (2022)
99. Yang, Z., Lei, H., Qian, W.: A hybrid formal verification system in coq for ensuring the reliability and security of ethereum-based service smart contracts. IEEE Access. **8**, 21411–21436 (2020b). https://doi.org/10.1109/ACCESS.2020.2969437
100. Li, Z., Lu, S., Zhang, R., Xue, R., Ma, W., Liang, R., Zhao, Z., Gao, S.: SmartFast: an accurate and robust formal analysis tool for ethereum smart contracts. Empir. Softw. Eng. **27**(7), 197 (2022)
101. Marescotti, M., Otoni, R., Alt, L., Eugster, P., Hyvärinen, A.E., Sharygina, N.: Accurate smart contract verification through direct modelling. In: Leveraging Applications of Formal Methods, Verification and Validation: Applications: 9th International Symposium on Leveraging Applications of Formal Methods, ISoLA 2020, Rhodes, Greece, October 20–30, 2020, Proceedings, Part III 9, pp. 178–194. Springer (2020)
102. Wang, Y., Lahiri, S.K., Chen, S., Pan, R., Dillig, I., Born, C., Naseer, I. Formal specification and verification of smart contracts for azure blockchain. arXiv preprint arXiv:1812.08829 (2018)
103. Mavridou, A., Laszka, A., Stachtiari, E., Dubey, A.: VeriSolid: correct-by-design smart contracts for ethereum. In: Financial Cryptography and Data Security: 23rd International Conference, FC 2019, pp. 446–465. Springer (2019)
104. Kalra, S., et al.: Zeus: analyzing safety of smart contracts. NDSS (2018)
105. Bhargavan, K., et al.: Formal verification of smart contracts: short paper. In: Proceedings of the 2016 ACM Workshop on Programming Languages and Analysis for Security, pp. 91–96 (2016)

106. Marescotti, M., Otoni, R., Alt, L., Eugster, P., Hyvärinen, A.E., Sharygina, N.: Accurate smart contract verification through direct modelling. In: Leveraging Applications of Formal Methods, Verification and Validation: Applications, pp. 178–194. Springer (2020)
107. Liu, J., Liu, Z.: A survey on security verification of blockchain smart contracts. IEEE Access. **7**, 77894–77904 (2019)
108. Wang, M., Wang, Z., Yu, B., Zhang, K.: WASAIUP: a demand-driven concolic fuzzer for EOSIO smart contracts. In: Proceedings of the 2023 IEEE 23rd International Conference on Software Quality, Reliability, and Security (QRS), pp. 150–161 (2023)
109. Choi, J., et al.: SMARTIAN: enhancing smart contract fuzzing with static and dynamic data-flow analyses. In: Proceedings of the 36th IEEE/ACM International Conference on Automated Software Engineering (ASE), pp. 227–239 (2021)
110. Nguyen, T.D., Pham, L.H., Sun, J., Lin, Y., Minh, Q.T.: sfuzz: an efficient adaptive fuzzer for solidity smart contracts. In: Proceedings of the ACM/IEEE 42nd International Conference on Software Engineering (ICSE), pp. 778–788 (2020)
111. Torres, C.F., Kol Iannillo, A., State, R.: ConFuzzius: a data dependency-aware hybrid fuzzer for smart contracts. In: Proceedings of the 2021 IEEE European Symposium on Security and Privacy (EuroS&P), pp. 103–119 (2021)
112. Wüstholz, V., Christakis, M.: Harvey: a greybox fuzzer for smart contracts. In: Proceedings of the 28th ACM Joint Meeting on European Software Engineering Conference and Symposium on the Foundations of Software Engineering (ESEC/FSE), pp. 1398–1409 (2020)
113. Feng, H., Ren, X., Wei, Q., Lei, Y.: MagicMirror: towards high-coverage fuzzing of smart contracts. In: Proceedings of the 2023 IEEE Conference on Software Testing, Verification and Validation (ICST), pp. 141–152 (2023)
114. Rodler, M., Paaßen, D., Li, W., Bernhard, L., Holz, T., Karame, G.O., Davi, L.: EF/CF: high-performance smart contract fuzzing for exploit generation. In: Proceedings of the 2023 IEEE 8th European Symposium on Security and Privacy (EuroS&P), pp. 449–471 (2023)
115. Shou, C., Tan, S.-H., Sen, K.: ItyFuzz: snapshot-based fuzzer for smart contracts. In: Proceedings of the 32nd ACM SIGSOFT International Symposium on Software Testing and Analysis (ISSTA), pp. 322–333 (2023)
116. Yang, H., Gu, X., Chen, X., Zheng, Z., Cui, Z.: CrossFuzz: cross-contract fuzzing for smart contract vulnerability detection. Sci. Comput. Program. **234**, 103076 (2024)
117. Mossberg, M., Manzano, F., Hennenfent, E., Groce, A., Grieco, G., Feist, J., Brunson, T., Dinaburg, A.: Manticore: a user-friendly symbolic execution framework for binaries and smart contracts. In: Proceedings of the 2019 34th IEEE/ACM International Conference on Automated Software Engineering (ASE), pp. 1186–1189 (2019)
118. Su, J., Dai, H.-N., Zhao, L., Zheng, Z., Luo, X.: Effectively generating vulnerable transaction sequences in smart contracts with reinforcement learning-guided fuzzing. In: Proceedings of the 37th IEEE/ACM International Conference on Automated Software Engineering (ASE), pp. 1–12 (2022)
119. Ashraf, I., et al.: GasFuzzer: fuzzing ethereum smart contract binaries to expose gas-oriented exception security vulnerabilities. IEEE Access. **8**, 99552–99564 (2020)
120. Durieux, T., Ferreira, J., Abreu, R., Cruz, P.: Empirical review of automated analysis tools on 47,587 ethereum smart contracts. In: Proceedings of the 42nd ACM/IEEE International Conference on Software Engineering (ICSE '20) (2020)
121. Pani, S., Nallagonda, H.V., Suman Prakash, V.R., Medicherla, R.K., Rajan, M.A.: Smart contract fuzzing for enterprises: the language-agnostic way. In: Proceedings of the 2022 14th International Conference on Communication Systems & Networks (COMSNETS), pp. 1–6 (2022)
122. Li, B., Pan, Z., Tianhui, H.: Redefender: detecting reentrancy vulnerabilities in smart contracts automatically. IEEE Trans. Reliab. **71**(2), 984–999 (2022)
123. Zhang, L., et al.: SeqFuzz: efficient kernel directed fuzzing via effective component inference. In: International Conference on Information Security and Cryptology. Springer Nature Singapore, Singapore (2025)

124. Olsthoorn, M., Stallenberg, D., van Deursen, A., et al.: Syntest-solidity: automated test case generation and fuzzing for smart contracts. In: Proceedings of the ACM/IEEE 44th International Conference on Software Engineering: Companion Proceedings (ICSE Companion), pp. 202–206 (2022)
125. Jiang, B., Liu, Y., Chan, W.: ContractFuzzer: fuzzing smart contracts for vulnerability detection. In: 2018 33rd IEEE/ACM International Conference on Automated Software Engineering, pp. 259–269. ASE (2018). https://doi.org/10.1145/3238147.3238177
126. Ashouri, M.: Etherolic: a practical security analyzer for smart contracts. In: Proceedings of the 35th Annual ACM Symposium on Applied Computing (2020)
127. Li, W., Wang, M., Yu, B., Shi, Y., Min, F., Shao, Y.: Grey-box fuzzing based on execution feedback for EOSIO smart contracts. In: Proceedings of the 2022 29th Asia-Pacific Software Engineering Conference (APSEC), pp. 1–10 (2022)
128. Maier, D., Fäßler, F., Seifert, J.-P.: Uncovering smart contract VM bugs via differential fuzzing. In: Reversing and Offensive-Oriented Trends Symposium, pp. 11–22 (2021)
129. Liu, C., Liu, H., Cao, Z., Chen, Z., Chen, B., Roscoe, B.: ReGuard: finding reentrancy bugs in smart contracts. In: Proceedings of the 40th International Conference on Software Engineering: Companion Proceedings (ICSE Companion), pp. 65–68 (2018)
130. Wu, S., Yu, Z., Wang, D., Zhou, Y., Liang, W., Wang, Z., Yuan, X.: DeFiRanger: detecting DeFi price manipulation attacks. In: IEEE Transactions on Dependable and Secure Computing, pp. 1–15 (2023)
131. Grieco, G., et al.: Echidna: effective, usable, and fast fuzzing for smart contracts. In: Proceedings of the 29th ACM SIGSOFT International Symposium on Software Testing and Analysis (2020)
132. Liu, Y., Li, Y., Lin, S.-W., Yan, Q.: ModCon: a model-based testing platform for smart contracts. In: Proceedings of the 28th ACM Joint European Software Engineering Conference and Symposium on the Foundations of Software Engineering (ESEC/FSE), pp. 1601–1605 (2020)
133. Lu, N., Wang, B., Zhang, Y., Shi, W., Esposito, C.: NeuCheck: a more practical ethereum smart contract security analysis tool. Softw. Pract. Experience. **51**(10), 2065–2084 (2021)
134. Mavridou, A., Laszka, A.: Tool demonstration: Fsolidm for designing secure ethereum smart contracts. In: Principles of Security and Trust: 7th International Conference, POST 2018, pp. 270–277. Springer (2018)
135. Zhang, P., Yu, J., Ji, S.: ADF-GA: data flow criterion-based test case generation for ethereum smart contracts. In: Proceedings of the IEEE/ACM 42nd International Conference on Software Engineering Workshops (ICSE Workshops), pp. 754–761 (2020)
136. Mughaid, A., Obeidat, I., Shdaifat, A., Alhayjna, R.'e., AlZu'bi, S.: Modelling and simulation for detecting vulnerabilities and security threats of smart contracts using machine learning. In: Proceedings of the 2023 Eighth International Conference on Fog and Mobile Edge Computing (FMEC), pp. 123–127 (2023)
137. Bragagnolo, S., et al.: SmartInspect: solidity smart contract inspector. In: International Workshop on Blockchain Oriented Software Engineering (IWBOSE), pp. 9–18 (2018)
138. Ferreira Torres, C., Jonker, H., State, R.: Elysium: context-aware bytecode-level patching to automatically heal vulnerable smart contracts. In: Proceedings of the 25th International Symposium on Research in Attacks, Intrusions and Defenses (2022)
139. Vivar, A.L., Orozco, A.L.S., Villalba, L.J.G.: A security framework for ethereum smart contracts. Comput. Commun. **172**, 119–129 (2021)
140. Yashavant, C.S.: SecSEC: securing smart ethereum contracts. In: Innovations in Software Engineering Conference, pp. 1–4 (2024)
141. Di Angelo, M., et al.: Smartbugs 2.0: an execution framework for weakness detection in ethereum smart contracts. In: 2023 38th IEEE/ACM International Conference on Automated Software Engineering (ASE). IEEE (2023)
142. Liao, J.-W., Tsai, T.-T., He, C.-K., Tien, C.-W.: SoliAudit: smart contract vulnerability assessment based on machine learning and fuzz testing. In: Proceedings of the 2019

Sixth International Conference on Internet of Things: Systems, Management and Security (IOTSMS), pp. 458–465 (2019)
143. Ressi, D., Romanello, R., Piazza, C., Rossi, S.: AI-enhanced blockchain technology: a review of advancements and opportunities. J. Netw. Comput. Appl. **2024**, 103858 (2024)
144. Yan, K., Zhang, J., Liu, X., Diao, W., Guo, S.: Bad apples: understanding the centralized security risks in decentralized ecosystems. In: Proceedings of the ACM Web Conference (WWW), pp. 2274–2283 (2023)
145. Ivanova, Y., Khritankov, A.: Regularmutator: a mutation testing tool for solidity smart contracts. Procedia Comput. Sci. **178**, 75–83 (2020)
146. Barboni, M., Morichetta, A., Polini, A., Casoni, F.: ReSuMo: a regression strategy and tool for mutation testing of solidity smart contracts. Softw. Qual. J. **32**(1), 225–253 (2024). https://doi.org/10.1007/s11219-023-09637-1
147. Barboni, M., Morichetta, A., Polini, A.: SuMo: a mutation testing approach and tool for the Ethereum blockchain. J. Syst. Softw. **193**, 111445 (2022)
148. Zhu, K., Wang, X., Chen, Z., Huang, S., Jie, W.: Evaluating ethereum reentrancy detection tools via mutation testing. In: Proceedings of the 2023 IEEE 34th International Symposium on Software Reliability Engineering (ISSRE), pp. 545–555 (2023)
149. Li, Z., Wu, H., Xu, J., Wang, X., Zhang, L., Chen, Z., Chen, Z.: MUSC: a tool for mutation testing of ethereum smart contracts. In: Proceedings of the 2019 34th IEEE/ACM International Conference on Automated Software Engineering (ASE), pp. 1198–1201 (2019)
150. Tikhomirov, S., Voskresenskaya, E., Ivanitskiy, I., Takhaviev, R., Marchenko, E., Alexandrov, Y.: SmartCheck: static analysis of ethereum smart contracts. In: Proceedings of the 2018 IEEE/ACM 1st International Workshop on Emerging Trends in Software Engineering for Blockchain (WETSEB), pp. 9–16 (2018)
151. Zhang, P., Xiao, F., Luo, X. SolidityCheck: quickly detecting smart contract problems through regular expressions. arXiv preprint arXiv:1911.09425 (2019)
152. Fei, J., Chen, X., Zhao, X.: Msmart: smart contract vulnerability analysis and improved strategies based on smartcheck. Appl. Sci. **13**(3), 1733 (2023)
153. Li, Z., Guo, W., Xu, Q., Xu, Y., Wang, H.: Research on blockchain smart contracts vulnerability and a code audit tool based on matching rules. In: Proceedings of the 2020 International Conference on Cyberspace Innovation of Advanced Technologies, pp. 484–489 (2020)
154. Chen, H., Zhao, X., Wang, Y., Zhen, Z.: SafeCheck: detecting smart contract vulnerabilities based on static program analysis methods. Secur. Priv. **2024**, e393 (2024)
155. Ferreira Torres, C., et al.: The eye of horus: spotting and analyzing attacks on Ethereum smart contracts. In: International Conference on Financial Cryptography and Data Security. Springer Berlin Heidelberg, Berlin, Heidelberg (2021)
156. Ivanov, N., Guo, H., Yan, Q.: Rectifying administrated ERC20 tokens. In: International Conference on Information and Communications Security. Springer International Publishing, Cham (2021)
157. Zhang, Y., Ma, J., Liu, X., Ye, G., Jin, Q., Ma, J., Zhou, Q.: An efficient smart contract vulnerability detector based on semantic contract graphs using approximate graph matching. IEEE Internet Things J. **10**(24), 21431–21442 (2023)
158. Dong, W., Zhou, T., Yan, D.: SolChecker: a practical static analysis framework for ethereum smart contract. In: Proceedings of the 2022 International Conference on Networks, Communications and Information Technology (CNCIT), pp. 179–186 (2022)
159. Praitheeshan, P., Pan, L., Zheng, X., Jolfaei, A., Doss, R.: SolGuard: preventing external call issues in smart contract-based multi-agent robotic systems. Inf. Sci. **579**, 150–166 (2021)
160. Chen, T., et al.: Tokenscope: automatically detecting inconsistent behaviors of cryptocurrency tokens in Ethereum. In: Proceedings of the 2019 ACM SIGSAC Conference on Computer and Communications Security (CCS), pp. 1503–1520 (2019)
161. Shah, N.K., et al.: Smart contract vulnerability detection techniques for hyperledger fabric. In: 2023 IEEE 8th International Conference for Convergence in Technology (I2CT). IEEE (2023)

162. Ye, J., Ma, M., Lin, Y., Ma, L., Xue, Y., Zhao, J.: Vulpedia: detecting vulnerable ethereum smart contracts via abstracted vulnerability signatures. J. Syst. Softw. **192**, 111410 (2022)
163. Lai, E., Luo, W.: Static analysis of integer overflow of smart contracts in ethereum. In: Proceedings of the 2020 4th International Conference on Cryptography, Security and Privacy, pp. 110–115 (2020)
164. Li, W., He, J., Zhao, G., Yang, J., Li, S., Lai, R., Li, P., Tang, H., Luo, H., Zhou, Z.: EOSIOAnalyzer: an effective static analysis vulnerability detection framework for EOSIO smart contracts. In: Proceedings of the 2022 IEEE 46th Annual Computers, Software, and Applications Conference (COMPSAC), pp. 746–756 (2022)
165. Ducasse, S., et al.: SmartAnvil: open-source tool suite for smart contract analysis. In: Blockchain and Web 3.0, pp. 192–222. Routledge (2019)
166. Liao, Z., Zheng, Z., Chen, X., Nan, Y.: SmartDagger: a bytecode-based static analysis approach for detecting cross-contract vulnerability. In: Proceedings of the 31st ACM SIGSOFT International Symposium on Software Testing and Analysis (ISSTA), pp. 752–764 (2022)
167. Ayub, M., et al.: Storage state analysis and extraction of ethereum blockchain smart contracts. ACM Trans. Softw. Eng. Methodol. **32**(3), 1–32 (2023)
168. Hu, T., et al.: Detect defects of solidity smart contract based on the knowledge graph. IEEE Trans. Reliab. **73**(1), 186–202 (2023)
169. Liu, Y., Li, Y., Lin, S.-W., Artho, C.: Finding permission bugs in smart contracts with role mining. In: Proceedings of the 31st ACM SIGSOFT International Symposium on Software Testing and Analysis (ISSTA), pp. 716–727 (2022)
170. Beillahi, S.M., et al.: Automated auditing of price gouging TOD vulnerabilities in smart contracts. In: 2022 IEEE International Conference on Blockchain and Cryptocurrency (ICBC). IEEE (2022)
171. Songsom, N., Werapun, W., Suaboot, J., Rattanavipanon, N.: The SWC-based security analysis tool for smart contract vulnerability detection. In: Proceedings of the 2022 6th International Conference on Information Technology (InCIT), pp. 74–77 (2022)
172. Wang, H., Li, Y., Lin, S.-W., Ma, L., Liu, Y.: VULTRON: catching vulnerable smart contracts once and for all. In: Proceedings of the 2019 IEEE/ACM 41st International Conference on Software Engineering: New Ideas and Emerging Results (ICSE-NIER), pp. 1–4 (2019)
173. Ramakrishnan, G., Rehan, M., Sujatha, G.: Solidity vulnerability scanner. In: Proceedings of the 2022 International Conference on Data Science, Agents & Artificial Intelligence (ICDSAAI), pp. 1–5 (2022)
174. Zhou, E., et al.: Security assurance for smart contract. In: 2018 9th IFIP International Conference on New Technologies, Mobility and Security (NTMS), IEEE (2018)
175. Dua, R.: Ethlint: linter for solidity code. GitHub (2024)
176. Azzopardi, S., Ellul, J., Pace, G.J.: Monitoring smart contracts: contractlarva and open challenges beyond. In: International Conference on Runtime Verification. Springer International Publishing, Cham (2018)
177. Ali, I.M. Efficient runtime protection for smart contracts. Diss. Hamad Bin Khalifa University (Qatar) (2023)
178. Ma, F., Fu, Y., Ren, M., Wang, M., Jiang, Y., Zhang, K., Li, H.: EVM: from offline detection to online reinforcement for ethereum virtual machine. In: Proceedings of the 2019 IEEE 26th International Conference on Software Analysis, Evolution and Reengineering (SANER), pp. 554–558 (2019)
179. Zhang, X., Sun, W., Xu, Z., Cheng, H., Cai, C., Cui, H., Li, Q.: EVM-Shield: in-contract state access control for fast vulnerability detection and prevention. IEEE Trans. Inf. Forensics Secur. **19**, 2517–2532 (2024)
180. Zhang, J., Gao, J., Li, Y., Chen, Z., Guan, Z., Chen, Z.: XScope: hunting for cross-chain bridge attacks. In: Proceedings of the 2022 IEEE/ACM International Conference on Automated Software Engineering (ASE), pp. 1–4 (2022)
181. Fortino, G., et al.: Detecting ethereum smart contract vulnerabilities via bytecode image analysis. IEEE Internet Things J. (2026)

182. Nassirzadeh, B., Sun, H., Banescu, S., Ganesh, V.: Gas gauge: a security analysis tool for smart contract out-of-gas vulnerabilities. In: Mathematical Research for Blockchain Economy, pp. 143–167. Springer (2023)
183. Stegeman, L.: Solitor: runtime verification of smart contracts on the ethereum network. Master's thesis, University of Twente (2018)
184. Wu, X., Du, X., Yang, Q., Liu, A., Wang, N., Wang, W.: TaintGuard: preventing implicit privilege leakage in smart contracts based on taint tracking at abstract syntax tree level. J. Syst. Archit. **141**, 102925 (2023)
185. Veloso, N.: Conkas: Concolic Analysis for Ethereum Smart Contracts. GitHub (2024). Accessed 11 June 2024
186. Norvill, R., Pontiveros, B.B.F., State, R., Cullen, A.: Visual emulation for ethereum's virtual machine. In: Proceedings of the 2018 IEEE/IFIP Network Operations and Management Symposium (NOMS), pp. 1–4 (2018)
187. Zhang, W., Banescu, S., Pasos, L., Stewart, S., Ganesh, V.: MPro: combining static and symbolic analysis for scalable testing of smart contracts. In: Proceedings of the 2019 IEEE 30th International Symposium on Software Reliability Engineering (ISSRE), pp. 456–462 (2019)
188. Chinen, Y., Yanai, N., Cruz, J.P., Okamura, S.: RA: hunting for re-entrancy attacks in ethereum smart contracts via static analysis. In: Proceedings of the 2020 IEEE International Conference on Blockchain, pp. 327–336 (2020)
189. Wu, J., Wang, Y., Wang, R., Chen, J., Zheng, Z.: Can neural networks help smart contract testing? An empirical study. In: Proceedings of the 14th Asia-Pacific Symposium on Internetware, pp. 79–89 (2023)
190. Kim, S., Hwang, S.K.: EtherDiffer: differential testing on RPC services of ethereum nodes. In: Proceedings of the 31st ACM Joint European Software Engineering Conference and Symposium on the Foundations of Software Engineering (ESEC/FSE), pp. 1333–1344 (2023)
191. Torres, C.F., Steichen, M., State, R.: The art of the scam: demystifying honeypots in ethereum smart contracts. In: Proceedings of the 28th USENIX Security Symposium (USENIX Security '19), pp. 1591–1607 (2019)
192. Fang, Y., Wang, C., Sun, Z., Cheng, H.: Jyane: detecting reentrancy vulnerabilities based on path profiling method. In: Proceedings of the IEEE 27th International Conference on Parallel and Distributed Systems (ICPADS), pp. 274–282 (2021)
193. Wang, S., Zhang, C., Zhe, S.: Detecting nondeterministic payment bugs in ethereum smart contracts. In: Proceedings of the ACM on Programming Languages 3, OOPSLA, pp. 1–29 (2019)
194. Ma, F., Xu, Z., Ren, M., Yin, Z., Chen, Y., Qiao, L., Gu, B., Li, H., Jiang, Y., Sun, J.: Pluto: exposing vulnerabilities in inter-contract scenarios. IEEE Trans. Softw. Eng. **48**(11), 4380–4396 (2022)
195. Bose, P., et al.: Sailfish: vetting smart contract state-inconsistency bugs in seconds. In: 2022 IEEE Symposium on Security and Privacy (SP). IEEE (2022)
196. Rodler, M., Li, W., Karame, G.O., Davi, L.: Sereum: protecting existing smart contracts against re-entrancy attacks. arXiv preprint arXiv:1812.05934 (2018)
197. Yang, Z., Liu, H., Li, Y., Zheng, H., Lin, W., Chen, B.: Seraph: enabling cross-platform security analysis for EVM and Wasm smart contracts. In: Proceedings of the ACM/IEEE 42nd International Conference on Software Engineering: Companion Proceedings (ICSE Companion), pp. 21–24 (2020)
198. Wu, J., et al.: Can neural networks help smart contract testing? An empirical study. In: Proceedings of the 14th Asia-Pacific Symposium on Internetware (2023)
199. Yao, Y., Li, H., Yang, X., Le, Y.: An improved vulnerability detection system of smart contracts based on symbolic execution. In: Proceedings of the 2022 IEEE International Conference on Big Data, pp. 3225–3234 (2022)
200. Krupp, J., Rossow, C.: teEther: gnawing at ethereum to automatically exploit smart contracts. In: Proceedings of the 27th USENIX Security Symposium (USENIX Security 18), pp. 1317–1333 (2018)

201. Ma, C., Song, W., Huang, J.: TransRacer: function dependence-guided transaction race detection for smart contracts. In: Proceedings of the 31st ACM Joint European Software Engineering Conference and Symposium on the Foundations of Software Engineering (ESEC/FSE), pp. 947–959 (2023)
202. Weiss, K., Schütte, J.: Annotary: a concolic execution system for developing secure smart contracts. In: Computer Security—ESORICS 2019, pp. 747–766. Springer (2019)
203. Chen, J., et al.: DefectChecker: automated smart contract defect detection by analyzing EVM bytecode. IEEE Trans. Softw. Eng. **48**(7), 2189–2207 (2022)
204. Frank, J., Aschermann, C., Holz, T.: {ETHBMC}: a bounded model checker for smart contracts. In: 29th USENIX Security Symposium (USENIX Security 20) (2020)
205. Li, P., Li, S., Ding, M., Yu, J., Zhang, H., Zhou, X., Li, J.: A vulnerability detection framework for hyperledger fabric smart contracts based on dynamic and static analysis. In: Proceedings of the 26th International Conference on Evaluation and Assessment in Software Engineering (EASE), pp. 366–374 (2022)
206. Liu, Y., Cai, L.: Honeytoken-Detector: a symbolic execution-based honeypot token detection tool. In: Proceedings of the 26th ACIS International Winter Conference on Software Engineering, Artificial Intelligence, Networking and Parallel/Distributed Computing (SNPD-Winter), pp. 134–139 (2023)
207. Hildenbrandt, E, et al.: Kevm: a complete semantics of the ethereum virtual machine (2017)
208. Fu, M., et al.: A critical-path-coverage-based vulnerability detection method for smart contracts. IEEE Access. **7**, 147327–147344 (2019)
209. Yang, S., Chen, J., Zheng, Z.: Definition and detection of defects in NFT smart contracts. In: Proceedings of the 32nd ACM SIGSOFT International Symposium on Software Testing and Analysis (ISSTA), pp. 373–384 (2023)
210. Torres, C.F., Schütte, J., State, R.: Osiris: hunting for integer bugs in ethereum smart contracts. In: Proceedings of the 34th Annual Computer Security Applications Conference (ACSAC), pp. 664–676 (2018)
211. Zheng, P., Zheng, Z., Luo, X.: Park: accelerating smart contract vulnerability detection via parallel-fork symbolic execution. In: Proceedings of the 31st ACM SIGSOFT International Symposium on Software Testing and Analysis (ISSTA), pp. 740–751 (2022)
212. Lin, S.-W., Tolmach, P., Liu, Y., Li, Y.: Solsee: a source-level symbolic execution engine for solidity. In: Proceedings of the 30th ACM Joint European Software Engineering Conference and Symposium on the Foundations of Software Engineering (ESEC/FSE), pp. 1687–1691 (2022)
213. Feng, Y., Torlak, E., Bodík, R.: Summary-based symbolic evaluation for smart contracts. In: Proceedings of the 35th IEEE/ACM International Conference on Automated Software Engineering (2020)
214. Jiang, B., et al.: WANA: symbolic execution of wasm bytecode for extensible smart contract vulnerability detection. In: 2021 IEEE 21st International Conference on Software Quality, Reliability and Security (QRS), p. 2021. IEEE
215. Prechtel, D., Groß, T., Müller, T.: Evaluating spread of 'gasless send'in ethereum smart contracts. In: 2019 10th IFIP International Conference on New Technologies, Mobility and Security (NTMS). IEEE (2019)
216. Wang, Z., Dai, W., Choo, K.-K.R., Jin, H., Zou, D.: FSFC: an input filter-based secure framework for smart contracts. J. Netw. Comput. Appl. **154**, 102530 (2020)
217. Keoleian, P.: pakala: a tool for packaging and publishing Python libraries. GitHub repository (2024). https://github.com/palkeo/pakala
218. Xue, Y., Ma, M., Lin, Y., Sui, Y., Ye, J., Peng, T.: Cross-contract static analysis for detecting practical reentrancy vulnerabilities in smart contracts. In: Proceedings of the 35th IEEE/ACM International Conference on Automated Software Engineering, pp. 1029–1040 (2020)
219. Xu, J., Shen, J., Tan, S.-H.: DoSChecker: an efficient and dedicated tool for detecting DoS vulnerability in smart contracts. In: Proceedings of the 2023 International Conference on Data Security and Privacy Protection (DSPP), pp. 22–31 (2023)

220. Gao, J., et al.: Easyflow: keep ethereum away from overflow. In: 2019 IEEE/ACM 41st International Conference on Software Engineering: Companion Proceedings (ICSE-Companion). IEEE (2019)
221. Qian, P., He, J., Lili, L., Shucheng, W., Zhen, L., Liwei, W., Zhou, Y., He, Q.: Demystifying random number in ethereum smart contract: taxonomy, vulnerability identification, and attack detection. IEEE Trans. Softw. Eng. **49**(7), 3793–3810 (2023)
222. Zhang, J., Li, Y., Gao, J., Guan, Z., Chen, Z.: SigUARD: detecting signature-related vulnerabilities in smart contracts. In: Proceedings of the 2023 IEEE/ACM 45th International Conference on Software Engineering: Companion Proceedings (ICSE-Companion), pp. 31–35 (2023)
223. Samreen, N.F., Alalfi, M.H.: SmartScan: an approach to detect denial of service vulnerability in ethereum smart contracts. In: Proceedings of the 2021 IEEE/ACM 4th International Workshop on Emerging Trends in Software Engineering for Blockchain (WETSEB), pp. 17–26 (2021)
224. Liu, Y., Li, Y.: InvCon: a dynamic invariant detector for ethereum smart contracts. In: Proceedings of the 37th IEEE/ACM International Conference on Automated Software Engineering (ASE), pp. 1–4 (2022)
225. Revere, R.O.: Solgraph: Visualizing Control Flow of a Solidity Contract. GitHub (2018). Accessed 14 June 2024
226. ConsenSys: Mythril: security analysis tool for ethereum smart contracts. GitHub (2018). Accessed 14 June 2024
227. Mueller, B.: Awesome MythX smart contract security tools. GitHub (2020). Accessed 14 June 2024

Chapter 10
Countermeasures and Best Practices in Smart Contracts

Abstract This chapter examines countermeasures and best practices designed to strengthen smart contract security, emphasizing the need for layered approaches that span prevention, containment, and recovery. It discusses proxy upgradeability as a means of overcoming immutability, circuit breakers and emergency stop for halting suspicious activity, defensive coding patterns such as check-effects-interactions and pull-over-push, and arithmetic protections including SafeMath. It highlights formal verification and property testing as rigorous methods for mathematically proving contract correctness, while emerging techniques in automatic repair and patch suggestion illustrate the growing role of automation and AI in vulnerability mitigation. In addition, it presents governance-based controls, including multisig wallets, DAO-led upgrades, and timelocks, as mechanisms to embed human consensus into security decisions, complemented by runtime monitoring platforms like Forta and OpenZeppelin Sentinel that enable real-time detection and response. Its comparative analysis evaluates countermeasures by scope, integration, and effectiveness, showing that preventive measures reduce common coding risks, upgradeability and governance provide corrective flexibility, and monitoring systems add responsive protection. Furthermore, its recommendations stress continuous security practices, reliance on audited libraries, automated analysis, formal verification for high-stakes protocols, cautious use of proxy patterns, emergency response readiness, thorough auditing, and governance structures aligned with transparency and accountability. As a final point, this chapter concludes that no single measure is sufficient; instead, resilient smart contracts demand carefully composed, multi-layered defenses that evolve alongside decentralized applications.
Smart contracts form the foundational logic of decentralized applications, automating value transfer, governance, and complex interactions on the blockchain [1, 2]. Yet their immutability, while critical for trust and transparency, also renders them uniquely vulnerable; any error, once deployed, can lead to irreversible financial loss or systemic compromise. As the scale and complexity of smart contract ecosystems grow, so too does the need for structured, multi-layered security approaches that extend beyond vulnerability detection. This chapter presents a comprehensive exploration of countermeasures and best practices designed to mitigate security risks in smart contracts [1, 3, 4]. It examines both theoretical strategies and practical

S. HajiHosseinKhani et al., *Understanding Cybersecurity for Smart Contracts*,
https://doi.org/10.1007/978-3-032-28863-9_10

implementations, encompassing preventative coding patterns, upgrade mechanisms, formal verification, runtime defenses, and governance controls. By evaluating how these techniques function individually and in combination, this chapter aims to equip developers, auditors, and protocol architects with a deeper understanding of how to design, deploy, and maintain secure smart contract systems that are resilient to evolving threats [4, 5].

10.1 Strategies to Mitigate Vulnerabilities

Mitigating smart contract vulnerabilities requires a combination of proactive and reactive strategies embedded early in development to address the unique immutability and security constraints of blockchain environments. This subsection presents a range of countermeasures that are used in practice to secure smart contracts. Each strategy is examined from both a theoretical and practical standpoint, illustrating how vulnerabilities can be addressed through sound architectural design, verified logic, modular patterns, and automated tooling. The focus spans from code-level practices, such as secure arithmetic and defensive interaction ordering, to system-level safeguards including proxy-based upgradeability, governance control, and real-time threat monitoring [1, 3, 6].

10.1.1 Proxy Upgradeability

One of the most critical challenges in securing smart contracts arises from their immutability [1, 2]. Once deployed to the blockchain, the contract's code cannot be modified, leaving no room for conventional patching if a vulnerability is discovered [3, 7]. To address this limitation, the concept of proxy upgradeability has emerged as a foundational countermeasure that enables the modification of contract logic while preserving user data and deployed addresses [1, 6, 8].

The core idea behind proxy upgradeability is the separation of contract logic and storage [2, 6]. In this pattern, a proxy contract serves as the single point of interaction for users, while delegating execution to a secondary implementation contract using the delegatecall opcode. Because the delegatecall runs in the proxy's context, all state changes affect the proxy's storage rather than the implementation. When vulnerability is discovered, or functionality needs to be extended, developers can deploy a new implementation contract and simply point the proxy to the new logic without losing any data or requiring users to migrate [9].

There are several variations of the proxy pattern, with the Transparent Proxy and the Universal Upgradeable Proxy Standard (UUPS) being among the most widely used [1, 8]. The Transparent Proxy pattern, popularized by OpenZeppelin, enforces access control by distinguishing between administrative and user interactions. In contrast, the UUPS model introduces a more gas-efficient structure by embedding upgrade logic directly in the implementation contract, thereby reducing indirection and simplifying governance.

A minimal example of a UUPS-style upgrade function may look as follows:

```
function upgradeTo(address newImplementation) external
onlyOwner {
   _setImplementation(newImplementation);
}
```

This simple function allows the contract owner to change the implementation address, effectively upgrading the contract logic. Of course, such upgradeability must be carefully protected to avoid unauthorized takeovers [1, 7]. Only privileged entities, such as multisig wallets or DAO governance, should be granted access to perform upgrades [4].

In practice, several tools have made proxy deployment and upgrade management safer and more accessible. The OpenZeppelin Upgrades Plugin provides standardized templates and deployment scripts compatible with Hardhat and Truffle environments, ensuring compliance with EIP-1967 storage slot standards. The OpenZeppelin Defender Admin platform further enhances the upgrade process by offering a secure dashboard where contract administrators can review, approve, and schedule upgrades in coordination with governance workflows [10].

Despite its power, proxy upgradeability introduces risks of its own. Developers must ensure the upgrade logic itself is sound and that each new implementation is thoroughly audited, as a flawed upgrade could permanently compromise the contract [3, 7]. Moreover, because the state is retained across upgrades, even small misalignments in storage layout between old and new implementations can lead to critical runtime errors or corruption.

Ultimately, proxy upgradeability is a robust countermeasure that balances technical flexibility with operational continuity [6, 10]. It enables post-deployment patching of vulnerabilities, facilitates the evolution of contract features, and supports long-term maintainability, an essential requirement for modern decentralized applications operating on a scale [1, 2, 9].

10.1.2 Circuit Breakers and Emergency Stops

In the dynamic and often unpredictable environment of blockchain-based applications, the ability to respond swiftly to emergent threats is essential. Circuit breakers, also known as emergency stop mechanisms, are preventive and corrective countermeasures designed to halt contract operations in the event of abnormal or malicious behavior. This strategy does not eliminate vulnerabilities outright, but it mitigates their impact by providing a mechanism to pause critical functionality before further damage occurs.

The core principle behind circuit breakers is operational containment. Contracts often hold substantial value or provide crucial financial services, making them prime targets for exploitation. If a vulnerability is discovered or suspicious activity is detected, such as a reentrancy loop, an unexpected flash-loan inflow, or a logic flaw in fund distribution, a circuit breaker can immediately freeze the contract's sensitive functions [6, 11, 12]. This pause buys valuable time for developers or governance mechanisms to investigate the issue, implement a fix (if upgradable), or migrate user assets to a secure environment [1, 9].

Implementing a circuit breaker in Solidity typically involves a paused state variable and a modifier that guards critical functions [9, 13]. The contract owner or an authorized role can trigger or lift the pause [4, 10]. A simple implementation looks like this:

```
bool public paused = false;


modifier whenNotPaused() {
  require(!paused, "Contract is paused");
  _;
}

function pause() external onlyOwner {
  paused = true;
}

function unpause() external onlyOwner {
  paused = false;
}

function withdraw(uint amount) external whenNotPaused {
  // critical logic
}
```

This pattern is foundational for emergency response in smart contracts and is supported by widely adopted libraries. The OpenZeppelin Pausable module, for example, provides reusable components that encapsulate this logic in a secure and auditable manner. Developers can simply inherit from the Pausable Base contract and integrate pause checks into their business logic, significantly reducing implementation risk [9, 13].

In more sophisticated architectures, circuit breakers can be coupled with automated triggers and monitoring systems. When integrated with platforms like OpenZeppelin Defender Sentinel, contracts can respond to predefined alerts, such as anomalous transaction volume or gas consumption, by automatically executing pause functions. This reactive defense model reduces the time window between exploit detection and response, potentially preventing cascading failures or massive financial losses [6, 10].

However, circuit breakers must be carefully balanced against usability and decentralization [7, 10]. In permissionless DeFi protocols, giving unilateral power to a single owner may raise concerns about centralization and abuse. For this reason, some systems implement governance-based emergency stops that require multisig or DAO consensus to trigger or lift a pause. This distributes power more equitably while still ensuring safety during crises [2].

While circuit breakers do not eliminate vulnerabilities at their source, they are an essential component of a defense-in-depth strategy. By enabling fast, controlled shutdowns of vulnerable functions, they limit damage, preserve user assets, and maintain stakeholder trust during high-risk situations. Their widespread adoption across major DeFi platforms underscores their value as a practical and reliable countermeasure to evolving threats.

10.1.3 Defensive Coding Patterns

Many smart contract vulnerabilities can be traced back not to exotic attack vectors but to predictable coding mistakes that could have been avoided through disciplined design patterns [1, 3, 13]. Defensive coding refers to a set of best practices and structural principles aimed at reducing a contract's attack surface from the outset. Rather than relying solely on post-deployment auditing or tooling, these patterns embed security-conscious thinking directly into the contract's architecture, helping to prevent critical classes of vulnerabilities such as reentrancy, access control bypass, gas griefing, and state inconsistency [1, 5, 12].

One of the most well-established defensive patterns in Solidity is the checks-effects-interactions pattern [13]. This simple yet powerful sequence mandates that all validations (checks) occur before any state changes (effects), and that all external calls (interactions) are deferred to the end of the function. This order prevents state inconsistencies during reentrancy, ensuring that malicious external contracts cannot exploit partially updated internal state [12, 14].

A typical implementation of this pattern looks like the following:

```
function withdraw(uint amount) external {
  require(balances[msg.sender] >= amount, "Insufficient
balance"); // Check
  balances[msg.sender] -= amount;
// Effect
  (bool success, ) = msg.sender.call{value: amount}("");
// Interaction
  require(success, "Transfer failed");
}
```

By reducing internal balance before interacting with the external recipient, this design ensures that even if the external call reenters the contract, the balance is already updated and thus cannot be exploited again. This structure proved especially important in the aftermath of the infamous DAO attack, which exploited improper ordering of state updates and external calls [7, 13, 15].

Another essential pattern is the pull-over-push payment model. Rather than automatically transferring funds to recipients (which could fail or be intercepted), contracts store balances and allow users to withdraw their funds manually. This avoids execution dependencies on unknown external addresses and ensures that funds are never locked due to failed transfers [1, 5].

In addition to ordering and flow design, access control mechanisms must be tightly scoped. Critical functions such as upgrades, withdrawals, or parameter updates should only be callable by authorized parties. This can be implemented using the onlyOwner modifier or, in more advanced systems, role-based access control via AccessControl modules provided by OpenZeppelin [2]. The lack of proper access restrictions has led to many avoidable exploits, in which attackers manipulated contract parameters or called privileged functions due to unguarded public visibility [9, 13].

Gas-related considerations also factor in defensive coding. Contracts should avoid code paths that consume unbounded gas or rely on assumptions about fixed gas stipends. Fallback functions, for instance, must remain simple to avoid denial-of-service (DoS) risks arising from out-of-gas errors. Moreover, assert() should be used only to enforce invariants, while require() should handle user-defined conditions, ensuring clear error propagation without excessive gas consumption.

To assist in enforcing these patterns, a range of practical tools exists. Slither, a popular static analysis tool, includes detectors for insecure design patterns, such as violations of checks-effects-interactions or use of dangerous low-level calls. Likewise, the SWC Registry maintained by ConsenSys classifies known vulnerability patterns with unique IDs and descriptions, providing developers with a reference catalog of security antipatterns to avoid. Incorporating these tools into the development pipeline helps reinforce defensive practices across teams and projects [4, 6].

Ultimately, defensive coding patterns are not just stylistic conventions; they are first-line countermeasures that can neutralize entire classes of exploits before they ever reach production. When consistently applied, these patterns serve as a foundational layer of security, enabling developers to build contracts that are not only functional but resilient by design [10].

10.1.4 Safe Math and Arithmetic Protections

Arithmetic operations are fundamental to the logic of most smart contracts, whether managing token balances, calculating interest, or enforcing thresholds. Yet in earlier versions of Solidity (prior to 0.8.0), these basic operations had a dangerous pitfall:

they used unchecked modular arithmetic, meaning that integer overflows and underflows would not trigger errors. This behavior allowed attackers to exploit logic that silently wrapped around values, often leading to critical breaches of balance, integrity, or access control mechanisms.

To address this, one of the earliest and most widely adopted countermeasures in the Solidity ecosystem was the SafeMath library. Developed by OpenZeppelin, SafeMath wraps arithmetic operations with overflow checks. If an operation results in a value outside the bounds of the unsigned integer type (e.g., uint256), the transaction reverts, preserving contract integrity.

A typical example of SafeMath usage looks like this:

```
using SafeMath for uint256;

function transfer(address recipient, uint256 amount)
public {
  balances[msg.sender] = balances[msg.sender].sub(amount);
// Checks for underflow
  balances[recipient] = balances[recipient].add(amount);
// Checks for overflow
}
```

In this case, if msg.sender does not have enough tokens, sub() will revert, preventing an underflow that would otherwise leave the sender with a massive balance. Similarly, add() ensures that the recipient's new balance remains within the allowable numeric range.

While SafeMath became an essential security tool in early Solidity development, a major improvement came with Solidity 0.8.0, which introduced built-in overflow and underflow protection. Arithmetic operations in this and later versions now revert automatically on overflow, making external libraries like SafeMath redundant in most cases. However, understanding and applying the principle behind SafeMath remains valuable, particularly for legacy contracts or developers working across multiple environments.

Beyond overflow protection, arithmetic safety also involves guarding against division by zero, incorrect assumptions about token decimals, and loss of precision in integer division. Developers must validate inputs and avoid unsafe mathematical assumptions, especially when dealing with user-controlled values or multi-token accounting logic [3, 6].

In terms of tooling, static analyzers such as Mythril and Slither can detect potential arithmetic vulnerabilities. For instance, they can identify unsafe operations, unguarded divisions, or failure to check the return value of critical calculations. In addition, the Securify analyzer flags dangerous arithmetic constructs and suggests appropriate fixes or safer alternatives.

In summary, arithmetic protections are a foundational countermeasure that prevents subtle bugs from escalating into full-scale exploits. While Solidity's built-in checks now handle most overflow and underflow cases, the legacy of SafeMath continues to inform secure development practices. Careful treatment of numerical operations through code, libraries, and analysis tools remains essential to the integrity of financial logic in smart contracts [10].

10.1.5 Formal Verification and Property Testing

While static analysis and manual auditing help identify known vulnerability patterns, they are often limited in scope and depend on human interpretation. In contrast, formal verification provides mathematical guarantees about the correctness and security of smart contracts. This countermeasure involves specifying desired contract properties in a formal language and using theorem provers or model checkers to exhaustively verify that the contract upholds these properties under all possible execution paths.

The central concept of formal verification is to shift from detecting bugs to proving their absence, at least with respect to a predefined specification. For example, a developer may want to formally prove that the total supply of a token never exceeds a hard cap, or that a withdrawal function cannot result in a negative balance. These properties are typically expressed as invariants, preconditions, and postconditions over the contract's state variables.

Consider the following formal specification for a simple ERC-20 token:

- Invariant: balances[account] ≥ 0
- Invariant: totalSupply = $\sum$ balances[all accounts]
- Precondition: msg.sender has sufficient balance to transfer
- Postcondition: msg.sender balance decreases by the amount
- Postcondition: recipient balance increases by amount

Once defined, these properties can be verified using formal tools that simulate or symbolically reason about every possible execution scenario. This process can catch subtle corner cases and logic errors that might otherwise escape both static analysis and testing.

Among the leading practical tools for formal verification in Ethereum is Certora Prover, a commercial-grade solution that enables developers to write formal specifications using the Certora Verification Language (CVL). This tool supports verification of complex behaviors in DeFi protocols and has been widely adopted by major platforms such as Aave, Compound, and Balancer. Another important tool is VeriSol, developed by Microsoft, which translates Solidity contracts into intermediate representations for formal verification against user-defined specifications. By enabling rigorous analysis of contract logic, VeriSol helps detect potential vulnerabilities early in the development process.

Building on a more foundational level, KEVM provides formal semantics for the Ethereum Virtual Machine using the K-framework. This tool verifies smart contracts at the bytecode level, providing precise execution models that reflect the contracts' actual behavior on the chain. In parallel, symbolic execution tools like Manticore and Mythril also contribute to formal reasoning. While primarily designed for dynamic analysis and property-based fuzzing, these tools offer limited support for verifying specific properties through symbolic exploration of execution paths.

The importance of formal verification becomes especially apparent in high-stakes applications such as lending protocols, decentralized exchanges, and DAO governance systems. In these contexts, a single flaw in logic can result in catastrophic financial losses or systemic failure, making rigorous formal analysis a critical component of secure smart contract development.

Despite its strengths, formal verification does have limitations. It requires substantial expertise in formal methods, and the specification itself must be both correct and complete. Moreover, because verification is performed against a fixed set of properties, any security assumption not explicitly stated will remain untested. Therefore, formal verification should be viewed as a complement, not a replacement, for other countermeasures such as testing, auditing, and runtime monitoring.

In recent years, integrating formal tools into CI/CD pipelines has become more feasible, lowering the barrier to adoption. Leading DeFi protocols now integrate property testing, symbolic reasoning, and formal proofs into their continuous security assurance process. Ultimately, formal verification provides one of the most rigorous and reliable means of securing smart contracts. By encoding and proving core system guarantees, it establishes a provable safety baseline, making it a vital countermeasure for high-assurance decentralized applications.

10.1.6 Automatic Repair and Patch Suggestions

As the complexity of smart contracts grows and the attack landscape evolves, the need to not only identify vulnerabilities but also automatically repair or mitigate them becomes increasingly important. Traditional detection tools typically highlight security issues, leaving it to the developer to understand, diagnose, and resolve them. In contrast, automatic repair tools aim to bridge the gap between vulnerability detection and resolution by offering patch suggestions or, in some cases, directly generating corrected code.

The theoretical foundation of automatic repair lies in pattern recognition and semantic analysis. When a tool identifies vulnerability, such as an unchecked external call, reentrancy risk, or unsafe arithmetic, it can map the finding to a known category with associated fix strategies. This is typically done by leveraging formal rules, code transformation templates, or even learning-based models trained on large corpora of secure and insecure code snippets. These strategies enable tools to synthesize code patches that either eliminate vulnerabilities or enforce constraints that block their exploitation.

For example, in the case of a reentrancy vulnerability, the recommended repair is often adding a reentrancy guard, a simple yet effective countermeasure that prevents recursive entry into a function [14]. A repair tool might automatically inject a nonReentrant modifier and ensure that all affected functions inherit its protection:

```
bool private locked;

modifier nonReentrant() {
 require(!locked, "ReentrancyGuard: reentrant call");
 locked = true;
 _;
 locked = false;
}
```

This pattern ensures that once a function begins execution, any recursive attempt to re-enter it via an external call will fail, thereby neutralizing one of the most common and dangerous classes of exploits in Ethereum.

Several practical tools now integrate automatic repair or patch recommendation features into the smart contract development process. One such tool is SmartShield, a framework that automatically fixes vulnerable smart contracts by rewriting them with safer constructs. It analyzes the contract code, identifies patterns associated with known vulnerabilities, often using classifications like the Smart Contract Weakness Classification (SWC), and applies targeted code transformations to mitigate or eliminate the detected issues.

In parallel, toolchains such as ReentrancyDetector combined with SmartFuzz go beyond detection by offering concrete suggestions for mitigating reentrancy vulnerabilities. These recommendations often include reordering state-changing operations or inserting appropriate guards to prevent recursive calls, effectively reducing the potential for exploitation.

Another widely adopted mitigation tool is ReentrancyGuard from OpenZeppelin. While not a repair tool in the strictest sense, it functions as a reusable contract module that developers can integrate to enforce non-reentrant behavior across multiple functions. Its ease of integration and standardized logic make it a practical follow-up measure after detecting reentrancy risks.

Beyond these established tools, emerging research is investigating AI-assisted approaches to vulnerability repair [6, 10, 16]. Techniques involving large language models and program synthesis are being explored to provide secure code completions and real-time patch suggestions during development. These AI-driven systems aim to embed security remediation directly into the developer's workflow, minimizing the time between vulnerability detection and response.

However, automatic repair systems are not without limitations. Generated patches must be carefully reviewed to ensure they do not introduce new vulnerabilities, break intended functionality, or conflict with business logic. In critical systems, no patch should be deployed without thorough testing, formal verification, or at least a manual audit. Additionally, many repair tools focus on common vulnerability types, and their effectiveness diminishes when applied to complex, protocol-specific logic.

Despite these challenges, automatic repair and patch-suggestion tools represent a promising direction for automating smart contract security. They allow developers to respond more quickly to known threats, reduce the cognitive burden of manual debugging, and promote secure-by-default coding practices. When integrated into a broader secure development lifecycle, they serve as a valuable layer of protection, turning identification into resolution and vulnerability into resilience.

10.1.7 Governance-Based Controls and Emergency Multisig

In decentralized systems, especially those handling large volumes of assets or operating as community-driven protocols, centralized control mechanisms, such as sole ownership, can pose both security risks and governance liabilities. To address these concerns while maintaining responsive control over contract behavior, many smart contract ecosystems incorporate governance-based controls and emergency multi-signature (multisig) schemes as core countermeasures [1, 2, 8]. These mechanisms allow privileged operations, such as pausing the protocol, upgrading contract logic, or executing fund transfers, to be governed by collective approval rather than unilateral decisions.

At the heart of this strategy lies the recognition that some security decisions, particularly those made in response to vulnerabilities or ongoing attacks, must balance urgency with the need to minimize trust. Governance-based controls distribute authority across a set of stakeholders, whether through token-weighted voting, multisig committees, or DAO (Decentralized Autonomous Organization) proposals, enabling decentralized risk management without sacrificing responsiveness.

One of the most common implementations is the multisignature wallet, often deployed via platforms like Gnosis Safe. These wallets require a predefined number of approvals from a group of trusted parties before an action can be executed. For example, a 4-of-7 multisig configuration means that at least 4 of the 7 signers must agree on an upgrade, pause, or fund transfer. This structure ensures that no single individual can execute critical functions, while still enabling relatively quick responses to detected vulnerabilities or governance decisions.

More decentralized systems may rely on on-chain governance frameworks where token holders propose and vote on actions affecting the protocol. Platforms like Compound Governor, Aragon, and Snapshot facilitate this model by allowing proposals to be submitted, deliberated, and passed via token-weighted consensus. Emergency actions, such as triggering a circuit breaker or upgrading to patch a discovered vulnerability, can be queued and executed by the governance contract once the vote passes, typically after a delay to allow community review.

These systems may also integrate role-based access control, in which governance assigns specific roles (e.g., upgrader, pauser, administrator) to designated accounts. For example, a DAO might assign the PAUSER_ROLE to its emergency response committee, while leaving the UPGRADER_ROLE under full governance control. This layered permissioning enables nuanced access to sensitive operations and reduces the risk of role abuse.

An important enhancement to this strategy is the use of timelocks, which introduces a programmable delay between the approval and execution of critical transactions. This delay allows the community to audit proposed changes, raise concerns, or exit the protocol if necessary. Tools like TimelockController in OpenZeppelin provide this functionality as a primitive governance.

However, the security of governance-based controls depends heavily on implementation details and participants' integrity. Inadequate quorum thresholds, weak multisig configurations, or poorly defined upgrade paths can lead to governance capture, insider abuse, or delayed responses in emergencies. Additionally, off-chain voting platforms like Snapshot rely on trusted relayers to execute votes, which introduces a centralization risk that must be mitigated through transparency and auditing.

Despite these challenges, governance-based controls remain one of the most powerful countermeasures in the smart contract security arsenal. By embedding human consensus in decision-making, they enable structured, democratic responses to vulnerabilities, upgrades, and emergencies. When combined with automation, access control, and timelocks, these systems transform critical contract functions from isolated risks into community-managed, auditable safeguards.

10.1.8 Runtime Monitoring and Reactive Defense

While pre-deployment analysis and secure coding practices form the foundation of smart contract security, they are not always sufficient to prevent or mitigate attacks that occur in live environments. Given the immutable nature of deployed contracts, once an exploit begins, it must be detected and contained in real time. Runtime monitoring and reactive defense systems have therefore emerged as critical countermeasures that operate alongside deployed smart contracts to observe, assess, and respond to abnormal behavior during execution [6, 7].

The core idea behind runtime monitoring is continuous surveillance of contract activity on the blockchain. These systems monitor for signs of exploitation, such as reentrancy loops, flash-loan manipulations, front-running attempts, or abnormal gas usage, and generate alerts or trigger predefined responses when suspicious behavior is detected. Unlike traditional security models that rely solely on preventive defenses, runtime monitoring enables dynamic, responsive defense, significantly reducing the window of opportunity for an attacker.

A practical example is a scenario in which a DeFi lending protocol observes a sudden, uncharacteristically large borrowing event accompanied by a flash loan. If this pattern matches a known exploit signature, the system can automatically pause sensitive functions (e.g., borrowing, withdrawing, liquidating) to limit financial loss while further investigation is conducted.

Forta, a decentralized threat-detection network, exemplifies the power of runtime defenses in blockchain environments. Forta agents operate off-chain and scan real-time transaction data for predefined attack indicators. When a suspicious transaction is detected, the agent emits an alert that can be consumed by an on-chain automation platform like OpenZeppelin Defender Sentinel. Sentinel can act upon the alert by invoking emergency functions in the target contract, such as pausing operations or blocking specific actors.

These systems enable automated responses that would otherwise require human intervention, providing a valuable layer of protection in high-speed, permissionless environments where attackers can drain funds within seconds. Sentinel, for instance, can monitor multiple smart contracts simultaneously and pause() if anomalous conditions are met, such as many failed transactions, sudden spikes in transaction frequency, or irregular function-call patterns.

Other platforms, such as Chainlink Keepers (now part of Chainlink Automation), offer programmable, event-driven responses to on-chain data changes. Developers can register conditions under which automated actions should be executed, enabling maintenance or protective logic without manual oversight. While Keepers are not explicitly designed as a security system, they can be configured to support reactive defense functions in specific contract designs.

However, implementing runtime monitoring comes with challenges. False positives must be minimized to prevent unnecessary disruptions to legitimate activity, while false negatives, missed threats, can undermine trust in the system. Moreover, response actions, such as pausing or blocking accounts, must be carefully designed to avoid centralization or abuse of control. Transparency in alerting logic, public auditability of agent code, and proper access governance are essential to maintaining trust in automated defensive systems [6, 10].

In sum, runtime monitoring and reactive defense represent a critical evolution in smart contract security: from static preconditions to dynamic, adaptive protection. These systems extend the contract's defense capabilities beyond its code by leveraging real-time data and automation to detect and disrupt attacks in real time. As DeFi protocols, DAOs, and other blockchain applications continue to scale in complexity and value, the integration of such intelligent surveillance mechanisms will be indispensable for maintaining secure and resilient ecosystems.

The countermeasures outlined in this subsection underscore a central principle of secure smart contract development: security must be designed, not assumed. From foundational techniques like checks-effects-interactions and reentrancy guards, to advanced methods such as formal verification and runtime monitoring, each strategy contributes to a layered defense model. Some address vulnerabilities at their source, others provide pathways for safe recovery, while a few operate at the governance or infrastructure level to enable coordinated response and resilience.

Importantly, these strategies are not mutually exclusive. Their effectiveness increases when combined, secure coding habits supported by automated analysis, upgradeability safeguarded by governance, and monitoring enhanced by well-defined emergency controls. Together, they enable decentralized systems to withstand not only known threats but also the inevitable emergence of new ones. As smart contract ecosystems continue to scale and mature, these mitigation strategies will remain essential, not only to defend against exploitation but to uphold the reliability, trust, and economic soundness of blockchain-based applications.

10.2 Comparative Analysis

Having examined the key strategies and tools used to mitigate vulnerabilities in smart contracts, this section provides a comparative analysis of these countermeasures along three critical dimensions: scope of protection, integration with existing systems, and effectiveness in real-world risk mitigation. By evaluating the strengths and limitations of each strategy, we aim to provide a practical framework for selecting and combining the most appropriate security mechanisms for a given decentralized application's context, architecture, and threat profile.

10.2.1 Scope of Protection

The scope of protection offered by a countermeasure refers to the range and depth of vulnerabilities it addresses. Some strategies focus on prevention, embedding safety at the design and code level; others offer containment or response, limiting the damage once a vulnerability is exploited or detected.

For instance, defensive coding patterns and SafeMath-style protections provide broad preventive coverage. They address common vulnerabilities such as reentrancy, overflows, access-control lapses, and gas griefing, making them foundational to almost all contracts. However, they are inherently limited to what the developer can foresee and encode at the time of writing.

In contrast, proxy upgradeability offers deeper but more targeted protection. It does not prevent vulnerabilities up front but allows developers to repair or extend contract logic after deployment, thereby addressing otherwise irreversible threats. Its effectiveness hinges on correct implementation and governance, and it does not protect against vulnerabilities in the upgrade mechanism itself.

Formal verification, on the other hand, offers rigorous protection against very specific failure modes. It excels in proving that a contract cannot violate defined invariants or safety conditions, but its scope is limited by the completeness and correctness of the formal specification. It does not inherently protect against undefined or emergent behaviors outside the model's scope.

Reactive strategies like runtime monitoring and circuit breakers are essential for post-deployment containment. Their scope is narrow in terms of direct protection; they cannot prevent vulnerabilities, but they are invaluable when immediate intervention is needed. Especially in DeFi protocols, where value can be drained within seconds, these countermeasures help detect and limit damage in real time.

Finally, governance-based controls and emergency multisigs provide a meta-layer of protection. Their scope is procedural rather than technical; they enable the protocol community or designated authorities to respond to security incidents, manage upgrades, or migrate assets. While they do not directly address code vulnerabilities, they are critical of the need to orchestrate broader protective measures. Thus, no single countermeasure offers total protection. Instead, their combined use, layered across prevention, detection, containment, and recovery, ensures that both known and unknown risks are meaningfully addressed across the smart contract lifecycle.

10.2.2 Integration with Existing Systems

The effectiveness of a countermeasure is closely tied to its ability to integrate seamlessly into real-world development workflows, toolchains, and decentralized ecosystems. Even the most robust security mechanism may remain underutilized or applied inconsistently if it imposes excessive complexity, disrupts system architecture, or requires specialized expertise beyond the capacity of typical development teams. Therefore, integration with existing systems, both technical and organizational, is a critical axis for evaluating the practical utility of smart contract mitigation strategies.

Among the most developer-friendly solutions are OpenZeppelin's modular libraries and contract templates, which facilitate the integration of defensive coding patterns, access control, pausable functions, and upgradable proxies. These components are designed to be compatible with widely used development frameworks, including Hardhat, Truffle, and Foundry. Their clear documentation, community support, and audit history make them the de facto standard for secure contract development, lowering the barrier to adoption without sacrificing robustness.

Proxy upgradeability, while highly effective for enabling post-deployment remediation, requires thoughtful architectural integration. It imposes additional design constraints, such as strict adherence to storage layout conventions and careful management of initialization logic. Nevertheless, modern tooling, such as the OpenZeppelin Upgrades Plugin and Defender Admin interface, abstracts away much of this complexity, enabling even non-experts to deploy and manage upgradeable contracts with confidence. In DAO-governed systems, integration may extend to on-chain governance modules or multisignature wallets, allowing upgrades to be coordinated in a decentralized but controlled fashion.

By contrast, formal verification remains a high-assurance strategy, but it is limited to integration in most production pipelines. Its effectiveness depends on the developer's ability to express security properties formally, and the system's compatibility with verification tools such as Certora, VeriSol, or KEVM. While some advanced protocols have embedded formal verification into their CI/CD processes, this remains a practice largely confined to high-value or high-risk contracts, where additional effort and cost are justified by the need for mathematical certainty. Broader adoption will depend on improved tooling, simplified specification languages, and integration into development environments.

Runtime monitoring and reactive defenses, including platforms such as Forta and OpenZeppelin Defender Sentinel, represent a new paradigm for post-deployment security that can be integrated with minimal changes to existing smart contract code. These systems operate off-chain or in parallel with the contract, offering alerts, anomaly detection, and automated triggers based on contract behavior. Their integration typically involves registering monitored functions, defining threat signatures, and configuring response actions such as pausing contracts or alerting administrators. Because these tools operate independently of the contract's core logic, they can often be adopted retroactively, making them especially valuable for legacy systems or third-party protocol integrations.

Governance-based controls, such as multisig schemes or DAO modules, require coordination at the organizational and protocol levels. Tools like Gnosis Safe, Compound Governor, or Aragon are designed to integrate with permissioned roles and administrative functions within smart contracts. They enable secure, transparent decision-making while introducing minimal technical overhead for projects, particularly in open-source projects with distributed teams. However, governance controls must be thoughtfully aligned with the protocol's decentralization goals, operational needs, and community expectations to avoid bottlenecks or overcentralization.

Ultimately, the degree to which a countermeasure can be integrated into existing systems determines not only its technical feasibility but also its long-term sustainability. Strategies that align well with mainstream development tools, protocol standards, and organizational workflows are more likely to be adopted consistently, maintained properly, and trusted by users and contributors alike. As the smart contract ecosystem evolves, integration will remain a key factor in translating theoretical security into practical protection.

10.2.3 Effectiveness in Risk Mitigation

While the design, theoretical soundness, and integrability of a countermeasure are important, its ultimate value lies in its effectiveness in reducing real-world risk. This effectiveness can be measured by the extent to which a strategy prevents vulnerabilities from being introduced, limits their exploitability when they do occur, and minimizes the damage when they are exploited.

Defensive coding patterns such as check-effects-interactions, reentrancy guards, and pull-over-push payment models have proven extremely effective in neutralizing some of the most common and historically devastating vulnerabilities. The reentrancy bug that led to the infamous DAO exploit, for instance, could have been entirely avoided with proper state handling order. These patterns, once adopted, drastically reduce the probability of critical design flaws and are easy to replicate across contracts. However, their effectiveness depends entirely on consistent application by developers and may be undermined by human oversight or project-specific complexity.

SafeMath and arithmetic protections, once essential for defending against underflows and overflows, are less central in modern versions of Solidity due to built-in safety checks. Nonetheless, their legacy demonstrates how small syntactic safeguards can have a significant security impact when used correctly. More broadly, automated libraries that encode best practices directly into their syntax can serve as effective guardrails for less-experienced developers.

Proxy upgradeability offers unmatched power in post-deployment risk management. It transforms an otherwise immutable system into a dynamically repairable one. This flexibility is especially important for protocols that manage large treasuries or evolve feature sets. The historical record shows that many major DeFi platforms, including Aave, Uniswap, and Compound, rely on upgradeable infrastructure to address vulnerabilities or rapidly changing requirements. However, the very power of upgradeability introduces new risks: unauthorized upgrades, storage misalignment, and governance capture. Therefore, its effectiveness is contingent on rigorous access control, community oversight, and extensive testing.

Formal verification is most effective in high-assurance environments where security properties can be precisely defined and proven. For example, lending protocols may require guarantees that loan repayments cannot exceed the loan amount, or that liquidation cannot occur below collateral thresholds. Formal methods have successfully proven such properties in production systems, thereby contributing to stronger guarantees in protocols such as MakerDAO and dYdX. However, the selective and resource-intensive nature of this approach means it does not scale universally across all contract types and is most valuable when applied to the most critical components.

Runtime monitoring and reactive defense systems, such as Forta and Defender Sentinel, have emerged as among the most practical and versatile risk mitigation tools. Their ability to detect threats in real time and trigger counteractions, such as pausing contracts or notifying operators, provides a vital defense layer that operates independently of the contract's original code. Notably, their impact has been observed in preventing cascading exploits across DeFi protocols, with early detection and swift action saving millions in potential losses. Their effectiveness is amplified when paired with well-defined circuit breakers and emergency governance procedures.

Finally, governance-based controls and emergency multisigs offer broad systemic protection. While not eliminating vulnerabilities per se, they provide the infrastructure for coordinated responses, upgrades, and asset recovery. Their impact has been most evident in DAO-managed ecosystems and community-driven projects, where proposals to fix bugs, migrate assets, or compensate users have demonstrated resilience in crisis. However, delays in decision-making, apathy in governance, or poorly designed voting mechanisms can reduce their responsiveness, limiting their effectiveness in the face of urgent threats.

In conclusion, the effectiveness of a countermeasure depends not only on its theoretical capability but on its real-world implementation, operational maturity, and responsiveness to evolving attack patterns. No single strategy can serve as a panacea. Instead, layered defenses that combine preventive, corrective, and reactive mechanisms offer the strongest mitigation against the diverse risks smart contracts face. An effective security posture embraces this multi-faceted approach, anticipating both known and unknown threats in a decentralized, adversarial environment.

The comparative analysis of countermeasures reveals a clear insight: smart contract security is not defined by any single strategy, but by the thoughtful composition of multiple, context-aware defenses. Each countermeasure contributes distinct strengths, whether by preventing vulnerabilities at the source, enabling recovery after deployment, or responding in real time to emergent threats. Their scope, ease of integration, and practical effectiveness vary, but when combined strategically, they form a layered security architecture capable of withstanding the evolving threat landscape. For developers and protocol architects, this analysis underscores the importance of selecting tools and practices that align not only with their technical stack but also with the protocol's governance model, user base, and asset exposure. As smart contracts continue to support increasingly valuable and complex systems, the strategic deployment of these countermeasures will be essential to building secure, trustworthy, and resilient blockchain applications.

10.3 Recommendations and Best Practices

While specific countermeasures offer targeted solutions to known vulnerabilities, long-term security in smart contract ecosystems depends on the consistent application of broader principles, those that guide design decisions, development workflows, auditing practices, and operational governance. This section consolidates insights from preceding strategies into a cohesive set of recommendations and best practices for developers, auditors, and protocol architects to enhance the security and resilience of their contracts.

First and foremost, security must be treated as a continuous process, not a one-time checkpoint. From the earliest stages of development, projects should follow a secure-by-design approach, incorporating well-established patterns such as checks, effects, and interactions, pull-over-push models, and minimal trusted roles. Security-conscious architecture, where modularity, clarity, and bounded scope are prioritized, reduces complexity and simplifies analysis.

Leverage mature, audited libraries and frameworks wherever possible. Reinventing low-level contract logic not only wastes resources but also increases the likelihood of introducing subtle bugs. Standardized modules provided by

OpenZeppelin and similar projects encapsulate common security features, such as reentrancy protection, pausable functions, and safe math operations, making them reliable building blocks for new contracts. Embed automated security analysis in the development pipeline. Static analysis tools such as Slither and Mythril, and symbolic execution engines like Manticore, should be used iteratively throughout development, not just before deployment. These tools, while not exhaustive, help catch a wide range of common issues early in the lifecycle, reducing the burden on final audits.

For high-stakes applications, invest in formal specification and verification of core logic. While formal methods require expertise and effort, they provide unmatched confidence in the correctness of critical operations. Properties such as balance invariants, authorization constraints, and upper/lower bounds on operations should be clearly documented and, where feasible, formally proven. Establish upgradeability with care. If a protocol requires future evolution, use proxy patterns judiciously and ensure upgraded paths are protected by governance or multisignature schemes. Mismanaged upgradeability introduces new vectors for takeover or state corruption, so version control, testing, and transparency are essential components of any upgradable system.

Define and implement emergency response protocols. This includes pausable contracts, multisig-controlled kill switches, and runtime monitoring systems that can identify and react to exploit patterns. Early warning mechanisms, especially those powered by services like Forta or Defender, should be tied to concrete response actions, whether automated or manual. Document and audit comprehensively. Clear documentation aids internal consistency, facilitates community review, and improves audit quality. Every deployed contract should be independently audited by experienced security professionals, and audits should be public whenever possible. Post-deployment bug bounty programs can further incentivize community participation in securing live systems.

Finally, governance should be aligned with security goals. Whether managed by DAOs or core development teams, decisions affecting contract upgrades, parameter changes, and emergency actions must be structured to ensure transparency, accountability, and timely execution. Multisigs, timelocks, and proposal vetting processes all play important roles in preventing governance-based exploits or inaction. Together, these recommendations reflect a shift in mindset from reactive patching to proactive resilience. Smart contract security is not simply a matter of patching bugs or adding guards, but of building systems that anticipate failure, enable recovery, and remain trustworthy even in adversarial conditions. By following these best practices, developers can contribute to a more secure and sustainable foundation for decentralized technologies.

10.4 Chapter Summary

This chapter explored the landscape of smart contract countermeasures, analyzing both their theoretical foundations and practical implementations across prevention, containment, and recovery domains. Strategies such as defensive coding, proxy upgradeability, formal verification, circuit breakers, and runtime monitoring were examined in depth, revealing distinct strengths and limitations in terms of vulnerability coverage, ease of integration, and operational resilience. Comparative analysis highlighted that while preventive measures help minimize the introduction of bugs, post-deployment mechanisms, ranging from upgrade paths to automated detection and response, are essential for addressing unforeseen threats in live environments. No single strategy offers complete protection; instead, layered combinations tailored to a protocol's architecture, governance model, and risk exposure are required. Ultimately, securing smart contracts demands not just technical precision but also adaptive, system-aware design that can evolve alongside the decentralized applications it aims to defend.

References

1. Zhou, H., Fard, A.M., Makanju, A.: The state of ethereum smart contracts security: vulnerabilities, countermeasures, and tool support. J. Cybersec. Privacy. **2**(2), 358–378 (2022)
2. Hewa, T.M., et al.: Survey on blockchain-based smart contracts: technical aspects and future research. IEEE Access. **9**, 87643–87662 (2021)
3. Sifra, E.M.: Security vulnerabilities and countermeasures of smart contracts: a survey. In: 2022 IEEE International Conference on Blockchain (Blockchain). IEEE (2022)
4. Yulianto, S., et al.: Security risks and best practices for blockchain and smart contracts: a systematic literature review. In: 2023 International Conference on Information Management and Technology (ICIMTech). IEEE (2023)
5. Hasanova, H., et al.: A survey on blockchain cybersecurity vulnerabilities and possible countermeasures. Int. J. Netw. Manag. **29**(2), e2060 (2019)
6. Soofiyan, S., Karami, A.: Ethereum smart contracts: a hierarchical analysis of vulnerability challenges and mitigation strategies. Clust. Comput. **28**(8), 543 (2025)
7. Nzuva, S.M.: Revisiting blockchain technologies and smart contracts security: a pragmatic exploration of vulnerabilities, threats, and challenges. Asian J. Res. Comput. Sci. **17**(7), 10–9734 (2024)
8. Capocasale, V., Perboli, G.: Standardizing smart contracts. IEEE Access. **10**, 91203–91212 (2022)
9. Bakhshi, A.: Securing Smart Contracts: Strategies for Identifying and Mitigating Vulnerabilities in Blockchain Applications. University of Central Arkansas (2024)
10. Alaba, F.A., et al.: Smart contracts security application and challenges: a review. Cloud Comput. Data Sci., 15–41 (2024)
11. Tjiam, K., et al.: Your smart contracts are not secure: investigating arbitrageurs and oracle manipulators in ethereum. In: Proceedings of the 3rd Workshop on Cyber-Security Arms Race (2021)
12. Alkhalifah, A., et al.: A mechanism to detect and prevent ethereum blockchain smart contract reentrancy attacks. Front. Comput. Sci. **3**, 598780 (2021)

13. Delmolino, K., et al.: Step by step towards creating a safe smart contract: lessons and insights from a cryptocurrency lab. In: International Conference on Financial Cryptography and Data Security. Springer Berlin Heidelberg, Berlin, Heidelberg (2016)
14. Xue, Y., et al.: Cross-contract static analysis for detecting practical reentrancy vulnerabilities in smart contracts. In: Proceedings of the 35th IEEE/ACM International Conference on Automated Software Engineering (2020)
15. Ji, S., Kim, D., Im, H.: Evaluating countermeasures for verifying the integrity of ethereum smart contract applications. IEEE Access. **9**, 90029–90042 (2021)
16. Hamdi, A., Fourati, L., Ayed, S.: Vulnerabilities and attacks assessments in blockchain 1.0, 2.0 and 3.0: tools, analysis and countermeasures. Int. J. Inf. Secur. **23**(2), 713–757 (2024)

Chapter 11
Challenges and Future Directions in Smart Contract Research

Abstract This chapter reflects on the trajectory of smart contract research, tracing its evolution from foundational studies of immutability, determinism, and trustless execution to modern advances in security, language design, and interdisciplinary inquiry. It highlights how landmark incidents such as The DAO and repeated DeFi exploits push research toward vulnerability taxonomies, formal verification methods, and diverse analyzers, while alternative languages like Vyper, Scilla, and Obsidian attempt to reduce common pitfalls. The discussion then examines persistent challenges: exploitable vulnerabilities in composable DeFi systems, gaps in formal specification and verification, scalability and gas cost constraints, limitations in language design, governance and upgradeability tensions, interoperability across heterogeneous blockchains, and unresolved legal and ethical ambiguities. These issues are framed as deeper trade-offs between flexibility and trust, scalability and decentralization, automation and accountability. Moving forward, this chapter outlines future directions, including mainstream adoption of formal methods with more accessible specification languages, co-design of safer smart contract languages, AI-enhanced analysis for vulnerability detection and stress-testing, privacy-preserving execution through zero-knowledge proofs and multiparty computation, secure cross-chain interoperability, adaptive governance frameworks, and legally informed contract architectures. Finally, it emphasizes that progress does not emerge from singular breakthroughs but from convergence across disciplines, cryptography, programming languages, distributed systems, economics, and law uniting formal rigor with human-centric governance to shape resilient, equitable decentralized infrastructures.

Smart contracts have evolved from experimental constructs into foundational components of decentralized systems, empowering a wide range of applications from decentralized finance (DeFi) to supply chain tracking and autonomous governance [1, 2]. Their unique capacity to execute verifiable code on distributed ledgers without intermediaries has redefined trust and automation in digital transactions [3, 4]. Over the past decade, smart contract research has made significant strides in addressing security vulnerabilities, improving expressiveness, and expanding the usability of blockchain platforms. However, despite this progress, the landscape remains riddled with challenges, many of which stem from the complexity of blockchain

S. HajiHosseinKhani et al., *Understanding Cybersecurity for Smart Contracts*,
https://doi.org/10.1007/978-3-032-28863-9_11

environments, the unpredictability of user behavior, and the trade-offs among decentralization, scalability, and security [5, 6].

This chapter provides a critical reflection on the state of smart contract research, drawing on insights from earlier chapters to identify lingering technical and theoretical obstacles. It also explores the unresolved issues that continue to hinder the reliability, safety, and scalability of smart contract systems in practice. As blockchain technology matures and adoption grows, new questions emerge about how smart contracts can evolve to meet the demands of more complex, data-driven, and legally significant interactions.

Looking ahead, this chapter outlines key avenues for future research that promise to address current limitations while opening new possibilities for innovation. These directions span from formal verification and language design to cross-chain interoperability, autonomous contract governance, privacy-preserving execution, and AI-enhanced analysis. By articulating both the limitations and the potential of smart contracts, this chapter aims to guide researchers, developers, and policymakers toward a more secure, functional, and inclusive decentralized future.

11.1 Summary of Previous Research

The evolution of smart contract research has been marked by a sustained effort to balance theoretical innovation with practical necessity. Early work in this field focused primarily on formalizing the notion of smart contracts and identifying their foundational properties, such as immutability, determinism, and trustless execution. Seminal studies examined Ethereum's architecture as a baseline, highlighting the trade-offs between expressiveness and verifiability in Turing-complete languages such as Solidity [1, 7].

Security has emerged as the central theme in smart contract research, driven by real-world incidents such as the DAO exploit, Parity wallet vulnerabilities, and repeated breaches of DeFi protocols. These events spurred the development of vulnerability taxonomies, formal verification methods, and an expanding ecosystem of static and dynamic analysis tools. Research has also explored the role of symbolic execution, fuzzing, AI-based vulnerability detection, and automated repair mechanisms, leading to a more rigorous approach to contract correctness and resilience [4, 5, 8].

At the language level, multiple studies have proposed safer alternatives to Solidity, including Vyper, Pact, Scilla, and Obsidian, each offering design constraints intended to reduce common pitfalls. Formal semantics and type systems have also been introduced to aid in the analysis of contracts before deployment. Meanwhile, other research threads have investigated patterns and anti-patterns in smart contract development, offering guidance to practitioners while informing the development of new frameworks and testing infrastructure.

Beyond security, smart contract research has increasingly embraced interdisciplinary perspectives. In DeFi, scholars have analyzed the economic dynamics of protocol design, incentive engineering, and mechanisms that are resistant to manipulation. Legal scholars have examined the challenges of aligning smart contracts with traditional contract law, while usability researchers have highlighted the barriers to adoption posed by non-intuitive interfaces and the difficulty of expressing real-world logic in code.

Collectively, these efforts have laid a robust foundation for smart contract science, charting its operational mechanics, illuminating its vulnerabilities, and offering the first generation of tools, languages, and theoretical models. Yet, as the ecosystem grows more complex and interconnected, new demands have surfaced that existing research has only begun to address.

11.2 Current Challenges and Unresolved Issues

Smart contracts, while revolutionary in concept and increasingly sophisticated in implementation, remain constrained by systemic, architectural, and socio-technical limitations. These challenges not only hinder the broader adoption of smart contracts but also signal deeper research questions that remain unresolved in both theory and practice [3, 5].

- Persistent Security Vulnerabilities in Evolving Environments
  The most pressing and visible challenge in smart contract ecosystems is the persistent presence of exploitable vulnerabilities. As observed in numerous DeFi exploits, even contracts that pass-through audits and formal verification can be compromised when executed in complex, adversarial environments. Attacks such as sandwiching, reentrancy, oracle manipulation, and logic bugs continue to cause significant financial damage. The problem is exacerbated by the increasing composability of protocols: one contract's behavior may change depending on its interaction with another, introducing emergent vulnerabilities that are difficult to anticipate in isolation [5, 8].
  While static and dynamic analysis tools have advanced, they are often limited to predefined vulnerability patterns and struggle to reason about economic logic, inter-contract dependencies, or interactions across multiple transactions. Additionally, the proliferation of upgradable and proxy-based contract systems introduces obfuscation and complexity that reduces the effectiveness of traditional detection methods.
- Gaps in Formal Specification and Verification
  Formal verification offers strong theoretical guarantees, yet its use in real-world smart contract development remains minimal. Writing correct formal specifications for smart contracts is inherently difficult, particularly when contracts implement complex financial behaviors or interoperate with external systems like oracles or cross-chain bridges. Many properties of interest, such as economic fairness, incentive compatibility, or resistance to market manipulation, cannot be easily expressed in current formal frameworks.

Moreover, existing tools (e.g., Coq, Why3, F* with translation layers for smart contracts) are either too heavyweight for typical developers or support only narrow subsets of Solidity. The translation of informal developer intent into precise mathematical specifications also remains a semantic bottleneck. Even when formal verification is applied, its guarantees are often brittle; one slight change in contract structure or compiler behavior may render proof obsolete.

- Scalability, Performance, and Execution Cost
  The resource constraints inherent to blockchain environments continue to limit the complexity and richness of smart contract logic. On Ethereum, for example, every operation incurs a gas cost, which forces developers to write highly optimized code at the expense of clarity, modularity, and security. This economic constraint discourages the use of defensive programming practices such as assertions, input validation, and structured exception handling [2, 6].
  Moreover, as the ecosystem shifts toward layer-2 scaling solutions (e.g., rollups, state channels, sidechains), a new class of challenges emerges. These include data availability issues, rollup fraud-proof vulnerabilities, bridging risks, and fragmentation of execution environments. Writing contracts that can seamlessly interact across these layers while maintaining state consistency, user trust, and security remains a complex and open problem.
- Language Design and Programming Abstractions
  The dominant language for smart contract development, Solidity, was not originally designed with formal verification, usability, or high-assurance safety in mind. Although improvements have been made, it still exhibits design flaws, such as default visibility settings, inconsistent data types, and ambiguous control-flow constructs, which contribute to security issues.
  Alternative languages (e.g., Vyper, Scilla, Pact, Obsidian, Move) have introduced stricter typing, formal semantics, and constrained expressiveness to mitigate risks, but they suffer from fragmented tool support and lack widespread community adoption. Most of these languages are either platform-specific or require developers to learn entirely new paradigms, which creates a steep learning curve.
  In addition, existing languages lack native support for expressing higher-level domain logic, such as contract negotiation, multi-party agreements, or regulatory compliance constraints. This limitation leads to either verbose, brittle code or the need to offload critical logic to off-chain components, reintroducing centralization risks.
- Governance, Upgradeability, and the Tension with Immutability
  One of the defining characteristics of smart contracts is their immutability, yet this same feature becomes a liability when contracts contain bugs, outdated logic, or misaligned incentives. To address this, many projects employ proxy patterns or upgradable contract frameworks. However, these introduce new risks, such as governance capture, upgrade abuse, and logic inconsistency between proxy and implementation contracts.
  Decentralized governance mechanisms, such as DAOs, are often used to manage upgrades and decision-making processes, but they come with their own chal-

lenges. Voting power tends to concentrate among wealthy stakeholders, and governance processes are susceptible to apathy, manipulation, or rushed proposals [1, 9]. Balancing flexibility with trust minimization remains an unresolved tension: how can smart contracts evolve without sacrificing their verifiability or decentralization?

- Interoperability and Cross-Chain Communication
  As the blockchain ecosystem diversifies, the ability for smart contracts to communicate across heterogeneous chains becomes increasingly important. Current cross-chain solutions (e.g., bridges, wrapped tokens, interoperability layers) rely heavily on external validators, message relayers, or trusted oracles, introducing new attack surfaces and points of failure [6].
  Semantic differences in execution models, consensus assumptions, and data availability across chains further complicate the development of portable or composable contracts. Research is still in its early stages on standardizing communication protocols, consensus-aligned state replication, and secure cross-chain function calls.
- Legal, Regulatory, and Ethical Ambiguities
  Smart contracts operate in a legally grey area. Their automated execution often clashes with the discretionary and interpretive nature of legal systems. It remains unclear how traditional contract principles, such as offer, acceptance, consideration, and enforceability, apply to autonomous code. Jurisdictional ambiguity, liability allocation, and consumer protection remain unresolved, especially in decentralized contexts where parties may be pseudonymous or globally distributed [1, 9].
  Furthermore, as smart contracts become more intertwined with governance, lending, insurance, and personal data handling, ethical considerations become more salient. Bias in contract logic, exclusionary access patterns (e.g., gas-based auctions), and the opaque decision-making of DAOs raise fundamental questions about fairness, accessibility, and accountability in decentralized digital infrastructures.

Taken together, these challenges reveal that the evolution of smart contracts is not merely a matter of improving code quality or optimizing performance; it is a deeply multidisciplinary endeavor that touches on language design, formal methods, system architecture, governance, economics, and law. Each unresolved issue reflects an inherent trade-off among flexibility and trust, scalability and decentralization, and automation and accountability. As smart contracts increasingly underpin critical financial and social infrastructure, addressing these issues will require collaborative advances that go beyond technical patchwork. The next phase of research must not only refine the tools and frameworks we use but also rethink the assumptions that shape how smart contracts are written, analyzed, governed, and interpreted within broader socio-technical systems. The following section explores these future directions in detail, outlining how the field might move toward more secure, expressive, and equitable smart contract ecosystems.

11.3 Prospective Future Research Directions

As the smart contract ecosystem matures, future research must evolve to address the fundamental limitations identified in the current landscape while pushing the boundaries of what decentralized computation can achieve. These future directions represent not just incremental improvements but potentially transformative shifts in how smart contracts are conceived, implemented, and integrated into complex, real-world systems [7].

One promising direction lies in the mainstream adoption of formal methods. While verification tools exist, they must be made accessible, modular, and composable to fit real-world development pipelines. Research can explore ways to automatically infer specifications from code, generate properties through learned patterns, and integrate proof assistants directly into IDEs. Advances in SMT solvers and model checkers tailored for smart contract semantics could help scale verification across large codebases. More fundamentally, the development of domain-specific specification languages tailored to common contract intents such as token issuance, auctions, or lending could lower the barrier to writing and verifying formal properties [3, 5].

Another fertile area of exploration is the co-design of smart contract languages with verification in mind. Rather than layering formal guarantees atop existing languages like Solidity, future languages could be built from the ground up with tractable semantics, restricted mutability, and built-in constraint logic. Such languages would prioritize predictability, safety, and analyzability over expressiveness, possibly through typed state machines, capability-based access control, or transaction-level logic gates. Simultaneously, toolchains must evolve to support the full contract lifecycle, from static analysis to fuzzing, symbolic simulation, and automated test generation, under a unified framework [6, 10].

The integration of AI and machine learning into smart contract tooling represents another exciting direction. Large language models (LLMs) and graph neural networks can be employed not only for vulnerability detection and classification but also for code completion suggestions, anomaly prediction, and intelligent refactoring. Future research might also investigate self-learning agents that simulate adversarial behaviors to stress-test contract logic under diverse economic conditions. Combining symbolic and neural reasoning could offer hybrid frameworks capable of detecting both structural and behavioral vulnerabilities in contract ecosystems.

In parallel, privacy-preserving smart contract execution will demand a novel architecture. Zero-knowledge proofs, secure multiparty computation (SMPC), and trusted execution environments (TEEs) are being investigated as means to enable verifiable yet confidential computation on-chain. However, integrating these into general-purpose contract logic poses open challenges in performance, composability, and developer usability. Research must focus on designing high-level abstractions that allow developers to reason about privacy boundaries without compromising expressiveness or trust guarantees.

Cross-chain interoperability also stands as a critical frontier. As multichain ecosystems become more interconnected, the need for secure, consistent, and verifiable communication across heterogeneous platforms will grow. Future solutions might involve cryptographic bridges without trusted third parties, state-anchoring techniques, or cross-domain virtual machines that abstract away consensus and execution models. Formalizing interoperability semantics and establishing safety guarantees for cross-chain atomicity will be vital to ensuring reliability in decentralized, interlinked systems.

Equally important is advancing research in smart contract governance, upgradeability, and resilience. Adaptive governance frameworks that balance automation with human oversight will require formal modeling of voting behaviors, incentive structures, and threat models. Moreover, embedding governance as a programmable and auditable component within contracts, rather than an external or ad hoc process, can provide both flexibility and accountability. Upgradeable contracts must be reimagined to retain the auditability and security of immutable code while supporting iterative evolution, perhaps through version-controlled compositional architectures or metaprogramming strategies.

Finally, interdisciplinary research at the intersection of law, ethics, and decentralized automation will become increasingly urgent. Legal scholars, technologists, and ethicists must collaborate to articulate frameworks for liability, enforceability, and fairness in automated agreements. Concepts like machine-readable legal clauses, dispute mediation protocols, and compliance-aware smart contracts may emerge as hybrid solutions that bridge the gap between code and law. Additionally, ethical design principles for algorithmic governance, such as transparency, inclusiveness, and non-discrimination, should be embedded in both protocol and contract logic [1, 9].

These directions signal that the future of smart contracts is not simply about writing better code but about reimagining the rules of digital interaction. As blockchain systems grow in complexity, scale, and societal impact, smart contract research must evolve into a truly multidisciplinary field, one that merges programming languages, distributed systems, economics, cryptography, and jurisprudence into a coherent vision for secure, autonomous, and equitable digital infrastructure.

11.4 Chapter Summary

This chapter examined the evolving landscape of smart contract research through the lens of persistent challenges and prospective innovations. It began by contextualizing the field's development, highlighting prior advancements in vulnerability detection, formal verification, language design, and decentralized governance. Building on this foundation, it identified a series of unresolved issues, ranging from compositional security and limited adoption of formal specifications to upgradeability constraints, fragmented language abstractions, and cross-chain interoperability risks. Each challenge underscored the inherent complexity of engineering reliable smart contracts within adversarial, decentralized ecosystems. Future directions were then explored, focusing on verifiable and privacy-preserving computation, AI-enhanced analysis, governance-aware upgrade frameworks, and legally informable contract architectures. These directions emphasized a growing need for tools and methodologies that are not only technically robust but also sociotechnically adaptive. The path forward for smart contract research is not defined by any singular breakthrough, but rather by the convergence of advances across disciplines, spanning cryptography, programming languages, distributed systems, and regulatory theory. Ultimately, securing and evolving smart contracts will require a holistic paradigm that unites formal rigor, compositional design, cross-chain trust, and human-centric governance within a scalable and inclusive decentralized infrastructure.

References

1. Khan, S.N., et al.: Blockchain smart contracts: applications, challenges, and future trends. Peer Peer Netw Appl. **14**(5), 2901–2925 (2021)
2. Wang, S., et al.: An overview of smart contract: architecture, applications, and future trends. In: 2018 IEEE Intelligent Vehicles Symposium (IV). IEEE (2018)
3. Zou, W., et al.: Smart contract development: challenges and opportunities. IEEE Trans. Softw. Eng. **47**(10), 2084–2106 (2019)
4. Chen, J., et al.: Maintenance-related concerns for post-deployed ethereum smart contract development: issues, techniques, and future challenges. Empir. Softw. Eng. **26**(6), 117 (2021)
5. Kannengiesser, N., et al.: Challenges and common solutions in smart contract development. IEEE Trans. Softw. Eng. **48**(11), 4291–4318 (2021)
6. Wang, S., et al.: Blockchain-enabled smart contracts: architecture, applications, and future trends. IEEE Trans Syst Man Cybern Syst. **49**(11), 2266–2277 (2019)
7. Sánchez, C., Schneider, G., Leucker, M.: Reliable smart contracts: State-of-the-art, applications, challenges and future directions. In: International Symposium on Leveraging Applications of Formal Methods. Springer International Publishing, Cham (2018)
8. Khaoulaj, Y., Hamdaoui, Y., Maach, A.: Survey on smart contract security: challenges, techniques, and future directions. In: International Conference on Advanced Intelligent Systems for Sustainable Development. Springer Nature Switzerland, Cham (2024)
9. Singh, J., Rani, S., Kumar, P.: Blockchain and smart contracts: evolution, challenges, and future directions. In: 2024 International Conference on Knowledge Engineering and Communication Systems (ICKECS), vol. 1. IEEE (2024)
10. Trivedi, C., et al.: A transformative shift toward blockchain-based IoT environments: consensus, smart contracts, and future directions. Secur. Priv. **6**(5), e308 (2023)

Chapter 12
Conclusion

Abstract This chapter concludes the book by reflecting on how smart contracts grow from a technical curiosity into a foundation for decentralized trust, reshaping law, governance, and digital transactions. It emphasizes that smart contracts are not just code but socio-technical instruments operating within volatile ecosystems, where correctness and resilience depend on context, incentives, and governance. It shows how security must be integrated throughout the contract lifecycle, with layered defenses, runtime monitoring, and community oversight replacing the notion of a "perfect" contract. It also highlights governance as a parallel challenge, balancing decentralized inclusiveness with the need for accountability and liability when failures occur. It underscores the importance of education, accessible tooling, and safer languages to lower barriers to secure development. Looking ahead, it points to privacy-preserving technologies, interoperability standards, zero-knowledge proofs, post-quantum cryptography, and evolving regulations as key forces shaping the future. Lastly, it positions smart contracts not merely as transactional scripts but as building blocks of digital civilization, requiring vigilance, ethical reflection, and responsible innovation.

Decentralized systems have fundamentally reshaped the architecture of trust, shifting reliance from centralized authorities to cryptographic consensus and autonomous code execution. At the heart of this transformation lies the smart contract, an innovation that merges logic with law, automates the enforcement of transactional integrity, and redefines how agreements are formed and enforced. What began as a technical curiosity has matured into a core pillar of decentralized finance, governance, digital identity, and beyond. Yet, the elegance of deterministic execution does not inoculate it against complexity or fragility. The evolution of smart contracts has exposed the intricate tension among formal rigor and practical flexibility, immutability and adaptability, and permissionless innovation and systemic risk.

Across the varied domains explored throughout this work, from foundational design patterns to emergent security challenges, from static detection methodologies to dynamic runtime analyses, a central theme emerges: smart contracts are not merely code. They are socio-technical instruments embedded in volatile ecosystems, operating under assumptions that may shift with technological innovation, adversarial ingenuity, or shifts in protocol governance. Their correctness and

S. HajiHosseinKhani et al., *Understanding Cybersecurity for Smart Contracts*,
https://doi.org/10.1007/978-3-032-28863-9_12

resilience cannot be evaluated in isolation; they must be understood in context, accounting for the blockchain layer they operate on, the composability of the protocols they interact with, and the economic incentives that drive both usage and exploitation.

Security, long treated as an external audit requirement, now demands integration into every stage of smart contract development and deployment. The attack surfaces are not static. They expand and evolve with cross-contract interactions, Layer 2 interoperability, MEV-driven transaction ordering, and the increasing modularity of DeFi protocols. Consequently, the paradigm of "secure-by-design" is not a singular goal but a continuous discipline. Formal verification tools, fuzzers, symbolic analyzers, and machine learning models have emerged as essential pillars of this discipline, but their success is contingent on precise assumptions, comprehensive coverage, and effective human interpretability. The notion of a perfect contract, a contract impervious to all conceivable attacks, is a mirage. What remains essential is not perfection, but a layered, probabilistic assurance strategy: a combination of static and dynamic defenses, runtime monitoring, upgraded mechanisms, and community-driven oversight.

Beyond technical design, the governance of smart contracts, who writes them, who upgrades them, who can pause them, and who bears liability when they fail, introduces a parallel axis of complexity. Decentralized governance offers inclusiveness but risks incoherence; centralized controls promise responsiveness but challenge trustlessness. The design of governance frameworks, DAOs, voting schemes, and emergency response mechanisms will increasingly define not just the success of individual contracts but the resilience of entire ecosystems. Future innovation must grapple with the duality of code as law and law as code, finding pathways that respect both cryptographic guarantees and the evolving needs of human institutions.

Education, accessibility, and tooling stand as critical enablers of sustainable growth. The learning curve for smart contract development remains steep, particularly when security principles are involved. Lowering this barrier, through robust development frameworks, better documentation, and domain-specific languages tailored for safety, will be essential to unlocking broader participation. As new developers, auditors, and protocol designers enter the space, the emphasis must shift from merely "getting it to work" to a deep understanding of why and how it works, and under what conditions it might fail.

Looking ahead, the trajectory of smart contract research and deployment will be shaped not only by advances in code analysis or protocol design but also by a deeper reconciliation between decentralized ideals and real-world constraints. Privacy-enhancing technologies, interoperability standards, zero-knowledge proofs, and post-quantum cryptography will all play increasingly central roles. Meanwhile, regulatory frameworks will evolve, sometimes in alignment with, and sometimes in opposition to, the ethos of permissionlessness. Navigating this interplay will require not just technical excellence, but also cross-disciplinary fluency, community consensus, and persistent commitment to public goods and open innovation.

The arc of smart contract development bends toward composability, automation, and self-enforcing coordination. But with these affordances come responsibilities, ethical, technical, and systemic. The vision of a trustless future cannot rest solely on the shoulders of code; it must be upheld by the collective vigilance of its builders, users, and stewards. As the boundaries between software and society continue to blur, smart contracts will increasingly serve not just as transactional scripts but as foundational constructions of digital civilization, requiring the same care, scrutiny, and philosophical rigor as the legal systems they aim to augment or replace.